CONVERSING WITH

Karl Barth addressed all the major themes of dogmatic theology, and in so doing made his own distinctive contribution to each of the ongoing conversations that constitute that theology. This book presents important new 'conversations with Barth' by leading contemporary theologians and Barth scholars. Each contributor offers their own distinctive emphasis to bring to light the ways in which the depths of Barth's work may illuminate or be illuminated by the work of other prominent thinkers who preceded or followed him. The conversations they host between Barth and other philosophers and theologians raise critical questions in the reading and appreciation of Barth's thought, and explore a wide range of themes in dogmatic theology.

This book not only adds to the comprehension of the riches of Barth's theology but also presents an important contribution to the ongoing conversations and debates alive in theology today.

Contributors: Nicholas Lash, John Webster, Timothy Gorringe, Graham Ward, George Hunsinger, Ben Quash, Mike Higton, John C. McDowell, Eugene F. Rogers Jr, Katherine Sonderegger, David Clough, David Ford.

Barth Studies

Series Editors

John Webster, Professor of Theology, University of Aberdeen, UK
George Hunsinger, Director of the Center for Barth Studies,
Princeton University, USA
Hans-Anton Drewes, Director of the Karl Barth Archive, Basel, Switzerland

The work of Barth is central to the history of modern western theology and remains a major voice in contemporary constructive theology. His writings have been the subject of intensive scrutiny and re-evaluation over the past two decades, notably on the part of English-language Barth scholars who have often been at the forefront of fresh interpretation and creative appropriation of his theology. Study of Barth, both by graduate students and by established scholars, is a significant enterprise; literature on him and conferences devoted to his work abound; the Karl Barth Archive in Switzerland and the Center for Barth Studies at Princeton give institutional profile to these interests. Barth's work is also considered by many to be a significant resource for the intellectual life of the churches.

Drawing from the wide pool of Barth scholarship, and including translations of Barth's works, this series aims to function as a means by which writing on Barth, of the highest scholarly calibre, can find publication. The series builds upon and furthers the interest in Barth's work in the theological academy and the church.

Conversing with Barth

Edited by

JOHN C. McDOWELL
University of Edinburgh, UK

and

MIKE HIGTON
University of Exeter, UK

ASHGATE

Published by
Ashgate Publishing Limited
Gower House
Croft Road
Aldershot
Hampshire GU11 3HR
England

Ashgate Publishing Company
Suite 420
101 Cherry Street
Burlington, VT 05401-4405
USA

Ashgate website: http//www.ashgate.com

British Library Cataloguing in Publication Data
Conversing with Barth. – (Barth studies)
   1. Barth, Karl, 1886–1968 2. Theology, Doctrinal
   I. Higton, Mike II. McDowell, John C.
   230' .092

Library of Congress Cataloging-in-Publication Data
Conversing with Barth / edited by Mike Higton and John C. McDowell. — 1st ed.
     p. cm — (Barth studies)
Includes bibliographical references and index.
     ISBN 0-7546-0568-X (hardcover : alk. paper) — ISBN 0-7546-0570-1 (pbk. : alk. paper) 1. Barth, Karl, 1886–1968. I. Higton, Mike. II. McDowell, John C. III. Series.

   BX4827.B3C58 2004
   230'.044'092—dc22   2003024707

ISBN 0 7546 0568 X (HBK)
ISBN 0 7546 0570 1 (PBK)

Typesetting by IML Typographers, Birkenhead, Merseyside
Printed and bound in Great Britain by TJ International Ltd, Padstow, Cornwall

Contents

Notes on Contributors

David Clough is Tutor in Ethics and Systematic Theology at Cranmer Hall, Durham. His book *Ethics in Crisis: Interpreting Barth's Ethics* will be published shortly, and he has also written on the theological significance of the Internet. He is currently researching a co-authored book on the shape of the Christian Just War and pacifist debate at the beginning of the twenty-first century.

David Ford is Regius Professor of Divinity in the University of Cambridge, and author of, amongst other publications, *Barth and God's Story, Self and Salvation: Being Transformed* and *The Modern Theologians*. He has also, with Mike Higton, edited an Oxford University Press Reader on *Jesus*. As well as writing on Barth himself, he has supervised many PhD students' work on Barth, and is one of those responsible for the recent increased popularity of Barth in English universities.

Timothy Gorringe is St Luke's Professor of Theological Studies in the University of Exeter and author of numerous books including *God's Just Vengeance: Crime, Violence and the Rhetoric of Salvation*, *Karl Barth: Against Hegemony*, *A Theology of the Built Environment* and *Furthering Humanity: A Theology of Culture*.

Mike Higton is Lecturer in Theology in the Departments of Theology and of Lifelong Learning at the University of Exeter, having moved there after ten years in Cambridge. He is the author of *Christ, Providence and History: Hans W. Frei's Public Theology* and *Difficult Gospel: The Theology of Rowan Williams*, and co-editor, with David Ford, of an Oxford Reader on *Jesus*.

George Hunsinger is McCord Professor of Systematic Theology at Princeton Theological Seminary, and former Director of the Center for Barth Studies there. He is author of *How to Read Karl Barth: The Shape of His Theology* and *Disruptive Grace: Studies in the Theology of Karl Barth*. He has also contributed to the volume that he has edited, *Karl Barth and Radical Politics*.

Nicholas Lash is retired Norris Hulse Professor of Divinity at the University of Cambridge. He has written widely, and his publications include *Theology on Dover Beach*, *Theology on the Way to Emmaus*, *Believing Three Ways in One God* and *The Beginning and End of Religion*.

John C. McDowell is Meldrum Lecturer in Systematic Theology at New College, University of Edinburgh. His doctoral study, under the supervision of Professor Nicholas Lash at the University of Cambridge, forms the basis of his book *Hope in Barth's Eschatology: Interrogations and Transformations Beyond Tragedy*. He has also authored articles on Barth's eschatology of election, theology of hope, evil and politics, as well as the tragic in George Steiner and the nature of theological honesty in Donald MacKinnon. Forthcoming articles of his concern Barth's politics, recent literature on Barth and the nature of theological practice in Donald MacKinnon.

Ben Quash is Dean of Peterhouse, Cambridge. He teaches widely in the area of nineteenth- and twentieth-century theology and Christian ethics, and is co-author of the recent *Balthasar at the End of Modernity*, as well as of a range of articles dealing with von Balthasar, Barth, Hegel, and the Eastern and Western mystical traditions. His Cambridge doctoral work, done under the supervision of David Ford, on von Balthasar's 'theodramatics' will soon be published. He is reviews editor for the journal *Studies in Christian Ethics*.

Eugene F. Rogers Jr is Professor of Religious Studies at the University of Virginia and author of *Thomas Aquinas and Karl Barth, Sexuality and the Christian Body: Their Way into the Triune God* and *After the Spirit*. He is also the editor of *Theology and Sexuality: Classic and Contemporary Reading*.

Katherine Sonderegger is Professor of Theology at Virginia Theological Seminary, responsible for the courses in Christian thought and tradition. She trained at Brown and Yale Universities and wrote her dissertation on Barth and his understanding of Jews and Judaism. *That Jesus Christ was Born a Jew: Karl Barth's Doctrine of Israel* stems from that dissertation. She has also published articles and delivered papers on Barth, in relation to current topics, such as North American feminism, as well as on his conversation partners, Schleiermacher and nineteenth-century academic theology.

Graham Ward is Professor of Contextual Theology at the University of Manchester. He is the author of *Barth, Derrida and the Language of Theology* and many other publications, two of his more recent being *Cities of God* and *True Religion*. He is also the senior executive editor of *Literature and Theology*.

John Webster has recently become Professor of Systematic Theology at the University of Aberdeen after having been the Lady Margaret Professor of Divinity at the University of Oxford, and is author of, amongst other publications, several articles and books on Barth, most notably *Barth's Ethics of Reconciliation, Barth's Moral Theology, The Cambridge Companion to Karl Barth* (ed.); and *Barth*. More recently, he has published *Word and Church, Holiness*, and *Holy Scripture*. He is a founding editor of the *International Journal of Systematic Theology*.

Preface

Nicholas Lash

'Globalization' is one of the buzzwords of the day, acknowledging the deepening, dangerous and unprecedented *interconnectedness* of every fact, event and circumstance; of wealth and poverty, disease, success and failure, life and death: 'We all make up one world, even if we are only gradually coming to recognize it' (Boyle, 1998, p. 9).

'No man is an island', said Donne, 400 years ago, 'every man is a piece of the continent, a part of the main' (John Donne, *Meditation XVII*). And yet, the scientific world-view emerging in Donne's day was one which saw the fundamental constituents of reality as minute particles, individuals, in emptiness. Today, even in physics the atomic individual entity has been dethroned and, guided by so-called 'chaos theory' (which is not, of course, about chaos at all, but about the unpredictable order of the world) 'every schoolchild knows' that rainfall in Topeka, Kansas, may follow from the flapping of a butterfly's wings in Tokyo. We have, once again, begun to learn the primacy of *relations*.

'One thing which has thus far escaped globalization is our collective ability to act globally' (Bauman, 2001, p. 52), to act on behalf not merely of this or that particular interest, but of the whole. The most urgent challenge that confronts the human race today is the requirement to imagine and to construct a global *politics* which can contain and counter the destructive violence unleashed by the unchecked operation of a global market. What shape such a politics may take we do not know. We have not been here before. Notwithstanding strenuous resistance from the 'rogue power' that is today's United States, the first beginnings may perhaps be glimpsed in the history of the United Nations and in the development of international law and instruments of international justice. One thing we can be sure of: the structure of a global politics will not be that of a 'world state'. Why not? Because the state is that institution on behalf of which the citizen is called to patriotic duty and, to put it very simply, it makes no sense to talk of patriotic duty to the *planet*, because the planet has no political opponents (see Boyle, 1998, pp. 175–6). It seems to me, moreover, that at least as important as the construction of appropriate institutions will be the development of what one might call a genuinely global *imagination*: a sense of solidarity with the whole of humankind – past, present, and to come.

In the development of such an imagination, Christianity undoubtedly has a part to play, and that is a positive assertion with no negative implications; many other traditions – political, philosophical, cultural, religious – also have their parts to play. It has a part to play not only because it has been around for a long time and continues to shape the identity of very many people (something like a quarter of the population of the planet is, at present, at least nominally Christian), but also on account of its own self-constituting narrative, or what we usually call the doctrine of the Church.

'Church', *'ecclesia'*, means gathering, assembly, congregation: a people summoned, called together for some task. This people is the human race – called, out of nothing, into common life, communion, in God. This does not make all human beings Christians. What we usually *call* 'Church' is that *particular* people which thus announces, symbolizes and dramatizes the fact and possibility and promise of the common peoplehood – exceptionless communion of the whole of humankind. (Such emphasis on the 'sacramental' character of Christian peoplehood fits neatly, it seems to me, with Dr Higton's proposal that 'the *Church Dogmatics* be seen as a school of figural interpretation', for, according to the ancient adage, *'sacramenta sunt in genere signi'*: sacraments are signs, or figures.)

The next step (which brings me, at last, to the theme of this collection) is to recognize that it would seem to be a necessary condition of the achievement and fostering of what I have called a 'global imagination' that humankind, in all its vast and frequently conflictual diversity, be brought, in some measure, into something like a common *conversation.*

References

Bauman, Z. (2001), 'Whatever Happened to Compassion?', in T. Bentley and D.S. Jones (eds), *The Moral Universe*, London: Demos.

Boyle, N. (1998), *Who Are We Now? Christian Humanism and the Global Market from Hegel to Heaney*, Edinburgh: T. & T. Clark.

Acknowledgements

This book has been some time in the making, and along the way we have been helped by many friends and colleagues – not least all those who agreed to write chapters for us. Many thanks are due in particular to our colleagues in Edinburgh and Exeter for supporting our work, and to various people who have engaged us in fascinating conversation about Barth and about the nature of conversation itself over the last few years: Jon Cooley, David Horrell, Steve Holmes, David Moseley, Susannah Ticciati, and the 'Karl Barth in Conversation' honours Class at New College in 2003.

Thanks are also due to *International Journal of Systematic Theology* and *Modern Theology* for permitting the publication of material from John C. McDowell (2002) 'Much Ado About Nothing: Karl Barth's Being Unable to Do Nothing About Nothingness', *International Journal of Systematic Theology* 4(3), pp. 319–35, and John C. McDowell (2003) 'Theology as Conversational Event: Karl Barth, the Ending of "Dialogue" and the Beginning of "Conversation"', *Modern Theology* 19(4), pp. 483–509, respectively.

Abbreviations

CD   Barth, K. (1956–1975), *Church Dogmatics*, Edinburgh: T. & T. Clark.
KD   Barth, K. (1932–1967), *Kirchliche Dogmatik*, Zollikon-Zurich: Evangelischer Verlag.

CHAPTER 1

Introduction: Karl Barth as Conversationalist

Mike Higton and John C. McDowell

There were two main reasons for conceiving this project. In the first place, we felt that something more ought to be done to shake off the nagging suspicions, commonly voiced, that Barth does not make a good conversation partner. James Barr's comment is representative of one kind of objection: Barth, he says, 'paid little attention to other people's opinions' (Barr, 1993, p. 31). Stating the problem in this way, of course, leaves Barr vulnerable to a lazy riposte – one that would simply rack up a list of Barth's approving citations or lengthy discussions of the ideas of other thinkers. His theological appreciation of Mozart's praise of creation, or of Heidegger and Sartre's limited but nevertheless instructive discussions of *nothingness* are well known, for instance. Such proof-texting is always frivolous, however, and leaves the core of Barr's suspicion fatally undamaged. Something more far-ranging is being claimed by Barr here: that Barth's theology illegitimately secures itself from critique; that it polices its narrow location assiduously and only lets in a few carefully vetted others when convinced that they can be of service.[1]

In the second place, we began this project not only because of our sense that this kind of suspicion depended upon an ill-judged account of what Barth was up to theologically, but for the far more positive reason that we are convinced that, in practice, Barth still remains a fascinating and important figure for the doing of theology today. We wanted not only to show that Barth was best understood as a conversational theologian, but also to encourage others to engage in wide-ranging, many-voiced conversations with him. Something of this conviction is already apparent in a claim of Paul M. van Buren's in 1964:

> If we would learn something of what it is like to be a man of the twentieth century in intimate conversation with the long past of theology (and thereby perhaps learn something more of that past than is easily discernible from these New World shores) it will be worth our while never to dismiss this man as a relic of an antique world or as a conservative or reactionary who will not move with the times. (Buren, 1964, p. xiv)

The recent increased rate of growth in secondary literature on Barth's theology is itself an indication of the value of this comment. Whilst there may have been times since his death when Barth's influence seemed to be a spent force, the vast majority of reflections on his theology published during the past five years or so should make us dubious about any such claim. Of course, the forms of reception of that influence differ widely from those who dine and converse with a welcome guest to those who attempt to flee from an intruder but, both to critical friend and to bemused enemy, Barth seems to present an inexhaustible field for redescription and engagement. However much we are willing to attribute to the self-absorbed dynamism of the academic Barth-studies industry, there must be something about his work which allows that industry to thrive – and, in any case, genuinely interesting readings and debates continue to be developed, particularly amongst those who, whilst enthusiastic about his theology, respect Barth's fear of being uncritically repeated (see Barth, 1963b, p. 12). More than 20 years on, we may echo John Webster's conclusion to a survey of Barth literature from 1975 to 1981: '… the understanding and critical reception of Barth's work is a task which is still not at all finished. There could hardly be a better testimony to a theologian's continuing fruitfulness' (Webster, 1982, p. 35).

Karl Barth: Conversationalist

A volume entitled *Conversing with Barth* is a viable project, we believe, because Barth saw himself standing within the spaces opened up for him by his past and found the shape of his thought subtly refigured through the various conversations he had with his contemporaries. Karl Barth was a conversational theologian. Yet we need to be careful to interpret that comment appropriately, for Barth has sometimes been misread by those who presuppose a different conception of what it means to be a conversationalist.[2] Barth says:

> You speak of conversation, but what does this mean? Conversation takes place when one party has something *new* and *interesting* to say to the other. Only then is conversation an event. One must say something engaging and original, something with an element of mystery. The Church must sound strange to the world if it is not to be dull …. We may read philosophers (and we should!) without accepting their presuppositions. We may listen respectfully (I have a holy respect for a *good* philosopher!). We can learn much from philosophy and science. But as theologians we must be obedient to the Word. (Barth, 1963b, p. 19)

Several things are noteworthy about this set of comments. First, Barth's interest in presuppositions betrays an interest in the particularity and difference that makes conversation possible. We do not converse because we share a common foundation, and can trade variations upon that agreed theme, but because we are different. Barth's reiteration of his commitment to determinatively ecclesial presuppositions is not a refusal of conversation, any more than is his recognition of the different presuppositions of the philosophers.[3] Conversation involves difference and the awareness of difference – neither the suppression nor the 'celebration' of difference, but a willingness to take it seriously. Put differently, Barth is aware that any conversation is always between a *particular* some*one* and a *particular* some*one* else; there can be no atemporal or acontextual conversation in which the conversation partners leave who they are behind in order to conduct a dialogue in so-called 'objectivity'.

We could compare this unembarrassed reliance on presuppositions which are not shared, but which need not isolate, with Harnack's 1923 complaint that Barth was 'unscientific' in his work – a complaint which seems to conflate reading guided by unshared presuppositions with a relativistic free-for-all. For Harnack, if there is no obviously objective reading of a text, then its meaning fragments into the chaos of readers' private preferences.[4] For him, only a hermeneutical objectivity grounded in universally shared assumptions can free readings from potential nihilism and for public discussion, interaction and assessment.

Barth's response exposes the unshared presuppositions in Harnack's own position. 'I think I owe it to you and our listeners', he says, 'to confess that I do consider my answers open to debate, but that still for the time being and until I am shown a better way I reserve all else to myself. Nonetheless, your objections cannot deter me from continuing to ask along the line of those answers' (Barth, 1972b, p. 40). Here, Barth subverts Harnack's own accusations by charging him with not listening and with methodological parochialism – the 'science' of theology may be broader than Harnack had imagined, but Harnack is unprepared to entertain any voices different from his own. Harnack's theology, then, is the one that is closed (ibid., p. 42). Even so, Barth continues, 'I would like to be able to listen attentively in the future to whatever *you* also have to say. But at this time I cannot concede that you have driven me off the field with your questions and answers, although I will gladly endure it when it really happens' (ibid., p. 52). Barth is unapologetic in naming the particular shape of his own presuppositions, those which set him on the particular path he was to tread – they are theological ones. As the 'But' in his claim cited earlier suggested ('*But* as theologians we must be obedient to the Word'), he is clearly not prepared to renege on his commitments. That would be to deny who he is.

Returning to that quotation, we can, second, note Barth's insistence that '[t]he Church must sound strange to the world if it is not to be dull'. Far from believing that his presuppositions bar him from conversation, by enclosing him in an impervious enclave, Barth instead believes that those presuppositions precisely enable him to converse. Despite what we have just been saying, this is not because he has some theory which would argue that, *in general*, particularity and conversation go together, but rather because the specific shape that his Christian identity takes is one that is constitutionally open to conversation – in a way that may or may not find partial parallels in the differing identities of others. So, for instance, it is precisely *because* he is a Christian that Barth is committed to a particular way of seeing the world in Jesus Christ that recognizes and generously admits its indebtedness to those who have spoken within the Christian Church past and present. This is not only clear in the lectures available as *Protestant Theology in the Nineteenth Century* (1972a), but as early as the Preface to the first edition of *Der Römerbrief*. There, Barth was able to claim that '[t]he understanding of history is an uninterrupted conversation between the wisdom of yesterday and the wisdom of tomorrow. And it is a conversation always conducted honestly and with discernment' (Barth, 1968, p. 1). This is not, for Barth, some general commitment to the role and possibilities of tradition, but a *theological* conviction that rests on a recognition that our activity as Christian theologians exists only in constant dependence, and also that this dependence is itself the fruit of an original, establishing and generative *absolute dependence*.[5] Prayer, then, is the origin of conversation, and a theology of grace demands attention to the notion that we converse because we have been conversed with – in Jesus Christ. We listen to the other because we listen to God – Christ is the divine Word and human hearing. The church lives in the faith that it is not engaged in dialogue only with itself.

Note the view of tradition, of handing-on, which is implied in this formulation, however. Barth is not satisfied with maintaining a commitment to some supposed identifiable set of theories or practices that could be carried through time in a pristine and immutable condition. He speaks of a conversation between yesterday and tomorrow, not of a sacred deposit delivered yesterday which we are charged to carry through to tomorrow. Barth could agree, in general, with Richard Roberts' rejection of '[t]he mechanical recapitulation of Christian doctrine merely as items in an inherited belief system, undertaken as though nothing had happened' (Roberts, 1997, p. 716). It is frequently noted, for instance, that Barth, despite being a Reformed theologian, has learned to read the Reformers critically, as one concerned with how they might speak to theology in the twentieth century rather than with the assumption that they said all that they needed to say in the sixteenth. His re-envisioning of the doctrine of election in *CD* II/2 is a good example of his avoidance of what Roberts calls a 'theological necrophilia' (Roberts, 1996, p. 192; see also Barth, 1972a, pp. 16f.; McFadyen, 2000, p. 50).

Third, our quotation from Barth's *Table Talk* indicates that Barth did not restrict the conversation to which his faith called him simply to the Christian tradition. William Stacy Johnson puts it well (although the term 'event' would seem better suited to Barth's descriptions than 'mystery') when he claims that:

> Respect for the mystery of God would seem to demand nothing less than a multidimensional approach to the theological task …. In his survey of *Protestant Theology in the Nineteenth Century*, for example, Barth professed a desire to attend to 'all the voices of the past,' and not merely the ones which have stood in official favor. This is necessary, he said, because one cannot anticipate in advance which voices will speak to the genuinely 'theological' elements in human endeavour. (Johnson, 1997, p. 37 referring to Barth, 1972a, p. 17)

Both in theory and in practice, Barth displayed a willingness to engage with secular philosophy. All kinds of extra-ecclesial claims and facts can become witnesses to the Gospel, and can be perceived as such in the light of a Christological hermeneutic: Barth's specifically Christian presuppositions provide him with an ear by which he can listen to voices from beyond the explicit pale of faith (Barth, 1990, p. 92; *CD* I/1, p. 176).[6] As Rowan Williams says, 'the church judges the world; but it also hears God's judgment on itself passed upon it by the world' (Williams, 2000, p. 330).

Bruce Marshall argues that:

> … on his [Barth's] account the range of theological discourse seems unlimited; he seems concerned to deny rather than assert that there are 'spheres' of discourse

'external' to theology .... Since theological discourse has no abiding 'outside', distinctions between discourse 'internal' and 'external' to theology, while in some respects perhaps provisionally useful, can in principle never be binding. Barth does not distinguish theology from other sorts of discourse primarily by locating a special subject-matter for it, still less by the principled exclusion or rejection of other kinds of discourse. What distinguishes theology is rather the particular way in which it strives to order all discourses: it interprets and assesses them by taking 'Jesus Christ as he is attested for us in holy scripture' as its primary and decisive criteria of truth and meaning .... Theology for Barth seems to be an open-ended project of understanding and judgement which, within the obvious limits of its human practitioners, aims at an estimate of all things – from Mozart to birth control, the rearmament of Germany to riding horses – oriented around this particular criterion. (Marshall, 1993, p. 456)[7]

Barth makes positive but critical use of, for instance, extra-ecclesial anthropologies (*CD* III/2) and of Mozart's music (*CD* III/3, pp. 297ff.), and his use of philosophy is too complex to be reduced to any single systematic scheme (Barth, 1986); he uses philosophy eclectically but pervasively in the service of theology, while taking care not to allow it to undermine or overwhelm the particularity of theology's witness to God in Christ. Thiemann describes this as 'the temporary borrowing of a tool to help us better understand the complex meaning of the Christian Gospel' (Thiemann, 1991, p. 82). A statement of Barth's renders the flavour of what he intends here. He admits that '[t]he central affirmations of the Bible are not self-evident .... Every possible means must be used ... not the least, the enlistment of every device of the conjectural imagination' in order to interpret it (see Barth, 1963b, p. 37f.). In this thematic context he famously declares:

God may speak to us through Russian communism, a flute concerto, a blossoming shrub or a dead dog. We do well to listen to Him if He really does .... God may speak to us through a pagan or an atheist, and thus give us to understand that the boundary between the Church and the secular world can take at any time a different course from that which we think we discern. (*CD* I/1, p. 55)[8]

Not only are these extra-ecclesial elements witnesses to God in Christ, they can function as critiques of the ways in which the churches performatively imagine the significance and import of that event. They are not significant because they shine a light complementary to that which shines in Christ, and the conversations we have with them are not intended to supplement the grace we find in Christ; rather, these conversations are an essential part of Barth's theology precisely because they take him deeper into Christ, into the one commanding criterion of his work.

The Virtue of Arguing

One of the differences of approach which has sometimes obscured, for commentators, Barth's commitment to conversation, is their assumption that conversation is fundamentally *irenic* – that it is seen best where friendly agreement flourishes, coupled with a willingness to differ on secondary matters. For Barth, on the other hand, quite a bit of his conversation takes the form of strident argument. Is this a failure? Is Barth's commitment to conversation vitiated by the form in which he conducts it – by the violence of his disagreement, by the sheer unstoppable momentum of his writing? There may indeed be much truth in this, and there is no doubt that Barth could, from time to time, be as unfair as theologians anywhere in his hasty characterizations and even hastier dismissals of others. But we must beware of stating this too strongly, as if Barth's willingness to argue, and to argue hard, were itself a sign of failure.

Donald Allen and Rebecca Guy speak for many when they take conflict, including argument, as 'generally mark[ing] the failure of social relations', and therefore as a social pathology (Allen and Guy, 1974, p. 239). But such a rejection of argument can only function where religious beliefs and practices are reduced to bland differences in choice, to matters of private taste about which it would be tasteless to kick up a fuss. Such a rejection can only function where religious practices, and indeed the shape of all our politics and ethical practices, are removed from the dangerous ultimacy of worship (the recognition of a universal scope worthy of our worship) to the local subjectivities of consumer choice. In other words, the rejection of argument, of serious disagreement, is possible only for a pluralism where all is allowed because nothing is taken seriously (see Placher, 1989, p. 81).

Barth's thought is resistant to this repressive tolerance, this easy, lazy pluralism which lets differences lie. The mark of a 'failure of social relations' can be found in Barth not where he argues, not where he engages in cheerful or bitter conflict (though we may sometimes regret his tone) but only where he ceases to believe that someone is worth arguing with, where he ceases to believe that someone is even worth contradicting. Where he argues, it is often the greatest compliment he can pay[9] – since to argue means both to maintain that the differences between his interlocutor and himself are real and that these differences matter. The very heat of his arguments is often a sign of his belief that the differences cut so deeply that addressing them is a matter of urgent duty: it is a sign that he regards engaging with the interlocutor as a very serious matter indeed.

At his best, Barth shows a startling willingness to think through an alternative point of view seriously, and not to rest content with surface differences but to chase these down into the deep theological divisions that underlie them. His determination to let his disagreements with others be thoroughly theological is not – at least, not always – a sign that he simply wishes to line other thinkers up against the chalk-marks of his own standards and dismiss all those that come in too short or too tall. Rather, he regards it as his duty to think through their claims from within his own frame of reference, not in the terms of some supposed neutrality,[10] because only in that way can he reach a genuine encounter with them, and only in that way can he genuinely be open to challenge by them. Only if he makes the effort to see how the interlocutor calls into question or contradicts the ways in which he has been faithful to his own deepest criteria can conversation be carried on. Only if he is willing to be so stridently critical can he be truly self-critical.[11]

As we have already suggested, this willingness – indeed, insistence – on pursuing disagreements to their roots, and thinking them through theologically, relies on a refusal to divide the world up into incompatible spheres, incommensurable conversations, or radically discrete epochs. This is most clear if we restrict ourselves to Barth's dealings with the wide stream of the Christian tradition: his insistence on criticizing his opponents theologically is itself based on the assumption that every theologian is dealing with the same God, with the same Christ, and that whatever we attribute to differences of cultural context, philosophical resources or rhetorical styles is secondary to a true grappling with that God, that Christ, that faith.[12] Barth's willingness to do theological battle with his opponents is itself a mark of his belief that they, too, are hearers of the same Word. Something similar is at work in his dealings with others beyond the theological tradition. The only way open to Barth if he wishes to take these others seriously is to take them theologically, and his willingness to do so – even when it is tempting simply to turn them all into yet more grist for his own theological mill, simply confirming him in his own prejudices – is, at its best, not a mark of closure, but of profound openness.

This sense of the unavoidable urgency and seriousness of theological talk, of the unavoidable urgency and seriousness with which we must enter conversation from our particular theological position and be willing to think through other claims and ideas theologically, accompanies and substantiates Barth's understanding of the fallibility and frailty of his own theology. However much his rhetoric sometimes lends itself to a sense of his theology's impervious strength, his work is never wholly without a sense of its own partial nature and its own necessary failure – and this sense is, in a hidden way, firmly present *in* (not just *despite*) his most trenchant theological grapplings with those with whom he disagrees. In our formation as listeners to the *Deus dixit* we have learned to hear distortedly; we must therefore constantly return to our source and become aware of our own preconscious, unconscious and even conscious temptation to idolatry – and that means both being open to challenge and being challenging. This is why Barth is able to announce to Harnack that:

> I do not intend to entrench myself in those positions in which you, honoured Sir, and our voluntary–involuntary audience in this conversation have seen me, simply because I know how frighteningly relative *everything* is that one can *say* about the great subject which occupies you and me. I know that it will be necessary to speak of it in a way quite different from that of my present understanding. (Barth, 1972b, p. 52)[13]

Something of the sense of the honesty of this generous and (self-)critical approach may be found in a comment Barth made towards the end of his life:

> Being truly liberal means thinking and speaking in responsibility and openness on all sides, backwards and forwards, toward both past and future, and with what

I might call total personal modesty. To be modest is not to be skeptical; it is to see what one thinks and says also has limits. This does not hinder me from saying very definitely what I think I see and know. But I can do this only in the awareness that there has been and are other people before and alongside me, and that still others will come after me. This awareness gives me an inner peace, so that I do not think I always have to be right even though I say definitely what I say and think. Knowing that a limit is set for me, too, I can move cheerfully within it as a free man. (Barth, 1977, pp. 34ff.)

That Barth did not, in the end, engage with everyone and everything theologically is testimony to the limitations of time and resources, as well as to sometimes problematic decisions about whose work was worth the effort. That he certainly did not understand all those with whom he did engage equally well does not itself undermine his sense of openness to, and respect of, others, but is testimony to the partiality and fragility of his all-too-human hearing. However, whilst the details of these absent conversations, and those conducted less well than we would like, may pose important questions about the manner of Barth's actual *practice*, they do less to indict his theological *theory* of conversation. As David Ford argues, 'there is only a limited number of exchanges any guest can take part in, and nobody needs to know what is going on in every conversation' (Ford, 1999, p. 271). Nevertheless,

I do not see how theology which is related to a God who relates to everything and everyone can in principle limit its questions and conversations .... [T]he central truths are such that they cry out to be related to the whole of reality and to every human being, with intensive conversation as one important way of doing this. (Ford, 2001, p. 566f.)

However unnecessarily pugilistic he may sometimes have been, Barth's trenchant commitment to the theological interpretation of his opponents, and to doing conversational battle with all comers, are not signs of arrogant failure, but of belief in God.

Conversing with Barth

The essays in this book explore in various ways Barth's openness to conversation, asking how much his theology was developed in explicit conversations with figures in and beyond the Christian tradition, and asking whether it can contribute to contemporary theological conversations without stifling them. This much is true by design, and a response by each author to our initial challenge to write about 'Barth in conversation'. However, a further, unplanned commonality emerged as the various papers were assembled – a commonality which perhaps suggests a broad front along which conversation with Barth is most urgent, most interesting and most productive. If the initial unifying theme was the openness of Barth's theology to conversation, this emergent unifying theme is the related openness of Barth's theology to the particularity, diversity, complexity and messiness of human life and history.

In Chapter 2 John Webster tackles the interlocking of these two themes directly, arguing that Barth's conversational way with the theological tradition rests firmly on a theological understanding of history. That understanding does not reduce the complexity and fragility of that history to a series of agreements or disagreements with some accessible deposit which would provide the true content of history – Barth does not, in Webster's phrase, approach the theological tradition's figures 'with a dogmatic checklist in hand'. Rather, Webster argues, Barth has both eyes open to these figures' struggle 'towards Christianness', their hopeful but fallible turning towards the one source of theology who is no more confined to Barth's possession than to theirs. This theological recognition of their humanity funds Barth's practice of conversation.

A similar question, as to whether Barth had time for history, is tackled by both Eugene Rogers (Chapter 9) and Mike Higton (Chapter 7). Rogers returns to the familiar question about Barth's pneumatology, and takes it in a new direction by pushing further Barth's conversation with Athanasius. He suggests that, once we have distinguished the tones of this conversation from those of Barth's louder conversation with Schleiermacher, the conversation with Athanasius might allow us to fill in some of the blanks in Barth's treatment of the Spirit – and that doing so might allow us to see how Barth's theology can be opened still further to the unpredictable flourishing of human freedom and doxology which the Spirit cultivates in history.

Mike Higton argues that Barth's practice of figural interpretation in his treatment of the doctrine of election, particularly when it is approached via a conversation with Hans Frei and Erich Auerbach's Dante, already demonstrates Barth's appreciation of the endlessly particular, endlessly surprising fulfilment of history. Barth's figural interpretation allows him to do justice to the historical density and irreducibility of Scriptural narratives, and also – potentially – to the historical density and irreducibility of creaturely existence in general. Recognizing this might allow us to use the *Dogmatics* in new, more productive ways.

Similar issues are raised by Ben Quash's investigation of Barth's understanding of human freedom in Chapter 6. Quash revisits the conversation between Barth and Hans Urs von Balthasar and, as well as tracing some of the profound commonalities linking the two theologians, puts forward the initially surprising suggestion that, despite the impression that von Balthasar tries to do more justice than Barth to the exercise of human freedom, it may well be Barth who has the more adequate framework. Where '[v]on Balthasar wants the *free* embrace of *obedience*', he says, Barth 'wants in the creature the *obedient* embrace of *freedom*'. Quash suggests that von Balthasar can still offer Barth a more robust account of human action's participation in Christ's action, but nevertheless argues that there might be, in Barth, a considerably more joyful celebration of the possibilities of creaturely freedom than has normally been recognized.

In Chapter 10 Katherine Sonderegger addresses these questions of obedience and freedom in a rather different way, by examining the nature of theology's responsibility to the givenness of Gospel history. Witness to this history structures and regulates Barth's dogmatics, and Sonderegger demonstrates that this regulation flows materially from a theology of the theologian's obedient hearing of the Word of God, a listening in order to assent which is itself the gift of proper freedom. Sonderegger contrasts this model with that of Robert Jenson, who proposes, instead, a rather different understanding of the theologian's task in history, centred on the model of the theologian as interpreter. Sonderegger argues that this model must be tested by the same criticisms which Barth levelled at Bultmann.

George Hunsinger (Chapter 5) addresses Barth's openness to the gradual stumbling growth of the Christian life in history, by hosting a conversation between Barth, Luther and Calvin. He explains that Barth's soteriology attempts to hold together Luther's insistence on the *simul iustus et peccator* with Calvin's insistence on the simultaneity of justification and sanctification. Hunsinger describes three related moves made by Barth in order to hold these together: a reconsideration of the meaning of our participation in Christ; a reconsideration of the meaning of Christ's presence to faith; and a reconsideration of the meaning of sanctification. Hunsinger suggests that, despite Barth's decisive advances in soteriology, a pressing question remains about the room which Barth leaves for growth, development and maturity in the Christian life and calls us to further theological work.

Graham Ward (Chapter 4) and Timothy Gorringe (Chapter 3) both examine the relationship between Barth and culture. Ward tackles the thorny issue of the possibility of Christian apologetics. What would it mean for one who is renowned for depicting theology as a conversation of faith with faith to conduct apologetics? Ward maintains that, for a Christian theologian, the one place it cannot operate from is some unmediated access to the Word in the world that could then be wielded like a weapon or used like a tool. While Ward notes in Barth's discourse an illegitimate attempt to police its own boundaries, by bringing Barth into conversation with Hegel he is also able to trace an admission in Barth of theology's own cultural embeddedness and its interdependence with the discourses of other disciplines.

Tim Gorringe's essay similarly explores the popular image of a Barth who had no time for culture, except in those hours he spent engrossed in Mozart's music. He suggests that, if instead of the narrower definitions of *Kultur* present in the German tradition we turn instead to the more variegated discussion of culture by such Anglo-Saxon voices as Arnold, Eliot, Williams and Eagleton, a different picture emerges. This is an unusual juxtaposition, but then Barth 'was always more surprising than a strict reading of his theology suggests'. On the one hand, culture has, Gorringe suggests, an entirely proper, if strictly limited, role for Barth; on the other, several of these Anglo-Saxon theorists of culture also have an inkling of culture's brokenness. In the face of various forms of 'barbarism' which confront both theologians and these theorists of culture, Gorringe suggests that there is room here for 'worthwhile engagement' or, at the very least, a 'fruitful contradiction'.

In Chapter 8 John McDowell also explores Barth's openness to culture, contrasting Barth's theological openness to Mozart's music with Donald MacKinnon's openness to tragic literature. By drawing on MacKinnon, McDowell is able to ask whether

Barth can do justice to that which ruptures thought and practice – that which Barth names *Das Nichtige* – whilst still holding fast to Christian, hope. He suggests that the nature of that hope cannot be allowed to elide too easily the questions that a reading of the tragic can put to it, and argues that, with MacKinnon's and tragedy's help, we can locate much in Barth that is open to the darkness of history and resistant to any too easily triumphant reading.

Lastly, David Clough (Chapter 11) examines one example of theology's sensitivity to the tragic in history, by exploring the way in which Barth allowed the clarity of his theological commitments to peace to be responsive to the extreme possibility of war. Clough explores Barth's understanding of the possibility of 'exceptional cases', in which obedience in the midst of history might need to take a form that opposes all the more general lines of the guidance which we have received from the Gospel; he examines John H. Yoder's criticism of this claim in the case of Barth's account of war, suggesting that, although Barth's acceptance of the possibility of exceptional cases is better justified than Yoder allowed, his handling of it in this particular case is nevertheless inadequate.

Notes

1 Richard Roberts puts his own version of this kind of criticism like this: Barth's isolation of theology after the *Römerbrief* of 1922 leads to the 'dangerously close collusion between his voice and that of God'. This entails a 'totalitarian' method that 'demands conformity and submission rather than critical investigation' (Roberts, 1991, p. xv).

2 An article by John Milbank on 'The End of Dialogue' provides a useful explication of this point. When complaining of the unchallenged assumptions of many involved in the talk of 'dialogue' in the area of religious pluralism, he argues that 'dialogue' is 'a profoundly ethnocentric illusion' that assumes a commonly recognized subject-matter by both (or all) participants, and that partners will progress to a sympathetic comprehension of each others' perspectives (Milbank, 1990, p. 177). 'The very idea that dialogue is a passage for the delivery of truth, that it has a privileged relationship to Being, assumes that many voices are coalescing around a single known object which is independent of our biographical or transbiographical processes of coming-to-know' (ibid.). 'Dialogue', in other words, may prove to be too ideological a discourse for theologians to participate in – too permented by a modern capitalist value system, and thus too easily preventative of the truth-of-difference.

3 David Burrell suggests that the nature of the pressure to perform on contemporary academic theologians could seriously disturb this primarily ecclesial space for conversation: 'The overweening academic context of a university can easily impel the theologians operating within it towards a conversation preoccupied with their academic colleagues rather than one focused on the community of believers' (Burrell, 2000, p. 21); '[I]t is easy to see how such an environment can lull the conversants into a certain set of presuppositions while marginalising other perspectives of the kingdom of God' (ibid., p. 22). Barth complained of the academic 'independence of theology in relation to other sciences.... It is indeed unfortunate that the question of the truth of talk about God should be handled as a question apart by a special faculty' (*CD* I/1, p. 5). Although this positioning may have been occasioned by current academic practice, it bestows on theology an honour simultaneously too great (as if it possesses 'special keys to special doors', and has a 'despair of the world') and too small (theology does not then show that what other disciplines say about it derives from 'alien principles', *CD* I/1, p. 6). Hence Barth announces that '[t]heology is the science which finally sets this task [talking of God], and this task alone, subordinating to this task all other possible

tasks in the human search for truth'. The word 'subordinating' is crucial here, suggesting reading all other disciplines theologically rather than ignoring them in order to do theology.

4   Harnack feels that Barth dispenses with historical science, and that this is a foolish move: 'his point of view … opens the gate to every suitable fantasy and to every theological dictatorship which dissolves the historical ingredient of our religion and seeks to torment the conscience of others with one's own heuristic knowledge' (in Barth, 1972b, p. 39). Barth complains of Harnack's accusation that he did not listen to others because he already knows both the questions and answers (Barth, 1972b, p. 40).

5   This admission undoes George Schner's comment that 'conversation' accords an active role to the theologian 'over the *receptive* moment of the religious attitude, an obvious debt to modernity's emphasis on rationality as constructive' (Schner, 2000, p. 30).

6   For an examination of this in the context of explicating Barth's critique of natural theology see McDowell (2002).

7   Elsewhere Marshall correctly argues that Barth's Christocentrism does not stipulate the details of the process of revelation's subjective appropriation, since, as Thiemann indicates, by the term 'revelation' Barth means primarily the *content* of our knowing of God (Marshall, 1987, p. 148f; cf. Thiemann, 1991, p. 84). In a statement that is not unrelated, Barth himself affirmed, 'No one can say how this is done, not even the most devout and learned theologians of all times have been able to hear the Christmas message' (Barth, 1959, p. 25).

8   Later in *CD* IV/3 Barth articulates the sense of this in terms of what he calls 'the little light of creation' (*CD* IV/3.1, §69.2).

9   Kenneth Surin argues that '[i]n this monologue, the pluralist … speaks well of the other but never to the other, and indeed cannot do otherwise because there really is no intractable other for the pluralist' (Surin, 1990, p. 200).

10 'But true education cannot rest with preferences, so an authentic theology will be called upon to present an alternative to a consumer society which so easily infects the exercise of academe as well, and we find that the best way to do that is by critically appropriating the fullness of a faith-tradition' (Burrell, 2000, p. 23).

11 'The inevitable outcome has been a sheer inattentiveness on the part of these thinkers to the intricacies and complexities and political configurations which circumscribe their reflections' (Surin, 1990, p. 202). '*Serious* dialogue indeed requires openness to change, but it also demands a sense of how significant changing one's faith would be' (Placher, 1989, p. 149).

12 These two together mean that Barth refuses a primarily historical or cultural analysis of other theologians. It is not that these are invalid – they can be done and no doubt should be done. But as a theologian, his task is different. It is to pay others the compliment of taking them seriously as theologians, even if that means claiming that they are utterly mistaken; and, for this task, historical or cultural analysis can only be a preparatory move.

13 Barth follows his opening remarks in his *Protestant Theology in the Nineteenth Century* with the claims that 'Of course, there is no method, not even a theological one, by means of which we can be certain of catching sight of theology. In this way, too, it can escape us, because we are inadequate to the task it poses' (Barth, 1972a, p. 15). Characteristically, however, Barth cannot let the matter rest there and comments on the risky but necessary venture of theology.

References

Allen, D.E. and R.F. Guy (1974), *Conversation Analysis: The Sociology of Talk*, The Hague: Mouton.

Barr, J. (1993), *Biblical Faith and Natural Theology: The Gifford Lectures for 1991*, Oxford: Clarendon Press.

Barth, K. (1959), *Christmas*, trans. B. Citron, Edinburgh and London: Oliver and Boyd.

Barth, K. (1963a), *Evangelical Theology: An Introduction*, trans. G. Foley, London: Collins.

Barth, K. (1963b), *Karl Barth's Table Talk*, ed. J.D. Godsey, Edinburgh and London: Oliver and Boyd.

Barth, K. (1968), *The Epistle to the Romans*, trans. E.C. Hoskyns, Oxford: Oxford University Press.

Barth, K. (1972a), *Protestant Theology in the Nineteenth Century: Its Background and History*, trans. B. Cozens and J. Bowden, London: SCM.

Barth, K. (1972b), *Revelation and Theology: An Analysis of the Barth–Harnack Correspondence of 1923*, ed. H.M. Rumscheidt, Cambridge: Cambridge University Press.

Barth, K. (1977), 'Liberal Theology – An Interview', in E. Busch (ed.), *Final Testimonies*, trans. G.W. Bromiley, Grand Rapids, MI: Eerdmans; see also <http://www.religion-online.org/cgi-bin/relsearchd.dll/showbook?item_id=417>.

Barth, K. (1986), 'The First Commandment in Theology', in H.M. Rumscheidt (ed.), *The Way of Theology in Karl Barth: Essays and Comments*, Allison Park, Pennsylvania: Pickwick, pp. 63–78

Barth, K. (1990), *The Göttingen Dogmatics: Instruction in the Christian Religion, Volume 1*, trans. G.W. Bromiley, Grand Rapids, MI: Eerdmans.

Buren, P.M. van (1964), 'Translator's Introduction', in K. Barth, *God Here and Now*, London: Routledge and Kegan Paul, pp. xiii–xviii.

Burrell, D. (2000), 'Radical Orthodoxy in a North American Context', in L.P. Hemming (ed.), *Radical Orthodoxy? A Catholic Enquiry*, Aldershot: Ashgate, pp. 20–30.

Ford, D.F. (1999), *Self and Salvation*, Cambridge: Cambridge University Press.

Ford, D.F. (2001), 'Salvation and the Nature of Theology: A Response to John Webster's Review of *Self and Salvation: Being Transformed*', *Scottish Journal of Theology*, **54**, pp. 560–75.

Johnson, W.S. (1997), *The Mystery of God: Karl Barth and the Foundations of Theology*, Louisville, KT: Westminster John Knox Press.

McDowell, J.C. (2002), 'A Response to Rodney Holder on Barth on Natural Theology', *Themelios*, **27**(2), pp. 32–44.

McFadyen, A. (2000), *Bound to Sin: Abuse, Holocaust and the Christian Doctrine of Sin*, Cambridge: Cambridge University Press.

Marshall, B. (1987), *Christology in Conflict: The Identity of a Saviour in Rahner and Barth*, Oxford: Basil Blackwell.

Marshall, B. (1993), Review of R.H. Roberts, *A Theology on its Way? Essays on Karl Barth*, *Journal of Theological Studies*, **44**, pp. 453–8.

Milbank, J. (1990), 'The End of Dialogue', in G. D'Costa (ed.), *Christian Uniqueness Reconsidered: The Myth of a Pluralistic Theology of Religions*, New York: Orbis, pp. 174–91.

Placher, W. (1989), *Unapologetic Theology: A Christian Voice in a Pluralistic Conversation*, Louisville, KT: Westminster John Knox Press.

Roberts. R.H. (1991), *A Theology on its Way? Essays on Karl Barth*, Edinburgh: T. & T. Clark.

Roberts, R.H. (1996), 'A Postmodern Church? Some Preliminary Reflections on Ecclesiology and Social Theory', in D.F. Ford and D.L. Stamps (eds), *Essentials of Christian Community: Essays for Daniel W. Hardy*, Edinburgh: T. & T. Clark, pp. 179–95.

Roberts, R.H. (1997), 'Theology and the Social Sciences', in D.F. Ford (ed.), *The Modern Theologians*, 2nd edn, Oxford: Blackwell, pp. 700–719.

Schner, G.P. (2000), 'Metaphors for Theology', in J. Webster and G.P. Schner (eds), *Theology After Liberalism: A Reader*, Oxford: Blackwell, pp. 3–51.

Surin, K. (1990), 'A "Politics of Speech"', in G. D'Costa (ed.), *Christian Uniqueness Reconsidered: The Myth of a Pluralistic Theology of Religions*, New York: Orbis Books, pp. 192–212.

Thiemann, R.F. (1991), *Constructing a Public Theology: The Church in a Pluralistic Culture*, Louisville, KT: Westminster John Knox Press.

Webster, J. (1982), 'Recent Work on Barth: A Survey of Literature Since 1975', *Themelios*, **7**(3), pp. 31–5.

Williams, R. (2000), *On Christian Theology*, Oxford: Blackwell.

CHAPTER 2

'There is no past in the Church, so there is no past in theology': Barth on the History of Modern Protestant Theology

John Webster

Near the end of the introductory chapter of *Protestant Theology in the Nineteenth Century*, Barth turns to discuss the proper attitude which theologians in the present are to entertain towards their predecessors. He writes:

> The Christian faith is not an authority which we are in a position to quote against others. That it is the basis for the mutual conversation between them and us may not be doubted for a moment, much less denied, no matter if we have a thousand reasons for such a verdict. (Barth, 2001, p. 14).[1]

This essay is an initial exploration of what is involved for Barth in that conversation – a conversation which deeply and intensively engaged him from before the beginning of his career as a theological professor until the end of his life. Careful and attentive reading of *Protestant Theology*, along with related materials from the *Church Dogmatics* and elsewhere, not only demonstrates that Barth is a good deal more perceptive, sophisticated and modest than interpreters of his work often allow him to be, but also raises some questions about the nature of the history of the Church and its theology which take us to the centre of the enterprise of historical theology.

Barth's various attempts to describe modern Protestant thought, and to articulate the nature of historical theology, have rarely been studied at any depth or with any systematic scope. In large part, this is because his work as dogmatician has usually been read and discussed in isolation from the texts in which he engages in other fields of theological inquiry: not only historical theology but also, crucially, exegesis and ethics. It is, of course, true that it is in dogmatics that Barth's powers were most fully deployed, and that his achievements as exegetical, moral and historical theologian are ultimately of ancillary value. Nevertheless, their neglect not only entails overlooking material of considerable important for understanding Barth's oeuvre in its full range, but also risks misjudgements about his dogmatics. Stripped of its exegesis and ethics, for example, the *Church Dogmatics* is a torso, and one which, moreover, attracts all manner of misinterpretations which can be corrected only by attending to what Barth has to say in its completeness. And the same is true of Barth's work in historical theology: he is a Church dogmatician and therefore acutely conscious that an essential aspect of the *dogmatic* task is that of 'serious attention' to, and 'mutual conversation' with, the theologians of the Church's past. Without an appreciation of what Barth is about in that conversation, aspects of his dogmatic work will remain closed to us.

If study of Barth's theology has a rather poor record in this matter, it is in some respects because many of the conventional lines of interpretation of his work were settled in advance of the widespread availability in the posthumous *Gesamtausgabe* of a good deal of material, mainly in the form of lecture texts, which Barth did not publish in his lifetime but which indicate that the full extent of his theological work cannot be understood without taking account of his thinking in the fields of ethics, exegesis and historical theology. In the historical field, particularly, three sets of lectures from his first professorate in Göttingen – those on Calvin (Barth, 1992), Schleiermacher (Barth, 1982a), and the Reformed confessional writings (Barth, 2002) – indicate how one central component in the transformation of the theological instincts which Barth acquired after 1916 into a coherent set of dogmatic principles was his intensive labour on central figures and texts in the Reformed tradition. These lecture cycles reinforce the fact that Barth's dogmatic work did not simply appear from nowhere; from its inception in Göttingen (Barth, 1991) through the Münster *Christliche Dogmatik* (Barth, 1982b) to the *Church Dogmatics* in Bonn and Basel, it grew from and fed upon an ever-increasing consideration of the history of the Church's theology and exegesis. It is, of course, true that the thoroughly historical character of Barth's tackling of dogmatic problems is already evident both in the *Christliche Dogmatik* and in the volumes of the *Church Dogmatics* (and would also have been plain to the hearers of his dogmatics cycle in Göttingen). For all that, however, one consequence of the relatively recent publication of his historical lectures from the 1920s has been to stimulate a fresh appreciation of the fact that Barth's work on the history of theology cannot simply be treated as a *violon d'Ingres*, but has to be seen as integral to his overall project as a biblical, Reformed dogmatician. Some of the best recent interpretation of Barth's work has begun to display how his development in the crucial period of the 1920s cannot be understood without a thorough grasp of his work in the areas of New Testament exegesis, and of the theological and confessional traditions which flowed from Calvin. This picture of Barth – so different from the conventional reduction of him to an eschatological opponent of liberalism – can be filled out further by looking in some detail at the *Protestant Theology* book.

This strangely neglected text is important for at least three reasons. First, it is the most substantial piece of historical theology which Barth published in his lifetime, and contains not only some of his most authoritative writing in the field but also, in the opening chapter, a substantial proposal about the nature and tasks of historical theology. Second, it has considerable significance for any attempt at understanding how Barth's thinking developed in Göttingen and Münster, since a good deal of the material is a revision of lectures first delivered in 1926. In particular, the text shows that – precisely in the period when Barth's theology is purported to have been driven by a transcendentalist repudiation of history – he felt it incumbent on him not only to immerse himself in the history of Protestant theology but also to place his own theological work in that trajectory. And, third, *Protestant Theology* may prove instructive in developing an appropriately critical posture towards the theological traditions of modernity. *Protestant Theology* shows Barth to be very far indeed from those critics of modern theology who consider themselves capable of extricating themselves neatly from its grip (whether for the purpose of retreat to a pre-modern Catholic synthesis, or for the purpose of advance into the fields of cheerfully anarchic free play). It is precisely as he struggles to come to terms with the dominant figures of modern theology that Barth shows himself, in very important respects, as a thoroughly modern theologian, taking up modernity's questions even when he turns inside out the answers developed with such skill by his forebears, and, above all, feeling responsible for shouldering (not evading or dismissing) its tasks as a responsible participant in its history.

Barth as Historian of Theology

Arriving at Göttingen woefully ill-prepared, as he felt himself to be, Barth worked assiduously to (re-)acquaint himself with and position himself vis-à-vis both the modern and the older traditions of Christian theology. The personal impact of what often seemed a Herculean labour for Barth is recorded in his correspondence with Thurneysen (see Barth and Thurneysen, 1972). Its public monument can be found in the record of Barth's teaching at Göttingen and Münster, in the published texts which grew from his lectures and addresses, and in his literary *Nachlass*. Indeed, it was not until 1924 that Barth ventured to lecture on dogmatics; before then, his teaching was exclusively in the fields of New Testament exegesis and historical theology. Thus in his Göttingen period from 1921 to 1925, only three of his 15 lecture courses were in dogmatics, and in Münster, of 20 lectures and seminars only four were in dogmatics and two in ethics, with four exegetical courses and ten courses which treated topics in historical theology. The most casual acquaintance with Barth's work in historical theology shows, of course, that he handled the material with an eye to his constructive, systematic interests, but it is surely remarkable that 15 of Barth's 35 courses in his first two professorates (just over three-sevenths) were attempts to come to terms with texts in historical theology.

At the beginning of his career, the field of his chair committed him to a special engagement with the Reformed tradition, and so he worked through the Heidelberg Catechism (Winter Semester 1921–22), Calvin (Summer Semester 1922), Zwingli (WS 1922–23) and the Reformed confessional writings (SS 1923); in Münster, Barth also ran a seminar on Galatians as interpreted in Luther's and Calvin's commentaries (SS 1927; WS 1927–28), and on the Reformation doctrine of justification (WS 1929–30). But alongside this, Barth also spent much energy on trying to give an account of the theological tradition which lay immediately behind him. He began this work with the remarkable set of lectures on Schleiermacher in WS 1923–24, but in

Münster the task expanded into lectures on 'The History of Protestant Theology since Schleiermacher' (SS 1926 and WS 1929–30); there were also seminars on Schleiermacher's *Glaubenslehre* (WS 1926–27) and on Ritschl (SS 1928). In the same period, Barth also ventured into medieval texts twice in his seminar: in SS 1926 into Anselm's *Cur deus homo* (the same theme was also treated in Bonn in SS 1930), and the *prima pars* of Aquinas' *Summa theologiae* in WS 1928–29. These lectures and seminars are in themselves ample testimony to the seriousness and zeal with which Barth worked on the history of Christian theology; behind them, moreover lay his deep and wide reading in those fathers and theologians of the Christian past who, as Barth put it in 1932 in the preface to the first part-volume of the *Church Dogmatics*, were:

> ... the voices which were in my own ears as I prepared my own text, which guided, taught, or stimulated me, and by which I wish to be measured by my readers. I never imagine that these voices say exactly what I say, but I do suggest that what has to be said and heard in dogmatics to-day is better understood, and in the last resort can only be understood, if we join in listening to these voices so far as concerns the Bible passages, i.e., the basic text upon which all the rest and everything of our own can only wait and comment. (*CD* I/1, p. xii)

This lasting preoccupation with the older and more recent traditions of Christian theology is, then, the context for the lectures on modern Protestant theology which were eventually published as *Protestant Theology*. The material had its first outing as lectures at Münster in 1926, two of which (those on Schleiermacher and Feuerbach) were published in *Zwischen den Zeiten* in 1927. Near the end of his stay at Münster, Barth repeated the cycle, with additional prefatory studies; later, he expanded the material once more for two sets of lectures in Bonn, one in WS 1932–33 on 'Vorgeschichte der neueren protestantischen Theologie (Aufklärung, Idealismus, Romantik)', and one in SS 1933 on 'Geschichte der protestantischen Theologie seit Schleiermacher'. As often happened, Barth ran out of time; neither course of lectures was completed, and the texts were laid aside until after the Second World War. At that point, Barth's son Christoph prepared the material for publication. Barth put them into print partly because copies of the lecture texts were circulating quite freely in various states of incompleteness and he wanted to make his judgements clear. But he also felt he ought to publish in order to hold in check some of his more ardent admirers who presented a very negative account of the theology of the nineteenth century, which they believed themselves to have learned from Barth, but from which he wished to distance himself. Already in the 1923–24 Schleiermacher course, Barth warned his cocksure hearers that:

> ... the aim of my lectures in not to make you hard on the universally venerated Schleiermacher but to see and know and learn to understand him with you, not to induce the arrogant view that you can become a match for him but to handle him modestly, not to condemn him but to comprehend him as he was and obviously had to be. (Barth, 1982b, p. xvi)

And he felt the same in 1946, writing in the foreword to *Protestant Theology*:

> I have allowed publication because I have constantly had occasion to wish and
> suggest that the attitude and approach of the younger generations of Protestant
> theologians to the period of the Church that is just past might be rather different
> from that which they now often seem to regard, somewhat impetuously, as the
> norm – misunderstanding the guidance they have received from me. I would be
> very pleased if they were (to put it simply) to show a little more love towards
> those who have gone before us, despite the degree of alienation they feel from
> them. (Barth, 2001, p. xii)

Protestant Theology finally appeared in 1947. Even after Christoph Barth's editing,
the material remains a little uneven. The lecture origins of the text are evident at a
number of points – some sections are rushed, and classroom hints on bibliography
and on how to draw up a time chart of the period have been left in (ibid., pp. 10–12).
With some exceptions (such as the sections on Kohlbrügge or Blumhardt) the lesser
nineteenth-century figures did not elicit Barth's best efforts, but alongside these
sections are some truly outstanding pieces of interpretation. The treatments of Kant,
Hegel and Schleiermacher are especially fine, as is the opening chapter on 'The Task
of a History of Modern Protestant Theology'. Stylistically, too, the lectures are not
wholly consistent, at times repetitive and sometimes lush: the opening pages of the
account of Rousseau are a case in point. Barth's very expansive style, which served
him so well in the long descriptive passages of the *Church Dogmatics*, is not always
as well suited to detailed discussion of historical material, and, as in the early lectures
on Calvin, Schleiermacher and the Reformed confessions, the best sections are those
where Barth leaves behind rather airy discussion of generalities to a more precise
engagement with the shape of the thought of one of his subjects. In *Protestant
Theology* it is only quite rarely that Barth offers the kind of detailed reading of
specific texts which can be found in the earlier cycles on Schleiermacher and the
Reformed confessions (not so much those on Calvin). The idiom of *Protestant
Theology* is less that of commentary and more that of a synthetic interpretation,
looking for the *grandes lignes* and seeking to expose the overall structure of his
subjects' thought. It is not wholly dissimilar to Tillich's approach in the Chicago
lectures which became *Perspectives on Nineteenth and Twentieth Century Protestant
Theology* (Tillich, 1967), though Barth's presentation has more vividness, colour and
warmth than that of Tillich, as well as a great deal more urgency. Barth betrays his
characteristic sense of struggling to grasp the otherness of the tradition which he tries
to set before his hearers in its integrity.

   He writes with a kind of reverent curiosity whose first task is simply to try and see
what is there and be instructed by it. 'Let it be said in warning,' Barth remarks in the
course of his account of Schleiermacher, 'that with every step which exceeds careful
listening and the careful asking of questions one may, not inevitably but very easily,
make oneself look ridiculous' (Barth, 2001, p. 413). The listening, as we have noted,
is less at the level of textual exegesis and more at the level of an attempt to give a

coherent thematic description, though, for all that, it is not for cursory or inattentive. The questioning is characteristically intense. A passage in the chapter on Hegel runs thus:

> The first question which arises is whether the Hegelian concept of truth can do justice to theology. Hegel thinks of truth as the thinking which is conceived as the pinnacle and centre of humanity. But has humanity *this* centre? *Has* it any such centre at all? Does not man always exist at the invisible intersection of his thinking and willing? Did not Kant's doctrine of the primacy of practical reason at least put forward a reminder of this unity in man? Was it not this with which Schleiermacher's teaching of the central significance of feeling was truly concerned? ... Is a theory of truth which builds itself upon the inner logic of a thought which is divorced from practice still the theory of man as he really is, the theory of his truth? Can the theory of truth be any other theory but the theory of practice? (Ibid., p. 403f.)

At first glance, the volley of questions appears pretty unfriendly, little more than a set of counter-propositions couched in the interrogative. But there is more here. The questions are not rhetorical, designed simply to dismiss Hegel and state the self-evidence of Barth's own views. They are better looked upon as questions which seek to penetrate that which they interrogate; their purpose is not to silence the object of questioning but to listen and respond as carefully as possible to its claim. It is questioning as a means of encounter, an energetic wrestling with the subject-matter rather than an undermining of it. The vigour of the questioning is a sign that, with the possible exception of the curiously tone-deaf chapter on Ritschl at the close of the book, Barth always takes his conversation partners very seriously.

Protestant Theology is full of surprises in other ways. It is by no means simply a history of dogmatics or even of religious and philosophical ideas; its human texture is much denser than the parallel volumes by Tillich (1967), Pannenberg (1997) or Rohls (1997), for example. The two chapters on 'Man in the Eighteenth Century' and 'The Problem of Theology in the Eighteenth Century' are especially noteworthy in this connection. The first teems not just with ideas, but with the sheer human variety of actions, places and human faces. He writes of the 'absolute man' of the eighteenth century:

> This absolute man, whether he is called Louis XIV or Frederick the Great or Voltaire, whether he lives the obscure life of a philistine with secret revolutionary thoughts or a friend of letters with liberal religious or even sceptical tendencies, or of a lady in her castle devoted to the mysticism of Tersteegen, or whether he sails the seas with James Cook or is a watchmaker in Geneva making tiny but useful improvements in the products of his handiwork ... this absolute man is eighteenth-century man, who appears to us more or less distinctly, more or less open or veiled in conventional drapings, in all the human faces of that century which are so different among themselves. (Barth, 2001, p. 22f.)

Again, Barth resists using 'Enlightenment' as the leading motif for the depiction of eighteenth-century Europe, and uses instead the notion of 'absolutism', for it is the civic and moral transformations of the eighteenth century which catch his eye. Furthermore, throughout the book Barth displays considerable independence of mind in the judgements which he reaches about individual figures. This comes across in (to give some random examples) his account of Lessing, in which Barth refuses to treat him as a mere emblematic figure of 'reasonable Christianity', or in his very generous reading of the first edition of Marheineke's *Dogmatik* for its theological and Trinitarian preoccupations. And, as we shall see, the complexity and subtlety of Barth's judgement is most evident in the handling of Schleiermacher: Barth is very far indeed from Brunner's drastically reductive reading in *Die Mystik und das Wort* (Brunner, 1924).

Protestant Theology is thus a work of real originality, very far indeed from the party piece of dialectical theology's banishment of the nineteenth century. The book has certainly been praised: Gerrish speaks of it as a collection of 'brilliant sketches by an astute theologian who was ... more than a little intoxicated with his own theological insight' (Gerrish, 1975, p. 123); Welch calls it 'a book of great power and insight, and within its limits the most provocative of all the works one could cite' (Welch, 1972, p. 8). Yet there has been little sustained analysis and assessment of the text, and virtually no attempt to relate what Barth does there to the many other places in his corpus which address questions of the nature and tasks of the history of the Church and its theology.[2] Those who have commented on the overall character of Barth's presentation have often been heavily critical, and the criticisms generally follow some well-defined tracks.

Some are of a more technical nature, concerning the way in which Barth conceives of the field of inquiry. Pannenberg, for example, although he believes Barth correct in identifying anthropocentrism as a key theme in the Protestant theological history of the nineteenth century, considers that (like Blumenberg in *The Legitimacy of the Modern Age* (1983)) Barth fails to trace its history behind the eighteenth century to the period of the magisterial Reformers (cf. Pannenberg, 1997, p. 23). Or, again, some criticize Barth's focus on individual theologians for its inadequate attention to the broad cultural background.[3] Because he offers an 'intensive' rather than an 'extensive' history (Lessing, 2000, p. 27), Barth betrays insufficient interest in lines of development, and tends to produce a set of critical portraits rather than an historical landscape. Others worry that Barth's attention is too focused on epistemological issues (see, for example, Williams, 1986, 1995; Gunton, 1986) – once again, a curious judgement about what Barth is doing, though one that has gained quite wide currency.

Other criticisms give a much more negative evaluation of the way in which Barth undertakes his history. Most commonly, Barth is held to be hostile in his presentation of the theology of the nineteenth century. Chapman, for example, writes that:

> Barth's influential writing of theological history undoubtedly possesses the virtue of simplicity and may well point to certain dangers in a theology which fails to engage sufficiently critically with the culture in which it emerges. Nevertheless his rhetorical dismissiveness of his theological teachers as guilty by

association, as well as the starkness of his dialectical terms, have served to isolate much earlier nineteenth-century German theology, and especially the theology of the early years of the twentieth century, from serious historical investigation. Indeed, after Barth the theology of the 'long nineteenth century' may be seen as something of an aberration, all attempts to accommodate theology to post-Enlightenment patterns of thought being regarded as an intellectual cul-de-sac. (Chapman, 2001, p. 11)[4]

Similarly, Rohls argues that Barth lacks any impartiality, assuming his own point of view and belabouring the nineteenth-century material for failure to agree with him.

> Since Barth ... conceives of the writing of the history of theology as a theological task, modern Protestant theology is judged on the basis of Barth's own standpoint. From that vantage point, however, it can only seem to be a history of unmitigated decadence in which, according to the common conviction of so-called dialectical theology, humankind presses more and more into the centre, at cost to God. (Rohls, 1997, p. xix)

Behind these critiques lies a larger unease, one which concerns Barth's theological project as whole but which has particular pertinence to his interpretation of the theology of the nineteenth century – namely, that Barth is a theological isolationist who feels it necessary to repudiate the correlation of history and theology so intricately constructed by his forebears. Chapman writes again, this time on the theological mood of the movement from which Barth's *Protestant Theology* sprang:

> Theology was isolated from a history identified with the meaningless slaughter of the fields of Flanders; it was consequently robbed of apologetic potential, except perhaps as a silent witness to the frailty of all human constructs. The alternatives to Troeltsch's theology which were to develop in the 1920s lost faith in the powers of history, and thereby succeeded in the sectarianization of theology as contact with the wider world of learning was severed in a world-view inspired by faith. All theology was destined to be dogmatics. (Chapman, 2001, p. 186)

Behind this judgement lies, it should be noted, a quite specific interpretation of Protestant theology in the 1920s. According to this account of the matter, the so-called 'dialectical theology' of the period is best understood as a symptom of a larger 'anti-historical revolution' which responded to the nineteenth century's *Enttheologisierung* of history by a forceful *Enthistorisierung* of Church and theology (see, for example, Graf, 1988; Nowak, 1987, 1997). Barth is to be considered the leading anti-historical theologian of the 1920s, and his break with the historical dogmatics of the late liberal period is emblematic of the alienation of Protestant systematics from historical culture. In Barth's case, the result of the alienation, it is claimed, is not only his extreme suspicion of the preceding generations of Protestant theologians, but also the precipitation of a crisis in Protestant historical theology. For when Barth comes to write about the history of Christian thought, he presents it as a narrative of the declension of Christian theology from adherence to the Gospel through adulteration with secularity. In the dialectical world of *Zwischen den Zeiten*, there can be no Church history or historical theology but only the invasion of the *saeculum* from the beyond. 'The house of history was no longer the dwelling-place of the Spirit' (Nowak, 1987, p. 162).

The *Protestant Theology* lectures are a very important text in deciding the adequacy of such an account of the matter. The claim, for example, that Barth is 'rhetorically dismissive' of the nineteenth century is certainly impossible to maintain from a close reading of the book, or from Barth's other materials on nineteenth-century theology. And beyond that, there are serious objections to the thesis that Barth is a leading theological *Antihistoriker*. Such a thesis succeeds only by establishing some general characteristics of a 'movement', rendering Barth as its representative figure, abstracting and maximizing features of his work which appear to support such a view (for example, his appeals to eschatology, his critique of the dogmatic foundations of liberal Protestant culture) and ignoring or underplaying the features of his work which tell against the interpretation (such as his ethico-political interests as a *Reformed* theologian).[5] If Barth had, in fact, been a kind of theological equivalent to Spengler, he would not have written such a humane, generous and often gentle text as *Protestant Theology*; he would (and could) have written a piece of polemic in the form of a study of the theology of the nineteenth century (which is exactly what Brunner did in *Die Mystik und das Wort*). That he chose not to do this indicates that, far from being a revolutionary seeking to sever his ties with the old regime, Barth did his work – even at the points of sharpest disagreement with liberal theology – out of a pervasive sense of participation in a common history with the theology of the recent and more distant past. He was, quite simply, no iconoclast. As we shall see, he understood his theological efforts as a contribution to a shared enterprise in which, in their different ways, theologians, both past and present, accept common responsibilities and undertake common tasks. And, what is more, to describe and reflect upon that common history involves respectful, courteous listening, intense questioning and counterquestioning, and, above all, a submission of both past and present to judgement by the object of theology which is the unifying factor in its history. Such an attitude can scarcely be called 'anti-historical'. Rather, it is much more an expression of a theology of history (and therefore of the history of the Church and its exegesis and dogmatics) which follows a quite different trajectory from that of, for example, Troeltsch and his modern disciples, but which for all that is no less concerned with the temporal career of Christian thought than the secularized histories which it opposes. In *Protestant Theology*, therefore, Barth is not so much an anti-historical theologian as a theological historian, 'describing and understanding' the history as a '*theological task*'. We now turn to a more detailed account of how Barth conceives of this task.

Barth as Theologian of History

In the course of the ethics of creation, Barth suggests that Christian activity may be regarded as truly secular and humane, in that:

> ... in what the Christian community does in fulfilment of its task, there takes place the very thing for the sake and in the context of which everything else must happen, which truly builds the world together and which is the ultimate goal of all else that is done, even though other men do not for the most part realise the fact. For may it not be that fundamentally world history is really Church history? (*CD* III/4, p. 485)

Like many of Barth's other claims, it startles because it is counterintuitive; Barth simply does not accept the convention that world history is the encircling context for the history of the Church. Instead, he proposes that world history is in an important sense enclosed by 'Church history'. He means this, however, in a very specific sense. By 'Church history' he does not refer simply to the factual record of the visible Christian community, externally viewed – that history may, indeed, be subsumed within the wider history of the world, in exactly the same way that Christianity may be subsumed within the category of 'religion'. In its deeper sense, 'Church history' is the history of the Church as 'that which God knows', 'the work of [God's] overruling of the Church' (*CD* III/4, p. 485). Defined by God's knowing and acting, Church history is the human historical visibility of the reconciling work of God in time. The business of describing Church history, and therefore the history of Church doctrine, is a '*theological* task' because it is concerned with the history of the Church not simply in its externality, but in its character as an episode in the divine knowing and forming of creaturely occurrence. Church history encloses world history, therefore, because (and only because) it is part of the history of God with us in which the nature and end of human history in its entirety emerges into visibility.[6]

Barth lays out in more detail the Christological dimensions of this view of history in his account of Christ's prophetic office near the end of the *Church Dogmatics*. In his office as prophet, the ascended Jesus Christ announces himself as the one who, in his reconciling work, has accomplished the complete 'alteration of the whole world situation' (*CD* IV/3, p. 191). That alteration does not so much modify as constitute world history; properly understood, world history now is the history of the conflict between, on the one hand, Jesus Christ's annunciation of his reconciling action and, on the other hand, the wickedness of human resistance to or ignorance of its effectiveness. 'The proclamation of Jesus Christ and its dreadful limitation are together the history which embraces and comprises, and thus controls and determines, the history of the world and the history of each and every man' (*CD* IV/3, p. 191).[7]

Though they find their most mature and spacious articulation in these last stretches of the argument of the *Church Dogmatics*, these convictions were formed very early in Barth's career. They can be found, for example, in the 1917 lecture on 'The Strange New World Within the Bible' (Barth, 1928b, pp. 28–50), or in the understanding of history and eschatology in the first *Römerbrief*,[8] and certainly undergird the project which Barth set himself in the 1920s of lecturing through the history of modern Protestant theology.

But Barth's claims about the nature of history need to be interpreted with some delicacy. By identifying the history of the Church as the true thread of the history of the world, Barth is not seeking to eclipse or erase 'ordinary' history by asserting the pre-eminence of an eschatological, transcendent stretch of time. The relation of world history and Church history is both more complex and less oppositional than such an interpretation would allow. It is, of course, true that, early on in his theological development, Barth breaks step with some of the most conscientiously-held principles of modern German Protestant theory about the nature of the history of Christianity. In the latter part of the nineteenth century, questions about the *theological* character of Church history and historical theology were a central concern of most accounts of the nature of the discipline.[9] In his 1890 *Antrittsrede* before the Berlin Academy, Harnack, placing himself explicitly in the tradition of Mosheim and Leibniz ('the founder of unpartisan and critical writing of Church history', Harnack, 1890, p. 788), expressed to his new colleagues his delight that 'following an old tradition you have a place for this science [that is, 'the history of Christianity'] among the disciplines with which this academy occupies itself' (ibid., p. 790). Harnack's claim that 'the fence which at one time separated the field of Church history from the field of general history has been torn down' (ibid.), is, of course, very far from positivism. Instead, it rather betrays a trust that historical science alone affords a comprehensive and critical view of human affairs and of the place of the Christian religion in the development of a humane culture. If Barth differs from his teacher, it is, in the end, because very early on in the process of theological reconstruction he began to work with quite a different ontology of history. In that ontology, priority is assigned to the being and action of Jesus Christ; he is the ontological, and therefore the noetic, ground of all creaturely time. The history of the Church, therefore, is not simply identical with the history of the Christian religion as a cultural magnitude, because the Church is that sphere in which Jesus Christ's reconciling work is confessed. Already in 1920 in an address to the same student conference at Aarau at which Barth lectured on 'Biblical Questions, Insights and Vistas' (Barth, 1928a, pp. 51–96), Harnack expressed a concern which has often been repeated as a charge against Barth, namely that this view of history threatens to become docetic and undermines the world-relation of faith (see Harnack, 1988).[10] But further probing of Barth's more general reflections on the nature of history, and of their application to the writing of the history of theology, shows this to be an overdrawn judgement, one which emphasizes Barth's dissonance from his liberal teachers but overlooks the complexity and nuance of his counterproposal.

One of the crucial elements of that counterproposal is a conviction which can be phrased in the following way: the history of the Church and its theology, like the history of reconciliation of which it is part, is not directly perceptible, but rather, because it shares in the spiritual visibility of the Church, is perceptible only in an indirect way. A theological interpretation of the history of the Church does not simply read off its verdicts from the empirical surface of events; rather, it reaches its judgements on the basis of a perception that those events are caught up in the divine governance of all things. But this 'governance' is not simply one more direct and open element in history of which we may give a report as if it were a natural or creaturely reality *tout court*. It can be spoken of only by speaking of the justifying and sanctifying work of God. In the same way that righteousness and holiness are not merely properties straightforwardly attributed to the Christian believer on the basis of his or her natural being and acts, but are attributed and perceived only in the event of grace, so also the history of the Church is what it is by imputation, and only as such truly known.

Barth makes explicit appeal to the notion of justification in a passage on the nature of Church history early on in the *Church Dogmatics*, when discussing 'true religion' (see *CD* I/2, pp. 325–61). Christianity can aspire to be described as such only when it demonstrates its apostolic character by fulfilling the principle 'When I am weak, then I am strong'. After a thumbnail sketch of the history of Christianity organized around this theme, Barth reflects on the necessary indirectness of any real apprehension of the history of apostolicity. Indeed, direct apprehension of Christian history suggests that the Church is not apostolic in that sense, but the very opposite: its history is simply 'a story of the distress which it makes for itself' (ibid., p. 337). The reality of grace and weakness 'can in the strict sense nowhere be perceived directly. Not even in the history of the Reformation!' (ibid.). And so 'we can speak of the truth of the Christian religion only within the sphere of the *iustificatio impii*' (ibid.). If, therefore, the history of the Church is to be that – *Church* history, the history of righteousness – it is only because 'we and our contradiction against grace stand under the even more powerful contradiction of grace itself' (*CD* I/2, p. 338).

Alongside the language of justification, Barth also deploys language of sanctification to explore the indirect perceptibility of the true history of the Church.

> The Church is the communion of saints, i.e., the fellowship of those who by the self-revelation of the King of Israel to which Scripture bears testimony are personally called: called out of the world; called into the community; called to faith in the kingdom of God and to the proclamation of this kingdom. Church history is the history of this fellowship within world history generally. And it is one of those special elements in world-occurrence which point to the divine world-governance. (*CD* III/3, p. 204)

Yet this by no means gives the theologian licence to interpret the history of the Church as directly bearing the marks of *historia sacra*. The Church, he writes, is not 'in a position either to proclaim directly or to prove to the general satisfaction its own status as the communion of saints'; it still lives within world occurrence and it is 'nowhere unequivocally distinguished from this occurrence. It can be perceived – and will be perceived – only as one phenomenon among others' (ibid., p. 205). Once again, then, the visibility of the history of the Church is spiritual visibility; if it becomes more than this – if its righteousness and holiness are directly attributed to it – then it is no longer history but mythology.

By appealing to theological doctrine concerning justification and sanctification in his ontology of the Church and its history, Barth is undertaking something rather more complex than the criticism that he is 'anti-historical' will permit. He is not assuming that the history of the Church can be disconnected from the wider history of humankind as if it were some quantifiable factor, an identifiably separate stretch of sacred time. The history of the holy Church takes place in, with and under the history of sinful world occurrence, and to pretend that it is visible to the naked eye is to misunderstand its holiness. Accordingly, it cannot be the task of the historian of the Church to sort through its past, assigning now this section to the category of holy events and now that one to the category of the unholy. Especially in writing the history of Christian thought, the historian may never rise above the record of ambiguity, for Church history never exists in absolute purity as 'unadulterated proclamation of the Word of God' (*CD* I/2, p. 803). Rather, it exists in

> ... sequences of thoughts and ideas which specifically choose, emphasise and underline, or again deny and suppress .... *In concreto* they always owe their origin and persistence to the specific currents of Church life (conditioned by the general historical situation), which emanate from the concrete personality of individual preachers and the character of their congregations. (Ibid., p. 802f.)

As Barth put it in an earlier comment on the history of dogma: '[T]he church is wholly and totally a part of history .... We should not be put off by recalling the humanly speaking unpleasant and suspicious and even wicked historical processes out of which the dogma developed' (Barth, 1991, p. 101f.). But what Barth will not allow is that this recognition requires the historian of the Church to refuse to see the subject-matter as anything other than mere religion, culture or ideology, any more than a frank admission of Christian impiety and worldliness requires us to suspend talk of the justification of the ungodly. What is required is a theological ontology of the time of the Church, one which indicates faith's perception that that time is not only the sphere of *confusio hominem* but also of *providentia dei*, and which therefore enables a complex and generous set of judgements about the Christian past.

It was the temptation of some of Barth's forebears either to collapse God and the processes of history into identity, or to naturalize historical occurrence so as to render talk of God's action simply *de trop*. The first temptation threatened Baur; the second, Troeltsch. Neither, on Barth's account of the matter, could see historical work as having a genuinely theological character. It would be easy enough to present Barth as reacting to both by setting up an antithesis between God and history. In one of the few alert critical discussions of Barth's historical writing, Peter Hodgson places him in a line of Protestant theology stretching from Kierkegaard, one which responded to the challenges raised by the prestige of historical science by proposing a purely *external* relation of faith and history. On Hodgson's account, this line was developed partly as a reaction to the immanentism and panentheism of which Baur is the representative figure. Because Baur's work edged towards making the 'internal relationships' between God and history into pure 'identity' (Hodgson, 1966, p. 268), Kierkegaard and his followers were tempted to the opposite stance, to '*separate* God and history, faith and historical knowledge, dogmatic theology and historical-critical theology, and to relate them only externally or paradoxically if at all' (Hodgson, 1966, p. 270).

For Hodgson, Barth's presentation of Baur in *Protestant Theology* is a case in point:

> Barth would remove Church history from the concept of history generally, and also, presumably, from the categories of historical knowledge. In so far as the history of the Church can be regarded as an authentically *theological* discipline, it can be of interest and concern only to the theologian, not to the historian. There can be no critical, scientific, and *at the same time* theological historiography; critical historical science is not part of an authentically *theological* discipline. History can be rightly understood only from within the framework of dogmatics. It is not clear in what sense Barth can meaningfully talk ... of an 'historical' theology or a 'Church history' and intend by these terms anything other than 'Church dogmatics'. And Church dogmatics, while not opposing itself to critical method (so it claims) is not an historical discipline as Barth exemplifies it. If 'Church history' is a theological discipline for Barth, then it is really Church dogmatics; if not, then it is simply a branch of secular historiography concerned with a particular range of historical phenomena to be empirically described, as Overbeck claimed it should be. (Hodgson, 1966, p. 270)

But, though it is phrased with some discrimination, in the end Hodgson's argument does not carry. Barth – unlike, for example, Pusey in his reaction to 'Germanism' – is not so much demarcating separate spheres of sacred and secular history which, as it were, touch only at their outer edges, if at all. He is distinguishing between primary and secondary agents. Divine action, the history of reconciliation which constitutes the history of the Church and is the true history of the world, is not action in a wholly distinct reality; it is action which accompanies, governs and perfects limited, culpable human action in history. In a telling paragraph in his Gifford lectures from the 1930s, Barth proposes that the fundamental theme and activity of 'the history of the Church in time' is 'exposition of Holy Scripture' (the context makes clear that he means not simply exegesis but the entirety of the Church's life under and from the Word) (Barth, 1938, p. 179). It is this which makes the history of the Church 'special history' (ibid., p. 180). But, crucially, within that history there are two subjects, God and humankind, and their relation is not simply one of dialectical confrontation but of ordered correspondence. Hence:

> Church history, i.e., the history of the Church's coming to terms with the theme given her in Scripture, cannot primarily be understood as the history of the human opinions, resolutions and actions which have emerged in the course of her coming to terms with her theme .... Church history must rather be understood as the history of the government of the Church by the Word of God, the history of the exegesis of Scripture accomplished by Scripture, i.e., by Jesus Christ Himself in the Church. *Scriptura scripturae interpres* – Scripture is the interpreter of Scripture. Of course we know this self-interpretation of Scripture at all times and in all places only as it is reflected in the human exposition visible in human opinions, resolutions and actions of every kind. But everything depends on our recognising this latter as something secondary, as the reflection of that real and genuine exposition, as the multiplicity of the attempts more or less successful to follow in the steps of that self-exposition of Scripture. (Ibid., p. 181)

Barth's response both to historical idealism and historical naturalism is thus not an estrangement of God and history, of the history of the Church and of the history of worldly occurrence, but a careful specification of the character of the Church's temporal career, as one of differentiated fellowship between the divine Lord and his human auxiliaries:

> There cannot but be a secondary subject of Church history and who else could that be at any time but man in his human opinions and resolutions? But it is just man who must learn to understand himself not as the primary subject but as this *secondary* subject; he must learn to follow, and not to take the initiative. (Ibid., p. 182)

The language here – of 'initiative' and 'following', like the differentiation between 'natural' and 'spiritual visibility' or the language of justification and sanctification – shows that the history of the Church is more than merely 'externally' or 'paradoxically' related to worldly occurrence; for Barth, it is *in* its secularity that the history of the Church is also, at the same time, the history of divine providence.

For Barth, we might say, the election of the history of the Church to be 'special' history does not entail its extraction from profane history so much as its appointment as a particular form of human action bearing a particular witness within that history. The task of the Church historian, therefore, is not to depict a separate sacral region, but simply and modestly to indicate that 'we have to say rather more about Church history than that it is merely part of secular history' (*CD* III/3, p. 206). In what does this 'something more' consist? Barth elaborates a number of answers in his discussion of the divine ruling in *Church Dogmatics* III/3: the fact that 'with all its insignificance and folly and confusion in history generally, [Church history] is still the central and decisive history to which all the rest is as it were only the background or accompaniment' (ibid., p. 207); that, although this can be maintained 'only in the demonstration of the Spirit and of power', nevertheless we are faced by Church history as the continuous trace of 'the One in whose name the Church offers its modest and equivocal service'; the fact that even in the midst of 'human pusillanimity and compliance and helplessness and weakness', the observer of Church history sees 'something persisting – a continuity' (ibid.) which can be called 'the economy which rules in its history' (ibid., p. 210).

These passages from Barth's doctrine of providence were written at the end of the 1940s, but they amplify and extend views which he first formulated nearly 30 years previously in his Göttingen lectures on Schleiermacher. Taking his students through the *Kurze Darstellung*, Barth notes that, in the tradition which followed Schleiermacher, 'the primacy of historians in theology, or theological historicism, is obviously established firmly and solidly and definitively' (Barth, 1982a, p. 172). And he reflects on this as follows:

> Schleiermacher's very clear-cut and radical attempt first to bring all the biblical, historical, and didactic data of theology under a common historical denominator,

and then dialectically to oppose to this a specific theological approach, could be regarded as a very promising one were it not that the cloven hoof of the consistent validity of the historical method on both sides of the antithesis betrays the fact that the dialectic is not authentic, that there will not really be any true *theological* approach, and that under this sign theology will be secretly betrayed and sold to the methods of empirical scholarship even though its special sphere will be preserved. That this takes place, and that Schleiermacher and those who follow him consistently rightly saw that it *has to* take place, has its basis in the fact that for him the object of theology is a phenomenon, a spiritual phenomenon to be sure, yet a psychical entity like any other, namely, what is called piety. This being so, it is hard to see how a universal historical or descriptive method, suitably modified to fit the subject, can fail to win out and achieve predominance in the theological area as well. (Ibid., p. 153)

We should not be misled into thinking that the word 'dialectic' here means that Barth believes the *theological* character of the various theological subdisciplines can only be maintained by negating their historical character, however. What Barth protests against is not history but historical reductionism, which mischaracterizes the object of theology. Later on, he remarks on the fact that, in Schleiermacher, theology 'becomes part of history in general' and that:

This makes sense. The Bible and the Church's present-day teaching are elements in history. It is not just an accidental and contingent and external task, but an inward and essential task of theological exegesis and the establishment of Church doctrine, to see and recognize and pay heed to this fact always and everywhere, not just in passing, but all the time. But we only take up the theological task when we dialectically oppose to this fact the further fact that these elements in history are only witnesses to revelation or to the view of revelation which is offered in the Church pending its better instruction. (Ibid., p. 174)

Such a passage might draw Hodgson's fire for espousing too paradoxical an account of the relation of theological and historical knowledge. But, even here, Barth insists that historical *Wissenschaft* is 'not just an accidental and contingent and external task', but 'inward and essential'.

Though we appear to have moved some way from the details of Barth's account of the history of nineteenth-century Protestant theology, this detour into his understanding of the nature of the history of the Church will prove illuminating in coming to terms with the kinds of judgement that he makes in *Protestant Theology*. We turn, finally, to a closer examination of that text.

Protestant Theology in the Nineteenth Century

'To describe and understand the history of Protestant theology from the time of Schleiermacher onwards is a *theological* task. Even as an object of historical consideration, theology demands theological perception, theological thought and theological involvement' (Barth, 2001, p. 1). On the basis of what we have seen so far about the way in which Barth understands the history of the Church in relation to the wider history of human affairs, it ought to be clear that, when he speaks of the history of the Church and its theology as a 'theological' task, he is not suggesting that this history can be treated as a segregated sphere. Barth is simply not an isolationist, whether in his ecclesiology or in his understanding of the intellectual task of theology. The 'theological perception, theological thought and theological involvement' required of the one who would describe Church history are not anti-historical. What makes them theological is the way in which they emerge from participation in the particular sphere of human history which we call the history of the Christian Church. That sphere is not hermetically sealed; it is 'special' not by virtue of achieved perfection, but in its existence in the movement of God's election of it within the wider scope of worldly occurrence. And so 'theological perception' of that history is simply perception of the fact that in – not *despite* – its confusion and contingency, it is caught up in God's reconciling activity. Theological perception is directed towards the special kind of visibility which the history of the Church has – a visibility which is neither the pure visibility of a cultural phenomenon nor the pure invisibility of a wholly ahistorical reality, but the spiritual visibility of the divine work taking shape in forms of human life and activity. '[I]t is,' Barth writes, 'a *conditio sine qua non* of the success of our undertaking that it should be approached theologically, in accordance with its subject-matter' (ibid.). Crucially, that subject-matter is the history of a *corpus permixtum*. What the historian of Christian thought must aspire to is, therefore, not absolute judgement, but something a good deal less pretentious: the kind of generous consideration of forebears made not by a spectator but a participant.

'Theological perception' is perception of the history of the Church, not as *historia sacra* but as *historia iustificata*, and, far from being in a position to issue Olympian judgements, it must take its place within, not above, the relativity and imperfection of its subject-matter. This theme forms the burden of the opening chapter of *Protestant Theology*; much ill-judged dismissal of the book could have been avoided if critics had bestirred themselves to study with care what Barth has to say there.

The 'theological involvement' required for the writing of the history of theology, Barth claims, demands 'special participation' (ibid.). At one level, Barth is simply extending a general principle of all historical interpretation – namely, that historical work cannot be undertaken from the detached position of the observer:

> Any knowledge of history that proved to be merely seeing, observing, establishing, is a contradiction in itself. Certainly the knowledge of human action – and that is what history is about – involves seeing, observing, establishing, but not in isolated theory. The theory of practice is the only possible theory where history is concerned. It is a seeing, observing, establishing where we ourselves are taken up in a particular movement, taken up in an action of our own which somehow encounters, corresponds to or even contradicts the action of another. We know history in that another's action somehow becomes a question to which our own action has to give some sort of answer. Without this responsible reaction to being questioned, our knowledge of history would be knowledge of facts, but not of living people; it would not be history but a form of science. (Ibid., p. 1f.)

Historical description is thus reflective participation in human affairs, for '[t]he subject-matter of history, the historical fact, is living man' and '[h]is actions become evident to us in their relationship to our own actions' (ibid., p. 2). In contrast to the 'idle onlooker' who declines to be 'involved in the matter' (ibid.), preferring to inspect history with unconcern, the proper stance of the historian is non-theoretical. In terms of the history of theology, this means that:

> ... no-one can understand the theology of the nineteenth century or of any other century unless in some way he has taken upon himself the burden of theological work. By this is meant not merely assuming the status of a theologian, but actively participating in his problems. This participation need not exclude critical, negative, sceptical attitudes within and even towards theology, provided that it is itself theological, provided that it does not represent an abandonment of the problem of theology, a *metabasis eis allo genos*, provided that the presupposition remains, even here, a readiness for one's own responsible involvement, practical reason. (Ibid.)

Much of this is, of course, common currency after Croce and Collingwood. What distinguishes Barth's account of history as practical reason is his appeal to theological categories to describe the special involvement required of the historian of theology – above all, his appeal to the category of 'Church':

> [S]erious theological work is forced, again and again, to begin from the beginning. However, as this is done, the theology of past periods, classical and less classical, also plays a part and demands a hearing. It demands a hearing as surely as it occupies a place with us in the context of the Church. The Church does not stand in a vacuum. Beginning from the beginning, however necessary, cannot be a matter of beginning off one's own bat. We have to remember the communion of saints, bearing and being borne by each other, asking and being asked, having to take mutual responsibility for and among the sinners gathered together in Christ. As regards theology also, we cannot be in the Church without taking as much responsibility for the theology of the past as for the theology of our present. (Ibid., p. 3)

This is, in effect, an appeal to tradition as both the setting and the theme of Church historical practice.[11] Appeal to tradition is simply the recognition of the fact that, in dealing with the history of theology, we are dealing with those who are *alive*. 'Augustine, Thomas Aquinas, Luther, Schleiermacher and all the rest are not dead, but living .... There is no past in the Church, so there is no past in theology. "In him they all live"' (ibid.). A certain attitude is therefore required of the theological historian: however critical he or she may find it necessary to be, the assumption undergirding historical work is (as Barth put it in his final Basel lectures) that 'the community itself may have been on the right track in the recent or remote past, or at any rate not on an altogether crooked path. Consequently, fundamental trust instead of fundamental mistrust will be the initial attitude of theology toward the tradition which determines the present-day Church' (ibid., p. 43). The first chapter of *Protestant Theology* tries to spell out what is involved in that trustfulness.

It is expressed, first, in an open attentiveness which allows the past to be itself and address us as such:

> The theology of any period must be strong and free enough to give calm and, attentive and open hearing not only to the voices of the Church Fathers, not only to favourite voices, not only to the voices of the classical past, but to all the voices of the past. God is the Lord of the Church. He is also the Lord of theology. We cannot anticipate which of our fellow-workers from the past are welcome in our own work and which are not. It may always be that we have an especial need of quite unsuspected (and among these, of quite unwelcome) voices in one sense or another. (Ibid., p. 3)

For Barth, this kind of loving attentiveness and suspension of our own concerns is a fundamental hermeneutical principle, deployed by him not only in relation to historical developments but also to the biblical texts.[12] In the case of the history of theology, it means that:

> ... [t]o hear someone else always means to suspend one's own concern, to be open to the concern of the other. Care will always be taken that this openness is not too wide. But the demand directed towards us, that we must know and may not evade, here or elsewhere, by qualifying it and weakening it, is for openness. The success of our preoccupation with the theology of the nineteenth century will depend upon the degree to which we can bring this openness to our particular concern. (Ibid., p. 10)

What Barth seeks to demonstrate in his book is thus 'the tranquil, attentive and open hearing of the involved participant which we cannot fail to give to the history of theology if we want to do theology in the Church, that is, on the only possible sphere for this undertaking' (ibid., p. 5).

Second, such attentive hearing of the past is incumbent upon the historian because in the sphere of the Church he or she stands under 'the demand for a sense of mutual responsibility' (ibid.). Acknowledging that his or her work is done as part of a common task, the theological historian can learn the modesty and reticence in judgement which come from the knowledge that he or she does not transcend and inspect but, rather, participates in the common life of theology in the community. We may suspect that this attitude did not come naturally to Barth himself. There are passages in the introductory chapter to *Protestant Theology* which sound more than a little autobiographical. 'The moment of one's own theological knowledge is always to some extent an intoxicating one .... The intoxication of such a moment represents a temptation which must now be mentioned.' It is tempting to consider ourselves correct in a way that gives us freedom to transcend our fellows from the past, and so, in the end, to fail to heed them. 'The one who is all too sure, illegitimately sure, that "we have brought it to so glorious a conclusion" cannot and may not notice carefully "what a wise man thought before us"' (ibid.). Barth is strongly aware that:

... [t]he description of the history of theology, and more particularly of recent theology, has largely been dominated by this pattern. I can think of a whole series of accounts where it is all too evident that the authors are not guiding us in a shared investigation of what the men of the past may be saying to us; rather, the one who has already made his discovery, who has done with listening, directs us with vigorous gestures to the position where he is now standing (not to say, sitting!). There is no question of being on the way. It is all too obvious that the figures of the past are to be explained to us only as positive or negative forerunners of the messiah of the time, however modestly he may be hiding his own appearance, his own knowledge (in this case his own *Dogmatics*) under the ample garb of the 'historian'. (Ibid., p. 6)

And Barth is also aware that his own theological discoveries may have promoted such an attitude:

I hope that anyone who feels from these lectures how good it is, after a long detour from Schleiermacher via Ritschl to Troeltsch, Seeberg and Holl, to arrive at 'dialectical theology' as the long-suspected and awaited salvation from all distress which has so far evaded everyone's grasp, will have made a mistake. (Ibid., p. 8)

For '[h]istory cannot be a proclamation of judgement' (ibid., p. 9). Certainly history can and must be written with decisiveness (without it, there would be no Churchly responsibility). 'We hear the voices of the ancients in order to give an answer by our own attitude and decision. But we do that for or against ourselves, not for or against them' (ibid., p. 8f.).

The root of this deferential and patient attitude towards our forebears is, very simply, that 'we are with them in the Church' (ibid., p. 10). This is not to sacralize the history of the community, but merely to say that, in all its imperfection, the history of the Church is the history of the *Church*, the place where, in the midst of short-comings, revelation is encountered and the confession is made. There is, therefore, a unity to the history of theology which the historian may not breach by consigning part of that history to the rubbish heap: 'over and above the differences a unity can continually be seen, a unity of perplexity and disquiet, but also a unity of richness and hope, which in the end binds us to the theologians of the past' (ibid., p. 13). And this means, further, that the historian of the Church may never allow confession of the Church's unity to be eclipsed by hostile judgement. '*Credo unam sanctam catholicam et apostolicam ecclesiam* is the reason for this, and if I am to pay serious attention to a theologian from the past, whether he is called Schleiermacher or Ritschl or anyone else, then I must be deadly serious about this credo' (ibid., p. 14). In the end, therefore, the historian can only remember that 'I and my theological work are in the Church only on the ground of forgiveness' (ibid.); that recognition is the ground of charity in historical judgement.

Whether Barth succeeds in living up to his own standards can only be decided on the basis of careful reflection upon his history as a whole. What is difficult to deny is the seriousness with which he tries to construct a positive account of the materials. 'In view of a mood which is widespread in theological circles today, it is necessary to remind ourselves that it has in no way been revealed to us that the nineteenth century was in whole or in part a time in which God withdrew his hand from the Church' (ibid., p. 13).[13] The best example of this is the chapter concerning the figure who, for Barth, always dominated the nineteenth century – namely, Schleiermacher. Barth's account of him – 'one is more strongly impressed every time one does consider him' (ibid., p. 412) – begins not with critique, but with an indication of why Schleiermacher must be treated as a weighty Christian theologian 'within the sphere of the Church and not elsewhere' (ibid., p. 415): his dedication of himself to Church and theology, despite his distinctions in other fields; the fact that he is never far from the situation of the preacher; his refusal to evacuate dogmatics into history; the sincerity with which he resisted the reduction of theology to apologetics; and, above all, his desire to be a modern man 'precisely because he was a theologian, and precisely upon the basis of his interpretation of Christianity' (ibid., p. 420). More-over, part of Schleiermacher's attraction for Barth is identical to that which attracts him to Calvin in the 1922 lectures on the reformer: that is, the perception on the part of both Calvin and Schleiermacher that the theme of the Christian faith is not single but twofold – God in relation to humankind. In a remarkable passage (remarkable not least because it offers a clear and early statement of most of the things which social Trinitarian critics believe Barth never said), Barth writes:

> Trinitarian thinking compels theology ... to be completely in earnest about the thought of God in at least two places: first, at the point where it is a question of God's action in regard to man, and, secondly, at the point where it is a question of man's action in regard to God. It is aware of God as the Word of the Father which is spoken to man and as the Spirit of the Father and of the Word which enables man to hear the Word. It cannot seek to have merely one centre, one subject, just because its subject is God. To the extent that it sought to resolve itself into a mere teaching of God's action in regard to man, into a pure teaching of the Word, it would become metaphysics. And to the extent that it sought to resolve itself into a teaching of man's action in regard to God, into a pure teaching of the Spirit, it would become mysticism. The one, however, would be just as little a pure teaching of the Word of God, as the other would be a pure teaching of the Spirit of God. A pure teaching of the Word will take into the account of Holy Spirit as the divine reality in which the Word is heard, just as a pure teaching of the Spirit of the Son will take into account the Word of God as the divine reality in which the Word is given to us. It was with this thought in mind that the Reformers propagated the teaching of the Word of God in its correlation with faith as the work of the Holy Spirit in man. (Barth, 2001, p. 444f.)

Though Barth is fearful that, in addressing himself to this theme, Schleiermacher reversed the proper priority of the divine over the human, he is clear that 'we must not condemn him for this out of hand .... A genuine, proper theology could be built up from such a starting point' (ibid., p. 445). If there is a weakness in Schleiermacher, therefore, it is a lack of full appeal to the resources offered by Trinitarian dogmatics: Spirit is too quickly correlated with faith, and insufficient attention devoted to the

Spirit's deity and his relation to the Logos. Hence the careful and respectful summary judgement that Barth offers: '*The Word is not so assured here in its independence in respect to faith as should be the case if this theology of faith were a true theology of the Holy Spirit*' (ibid., p. 457).[14]

The treatment of Schleiermacher is instructive for what it indicates of the way in which Barth reaches judgements about the history he presents. Two features of those judgements are especially noteworthy. One is that judgements about the theology of others may not proceed from a confident sense of the 'Christianness' of our own theological positions. 'Christianness' is not a property that any theology or any theologian may possess, and so not a property that we can ascribe to ourselves or deny to others. In an important passage, Barth writes:

> The factor which is decisive in making a theology theology does not belong to the motifs whose presence can be asserted or denied in anyone's work. Even of Luther or Calvin it cannot simply be said that they represented and proclaimed the Christian faith, the Gospel. The Gospel in the full sense of the word ... is represented and proclaimed *ubi et quando visum est Deo*, not at the point where, applying this or that yardstick, we feel we can affirm the Christian quality of a theology or philosophy .... The Christian quality of a theology does not belong to the motifs of a theology which can be vouched for, just because it is always the motif ... which is to be questioned. (Ibid., p. 414)[15]

Second, therefore, in making judgements about the history of theology, the historian will not be looking for signs of realized dogmatic perfection so much as indications that the theology under consideration retained a Christian integrity in addressing itself to the concerns by which it was faced. The historian is required to ask whether this or that theology sought to address its situation by looking to the resources of the Christian Gospel, however incomplete or muddled its attempts may have proved. As he passes in review the figures on whom he writes, Barth is not inspecting them with a dogmatic checklist in hand. He is trying to discern how they have struggled towards Christianness, not by merely announcing some position, but by seeking to set themselves face-to-face with the matter of theology in humility and hope. Barth is characteristically critical of theologians who he believes have cared little for such integrity or who considered themselves to possess it in ample measure, and characteristically laudatory of those who fought to maintain integrity in addressing the culture. Moreover, he is clear that theology may be helped to discover and exercise such integrity precisely in its conversations with philosophy. The question which Barth takes to both Kant and Hegel is: can philosophy remind theology of its proper task? In particular, can theology learn to return to, and draw upon, the resources of its understanding of revelation in order to have fruitful and helpful things to say to its conversation partners?

Barth did not write the history of the nineteenth century as a bleak episode of compromise and vacillation; indeed, he believes himself forbidden to make such judgements by the nature of the object, which is the history of God's sanctification of human thought and speech in the life of the Church. He is no less relentless in his magnanimity than in his criticism; never contemptuous; always in solidarity with his subject; and, more than anything, constrained by theological conviction to maintain (against most of his detractors, many of his supporters and even, on occasions, against himself) that 'evangelical theology ... did exist in the nineteenth century' (Barth, 1961, p. 11).

Notes

1   The pagination of the 2001 printing differs slightly from previous editions.
2   The chief exception is a strange article by H. Gauss (1949) which by and large fails to come to grips with Barth's text.
3   Cf. Rohls (1997, p. xix) – an odd judgement in view of the material on the eighteenth century.
4   Chapman (2001, p. 11) is forced to admit that Barth is 'often surprisingly sympathetic' to his subject-matter ('surprisingly' because one can already assume in advance that Barth will be a hanging judge when it comes to the theology of others?).
5   F.W. Graf's essay 'Die "antihistorische Revolution"' is particularly prone to these problems (Graf, 1988). His reconstruction of the 'anti-historical' world-view, for example, is largely assembled out of phrases or motifs (but not arguments) from a number of quite minor figures considered to be Barth's sympathizers in the 1920s which, when put together, are presented as indicative of a universally perceived religious and cultural malady. There is little sustained presentation of Barth himself, and almost no attention to the larger scope of his theology. Simply as a piece of *historical* analysis, what Graf offers leaves much to be desired.
6   It is this which distinguishes what Barth has to say from the initially similar-sounding affirmations of W. Pannenberg in his account of the relation of Church history to general history in *Theology and the Philosophy of Science* (Pannenberg, 1976, pp. 390–403). Pannenberg argues that 'Church history is ... not a branch of history, naturally subordinate to general history. On the contrary, it unites in itself what in secular history is divided into specialised areas' (ibid., p. 395). Like Barth, Pannenberg suggests that history is a totality organized around a single theme, the clue to which is to be found in a consideration of divine action (see ibid., p. 396f.). But where Barth starts from the *particula veri* of the Christian Gospel of reconciliation, to which all else is subordinate, Pannenberg's starting point, though at first it seems to be very specific, is in fact much more general – namely, the history of religion (of which the Church's history is an instance). 'Church history is the treatment of Christianity from the point of view of the history of religion' (ibid., p. 393); indeed, 'history in general is the history of religion, right down to all the processes of secularisation and emancipation, because the concern of religion involved no less than the whole of reality and human destiny' (ibid., p. 394). And so for Pannenberg, this starting point has the advantages that it does not compromise the proper methodological secularity of the study of history, and, in avoiding starting from dogmatics, has greater apologetic utility in showing 'how far in this historic experiential situation [that is, Church history] the God of the Christian tradition had manifested himself to the participants as the all-determining reality' (ibid., p. 399). There are clear differences here concerning the ontology of the Church and the visibility of its history, as well as concerning the perceptibility of divine action and its relation to general historical experience.
7   Barth's conception of the self-proclamation of Jesus as constitutive of history should not be collapsed, as it is by K. Hafstadt, into an idea of history as constituted by speech-events; the notion of speech-event is far too narrow to bear the full weight of Barth's conception of Jesus' prophetic action, which gathers into itself the entirety of the economy of salvation, and has reference to the comprehensive ontological scope and force of the person and work of Christ (Hafstadt, 1985).
8   On this see McCormack (1995, pp. 141–55), and MacDonald (2000) – though one may legitimately wonder whether MacDonald's elaborate cultural genetics is a necessary part of his account of Barth's understanding of a '*theological* historicality' (2000, p. 18).

9 See, for example, the relevant sections of the survey article by E. Stöve (1989) and Markschies *et al.* (2001). Further, see Mühlenberg (1988) and Uhlig (1985). For more recent materials, see, for example, Hempelman (1997) and Herms (1997).

10 For only one more recent example of the charge, see Dantine (1968).

11 On the theme of tradition, see Barth (1963, pp. 42–47).

12 See the discussion of biblical interpretation in *CD* I/2, pp. 463–72; on this theme, see now Burnett (2001, pp. 95–220).

13 Barth's positive reading of the modern history of Christianity finds fullest expression in his tiny sketch of post-Reformation Church history in *CD* IV/3 (pp. 19ff.); his praise there of modern theology as a form of outreach into the world which 'even in its weaker as well as its stronger elements belongs to the credit side of the total picture' (ibid., p. 32) is noteworthy, especially when compared with the much more cautious account in *CD* I/2 (pp. 335ff.), where Barth judges that the victories of the Church and its theology in the age of mission were 'Pyrrhic victories' (ibid., p. 336). In this context, Barth's 1957 lecture to the *Goethegesellschaft* (Barth, 1961, pp. 9–33) offers a very generous reading of the nineteenth century tradition, which draws on the opening chapter of *Protestant Theology*.

14 In this light, J.E. Thiel's view that Barth's early interpretation of Schleiermacher is 'one-sided, thoroughly polemical and even a-historical', and that, in his monologue, Barth 'does not seek nuanced understanding but rejects the possibility of dialogue with a flurry of sweeping accusations and condemnations' (Thiel, 1988, p. 11) is simply absurd. Alice Collins' (1988) argument that only later does Barth move to a more conciliatory relationship to Schleiermacher founders on the fact that, already in the 1920s, Barth's attitude is very far from dismissive.

15 On this, see a parallel set of statements in Barth (1981, pp. 33–38).

References

Barth, K. (1928a), 'Biblical Questions, Insights and Vistas', in *The Word of God and the Word of Man*, London: Hodder and Stoughton.

Barth, K. (1928b), 'The Strange New World within the Bible', in *The Word of God and the Word of Man*, London: Hodder and Stoughton.

Barth, K. (1938), *The Knowledge of God and the Service of God According to the Teaching of the Reformation*, London: Hodder and Stoughton.

Barth, K. (1961), 'Evangelical Theology in the Nineteenth Century', in *The Humanity of God*, London: Collins.

Barth, K. (1963), *Evangelical Theology: An Introduction*, London: Weidenfeld and Nicolson.

Barth, K. (1981), *Ethics*, trans. G.W. Bromiley, Edinburgh: T. & T. Clark.

Barth, K. (1982a), *The Theology of Schleiermacher. Lectures at Göttingen, Winter Semester of 1923/24*, Edinburgh: T. & T. Clark.

Barth, K. (1982b), *Christliche Dogmatik im Entwurf* in *Karl Barth Gesamtaugabe*, vol. II, ed. G. Sauter, Zürich: Theologische Verlag.

Barth, K. (1991), *The Göttingen Dogmatics. Instruction in the Christian Religion. Vol. 1*, Grand Rapids: Eerdmans.

Barth, K. (1992), *The Theology of John Calvin*, Edinburgh: T. & T. Clark.

Barth, Karl (2001), *Protestant Theology in the Nineteenth Century: Its Background and History*, London: SCM.

Barth, K. (2002), *The Theology of the Reformed Confession, 1923*, Louisville, KT: Westminster John Knox.

Barth, K., and E. Thurneysen (1972), *Karl Barth–Eduard Thurneysen: Briefwechsel II: 1921–1930*, Zürich: TVZ.

Blumenberg, H. (1983), *The Legitimacy of the Modern Age*, Cambridge, MA: MIT Press.

Brunner, E. (1924), *Die Mystik und das Wort*, Tübingen: Mohr.

Burnett, R.E., (2001), *Karl Barth's Theological Exegesis: The Hermeneutical Principles of the Römerbrief Period*, Tübingen: Mohr.

Chapman, M. (2001), *Ernst Troeltsch and Liberal Theology: Religion and Cultural Synthesis in Wilhelmite Germany*, Oxford: Oxford University Press.

Collins, A. (1988), 'Barth's Relationship to Schleiermacher: a Reassessment', *Studies in Religion*, **17**, pp. 213–24.

Dantine, W. (1968), 'Der Welt-Bezug des Glaubens: Überlegungen zum Verhältnis von Geschichte und Gesetz im Denken Karl Barths', in W. Dantine and K. Lüthi (eds), *Theologie zwischen Gestern und Morgen: Interpretationen und Anfragen zum Werk Karl Barths*, Munich: Kaiser, pp. 261–301.

Gauss, H. (1949), 'Philosophische Randbemerkungen zu Karl Barth, *Die protestantische Theologie im 19. Jahrhundert*', *Theologische Zeitschrift*, **5**, pp. 123–43.

Gerrish, B. (1975), Review of K. Barth, *Protestant Theology, Church History*, **44**, p. 123.

Graf, F.W. (1988), 'Die "antihistorische Revolution" in der protestantischen Theologie der zwanziger Jahre', in J. Rohls and G. Wenz (eds), *Vernunft des Glaubens: Wissenschaftliche Theologie und kirchliche Lehre. Festschrift zum 60. Geburtstag von W. Pannenberg*, Göttingen: Vandenhoeck und Ruprecht, pp. 377–405.

Gunton, C. (1986), 'Barth and the Western Intellectual Tradition. Towards a Theology after Christendom', in J. Thompson (ed.), *Theology Beyond Christendom*, Allison Park: Pickwick, pp. 285–301.

Hafstadt, K. (1985), *Wort und Geschichte: Das Geschichtsverständnis Karl Barths*, Munich: Kaiser.

Harnack, A. von (1890), 'Antrittsrede' in *Sitzungsberichte der königliche preussischen Akademie der Wissenschaften zu Berlin*, Berlin: Verlag der königliche Akademie der Wissenschaften.

Harnack, A. von (1988), 'What Has History to Offer as Certain Knowledge Concerning the Meaning of World Events?', in H.M. Rumscheidt (ed.), *Adolf von Harnack: Liberal Theology at Its Height*, London: Collins, pp. 45–63.

Hempelmann, H. (1997), '"Erkenntnis aus Glauben": Notwendigkeit und Wissenschaftlichkeit von Kirchengeschichte und kirchlicher Zeitgeschichte als theologische Disziplinen', *Kirchliche Zeitgeschichte*, **10**, pp. 263–304.

Herms, E. (1997), 'Theologische Geschichtsschreibung', *Kirchliche Zeitgeschichte*, **10**, pp. 305–30.

Hodgson, P.C. (1966), *The Formation of Historical Theology. A Study of Ferdinand Christian Baur*, New York: Harper.

Lessing, E. (2000), *Geschichte der deutschsprächigen evangelischen Theologie von Albrecht Ritschl bis zur Gegenwart. Band 1: 1870–1918*, Göttingen: Vandenhoeck und Ruprecht.

McCormack, B.L. (1995), *Karl Barth's Critically Realistic Dialectical Theology: Its Genesis and Development 1909–1936*, Oxford: Clarendon Press.

MacDonald, N.B. (2000), *Karl Barth and the Strange New World Within the Bible: Barth, Wittgenstein and the Dilemmas of the Enlightenment*, Carlisle: Paternoster Press.

Markschies, C. *et al.* (2001), 'Kirchengeschichte/Kirchengeschichtsschreibung', in *Die Religion in Geschichte und Gegenwart*, 4th edn, vol. 4, pp. 789–91, 1170–79.

Mühlenberg, E. (1988), 'Dogmatik und Kirchengeschichte' in J. Rohls and G. Wenz (eds), *Vernunft des Glaubens: Wissenschaftliche Theologie und kirchliche Lehre. Festschrift zum 60. Geburtstag von W. Pannenburg*, Göttingen: Vandenhoeck and Ruprecht, pp. 436–53.

Nowak, K. (1987), 'Die "antihistorische Revolution". Symptome und Folgen der Krise historischer Weltorientierung nach dem Ersten Weltkrieg in Deutschland', in G.H. Renz and F.W. Graf (eds), *Troeltsch-Studien*, Gütersloh: Mohn, pp. 133–71.

Nowak, K. (1997), 'Wie theologisch ist die Kirchengeschichte? Über die Verbindung und die Differenz von Kirchengeschichtsschreibung und Theologie', *Theologische Literaturzeitung*, **122**, pp. 3–12.

Pannenberg, W. (1976), *Theology and the Philosophy of Science*, London: Darton, Longman and Todd.

Pannenberg, W. (1997), *Problemgeschichte der neueren evangelischen Theologie in Deutschland: Von Schleiermacher bis zu Barth und Tillich*, Göttingen: Vandenhoeck und Ruprecht.

Rohls, J. (1997), *Protestantische Theologie der Neuzeit I: Die Voraussetzungen und das 19. Jahrhundert*, Tübingen: Mohr.

Stöve, E. (1989), 'Kirchengeschichtsschreibung', *Theologische Realenzyklopädie*, **18**, pp. 535–60.

Thiel, J.E. (1988), 'Barth's Early Interpretation of Schleiermacher' in J.O. Duke and R.F. Streetman (eds), *Barth and Schleiermacher: Beyond the Impasse,* Philadelphia: Fortress Press.

Tillich, P. (1967), *Perspectives on Nineteenth and Twentieth Century Protestant Theology*, London: SCM.

Uhlig, C. (1985), *Funktion und Situation der Kirchengeschichte als theologische Disziplin*, Frankfurt am Main: Lang.

Welch, C. (1972), *Protestant Thought in the Nineteenth Century. Vol. 1: 1799–1870*, New Haven, CT: Yale University Press.

Williams, S. (1986), 'Barth, Buddeus and the Eighteenth Century', *Modern Theology*, **2**, pp. 309–19.

Williams, S. (1995), *Revelation and Reconciliation*, Cambridge: Cambridge University Press.

CHAPTER 3

Culture and Barbarism: Barth amongst the Students of Culture

Timothy Gorringe

Discussion of Barth's theology of culture faces a twofold embarrassment. First, Barth began his career with a violent rejection of the nineteenth-century tradition of the *Kulturprotestantismus*. Stung by both of Barth's Romans commentaries, and by the Tambach lecture, Harnack indignantly asked him, 'If God is simply unlike anything said about him on the basis of the development of culture, on the basis of the knowledge gathered by culture, and on the basis of ethics, how can this culture and in the long run one's own existence be protected against atheism?' Barth replied by pointing, as an example of culture, to 'the statements of the war theologians of all countries' and maintaining that such theology actually sowed atheism since it came out of polytheism. Barth's theology, Harnack felt, consigned Goethe and Kant to barbarism. Barth replied that the Gospel had as little to do with barbarism as with culture (Rumschiedt, 1972, pp. 30, 33).

There is no evidence that Walter Benjamin knew of this exchange, but we cannot but be reminded by it of the famous sixth thesis on the philosophy of history which he wrote in 1940, fleeing from the Nazis. Benjamin saw history as the story of the victors, who carry the spoils in their triumphal procession. These spoils are called cultural treasures, and a historical materialist, Benjamin noted, 'views them with cautious detachment':

> For without exception the cultural treasures he surveys have an origin which he cannot contemplate without horror. They owe their existence not only to the efforts of great minds and talents who have created them, but also to the anonymous toil of their own contemporaries. There is no document of civilisation which is not at the same time a document of barbarism. (Benjamin, 1992, p. 248)

Augustine writing on Rome, Luther debating with Erasmus, Barth rejecting cultural Protestantism: all have this same sense of the ambivalence of culture. All three of them are emphatically men of the senses, valuing music, letters and art, but all three see the barbarism attached to culture and each comments on this in texts of classic status.[1] In different ways all three write amongst ruins: Augustine after the sack of Rome; Luther during the passing of one age and the birth pangs of another; and Barth amidst the cultural chaos caused by the First World War.

A second embarrassment in discussing Barth's theology of culture stems from the comparison Barth himself made, as early as 1926, between his theology and that of

Paul Tillich. Even at that early date, when Tillich was still a professor of philosophy, his interest in culture was notable; 30 years later he was to become the champion of a theology of a culture. His theological method, which found the divine in whatever was a matter of 'ultimate concern', was a simple and effective way of discussing cultural matters theologically; for this method, however, Barth had nothing but scorn. In return he was characterized by Tillich as one who stood outside the great cultural stream, casting stones at those who were being carried by it.

In the Anglo-Saxon world, at least, this caricature has stuck. Barth's interest in Mozart is well known – not so his rapt attention before Michelangelo's *Pieta*, in the Vatican, before Botticelli's great paintings in the Uffizi, before Rembrandt's *Night Watch* in Amsterdam. His deep knowledge of German literature, of Schiller (on which Julicher commented ironically in his review of the first Romans commentary) and of Goethe, his magnificent essays on the eighteenth century, his profoundly empathetic friendship with Carl Zuckmayer – these are either overlooked or regarded as inconsistencies. Barth himself is undoubtedly partly to blame. In 1967 Zuckmayer suggested to Barth the possibility of worshipping God 'in the presence and even in the bark of some Alpine tree'. 'From you', Barth wrote, 'as distinct from theologians, I am willing to accept such things and to take them in good part' (Barth and Zuckmayer, 1977, p. 12). Barth was 81 when he wrote this; it is difficult to imagine him doing so even five years earlier, and one might be forgiven for suggesting that perhaps Barth was adopting a form of the doctrine of double truth – that something might be true for the poet and false for the theologian, or vice versa. Barth's single-minded 'Christocentricity' was precisely his attempt to avoid any such running on parallel tracks, and it helps confirm the impression of his indifference to culture.

Barth, Benjamin and Tillich all write within the German tradition of *Kultur*, anglicized by Matthew Arnold as 'the best that has been thought and known in the world'. Beginning with Arnold, or perhaps with Coleridge, there is a very distinctive Anglo-Saxon appropriation of this tradition, an appropriation far more attentive to the value of working-class culture than its Continental neighbour, often sceptical of the value of high culture, and concerned with barbarism in different ways. In this chapter I want to propose an Anglo-Saxon extension of the conversation between Barth and Zuckmayer, bringing Arnold, Eliot, Williams and Eagleton into the circle. In doing so we can perhaps break the spell of the Barth–Tillich confrontation and move into rather different territory in the discussion of culture.

Though by no means an anglophile, Barth enjoyed his visits to Britain and his conversations with his pragmatic neighbours, so sceptical of grand theological schemes. I will let the British begin the conversation and then consider what we may take to be Barth's reply in the light of his 1926 essay on 'Church and Culture', his lectures on education, given two years later, and his thoughts, 30 years later, on the relation of the great light and the lesser lights.

Culture: The English Tradition

In *The Long Revolution*, first published in 1961, Raymond Williams outlines a threefold definition of culture first as an ideal, the discovery and description of timeless values; second, as record – culture as tradition; and third as the description of a particular way of life (Williams, 1965, p. 57).[2] His interest is in the relations between these aspects. Cultural analysis is, according to him, essentially concerned with the analysis of patterns, looking at the relationships between elements in a whole way of life. What this yields us, characteristically, is an account of 'the structure of feeling' in any given society, 'a particular sense of life, a particular community of experience hardly needing expression' which is the culture of a period, 'the particular living result of all the elements in the general organization' (ibid., p. 64). Three years earlier, in one of his greatest essays, he put this point differently by insisting that 'culture is ordinary'.

> We use the word culture in ... two senses: to mean a whole way of life – the common meanings; to mean the arts and learning – the special processes of discovery and creative effort. Some writers reserve the word for one or other of these senses; I insist on them both, and on the significance of their conjunction. (Williams, 1989, p. 4)

This insistence on conjunction was precisely what was lost in the German tradition of *Kultur*. Nothing expresses this more obviously than Schleiermacher's observation, in the first of the 1799 *Speeches*, that it was useless to appeal to the working class, who simply did not have the time needed to attend to things of the Spirit. Hence it was the *cultured* despisers who had to be addressed. Paradoxically, this was never the case in the most class-conscious society in Europe. Thus in *Lyrical Ballads*, published the year before the *Speeches*, it is the peasantry which is, as it were, the bearer of the most valuable things in culture, as they were for Scott in *Border Ballads*. Arnold was indisputably influenced by the idea of *Bildung*, and he acknowledges his debt especially to Lessing and Herder, and yet in *Culture and Anarchy* it is his own middle class, the Philistines, who are the target, who he wants to redeem from the work ethic, from that dismal utilitarianism which he appropriately calls 'machinery'. Culture, for Arnold, was the study of perfection, by which he meant the possibility of sympathy which he missed in the fervent religion of his day. Culture was to be the leaven of that religion, to supply it, in T.S. Eliot's rather sour phrase, with 'ethical formation and some emotional colour' (Eliot, 1948, p. 28). For all his championing of high culture Arnold was no elitist. For him, the men of culture were 'the true apostles of equality':

> The great men of culture are those who have had a passion for diffusing ... for carrying from one end of society to the other, the best knowledge, the noblest ideas of their time ... to make it efficient *outside the clique of the cultivated and learned*, yet still remaining the *best* knowledge and thought of the time. (Arnold, 1909, p. 31)[3]

Arnold's caricatures of the working class, addressed to the Philistines, are crude and inaccurate enough, but there is no doubting his levelling sentiment – a levelling to be accomplished by education.

Arnold was, as he describes himself, a Philistine and the son of a Philistine; likewise, Raymond Williams, the greatest cultural theorist in Britain in the twentieth century, was born, and always kept his roots, in the working class. For him, the observable badness of much popular culture was not, in fact, a true guide to the state of mind and feeling of the working class. On the contrary he found there 'as much natural fineness of feeling, as much quick discrimination, as much clear grasp of ideas within the range of experience, as I have found anywhere' (Williams, 1989, p. 12). He wrote these words in 1958; I have not been able to find an instance of his revisiting this theme prior to his death 30 years later. In 1958 he also observed that 'the central problem of our society, in the coming half century, is the use of our new resources to make a good common culture' (ibid., p. 10). Less than a decade after he wrote this, the *Sun* became Britain's best-selling newspaper, a position it has retained ever since, and the process of the commercialization of television, in its infancy when Williams wrote that essay, culminated with Sky TV. The working-class culture which Williams grew up with, for which education was one of the highest priorities, has evaporated into a new populism which scorns education. In 1958 'culture vulture' was the sneer of some intellectuals, but the 'guilt ridden tic at the mention of any serious standards whatsoever' which Williams discerned even then has now become characteristic of an entire culture. Williams agreed with Arnold that 'a desire to know what is best, and to do what is good, is the whole positive nature of man' (ibid.). The political, environmental and ecological choices made by the democracies of the North during the past 40 years call that statement into question, to say the very least. Williams believed in the necessity and efficacy of education as passionately as Arnold, describing it as 'the process of giving to the ordinary members of society its full common meanings, and the skills that will enable them to amend these meanings, in the light of their personal and common experience' (ibid., p. 14). This vision was abandoned, in Britain, under Margaret Thatcher, and has never been recovered. If anything, the emphasis on education as training for jobs and making 'useful' (that is, conforming) citizens has grown stronger.

T.S. Eliot's *Notes Towards the Definition of Culture* appeared ten years before Williams' 'Culture is Ordinary', but he had been working on it for some years – that is, through the war and while he was writing the *Four Quartets*. Like Williams, he offers a threefold definition of culture, but instead focuses on the individual, the group and society as a whole. Though he was worried by the prospect of a disintegration into a mass of competing subcultures, his vision of a healthy culture was the coexistence of classes, whose boundaries were porous, and who would be led by an intellectual elite not identical with those in power.[4] Although he talks incautiously of 'superior' and 'inferior' people he, too, is committed to no vision of *Kultur*. On the contrary:

> To treat the 'uneducated' mass of the population as we might treat some innocent
> tribe of savages to whom we are impelled to deliver the true faith, is to encourage
> them to neglect or despise that culture which they should possess and *from which
> the more conscious part of culture draws vitality*; and to aim to make everyone
> share in the appreciation of the fruits of the more conscious part of culture is to
> adulterate and cheapen what you give. (Eliot, 1948, p. 106, emphasis added)

Part of his emphasis on the need for difference was an appreciation for the role of
regional culture which gives what is, in many ways, a very dated piece of work a more
contemporary feel. The different class and regional cultures would contribute to a
positive form of conflict, which would diffuse the animosities which can otherwise be
focused on another nation. Unlike either Arnold or Williams, Eliot was no great
enthusiast for education. The headlong rush to educate everybody, he believed, meant
the necessary lowering of standards, what today we call 'dumbing down', 'destroying
our ancient edifices to make ready the ground upon which the barbarian nomads of
the future will encamp in their mechanised caravans' (ibid., p. 31).

Of these Anglo-Saxon writers only Arnold and Eliot explore the relationship
between religion and culture. For Arnold, as we have seen, culture takes further and
sweetens the necessary moral influence of religion. Eliot, on the other hand, proposed
a dialectical understanding of religion and culture in which they were both identical
and different. He maintained their identity on the grounds that no culture has emerged
except in relation to religion.[5] It is religion, rather than culture, that he defines as the
'whole way of life of a people from birth to the grave, from morning to night and even
in sleep'. But, he adds, 'that way of life is also its culture' (ibid.). At the same time, a
contrast between religion and culture was necessary, for without it an inferior culture
and religion resulted. Identity, Eliot maintained, worked on the unconscious, and
difference on the conscious level. Eliot was perfectly well aware of the dehumanizing
potential of religion, of the possibility that 'elements of local culture – even of local
barbarism – may become invested with the sanctity of religious observances, and
superstition may flourish instead of piety' so that people *slip back* to a primitive unity
of religion and culture (ibid., p. 71). On the other hand, in the background is quite
clearly his vision of an organic English society, sustained by some kind of residual
Christian belief, reaching back seamlessly into the non-Christian past, engaged in a
struggle against Nazi barbarism, as this appears in *East Coker*. His background is
therefore quite different from Barth's ferocious opposition to religion, which
emerged from his perception of the way in which it was used to sustain barbarism in
the First World War.

When Eliot says that culture cannot be preserved without religion and that religion
equally needed 'the preservation and maintenance of culture', he only superficially
resembles Harnack. Whereas, by 'culture' Harnack meant Goethe and Kant, Eliot
meant, in a notorious description, 'Derby Day, Henley Regatta, Cowes, the twelfth of
August, a cup final, the dog races, the pin table, the dart board, Wensleydale cheese,
boiled cabbage cut into sections, beetroot in vinegar, nineteenth century Gothic
churches and the music of Elgar' (ibid.). But although no one will dispute that bishops

in gaiters are part of culture, to argue that Derby Day and the dog track are part of religion is so to redefine religion as to make it incompatible with faith. Barth had no such folkloric idea of religion in view when he declared faith and religion mutually opposed in *Church Dogmatics* I/2, but it would simply have strengthened his case.

While Eliot was reflecting on the problems of culture, Adorno and Horkheimer were mimeographing their attack on the culture industry, not just an analytic but a prescient account of what was to come. For culture came to centre-stage at the end of the twentieth century partly because it has been put to good use by Capital. Whereas Arnold's Philistines had no use for culture, today's Philistines have realized that they can make money from it. Other factors are also involved in the contemporary centrality of culture – above all, the struggles against colonialism and the rise of identity politics all over the world. In the face of this centrality Terry Eagleton calls for culture to be put back in its place, since it cannot alleviate the primary problems of the new millennium – war, famine, poverty, disease, debt, drugs, environmental pollution and the displacement of peoples (Eagleton, 2000, p. 130). To accord too high a significance to the arts is to lay on them a burden they cannot bear, and will lead them to crumble from the inside (ibid., p. 16). Eagleton sees a contest between culture as civility, culture as identity and culture as commercial (ibid., p. 64). He agrees with Eliot that culture is dependent on religion, but points out that it then finds itself caught in a double bind. If it comes adrift from its roots in religion it is enfeebled; if it clings to those roots it is condemned to irrelevance (ibid., p. 67). It is capitalism above all which is destroying this religious relevance, for 'the market is the best mechanism for ensuring that society is both highly liberated and deeply reactionary' (ibid, p. 71).

Eagleton agrees with Frank Farrell that the clash between modernity and postmodernity has its roots in late medieval theology, between realists and nominalists, the one believing that God respects the world God has created, the other that God has absolute freedom vis-à-vis creation (Farrell, 1996). It is an old Catholic argument that nominalism passed over into Protestantism. The Protestant, it is claimed, imbues with meaning a world which is otherwise stripped of significance. In this sense, Eagleton understands postmodernism as a belated form of Protestantism as, in its view, it is culture that makes the world (Eagleton, 2000, p. 84). The political result is the culture of identity and small-scale contests for minority rights. Eagleton, by contrast, restates the classic Thomist synthesis of nature and grace in understanding human beings as 'cusped between nature and culture' (ibid., p. 99). Like a good Thomist he wants both sides to be honoured: crucial to the cultural side is political mobilization, which cannot be reduced to culture as civility or as art. Like both medieval and Reformation theologians, and like Eliot and Williams, he wants a common culture as a result – one that is 'continuously remade and redefined by the collective practice of its members', *ecclesia semper reformanda*. Whereas the theologian finds the origin of this in the *promissio inquieta*, Eagleton insists that such a society is inseparable from radical socialist change (ibid., p. 119). Here, a fourth form of culture – culture as radical protest – plays its role, in returning the cultural to the material, grace to nature. In such protest, religion, too, may claim to shape the future. Although it is identified as a form of the past, it points beyond that part insofar as it inspires challenges to the dominant culture. Thus, 'While postmodernism declares an end to history, these forces continue to act out that more modernist scenario in which the past returns, this time as future' (ibid., p. 123).

Barth on Culture

It is time, now, to bring Barth back into this conversation, and I will concentrate on his 1926 article, 'Church and Culture' which he wrote when he was just 40 years old. In looking at this we have to remember Barth's remarks to Bethge, Bonhoeffer's biographer, about the danger of judging someone by their early writings (Barth, 1971, p. 122).[6] Nevertheless, by this stage Barth had already moved to the threefold form of Dogmatics which was to shape his mature work, and he uses it to structure his paper. If we look at the 1928 *Ethics*, and compare them with the only part of the mature ethics we have, *Church Dogmatics* III/4, we can see that there are parts which are taken over word-for-word, but that the subdivisions have changed beyond recognition, and that the whole is greatly expanded. Barth dealt with culture partly in the section on work in III/4, but he would have taken it up further both in IV/4 and in the ethics of redemption, where he had promised to say something about Marlene Dietrich! We have a pointer, then, to what his mature thought might have offered, but not the finished article.

Tillich, who had written on 'Church and Culture' in 1924, is in view from the start, and, as always, his method is rejected. Tillich had begun with a sociological account of the Church. We can certainly learn from that, says Barth, but it misses what is essential. He defines the Church instead as 'the community of faith and obedience living from the Word of God, the community of sinful men' (Barth, 1962, p. 334). It is this last phrase, according to Barth, that brings the sociological dimension into the picture. That the Church witnesses to the true goal of culture does not mean that it speaks from a superior position. The Church, necessarily 'swims along in the stream of culture', but its task is to witness to the Word that establishes culture. Turning to this, Barth finds in *Religion in Geschichte und Gegenwart* the definitions, 'the sum of the aims proceeding from human activity and in turn stimulating human activity' or 'the idea of the final goal and the totality of norms by which human activity should be guided'. If these are our definitions, he says, 'the Church could only speak negatively and polemically on the significance of culture. The two entities would not only exist on different levels, but on mutually exclusive levels, as truth and error' (ibid., p. 337). This is Tillich's stone-throwing Barth, and hostile enough in all conscience. The two definitions are excessively general, but with some charity we might align the first with Williams' third definition – culture as a way of life – and the second with culture as art – *Kultur*. Why should the Church view 'this so-called culture with horror, as an impossible fantasy and an idol' (ibid., p. 338)? Barth's answer refers directly to Terry

Eagleton's description of humankind as 'cusped between nature and culture'. The task of culture, according to Barth, is the realization of our humanity. The problem is that we exist as soul and body, spirit and nature, and we have to bring these into unity. Spirit must mould nature, and nature actualize spirit. Because we fail to do this 'Christian preaching ... has met every culture, however supposedly rich and mature, with ultimate sharp scepticism' (ibid, p. 339).

Why does Barth define the cultural task in term of the realization of *unity*? In this lecture he gives us no clue, and it is certainly not self-evident, but perhaps we can find the answer in his reflections on what he calls dissipation in *Church Dogmatics* IV/2, published in 1955. He has already argued that human beings must be understood as a union of a ruling soul and a serving body. Here he argues that a split in *either* direction, privileging either the body at the expense of the soul *or the soul at the expense of the body*, leads to a ruinous dissipation. If we choose one or other form of that dualism, he argues, we reject God. For Barth, dissipation, the falling apart of body and soul, leads to the loss of our humanity. He does not say so, but we might say that any such dissipation is always a prelude to barbarism.

The human task, Barth argues, is set us by God's Word. It is, in Paul Lehmann's phrase, 'to make and to keep human life human'. It is this task that is what we mean by 'culture', and as such it emerges as response to the Word of God. Of course, in historical terms this is complete nonsense, since culture long pre-dates the emergence of what Barth speaks of as revelation, but, as we would expect, he has an answer to this objection, which emerges in the course of his exposition of culture in relation to creation, reconciliation and redemption.

Clearly differentiating himself from the Thomist principle alluded to by Eagleton, Barth instead approaches creation through the *extra calvinisticum*, the doctrine that the Logos, Jesus Christ, fills heaven and earth. Beginning from this standpoint we can recognize the truth of the statement that grace does not destroy, but perfects, nature. There is no question of total depravity because human beings are capable of hearing the promise: 'The term *culture* connotes exactly that promise to man: fulfilment, unity, wholeness within his sphere as creature, as man, exactly as God in his sphere is fullness, wholeness, Lord over nature and spirit, Creator of heaven *and* earth' (ibid., p. 343). Because this is the case culture can, in fact, be a witness to the promise, a reflection of the light of the incarnate Logos. Whilst there is no place for a sanctifying of cultural achievement, *à la* Schleiermacher, 'there is even less place for a basic blindness to the possibility that culture may be revelatory, that it can be filled with promise'. Thus, '[t]he Church will not see the coming of the kingdom of God in any cultural achievement, but it will be alert for the signs which, perhaps in many cultural achievements, announce that the kingdom approaches' (ibid., p. 344). Culture, then, has a sacramental, or signifying role. Compare Terry Eagleton's dictum that '[a]rt defines what we live for, but it is not art for which we live' (Eagleton, 2000, p. 64).

We can compare this account of the significance of the *regnum naturae* for our appreciation of culture with Barth's mature thought on 'the lesser lights' in *Church Dogmatics* IV/3, published more than 30 years later in 1959. Barth expounds Jesus as the Light of Life, the one Word of God alongside which there is no other. Precisely because this is the case, however, 'the sphere of his dominion and Word is … greater than that of the kerygma, dogma, cultus, mission and the whole life of the community'. There are in fact 'parables of the kingdom' outside the Church: 'In the narrow corner in which we have our place and task we cannot but eavesdrop on the world at large' (*CD* IV/3, pp. 116–17). While human beings may deny God, God does not deny human beings: 'Even from the mouth of Balaam the well-known voice of the Good Shepherd may sound, and it is not to be ignored in spite of its sinister origin' (ibid., p. 119). The community has, in fact, always heard words from that world in which it recognizes with joy its own message. The truth of such words is to be measured by Scripture, by Church confession and by their fruits. There will also be words addressed to the Church of affirmation and criticism, address and claim and therefore of a summons to faith and repentance. (Perhaps Overbeck is in view. We could also think of Ricoeur's three 'masters of suspicion', Marx, Nietzsche and Freud.) The work of all such words is to lead the community more deeply in to the given Word of the Bible. Scripture relativizes these words; however, '[t]o relativise means critically to set something in its limited and conditioned place. But it also means positively to set it in the relationship indicated by the limits of this place' (ibid., p. 163). Here, too, then, culture, and not just *Kultur*, but all three of Williams' senses, is affirmed as a place of God's operation.

I return now to the 1926 essay and to the significance of the doctrine of reconciliation for culture. The kingdom of Christ stands 'in the midst of enemies'. Nevertheless reconciliation is a fact and this means that faith is lived out 'as the proclamation of the righteousness of God in the valley of death'. From this point of view, culture is the law in reference to which the justified and sanctified sinner practises faith and obedience. The promise implicit in creation is here law and command – the command to be human, a task which has to be actualized. 'The standard for such distinctions is always unity, the destined character of man, that man find himself as a whole' (Barth, 1962, p. 346).

From the perspective of redemption 'culture is the limit set for men, on the other side of which God himself, in fulfilment of his promise, makes all things new' (ibid., p. 347). Redemption for Barth, at this stage, is not about the Spirit, but about eschatology. Eschatology means that culture, as formed reality and real form, is the process of becoming. The Church confronts society with eschatological anticipation:

> Not with an undervaluation of cultural achievement, but with the highest possible evaluation of the goal for which it sees all cultural activity striving. Not in pessimism, but in boundless hope. Not as a spoilsport, but in the knowledge that art and science, business and politics, techniques and education are really a game – a serious game, and game means an imitative and ultimately ineffective activity – the significance of which lies not in its attainable goals but in what it signifies. (Ibid, p. 349)

An obvious objection to put to Barth here – an objection raised more by George Steiner than by my Anglo-Saxon interlocutors – is that the concept of 'game' is inadequate to the tragedy of the human situation. On the other hand, to the extent that Barth has *Kultur* in mind, we can compare Eagleton's insistence that culture needs to be put in its place, as compared with political struggle to make the world a better place. And we recall that, between 1938 and 1942, Barth preached resistance to Hitler as God's command.

Barth includes education in his list, and that education is a central component of culture is a key doctrine for any contemporary state, appropriated in different ways by both Arnold and Williams. Barth lectured on education in his 1928 *Ethics*. How does what he has to say compare with their views?

In the 1928 *Ethics* Barth already understood ethics as command, and, as in the lecture on culture, envisaged a threefold command of God the Creator, Reconciler and Redeemer. Under the first came the Command of Life, and then calling, order and faith; under the second came the Command of Law, and then authority, humility and love; and under the third came the Command of Promise, and then conscience, gratitude and hope. It was under authority that he chose to deal with education.

The concern of both Arnold and Williams is, by and large, the extension of education to those classes which have not hitherto enjoyed it. Barth's concern, by contrast, is more the nature of pedagogy, especially in the context of Weimar and ideas such as those of the Rudolf Steiner schools. He has profound things to say, which invite comparison with Simone Weil's reflections on education. In the context of this debate I will, however, concentrate on only one strand of this, namely the role of education in fitting us for our human task. We have seen that Williams indignantly rejects the utilitarian justification of education as something that fits us for a job. Barth argues that the goal of education is to fit a person for their position in the world. To be fit is to be able to do what is required. Having a calling does not mean living one's own life, developing one's own talents and interests. It means, rather, being claimed for, and required to bear, a particular place in human society and history with one's own particular abilities. All the real education that comes to us consists of being directed by men, in God's service, to this place and these limits or abilities being oriented to what is required, to a goal set for us (Barth, 1981, p. 14). The claim that I put before my pupil is not my personal claim, but the awaiting claim of life which is to be proclaimed through me. The pupil's life is a life that is required by God. But pupils are sinners and do not understand that their lives are required by God. Teaching, then, is this proclamation.

This is put in an idiom which would probably have been anathema to Williams (though he might have recognized in it the rhetoric of the Chapels), but it seems to me to represent the same serious view of the way in which education contributes to culture as a way of life. Contrary to appearances, this, too, is what Eliot may be construed to be seeking, for, in rejecting education for all, he is in fact rejecting the universalization of *Kultur* and tacitly recognizing that education is a far wider matter. The contradiction of which Barth speaks can come, after all, in learning agricultural or industrial skills, and is not limited to the classroom.

Culture, Barbarism and Redemption

On the face of it, little would result from putting Barth and my Anglo-Saxon protagonists in the same room, but Barth's friendship with Zuckmayer illustrates the way in which he was always more surprising than a strict reading of his theology might suggest. His remarks on Ernst Ginsberg suggest that, had he lived and worked within the English-speaking world, he would have certainly known Eliot's poetry, which is far greater and more profound than his prose (Barth and Zuckmayer, 1977, p. 14). With all of his interlocutors he shares a serious and passionate concern for fullness of life. The vocabulary and the standpoints differ but, in one form or another, all these writers recognize a brokenness in human culture, a need for amendment, which Barth speaks of in terms of sin and redemption. He would say that their account of 'sin' was not nearly deep enough, that politics and social change, necessary as they are, cannot remedy the human condition. On the other hand, these practitioners of the Word would say that his account of the Word attributed to the Christian revelation an importance deeply implausible in the light of its actual results, both in terms of its history and in terms of what Williams called its 'residual' status. All, however, recognize the tension between culture and barbarism. Arnold (1909), drawing on the Romantic protest against industrialism, found barbarism not in 'heathen lands afar', but in the priorities of the English middle and upper classes, and proposed culture, the struggle for perfection, as a remedy. He puts his faith, ultimately, in those few in each class who see the point. He does not see, as Benjamin does, that culture is not just the opposite of barbarism, but also part of the problem. Here the other parties to this discussion are far clearer-sighted. In his allusions to the English Civil War in Little Gidding (Eliot, 1944) Eliot almost suggests Benjamin's dictum:

> Whatever we inherit from the fortunate
> We have taken from the defeated
> What they had to leave us – a symbol.

But in the light of the dialectic of the Christian revelation, of strength in weakness, Eliot continues:

> A symbol perfected in death.
> And all shall be well
> By the purification of the motive
> In the ground of our beseeching.

Eliot understands perfectly well that there is no redemption through culture, but that culture needs redemption. Williams and Eagleton understand this too, but look for redemption in political movements, at the same time recognizing that such movements cannot mobilize people as faith can, nor reach the depths it does.

The Jews, said Benjamin, in his concluding thesis on the philosophy of history, were prohibited from investigating the future, but commanded to remember. As a result, every second of time was turned into the strait gate through which the Messiah might enter (Benjamin, 1992, p. 255). What has been omitted from reflection on culture, said Barth, at the close of his reflections, 'is the insight that all Christendom and its relation to culture depends entirely upon hope; that the difference between reconciliation and redemption is a fundamental difference, and so also is that between reconciliation and creation. Upon the knowledge of the limit depends also the knowledge of the promise and the law' (Barth, 1962, p. 354).

> The dove descending breaks the air
> With flame of incandescent terror
> Of which the tongues declare
> The one discharge from sin and error.
> The only hope, or else despair
> Lies in the choice of pyre or pyre–
> To be redeemed from fire by fire.

In a situation where the barbarians are not just at the gates, but have been ruling us for quite some time, this seems to me a doctrine that should bring theologians and cultural theorists into worthwhile engagement or, at the very least, to a fruitful contradiction.[7]

Notes

1 Augustine in *The City of God*, Luther in *The Bondage of the Will*, and Barth in second *Romans*.
2 In *Culture and Society 1780–1950*, published in 1958, Williams defined culture as an individual habit of mind, an account of the intellectual development of society as a whole, the arts and the whole way of life of a people (Williams, 1963, p. 16).
3 Arnold italicizes the word 'best'; other italics are mine. Against this, Terry Eagleton points out that Arnold refused to take sides over the question of slavery in the American civil war (Eagleton, 2000, p. 17).
4 As Eagleton puts it, his vision is of a situation where '[a] priestlike clerisy, composed of individuals not utterly dissimilar to T.S. Eliot, will consciously nourish spiritual values, but these will be disseminated to the people and lived out by them obliquely, unreflectively, in the rhythm and texture of their lived experience' (Eagleton, 2000, p. 117).
5 He provides few grounds for this assertion, but does argue that all theological issues have cultural consequences, and that, therefore, Athanasius should be recognized as one of the great builders of Western civilization (Eliot, 1948, p. 77).
6 Barth wrote: 'It is unthinkable – and I put myself in his place now – what people would have done to me had I died … after the publication of the first or even the second Epistle to the Romans or after the appearance of my *Christliche Dogmatik im Entwurf.*'
7 I allude, of course, to the close of Alasdair MacIntyre's *After Virtue* (1981, p. 263).

References

Arnold, M. (1909), *Culture and Anarchy*, London: John Murray.
Barth, K. (1962), 'Church and Culture' in *Theology and Church*, trans. L.P. Smith, London: SCM.

Barth, K. (1971), 'Letter to Eberhard Bethge' in *Fragments Grave and Gay*, trans. E. Mosbacher, Glasgow: Collins.

Barth, K. (1981), *Ethics*, trans. G.W. Bromiley, New York: Seabury.

Barth, K. and C. Zuckmayer (1977), *A Late Friendship: The Letters of Karl Barth and Carl Zuckmayer*, trans. G.W. Bromiley, Grand Rapids, MI: Eerdmans.

Benjamin, W. (1992), *Illuminations*, trans. H. Zohn, London: Fontana.

Eagleton, T. (2000), *The Idea of Culture,* Oxford: Blackwell.

Eliot, T.S. (1944), *Four Quartets*, London: Faber.

Eliot, T.S. (1948), *Notes Towards the Definition of Culture*, London: Faber.

Farrell, F. (1996), *Subjectivity, Realism and Postmodernism*, Cambridge: Cambridge University Press.

MacIntyre, A. (1981), *After Virtue*, London: Duckworth.

Rumscheidt, H.M. (1972), *Revelation and Theology: An Analysis of the Barth–Harnack Correspondence of 1923*, Cambridge: Cambridge University Press.

Williams, R. (1963), *Culture and Society*, Harmondsworth: Pelican.

Williams, R. (1965), *The Long Revolution*, Harmondsworth: Pelican.

Williams, R. (1989), 'Culture is Ordinary' in *Resources of Hope*, London: Verso, pp. 3–18.

CHAPTER 4

Barth, Hegel and the Possibility for Christian Apologetics

Graham Ward

Why does the possibility of Christian apologetics matter? Any attempt to answer this question requires considering the nature and significance of theological discourse, and that consideration in turn requires thinking through the context in which such discourse arises. For whom is theology written and for what purpose? Or, who does the theologian address and what is the task undertaken in the address? Christian apologetics situates the theological task with respect to the gospel of salvation in Christ freely offered to the world – a world not divorced from Christ but whose meaning is only known with respect to Christ as the one through whom all things were made and have their being. As such, apologetics orientates theological discourse towards a specific cultural and historical negotiation concerning public truth. Its task is evangelical and doxological. Upon the basis of apologetics rests, then, the Christian mission not only to disseminate the good news, but also to bring about cultural and historical transformations concomitant with the coming of the Kingdom of God. This is why the possibility for Christian apologetics matters – for its task makes manifest the polity of the Christian Gospel, its moral, social and political orders. Its task is Christological insofar as it is the continuation of, and participation in, the redemptive work of Christ. Without the orientation of Christian apologetics towards the world, the theological task is merely an exercise in navel-gazing. And while a reflexivity has necessarily to be intrinsic to theological work – for the theologian attempts to speak in the name of Christ, and that is a presumption the theologian must continually be scandalized by – that reflexivity cannot be the *telos* of the theological work.

The possibility for a Christian apologetics, then, is fundamental to the theological task. Apologetics has a theological warrant for the work it undertakes in the operation of the Word in the salvation of the world. But it has no unmediated access to that Word such that it can be wielded like a weapon or used like a tool. The basis upon which apologetics engages the Word with the world requires an understanding of both the character of that Word and the character of the world. This dual understanding involves an immersion in the words and works that bear witness to the Word and the words and works that characterize any particular cultural context. And here lies the dialectical risk that theology must run. On the one hand, in under-standing the Word theology comes to understand itself (what it has to say, what is the *charism* it has been given to deliver). In understanding itself, it must receive the revelation of Christ that comes from that time and place 'before the foundations of the world'. It must participate in that grace whereby the eternal makes provision for, and maintains, the temporal, challenging all that is fallen and misconceived. On the other hand, the theologian is situated within the world. Being situated in the world at a particular time, in a particular cultural situation, he or she takes up the theological task with the resources of the tradition and a mind-set formed in and through the words and works that constitute this *habitus*. The theologian can only understand the faith held and practised by the Christian Church, the theological task this enjoins and the people to whom this task is addressed, through what is culturally and historically available. The theo-logic of theology itself, the faith that seeks understanding, is then constituted in a cultural negotiation between the revelation of Christ to the Church (rooted in the Scriptures, the sacraments and the tradition of their interpretation and application) and the 'signs of the times'. Both the danger and the possibility of apologetics lie in the degree of critical difference between the Christian *evangelium* and the ways in which the world produces and maintains its own historical self-reflection. But, and this remains fundamental, neither can be accessed without the other. The secular world is never confronted as such, without first being constructed as a homogeneous cultural order from the standpoint of Christian difference; while the Christian difference is never defined as such without also being constructed as a homogeneous religious culture from the standpoint of the irreligious or de-divinized world-view. This is why, in attempting to demonstrate the necessity of Christian apologetics, and its possibility, the work of Karl Barth is important. For Barth, while opposing dogmatics as the study of God's self-revelation in the service of the church to the *Kulturprotestantismus* of apologetics, not only alerts the Christian theologian to the dangers of such a project, his dialectical method performs his own wrestling with the relation between the Word of God and the words and works of the world.[1]

'[A]s long as he [*sic*] is an apologist the theologian must renounce his theological function,' Barth writes in one of his perceptive analyses of Schleiermacher (Barth, 2001, p. 428).[2] He thought that Schleiermacher had failed as a theologian on exactly this score, and led many another nineteenth-century theologians in tow. As his own twofold introduction to the *Church Dogmatics* – 'The Task of Dogmatics' and 'The Task of Prolegomena to Dogmatics' – makes plain, theology may be exegetical, dogmatic or practical, but since its task is to examine 'the agreement of the Church's distinctive talk about God with the being of the Church' it has no role to play vis-à-vis the 'secular or pagan' (*CD* I/1, pp. 4–5). Theology so conceived speaks from faith to faith. Where it involves itself with unbelief, it is not 'pure unbelief' (ibid., p. 32), but those forms of unbelief within the Church itself, within interpretations of the faith, among heresies. But the seriousness with which unbelief has to be taken when it lies outside the Church or interpretations of the faith, means that, first, it cannot take the theological task itself 'with full seriousness' (ibid., p. 30), and, second, it can only proceed on the assumption that the dogmatic task of the faith coming to an understanding of itself is completed. The theologian, therefore, compromises himself or herself when 'He [*sic*] must present himself to [the educated among the despisers of religion] in a part which is provided for in their categories' (Barth, 2001, p. 428). Where the task of theology accomplishes a genuine apologetics, it does so only as a byproduct of its exegetical, dogmatic and practical tasks. This genuine apologetics is recognized by its effectiveness. That is, it produces an event of faith that is otherwise beyond all human polemical endeavours; the work of theology is 'empowered and blessed by God as the witness of faith' (*CD* I/1, p. 31). This effect cannot be prescribed or planned for in advance. The unbeliever overhears a conversation, internal to faith, seeking its own understanding through which occurs the speaking of God's Word, a revelation that 'itself creates of itself the necessary point of contact' (ibid., p. 29).

If theological apologetics is to avoid the construction of follies, it must examine why it can speak – and speak not only to, for and in the Church, but to, for and in the world beyond the Church. Theology needs to expound the grounds on which it can be apologetic without ceasing, in that task, to be theological. And, again, Barth is important here, because he himself asked these questions – even if we may decide to depart from both the answers he gave to, and his framing of, those questions. Weaving in and out of a conversation with Barth, what kind of a theological basis for apologetics can be found?

Much of Barth's polemic against apologetics and *Kulturprotestantismus* is a mellower form of the 'infinite qualitative difference' between God's Word and human words found in his commentaries upon Romans. There, in his first commentary (1919) he could announce, 'That you as Christians are to have nothing to do [*nichts zu tun habt*] with monarchism, capitalism, militarism, patriotism and liberalism is so obvious that I need not say anything' (Barth, 1963, p. 381). Proclaiming the new world in Christ, and God's countercultural NO – intensified in the second edition of the commentary – Barth's eschatological fervour was reactive and addressed explicitly at the Protestant theologians who he felt had betrayed the *evangelium*. But it is exactly at the point of what Christians are to do or not do that a theological analysis aware of its own cultural embeddedness has to begin. For Barth's sentiment in the first editions of *Romans* is naïve, but the grounds on which it is naïve need to be made explicit. It is the very fact that Christians act [*zu tun*] in the world, even if their actions are graced and therefore eschatologically informed, that means they cannot be inoculated against an involvement in 'monarchism, capitalism, militarism, patriotism and liberalism'. Barth's radical separatism, at this point in his work, betrays, in fact, an inadequate mode of dialectical thinking.[3] It is inadequate because it is unable to think through the relationship of this God of cultural judgement to Barth's equal insistence, against Harnack among others, that Christians are not neutral subjects in the events of the world; they cannot remain indifferent to the social, political and economic circumstances in which they live. In fact, one of the most interesting forms of analysis of Barth's work, Barth's relationship to radical politics, enables us to appreciate how encultured Barth's theological thinking is. Marquardt might have overstretched the early work of Barth in suggesting its affinities with the writings of Lenin, but nevertheless he, and more recently Tim Gorringe (who has compared

Barth's thinking to Gramsci's), have shown how contextual Barth's theology is.[4] This early dialectical thinking, then, fails to adequately account for what Christians *do* [*zu tun*], whilst too quickly prescribing what they *should do*. This is interesting because Barth's approach to dialectics in the first edition of *Romans* – whilst emphasizing *Krisis* and *Diakrisis* – is much more Hegelian. That is, it is a dialectic between the Word and the world which operates through the processes of encounter and sublation of the world. It is, then, committed to the historical and the unfolding of that history through what people do [*zu tun*]. Michael Beintker observes Barth's concern with dynamics, growth and movement in the earlier text and his emphasis on thinking as always in flight and concludes: 'Damit ist die Dialektik von Romer I als bewegungs-massiges Denken derjenigen Hegelscher Philosophie sehr nahe' (Beintker, 1987, p. 113).

In the second edition of Romans, the deepening emphasis on what Michael Beintker calls the 'widerspruchsvollen Komplexität profaner Weltlichkeit' means that 'Der Theologie kann allerdings die Komplexität profaner Weltlichkeit nicht von der Beziehung zwischen Gott und Mensch isolierien' (Beintker, 1987, pp. 58–59).[5] Dialectical theology (Barth's *Realdialektik*) as 'total contradiction' [*widerspruchs-vollen*] submerges incommensurability into theological mystery and weds theological mystery to a highly voluntarist notion of God. The inadequacy of the dialectic, then, arises because Barth needs to give more nuanced accounts of history, agency and power so that he can reflect more upon the method of his own discourse. He needs to think through the relationship between dialectic as *Denkform* and the noetic and 'ontological connexion between Christ and creation' (*CD* III/1, p. 51) – the dialectics of salvation. He needs to negotiate dialectic as *widerspruchsvollen Komplexität* with dialectic as process. He needs to wrestle not only with Kierkegaard, but with Hegel.[6] Beintker, with respect to examining Barth's dialectic in the second edition of Romans and noting the 'not uncomplicated relationship between Barth and Hegel', points to 'eine Strukturverwandtschaft zwischen Hegel und Barth im Blick auf das Synthetische als Ur- and Zieldatum' (Beintker, 1987, p. 72). But this 'structural resemblance' cannot be developed until Barth reconsiders the time and eternity paradox in terms of a lesson Overbeck taught him concerning the operation of *Urgeschichte*. For, as Robert E. Hood observed, for Overbeck the 'Urgeschichte is the telos toward which all history is moving; yet, it is not an abstraction from history' (Hood, 1985, p. 10). Barth will only be able to begin this reconsideration when he develops his doctrines of the Trinitarian God, creation and reconciliation. As we will see, this will lead to a critical interplay between the dialectical strategy in the first edition of Romans and the dialectical strategy in the second.

By the time we come to the introduction to the *Church Dogmatics*, a more adequate dialectic is evident. Here Barth's sharp certainties and clear-cut distinctions are always intentionally compromised by his recognition of the impossibility, and yet necessity, of the theological task itself. He proceeds by identifying clear loci – the Church, on the one hand, unbelief, paganism, heathenism, on the other. But then he qualifies the Church by speaking of the Roman Catholic, Evangelical and Protestant

Modernist struggles to be the Church: 'the Church must wrestle with heresy in such a way that it may be itself the Church. And heresy must attack the Church because it is not sufficiently or truly Church' (*CD* I/1, p. 33). Faith and the Church are located within this paradoxical struggle that constitutes Barth's dialectical method. They are not, then, objects as such, nor can they therefore be identified as such. They are positions under constant negotiation – positions articulated only once he has embarked on the way of the theological inquiry, and, even then, '[w]e have to state quite definitely that our own understanding of the being of the Church is in no sense the only one' (ibid., p. 32). Those little words 'quite definitely' betray much – a polemic conducted with respect to both Roman Catholicism and Protestant Modernism in which Barth is 'quite definite' both with respect to his dogmatic certainties (about apologetics) and his uncertainties (the 'intractability of faith' whereby 'divine certainty cannot become human security' (ibid., p. 12)).

The same dual strategy is evident with respect to his other, determinative loci – unbelief. His claim that Christian dogmatics 'speak in the antithesis of faith to unbelief' (ibid., p. 30) marks a precise border between belief in God and godlessness. It is a border separating theology as a science from the other secular sciences – a border maintained through the lack of any 'ground of common presuppositions' (ibid., p. 31); hence the impossibility of apologetics. But then there are degrees of this unbelief, since there are other accounts of the faith 'in which we hear unbelief express itself' (ibid.) and Barth ends the opening section on 'The Task of Dogmatics' by claiming that any success for this work is only possible 'on the basis of divine correspondence to this human attitude: "Lord, I believe; help thou my unbelief"' (ibid., p. 24). So when does unbelief become 'pure unbelief'? And since the negotiations to understand the faith constitute an ongoing wrestling with possible tragic consequences, when is faith ever without unbelief?

So what happens to the coherence of Barth's understanding of apologetics if the criteria governing that understanding are both identified and qualified, and stated quite definitely with respect to both their identification and qualification? Who identifies the presuppositions that radically distinguish the grounds of difference between the task of theology and the tasks of other sciences? Who judges when the event of faith has taken place? Does this event of faith proffer a 'pure faith' unmixed with unbelief? How are the degrees of faith and unbelief calibrated? Who discerns when theological discourse has been 'empowered and blessed by God'? The Church? Which Church? The contested and contestable Church?

We can confront the problems here from another direction. We can ask why, although theology is human words answering to and working within the operation of the Word of God, there can be no 'human security' in the knowledge of God. Why must theology always be procedural, or 'on its way'? Why do we always seem 'to be handling this intractable object with inadequate means?' (ibid., p. 23) For Barth, there are four aspects implicated in any answer to these questions. The first two are theological aspects, and the second two are anthropological aspects. First, there is the nature of the difference and the divide between the gracious addresses of God in Jesus

Christ to human beings. Second, there is the operation of 'the free grace of God which may at any time be given or refused' (ibid., p. 18) – a freedom whose logic lies in the depth of God's self. Third, there is, from the human perspective, the need to speak in and from faith: 'the presupposition of an anthropological *prius* of faith' (ibid., p. 39). The reception and operation of this faith is manifestly associated with the two theological aspects treated above. But, even so, this mimetic activity of human beings, the 'Christian utterance', the 'humanly speaking' which constitutes 'the work of human knowledge' (ibid., p. 15) is an 'act of human appropriation'. And this appropriation of the Word in human words is constantly in question because it 'is by nature fallible and therefore stands in need of criticism, or correction, of critical amendment and repetition' (ibid., p. 14). This fallibility in appropriation and representation – for there do seem to be two acts for Barth, human speaking and the act of appropriation – is related to the fallen, sinful nature of being human. This fallenness is the fourth of the aspects implicated in any answer to questions concerning theology's self-reflexive process, inadequate means and partial delivery of truth.

These aspects make a threefold assumption about theology. First, there is a pure, ahistorical truth – associated with the Word – that is being pursued through the contingencies and vicissitudes of historical Christian living and thinking. Second, there are better (and therefore worse) appropriations of this truth, the measurement of which is again ahistorical: Anselm is a high point, as is Luther; Aquinas is a lower point, as is Schleiermacher. Third, it is assumed that obedience to the Word, if followed through by all Christians, would lead to a consensus and agreement on all matters of doctrine – would lead, that is, to a Church dogmatics that all Christians could subscribe to whatever their time, place, race or gender.

Putting to one side the voluntarist account of God as the agent of grace, which seems to render all events of grace arbitrary interruptions into creaturely existence,[7] and putting aside the way in which this characterization of both God and God's agency constructs another clear-cut and categorical distinction between God and godlessness, God's self-presence and God's utter absence in creation; putting aside, then, two major theological reservations about this account of God vis-à-vis the world, Barth is emphatic that the realm in which theological inquiry is either blessed or is mere idle speculation is discursive. It reduces down to 'Christian speech [that] must be tested by its conformity to Christ. This conformity is never clear and unambiguous' (ibid., p. 13). Thus, that which dogmatics investigates is nothing other than 'Christian utterance' (ibid., p. 12).[8]

Barth points out that this attention paid to Christian utterance by dogmatics makes theological inquiry a 'self-enclosed circle' of concern (ibid., p. 42), and the self-enclosed nature of this concern means that theology takes itself, rather than extra-ecclesial concerns, seriously. Dogmatics cannot be anything other than unintentionally apologetic because of the self-enclosure of Christian utterance. The moment it steps out of this enclosure to speak to those without faith it adopts alien categories. 'Apologetics is an attempt to show by means of thought and speech that the determining principles of philosophy and of historical and natural research at some given point in time certainly do not preclude, even if they do not directly require, the tenets of theology' (Barth, 2001, pp. 425–26). But it is at this point that a critical intervention can be made. Discourse is recognized as fundamental. It defines the faithfulness of dogmatics and the unfaithfulness of apologetics, while betraying the incomplete and fallible nature of all dogmatic inquiry. But who can police the boundaries of any discourse, Christian or otherwise? Put more precisely, who can ensure the self-enclosure when the constitution of that enclosure is a question of language and representation? Does the belief in the self-enclosure of certain linguistic practices not presuppose the distinct separation of different discourses and forms of reason? Barth points to as much when he declares: 'There has never been a *philosophia christiana*, for if it was *philosophia* it was not *christiana*, and if it was *christiana* it was not *philosophia*' (*CD* I/1, p. 6). Theological discourse or Christian thinking is rendered utterly distinct from philosophical discourse, historical discourse or scientific discourses of various kinds. But who defines and maintains the autonomy of these discourses? Doesn't Barth's description of research conducted on the basis of 'determining principles' sound like the academic rationale for distinct and jealously guarded faculty boundaries in a post-Berlin university? For – and this is the main point I wish to make here – if discourses are not bounded, if discourses exceed institutional, contested and contestable framings, then an apologetics can proceed without the theologian *necessarily* renouncing his or her 'theological function'. Recently, Kathryn Tanner, in a critical discussion of postliberalism's Barthian account of the autonomy of discrete language games (of which Christianity would be one), has observed that contemporary cultural anthropology argues strongly against the corollary of this thesis which suggests that 'Christians have a self-sustaining society and culture of their own, which can be marked off rather sharply from others' (Tanner, 1997, p. 96).[9] Christian utterance is constructed out of the cultural materials at hand. It is not homogeneous but always hybrid, improvised and implicated in networks of association that exceed various forms of institutional, individual or sectarian policing. Furthermore, since Christians are also members of other associations, networks and institutions, what is both internal and external to Christian identity (and its continuing formation) is fluid.

What is significant is that in the very performance of his dialectic, the very process of the realization of his thoughts, Barth reweaves what he has already woven in a manner that suggests a negotiation with a thesis he has already negated. And it is this aspect of his dialectic that I wish to examine with respect to Hegel. For, while Barth suggests Christianity is self-defining and must be so in order to protect itself from the corrupting external influences of secular society, he himself reveals how interdependent Christian utterance is upon the discourses of other disciplines. His own writing demonstrates how vocabularies and categories are not discrete and how Christianity always defines itself in terms of that to which it allies itself or from which it distinguishes itself. In defining the dogmatic task Barth employs categories like 'knowledge', 'consciousness', 'conception', 'understanding', 'formal' and 'ontological-ontic'; he refers continually (though admittedly not depending on their investigations) to Plato, Aristotle,

Descartes, Kant and Heidegger; he situates his task with respect to the older Protestant orthodoxy, to 'historical development of at least the last two or three hundred years' (*CD* I/1, p. 9) and to the medieval writings of Anselm, Bonaventura and Aquinas; and he speaks of 'other sciences' social, psychological and natural. Barth can then only proceed to define his particular form of Protestantism on the basis of shared vocabularies, categories and reference points that stand 'outside' and other to his thesis. The German language he writes, while translating these other discourses into his own Christian thesis, is working across other languages such as Greek and Latin. His is not a 'self-enclosed' discursive reflection; and neither *can* Christian theology or Christian living be self-enclosed. As the dialectic issues from an understanding of the ongoing and yet to be perfected Word and work of God in the act of reconciling the world to Himself, so Christian theology can neither be completely systematized nor, *a priori*, stake out the limits of what is in and what is outside Christ. Theology *is* a cultural activity; the dialectic it is implicated in is, simultaneously, transhistorical, historical and material. And, here again, Barth encounters Hegel.

It is, I suggest, Hegel more than Schleiermacher who lies behind Barth's categorical assertion that '[t]here has never been a *philosophia christiana*, for if it was *philosophia* it was not *christiana*, and if it was *christiana* it was not *philosophia*'. For it is Hegel who poses the challenge of the relationship between philosophy and theology by conflating the dialectic of reason with Trinitarian procession. Thus it follows that 'everything that seems to give theology its particular splendour and special dignity appears to be looked after and honoured by this philosophy in a way comparably better than that achieved by the theologians themselves' (Barth, 2001, p. 382).[10] The language of appearance is telling here – Barth (with a number of Hegel scholars before and after him) is not quite certain where Hegel, the orthodox Lutheran, falls into heterodoxy. But, Barth nevertheless wishes to point out that Hegel's work consummates the Prometheanism of human confidence in the act of thinking, in the Enlightenment categories such as mind, idea, concept and reason, and which he views as inimical both to dogmatics and the dialectical encounter with the Word of God that is the contents of dogmatics. It is Hegel, then, who proclaims the possibility of a *philosophia christiana* – and Aquinas who Barth consistently brackets with Hegel. Barth's reading of Aquinas is wrong and his persistent reading of Hegel's dialectical method as 'thesis, antithesis and synthesis', with an emphasis on consummation of the absolute, owes more to left-wing Hegelians after Hegel (Strauss and Marx, in particular) than Hegel himself.[11]

Nevertheless, his observation that, for Hegel, 'God is only God in his divine action, revelation, creation, reconciliation, redemption; as an absolute act, *actus purus*' demonstrates how close Hegel (and Aquinas) is to Barth (ibid., p. 385). And, characteristically, in Barth's short, but excellent, analysis of Hegel in *Protestant Theology in the Nineteenth Century*, the condemnation of the univocity of *Geist* and reason that reveals Hegel's inability to take seriously either sin or God's freedom with respect to confronting human beings in their sin, is offset by a recognition of the unfulfilled and 'great promise' in Hegel's work (ibid., p. 407). 'Doubtless, theology could and can learn something from Hegel as well. It looks as if theology had neglected something here, and certainly it has no occasion to assume an attitude of alarm and hostility to any renaissance of Hegel that might come about' (ibid., p. 403). When we examine what it is that remains promising for Barth in Hegel it is in fact the Trinitarian-informed reflexivity of his dialectic. Though Barth chides him for his unsatisfactory doctrine of the Trinity, he applauds Hegel's reminder 'of the possibility that the truth might be history' and that theology's knowledge 'was only possible in the form of a strict obedience to the self-movement of truth, and therefore as a knowledge which was itself moved' (ibid., pp. 401–402). Furthermore, in Hegel's commitment to theology as a material practice participating in the unfolding of a history of God's own self-unveiling, theology is reminded 'of the contradictory nature of its own knowledge'. For 'Hegel with his concept of mind, must wittingly, or unwittingly have been thinking of the Creator of heaven and earth, the Lord over nature and spirit, precisely by virtue of the unity and opposition of *dictum* and *contra-dictum*, in which Hegel had the spirit conceiving itself and being real' (ibid., p. 402).

There are three things, then, that Barth recognizes of theological value in Hegel: history as a material process informed by God; theology as a discursive practice participating in what he will elsewhere conceive as '[t]he covenant of grace [a]s *the* theme of history' (*CD* III/1, p. 60); and the need for theology to be reflexive about that practice because the words and works of human beings can never be identical to the unveiling of God.

The question remains as to the extent to which Barth integrated these insights into his own theological thinking. Such an integration had certainly not taken place when Barth gave the lecture on Hegel in the early 1930s, although there is a hint of what he will develop as he and the Christian Church stood in the twilight of a global history of world-occurrence. For in what appears almost to be an aside in the Introduction to the *Church Dogmatics*, he observes: 'The separate existence of theology signifies the emergency measure on which the Church has had to resolve in view of the actual refusal of the other sciences in this respect' (*CD* I/1, p. 7). The observation points not to a pragmatism, but to the temporal specificity about theology's task. Its 'separate existence' is a response to a culture and a historical moment when the theological is despised.[12] As with his view of discrete discourses for discrete disciplines, the dogmatic in opposition to the apologetic task of theology becomes a cultural production (and a cultural producer in its own right), one that *necessarily*, on Barth's own axioms, 'stands in need of criticism, or correction, of critical amendment and repetition'. The necessity comes about when Christian theology, and therefore the task of the Christian theologian, is elsewhere implicated in a different kind of cultural productivity. By the end of the Second World War – when Barth was completing the opening volume of his doctrine of creation – history, the theological practice of participating in that history and the need to consider more carefully that biblical witnesses 'speak as men, and not as angels or gods' (*CD* III/1, p. 93) give rise to a different reflection and a new kind of dialectic.

> Thus we have to reckon on their part with all kinds of human factors, with their individual and general capacities of perception and expression, with their personal views and style, as determined by age and environment, and of course with the limitations and deficiencies of these conditioning factors – in this case the limitations of their imagination. (Ibid., p. 93)

Barth is specifically examining the creation stories as the Word of God, but in his development of the category of 'saga' and his recognition of the different genres of biblical writing, he speaks more generally of biblical witness. The commitment to a God who does not transcend history but informs it at every point, to an account of eternity as the origin and *telos* of the history, not its erasure, leads to an understanding of biblical discourse as culturally and psychologically 'determined'. I am not going to follow the psychological trajectory of Barth's thinking as such; I shall only comment that 'personal views', expression and style – and, some would even say, individual levels and direction of perception – cannot be divorced from the 'conditioning factors' of 'age and environment'. But in my concern to assess the possibility for apologetics that begin from a Christian theological standpoint, this recognition of the cultural embeddedness of biblical discourse is an important move towards seeing that theological discourse cannot be simply self-referring and 'overheard' by other publics. Biblical witness borrows materials and forms of representation, and refigures them for its own purposes. The accounts that it furnishes of things prehistorical or historical involve cultural negotiations, 'textual relationships' (ibid., p. 87) and human knowing that 'is not exhausted by the ability to perceive and comprehend' (ibid., p. 91). Barth even employs Schleiermacher's hermeneutical category of 'divination' to speak of the way in which the writer has to divine the vision of the true historical emergence (the operation of God in creation) that preceded the 'historical' events so cherished by professional historians and historicism. The questions of 'depiction and narration' issue not from discussing the abstractions of time and eternity, but the covenant of grace that *is* the theme of God's history. Time is in God, and therefore, although the truth of God's Word is eternal, it is also highly specific: 'Creation is not a timeless truth … there are no timeless truths; truth has a concretely temporal character' (ibid., p. 60).

Of course, Barth's attention here is to biblical witness and biblical writing. But since this witness and writing must be the source and prototype for all Christian witness and writing, the cultural and historical embeddedness of his own discourse must follow, although Barth says little about this. In fact, again almost as an aside, he writes: 'concerning the ground and being of man and his world, we are referred to our own metaphysical and scientific genius, or to our own powers in the construction of myth or saga' (ibid., p. 61). Christian theology tells God's story in the place any theologian finds himself or herself situated. Such storytelling cannot but rehearse and refigure the language, ideologies, cultural assumptions, fears, guilts and dreams of its times. The theologian attempts to read the signs of those times in terms of the continuing covenant of grace, but in reading those signs cultural negotiations are set in operation. Theological discourse is involved in the wider cultural dissemination and exchange of signs. Other people will be telling the story of what is from where they are and possibly using some of the same materials and reference points. And while Christian theology (like the biblical witnesses) speaks of the 'genuinely historical' (ibid., p. 66) relationship between God and human beings – such that cultural relativism is not a question raised – Christian theology cannot transcend the historical and cultural determination and conditions. If it cannot transcend them, then it equally cannot distil for itself some purely theological discourse.

Christian theology is therefore implicated in cultural negotiations, and to that extent is engaged in an ongoing apologetics. Barth, it seems, moves towards an integration of what Beintker (after Henning Schroer) termed the 'complimentary' and 'supplementary' of paradox. Barth's forges a theological method that brings together, in a creative tension, the synchronic dialectic of Kierkegaard's 'infinite qualitative difference' with the diachronic dialectic of Hegel's 'possibility that the truth might be history' and that theology's knowledge 'was only possible in the form of a strict obedience to the self-movement of truth, and therefore as a knowledge which was itself moved'. The synchronic and the diachronic can supplement each other in the work of the theologian with respect to the world.

Allow me now to pursue this further by referring back to the third of Barth's affirmations about Hegel's project: the need for theology to be reflexive about that practice because the words and works of human beings can never be identical to the unveiling of God. For Beintker characterizes the 'complimentary' use of paradox as involving an asymmetrical relationship between thesis and antithesis, such that the reconciliation or sublation proceeds through the absorption of the latter by the former. This is parallel to the asymmetrical relation in Hegel's thinking between the in-itself and the for-itself such that, in the dialectical process of being with oneself in an other, the other is integrated into one's own projects. In this way the other fulfils and perfects the same; it becomes part of the free activity of the subject. Barth's description of the dialectic of sexual difference bears something of this Hegelian model (see Ward, 2000, pp. 183–202). But since theology moves between Christ's Word and a cultural situation in which '[t]here are no forms, events or relationships … unmistakeably confused by man in which the goodness of what God has created is not also effective and visible, the only question being how this is so' (ibid., p. 698), then it has no unqualified access to that asymmetrical relationship. And, if this is so, it may not so easily take up the 'complimentary' use of paradox that judges the other only to have value with respect to the same. It cannot judge and subjugate the world to its own discourse. For theology cannot leave out the possibility that, in this cultural other, God is at work, and engagement with this other may mean that it is not subordinated but allowed to challenge radically the theological project. Cultural negotiation must run such a risk – the risk of being disrupted. The 'supplementary' use of paradox allows for what George Hunsinger (2000) has recently termed 'disruptive grace'. But the 'supplementary' use of paradox is also asymmetrical, and it is at this point that the theologian needs to cultivate a healthy agnosticism with respect to what he or she knows. Space must be allowed, on the basis of what theology understands about itself and the God with whom it has to do, for the other to speak. This enables the cultural engagement of Christian apologetics to be a negotiated engagement.

The last reference to Hegel, whose dialectic I am suggesting opens Barth's theology to the possibility of apologetics as Christian cultural negotiation, comes in *Church Dogmatics* IV/3.2 and the development of his doctrine of reconciliation. Here, Barth's dialectical structure is firmly in place in a discussion of the interface between *Hominum confusione et Dei providentia* in the call of Christ to all humanity. However, he seeks a third way beyond the antithesis, and this is where he introduces Hegel. Again, it is the Hegel of the thesis–antithesis–synthesis – Hegel reduced to a formula that can then be haughtily dismissed. What Barth wishes to avoid is a *tertium quid*. So what he offers 'the Christian community as *it is required* to go beyond that twofold view' (emphasis added) is the 'reality and truth of the grace of God addressed to the world in Jesus Christ' (*CD* IV/3.2, p. 706). What this amounts to is that the Christian community is enjoined to speak to the world about Jesus Christ while recognizing that, on the one hand, Jesus Christ 'is not a concept which man can think out for himself, which he can define with more or less precision, and with the help of which he can then display his mastery over … this problem of this antithesis' (ibid.); while, on the other hand, understanding that '[w]e think and speak like poor heathen, no matter how earnestly we may imagine that we think and speak of it [the grace of God addressed to the world in Jesus Christ]' (ibid., p. 707). Which leaves us where exactly? With the knowledge of the *diastasis*, concerning which there is no 'real synthesis', although the fallible Christian community as the bearer of, and witness to, a better hope testifies to the work and Word of God as a 'new thing in relation to that contradiction' (ibid., p. 708). It not only testifies, but in testifying seeks to participate in the unfolding of that new world; and so it attempts to perform and produce that 'new thing'.

Furthermore, its practice of transformative hope, executed in the name of Christ, is disseminated through the world because the living community of the Church is implicated in other 'communities' and practices. Those characterized as the community of the Church participate in the operations of other desires that are not *prima facie* theological, only *de jure* theological because Jesus Christ is both the 'loftiest, most luminous transcendence' and 'heard in the deepest, darkest immanence' (Barth, 1961, p. 46). These members of the community of the Church are also members of other forms of fellowship, other bodies – industrial, commercial, agricultural, political, sporting and domestic. Barth, too, was a member of a political party. To return to a moment mentioned earlier in the first editions of *Romans*, it is because Christians are involved in 'monarchism, capitalism, militarism, patriotism and liberalism', among other things (things working against the hegemony of such ideologies), that the work and words of the living community extend out into the 'deepest, darkest immanence' in their testimony to and performance of a 'new thing'. This movement in, through and beyond the Church, in through and beyond the Church's endless cultural negotiations, is not a dialectic of progress or growth, because it moves between mysteries and confusion, but it is nevertheless teleologically driven. It is, then, a positive dialectic tracing and performing what Hegel called 'the march of God in the world' (Hegel, 1991, p. 279). We may not like Hegel's metaphor, but I suggest, on this basis, that an apologetics, no longer saddled with defining itself against *Kulturprotestantismus,* can proceed: reading and producing the signs of the times, and negotiating a role in defining public truth; taking its own historical and cultural embeddedness with all theological seriousness.

Notes

1   I am aware that, by giving emphasis to the Church as the body of Christ and the role of the sacraments in creating, sustaining and fostering the growth of that body, these are more Catholic elements than Barth would have espoused. But I am not trying to reproduce Barth's theology in this essay; rather, I wish to engage it in developing a theological project with respect to the Christian faith today. The Church is not today where Barth once was.

2   It needs to be pointed out that, on the basis of his exposure to and researches in nineteenth-century German theology and his in-depth analysis of Schleiermacher's work during his Göttingen employment, Barth conflates 'apologetics' with '*Kulturprotestantismus*'. For an understanding of theologically driven apologetics see Edwards *et al.* (1999).

3   I am saying nothing here that Barth did not admit, almost 40 years later, in his 1956 address 'The Humanity of God'. See Barth (1961, pp. 37–65).

4   See Marquardt (1972) and Gorringe (1999). Of course, the work of George Hunsinger's edited volume (1976) and also Bruce McCormack's (1995) should also be added here.

5   Beintker distinguishes this form of dialectic from the form in the first edition of *Romans* by differentiating between the employment of 'complimentary' and 'supplementary' paradoxes. In the complimentary *Paradoxdialektik* an asymmetrical relationship holds between the thesis and the antithesis, but (to use the Hegelian term) the thesis can sublate the antithesis and hence move forward. With the supplementary employment of paradox no movement is possible because the two terms are radically antithetical to each other.

6   As several commentators have pointed out (including Barth himself), beyond appreciating the theological importance of concepts such as paradox, either/or, the moment, difference, and fear and trembling Barth never really undertook a thorough study and analysis of dialectic. See Beintker (1987, pp. 230–38). It is surprising that, to my knowledge, only in the chapter on Hegel in *Protestant Theology in the Nineteenth Century* does Barth really engage with Hegel's thinking. The early distinction he makes between Hegel's *Dialektik* and Kierkegaard's *Realdialektik* in *The Göttingen Dogmatics* goes unelaborated (Barth, 1990, p. 77). Later, in the *Church Dogmatics*, considering Hegel's dominance in German thinking with respect to construals of history, reconciliation and community, he appears mainly as a name in a list of other names. There is neither refutation nor quotation of Hegel in the section almost screaming for comparative and penetrating analysis – *CD* III/1, 'Creation, History and Creation History'. We will come to the reference in *CD* IV/3, 'The Holy Spirit and the Sending of the Christian Community' later.

7   I put 'seems' because the critics of Barth on this very point may have missed something. There is a question here as to whether the events of God's grace are arbitrary and interruptive only from the human perspective. That is, as far as God is concerned, is there a continuum of activity with respect to creation such that the veiling and unveiling of God's self is what human beings in their darkened and unredeemed state discern. Or is creation so wholly other from God, not only in its fallenness – which can only be contingent with respect to the determination of divine salvation – but in its essence, such that any divine activity with respect to creation enters it from an ontologically distinct and prior

exteriority? When Barth is developing his doctrine of creation, based on his *analogia relationis*, he is emphatic that time and creation are not in contradiction to the eternal Godhead, but 'in Him'.

8   Of course, this idea of the dogmatic task as investigating what Christians say and do developed into postliberalism's distinction between first- and second-order discourses. The assumed role of the dogmatician is, then, both diagnositic (with respect to its investigation into Christian utterance) and regulative (with respect to bringing that utterance into a better understanding of its relation to the Word). It is not only doubtful that such a distinction can be made between practice and theory, it is not only questionable whether the distinction should be made (which privileges academic theologians, or at least sets them as a class apart from others by reinforcing a dualism between practical and dogmatic theology), it is manifest from Barth's own writings how little account is given of the Christian utterances (apart from other academic theologians). We gain little insight into the actual everyday living of this church with respect to which and for which Barth is writing his dogmatics. The question of authority – for whom is this task being undertaken, with what jurisdiction and to whom is it addressed – hollows Barth's text.

9   Interestingly, although critique of postliberalism continues unabated, all Tanner's references to Barth – the theological spinal cord of postliberalism – are uncritical and affirmative.

10 This repeats his conclusion about Hegel's speculative Trinity in *The Göttingen Dogmatics*, where he observes Hegel's 'replacement of the Christian Trinity by a logical and metaphysical Trinity and by the relegation of the Christian Trinity to the sphere of naïve, symbolical, and inadequate conceptions' (Barth, 1990, p. 105). But nothing positive about Hegel's thinking is said in this earlier work. By the time the last form of the lectures on the history of nineteenth-century Protestant theology were given (in winter 1932–33), Barth is much more appreciative of Hegel's potential.

11 Elsewhere Barth makes evident that he interpreted the relationship in Hegel's thought between *Sittlichkeit* and *Staat* as the deification of German nationalism that courted the hubris leading to the betrayals by the theological establishment in the First World War. This, too, is a wrong reading of Hegel's *Elements of the Philosophy of Right*. See Wood (1991); Lakeland (1982); Shanks (1991); Ward (2000, pp. 137–46). Hegel would in fact concur with Barth's own judgement (albeit with a different doctrine of the Trinity): 'the State as such belongs originally and ultimately to Jesus Christ' (Barth, 1968, p. 118).

12 In his study, *Christ and Culture*, H. Richard Niebuhr points out the association between the Christian response to the cultural and the cultural response to Christianity. He does not develop this insight to any depth, but, significantly, the first of his five models for the 'enduring problem' of Christian theology with respect to its cultural context, Christ against culture, first arises because of the persecution of the Church. This defines the Church as a new creation in Christ, totally separate from what Barth called 'world-occurrences', and a Christology emphasizing Christ as King, Lord and Lawgiver. See Niebuhr (1951, pp. 45–115).

References

Barth, K. (1961), *The Humanity of God*, London: Collins.

Barth, K. (1963), *Der Romerbrief*, 1st edn, Zurich: EVZ.

Barth, K. (1968), 'Church and State' in *Community, State and Church*, trans. A.M. Hall *et al.*, Gloucester, MA: Peter Smith.

Barth, K. (1990), *The Göttingen Dogmatics: Instruction in the Christian Religion*, I, trans. G.W. Bromiley, Grand Rapids, MI: Eerdmans.

Barth, K. (2001), *Protestant Theology in the Nineteenth Century*, trans. B. Cozens and J. Bowden, London: SCM.

Beintker, M. (1987), *Die Dialektik in der 'dialektischen Theologie' Karl Barths*, Munich: Ch. Kaiser Verlag.

Edwards, M., M. Goodman and S. Price (eds) (1999), *Apologetics in the Roman Empire: Pagans, Jews, and Christians*, Oxford: Oxford University Press.

Gorringe, T. (1999), *Karl Barth: Against Hegemony*, Oxford: Oxford University Press.

Hegel, G.W.F. (1991), *Elements of the Philosophy of Right*, trans. H.B. Nisbet, Cambridge: Cambridge University Press.

Hood, R.E. (1985), *Contemporary Political Order and Christ: Karl Barth's Christology and Political Praxis*, Allison Park: Pickwick Publications.

Hunsinger, G. (ed.) (1976), *Karl Barth and Radical Politics*, Philadelphia: Westminster.

Hunsinger, G. (2000), *Disruptive Grace: Studies in the Theology of Karl Barth*, Grand Rapids, MI: Eerdmans.

Lakeland, P. (1982), *The Politics of Salvation: The Hegelian Idea of the State*, Albany, NY: SUNY.

McCormack, B. (1995), *Karl Barth's Critically Realistic Dialectical Theology: Its Genesis and Development 1909–1936*, Oxford: Oxford University Press.

Marquardt, F.-W. (1972), *Theologie und Socialismus: Das Beispiel Karl Barths*, Munich: Grunewald.

Niebuhr, H.R. (1951), *Christ and Culture*, New York: Harper & Row.

Shanks, A. (1991), *Hegel's Political Theology*, Cambridge: Cambridge University Press.

Tanner, K. (1997), *Theories of Culture: A New Agenda for Theology*, Minneapolis: Fortress Press.

Ward, G. (2000), *Cities of God*, London: Routledge.

Wood, A. (1991), 'Introduction', in G.W.F. Hegel, *Elements of the Philosophy of Right*, trans. H.B. Nisbett, Cambridge: Cambridge University Press, pp. vii–xxxii.

CHAPTER 5

A Tale of Two Simultaneities: Justification and Sanctification in Calvin and Barth[1]

George Hunsinger

In memoriam Heiko A. Oberman

In a telling remark Hans Urs von Balthasar once observed that Karl Barth rejected all talk of growth or progress in the Christian life. Barth rejected 'all discussion of anything in the realm of the relative and temporal,' von Balthasar claimed, but that is the realm in which we must look for 'a real and vibrant history' of human beings with their redeeming Lord and God (von Balthasar, 1992, p. 371). Although this remark is sweeping and would need to be refined before it could be accepted, von Balthasar raises an important question and points us in the right direction. As we shall see, it is false to state that Barth allows no place for growth or progress in the Christian life, but it is not false to observe that he has very little to say about it. Why should that be? What is it about Barth's soteriology that militates against the ideas of growth or progress? How does Barth propose that we understand the doctrine of sanctification, for example, if not by means of healing, growth, or gradual progress? If we examine such questions carefully, we will not only enter into the heart of Christian soteriology, but also into very deep problems that the Reformation left unsettled in its own ranks. A satisfactory resolution of these problems, which are still outstanding, is of the greatest importance for ecumenical theology today.

A Tale of One Simultaneity: John Calvin

No one would ever think of accusing John Calvin of the liability that von Balthasar found in Barth. No one would ever accuse Calvin, that is, of rejecting all talk of growth or progress in the Christian life. Calvin was, of course, familiar with such accusations. They were, in one form or another, a standard item in Roman Catholic attacks on the Reformation, especially as exemplified by Luther. The message of justification by faith alone, Catholic critics charged, evacuated the Christian life of its significance. Justification as taught by the Reformation made all efforts at progress in the Christian life superfluous. It led to quietism, lethargy and weak resignation. Evidently Calvin felt that Reformation soteriology, as he had inherited it, was not invulnerable to this line of attack. Roman Catholic polemics were assaulting an unguarded flank. The strategy of Calvin's remedy was to reverse the customary order of presentation. Instead of beginning with justification and moving only from there to sanctification (or 'regeneration,' Calvin's preferred term), he began with sanctification instead, postponing all detailed consideration of justification until the discussion of sanctification was complete. He thereby hoped to show 'how little devoid of good works is the faith' (*Institutes*, III.11.1),[2] and thus that sanctification or 'real sanctity of life' was actually inseparable from justification or 'the gratuitous imputation of righteousness' (III.3.1, Allen).[3] Far from making growth and progress in the Christian life superfluous, sanctification followed from union with Christ no less than did justification. The two were inseparable and concomitant.[4]

Calvin's strategy of reversal was based on a logical point. Justification and sanctification, he argued, were given to faith 'simultaneously' (*simul*). Since the one was never given without the other, the order in which theology presented them was flexible. It made no essential difference whether one moved from justification to sanctification, or else from sanctification to justification, as long as one realized that both followed together from union with Christ by faith. The order of presentation could be chosen to meet the needs of the situation. If, as seemed actually the case, justification was being emphasized at the expense of sanctification by attacker and defender alike, there was every reason to redress the imbalance by considering sanctification first. Since the two were given to faith simultaneously, the strategy of reversal would only serve to underscore the essential point that there was no justification without sanctification, and no sanctification without justification.

Calvin's *simul* can be illustrated by a few characteristic statements. 'The Lord freely justifies his own', wrote Calvin, 'in order that he may at the same time [*simul*] restore them to true righteousness by sanctification of his Spirit' (III.3.19). Those who belong to Christ, it seems, are restored to righteousness in two ways at the same time. On the one hand, Christ freely justifies them so that in him they are completely righteous before God. On the other hand, they are also restored to righteousness gradually in themselves 'by sanctification of his Spirit'. Righteousness is a free gift that is given at once categorically (justification) and yet also as a process of growth in the Christian life (sanctification). In Christ we are completely righteous by faith. In ourselves we are also set in the process of becoming righteous. Note that, for Calvin, our righteousness in Christ is no less actual than the righteousness that develops gradually and indeed slowly within us. The distinction between being righteous in Christ (*in Christo*) and being righteous in ourselves (*in nobis*) is not a distinction between a 'legal fiction' and a true state of affairs. It is a distinction between two aspects of a single reality within the context of a complex Christocentric eschatology. In Christ we are already as perfectly righteous as we will ever need to be *coram Deo* we are not yet as righteous as we shall be on the Last Day, and we are in process of becoming righteous existentially here and now.

For Calvin, sanctification, like justification, is always the free gift of God. It is not a human work, and it has no basis in human merit. It is the work of the Holy Spirit in the Christian life. It is the Spirit's gradual impartation to the believer of Christ's own righteousness (sanctification) – a righteousness that has already been imputed to the believer both instantaneously (*statim*) and totally (*totus*) upon the believer's transition from lack of faith to faith. The operative distinctions for this peculiar relation are thus: in Christ / in us, completely / partially, instantaneously / gradually, by imputation / by impartation, by grace alone without works (justification) / by grace alone yet not without works (sanctification). When justification and sanctification are said to be given to faith *simultaneously*, it is this complex – or perhaps better, duplex – soteriological relation with its various aspects and distinctions that is meant.

Here is another instance of Calvin's use of *simul* for this double phenomenon:

> Do you wish … to attain righteousness in Christ? You must first possess Christ; but you cannot possess him without being made partaker in his sanctification, because he cannot be divided into pieces. Since, therefore, it is solely by expending himself that the Lord gives us these benefits to enjoy, he bestows both of them at the same time [*simul*], the one never without the other. Thus it is clear how true it is that we are justified not without works yet not through works, since in our sharing in Christ, which justifies us, sanctification is no less included [*non minus continentur*] than justification. (III.16.1, translation revised)

Once again, the believer is said to enjoy two distinct benefits or, better, a single twofold benefit. They represent two complementary and mutually necessary ways of attaining righteousness in Christ. The one is 'to possess Christ'; the other is to be made a 'partaker in his sanctification'. To possess Christ (*possidere*) corresponds to justification, for to possess Christ by faith is to possess his righteousness. Partaking of Christ (*participare*) then corresponds to sanctification, for possessing his righteousness by faith cannot occur without that righteousness also becoming ever more fully our own at the existential level. Possessing and partaking (or partaking with a twofold blessing) are bestowed simultaneously, and never the one without the other.

Therefore, both the categorical and the relative, the instantaneous and the gradual – righteousness in both senses (total / partial), or in both aspects (in Christ / in us) – are gifts of the one Lord Jesus Christ, and both are essentially gifts of himself. He bestows them solely by bestowing or 'expending' (*erogare*) himself. The believer receives these gifts, or this one twofold gift, and 'enjoys' (*fruor*) them, but does not earn or merit them. Although we are not justified *through* works, we are not justified *without* them. That is, the good works consequent upon justification are the fruits of faith's union with Christ. They are the work of Christ by his Spirit within our hearts and lives. They presuppose, but do not effect, our reconciliation with God. It is not our own existential or actual righteousness, but Christ's righteousness as enacted for our sakes, and grasped only by faith, 'by which alone we are reconciled to God' (III.16.1).

In short, justification is the free gift of righteousness in Christ, perfect and indivisible, even as sanctification is the gradual impartation of this righteousness existentially here and now. It is Christ himself and Christ alone who holds these two benefits together. 'Christ contains both of them inseparably in himself' (III.16.1). The one (sanctification) can no more be divided from the other (justification) than Christ can be 'divided into pieces'. Giving us himself by grace through faith, he also gives us his righteousness, for he himself just *is* our righteousness (1 Cor. 1:30) – in two distinct but inseparable modes (justification and sanctification), which for all their distinctness are bestowed, as we have seen, in and with one another. 'Christ justifies no one whom he does not at the same time [*simul*] sanctify. These benefits are joined together by an everlasting and indissoluble bond' (III.16.1).

> Just as Christ cannot be divided into parts, so also these two blessings, which we receive in him [*percipimus*] at the same time [*simul*], are inseparable: justification and sanctification. To those whom God receives into grace, therefore, he at the same time [*simul*] gives the Spirit of adoption, by whose power he re-forms them in his own image. (III.11.6, Allen, translation revised)[5]

Just as being received into divine grace here alludes to justification, so being given the re-forming power of the Spirit alludes to sanctification, and both are not only inseparable through our union with Christ, but are given and received at the same time.

This double gift of salvation (justification and sanctification) is famously described by Calvin as a double grace (*duplex gratia*).

> Christ was given to us by God's generosity, to be grasped and possessed by us in faith. By partaking of him, we principally receive a double grace: namely, that being reconciled to God through Christ's blamelessness, we may have in heaven instead of a Judge a gracious Father; and secondly, that sanctified by Christ's Spirit we may cultivate blamelessness and purity of life. (III.11.1)

Note that Christ is again central, and that our relation to Christ is again one of possession and participation. The double grace is said to be received through participation in Christ (*cuius participatione*), and this participation takes place through faith. Everything depends on our partaking of Christ by faith. 'As long as Christ remains outside of us, and we are separated from him, all that he has suffered and done for the salvation of the human race remains useless and of no value for us' (III.1.1). Christ cannot share with us what he has received from the Father unless he becomes ours by grace, so that we partake of him by faith (III.1.1).

Union and communion with Christ thus set the immediate relevant context within which justification and sanctification are divinely bestowed and humanly received. This union can be described as a *koinonia* – a relation of mutual indwelling. By grace through faith, the believer dwells in Christ even as Christ dwells in the believer. Dwelling in Christ, the believer possesses Christ and so also the reconciliation with God accomplished by Christ's blameless obedience (*innocentia*) as it reached its climax in his death on the cross. The believer can therefore stand before God without anxiety as before a gracious Father as opposed to a hostile judge. Dwelling in the believer, Christ breaks the dominion of sin in the human heart by bestowing the gift of his Spirit. Sanctified by the Spirit's indwelling, the believer is freed to cultivate (*meditari*) that blamelessness (*innocentia*) and purity of life (*puritatem vitae*) which had otherwise been forfeited by sin (III.11.1).

It is noteworthy, however, and also unexpected, that, for Calvin, the twofold gift of grace correlates not with a single, but with a double, divine acceptance. Against those who would interpret certain Scripture passages to mean that we may gain God's favour for ourselves not by God's gift alone but by means of our own right efforts, Calvin retorts: 'But you can in no way make the Scriptures agree unless you recognize a double acceptance of man before God [*duplicem hominis apud Deum acceptionem*]' (III.17.4). The one acceptance is based on Christ's work apart from us (justification), while the second acceptance is based on Christ's work in us by his Spirit (sanctification). The first acceptance presupposes that, although in ourselves we are wholly unrighteous as sinners, in Christ and clothed in his righteousness we are nonetheless wholly righteous before God. The second acceptance, however, depends on our becoming righteous at the existential level. The actual righteousness that God works in us by his Spirit also makes us acceptable to God. At this level, states Calvin, God does indeed accept believers by reason of their works, but only because those works are effected in them by his Spirit. 'This is the acceptance ... in which even the works of believers after their vocation are approved by God; for the Lord cannot but love and accept those good effects which are produced in them by his Spirit' (III.17.5, Allen). Because 'regeneration is a reparation of the Divine image in us', the second mode of acceptance, related to human works, occurs because God accepts and beholds in his children 'the marks and lineaments of his own countenance' (III.17.5, Allen). 'But it must always be remembered that they are accepted by God in consequence of their works, only because, for their sakes and the favour which he bears to them, he deigns to accept whatever goodness he has liberally communicated to their works' (III.17.5, Allen).

This teaching of a second mode or basis of acceptance would seem to place Calvin on thin ice. For to make it plausible, he has to adopt lines of argument that come perilously close to the Roman Catholic ideas that the Reformation had set out to overcome. Note well that Calvin is not just saying that sanctification is the concomitant of justification in the Christian life. He is also saying that our acceptance before God does not rest on justification alone – potentially a momentous assertion. He insists that a second, complementary basis for our acceptance lies in the actual righteousness of our own lives, in our sanctification. Does this mean that justification in itself is not enough? Does it mean that sanctification is also in some sense necessary if the believer is to be rendered acceptable before God? Is sanctification not just a fruit of union with Christ, but a condition for the possibility of divine acceptance? The idea that sanctification is at once a human work and yet also a gift of grace is, of course, familiar in Roman Catholic soteriology, appearing in both Augustinian–Thomistic and Franciscan forms.[6] Moreover, the worry that justification is not enough in itself to make us acceptable before God is a standard Roman Catholic objection to Reformation soteriology. With this idea of a twofold acceptance – which would have been unthinkable to Luther – has Calvin sold the Reformation down the river?

It would be unfair if we failed to note that Calvin surrounds his teaching of a second acceptance with heavy qualifications. He is, after all, trying to make sense of certain scriptural passages – seized upon by the Reformation's opponents – that are not easy to align with the doctrine of justification by faith alone. He rejects every suggestion that good works bring merit:

> It is beyond a doubt that whatever is praiseworthy in our works proceeds from the grace of God; and that we cannot ascribe the least portion of it to ourselves. If we truly and seriously acknowledge this truth, not only all confidence in merit, but likewise all idea of merit immediately vanishes. (III.15.3, Allen, translation revised)

> Where remission of sins has been previously received [*justification*], the good works which succeed [*sanctification*] are estimated far beyond their intrinsic merit; for all their imperfections are covered by the perfection of Christ, and all their blemishes are removed by his purity, that they may not be scrutinized by the Divine judgement. The guilt, therefore, of all transgressions, by which men are prevented from offering anything acceptable to God, being obliterated, and the imperfection, which universally deforms even the good works of believers, being buried in oblivion, their works are accounted righteous, or, which, is the same thing, imputed for righteousness. (III.17.8, Allen)

With statements like these Calvin seems well within the bounds of Reformation soteriology. Neither Thomas nor Scotus could have suggested, for example, that *absolutely nothing* praiseworthy in our works proceeds from us, since they both subscribed to the idea of merit in various ways. Calvin, by contrast, seems to hold that in doing good works the believer, while consenting to the operation of grace, does nothing that essentially contributes to it. The believer cooperates with the operation of grace without effecting the praiseworthy result. Moreover, since all one's good works are still unacceptable to God by virtue of their deformation by sin, even the believer's best works can be rendered acceptable only by the imputation of Christ's righteousness. Clearly, for Calvin the free grace of justification prevails over the imperfections of sanctification at every point. In a way foreign to standard Catholic soteriology, sanctification is completely merit-free, while even the best of good works (being marred by sin) is still unacceptable apart from the threefold basis of Christ, grace, and faith alone – but on that basis the believer's works are acceptable indeed.

Nevertheless, doubts and ambiguities remain. Not only Calvin's rejection of merit, but also his careful regulation of sanctification by justification would both seem to militate powerfully against his curious suggestion of a second ground or mode of acceptance. We might muse that not all his soteriological ideas were formulated with sufficient care, so that sometimes his *duplex*-complex got the better of him! Unfortunate, stray remarks would sometimes seem to occur one or two standard deviations out from the bulge at the middle of the bell-shaped curve. Among the most perplexing of these atypical ideas is the discussion that goes so far as to make good works into 'inferior causes' (*causas inferiores*) of our salvation (!) (III.14.21). Even with Calvin's tortured qualifications, it is hard to see how this statement can be retrieved, or why it should have been ventured at all.

More serious, however, is a matter that underlies these worries, for it concerns Calvin's basic soteriological orientation. 'For Luther,' writes Heiko Oberman, 'the *locus* of the *gloria dei* is the *iustificatio impii*, while for Calvin it is the *iustificatio iusti*' (Oberman, 1986, p. 238). Luther insisted repeatedly that God's grace really comes to lost sinners. For him, this word was our only hope, the abiding good news, something we needed to hear afresh each day. We could never outgrow our need for this news, for even after baptism we still remained sinners in ourselves. Grace was God's abiding '*Nevertheless*' that depended on nothing other than itself, and certainly on nothing in us, to bring us mercy, light and life.

None of this was, of course, denied by Calvin but, as Oberman suggests, matters could sometimes go off in a curiously different direction:

> When we hear mention of our union with God, let us remember that holiness must be its bond; not because we come into communion with him by virtue of our holiness. Rather, we ought first to cleave unto him so that, infused with his holiness, we may follow whither he calls. (III.6.2)

Not only do we not come into communion with God by virtue of our holiness, Luther might have objected, but neither do we remain there by any such precarious bond. Calvin here speaks of our holiness, Luther might have continued, where he ought properly to speak only of Christ as received by faith alone. Christ himself is, and remains, the only bond of our union with God. We do not remain in communion with God because of our holiness, so Luther would have insisted, but despite our actual unholiness, by sheer grace. Nor, he might have added, does our ability to do good works depend on our being 'infused' (*perfusi*) with Christ's holiness, but again on the grace that breaks in anew each day upon our really persisting lack of holiness. It was Thomas Aquinas who wrote that 'God gives grace only to the worthy, but he himself makes them worthy by grace'.[7] In these admittedly odd passages (offset by the bulk of Calvin's teaching), does not Calvin seem to approximate something all-too-similar – that 'God gives grace only to the holy, but he himself makes them holy by grace'? Does the God of 'double acceptance' actually give grace only to the holy, Luther might ask, once they have first been justified by faith? Does God really regard the works of the saints as 'inferior causes' of their own salvation? Or does grace come only to lost sinners – even after their baptism – even if, by the promises of God, it really does come to them? Can the assurance of faith that was rightly so important to Calvin really rest secure if our position before God depends finally not on a single, but a double, acceptance?[8]

A Tale of Another Simultaneity: Martin Luther

Markedly different from Calvin's *simul*, the simultaneity relation that impressed itself so indelibly upon Luther was that of *simul iustus et peccator*. It cannot be insignificant that, as Richard Wevers' exhaustive concordance shows, the phrase *simul iustus et peccator* does not appear in Calvin's *Institutes* (Wevers, 1992). Calvin's *simul*, as we have seen, led him to develop a form of soteriological gradualism. 'Christ is not outside us but dwells within us,' he wrote. 'Not only does he cleave to us by an invisible bond of fellowship, but with a wonderful communion, day by day, he grows more and more into one body with us, until he becomes completely one with us' (III.2.24). Calvin saw the existential aspect of salvation primarily as a matter of growth, healing and gradual progress by degrees.

By contrast, Luther saw the existential aspect of salvation rather differently. For him, it was subject to a process that was not so much gradual as perpetual. In other words, where Calvin posited a process of 'more and more', Luther posited one of 'again and again'. Luther wrote:

> Forgiveness of sins is not a matter of a passing work or action, but of perpetual duration. For the forgiveness of sins begins in baptism and remains with us all the way to death, until we rise from the dead, and leads us to life eternal. So we live continually under the forgiveness of sins. Christ is truly and constantly the liberator from our sins, is called our Savior, and saves us by taking away our sins. If, however, he saves us always and continually, then we are constantly sinners. (Luther, 1960, p. 164)

Christ comes daily, continually and without interruption, every day and every hour – to sinners. 'Daily we sin, daily we are continually justified' (Luther, 1960, p. 191). Although Luther, like Calvin, also knows of salvation as a gradual process, unlike Calvin, he subordinates all gradualism to the perpetual advent of grace, which confronts sin continually afresh, and continually overcomes it *as a whole*.

Sin and righteousness, for Luther, are categorical terms. Although in themselves they admit of degrees, they are mutually exclusive in relation to one another. *Coram Deo* where there is sin, there is no righteousness; and where there is righteousness, there is no sin. 'Partial righteousness does not justify' (ibid., p.127). Slight gradual improvements in sinners avail for nothing before God. Luther's *simul* is inseparable from Luther's *totus*. The great doctrine of *simul iustus et peccator* describes a *totus/totus* relation. The baptized believer who is still completely a sinner is also, at the same time, completely righteous in Christ. The relationship between the two predications is not static, as in a frozen paradox, but eschatological. *Peccator* refers to the old sinful humanity. It lives on in the present as the past that was crucified with Christ. *Iustus* refers to the new redeemed humanity. It breaks in on the present continually as the future that was risen with Christ. The Christian life is a constant turning from the past to the future, from oneself as sinner to oneself as righteous, in the form of a constant turning to Christ – who exchanged his righteousness for our sin, that we might exchange our sin for his righteousness. We participate in this great exchange once and for all through faith, and thereafter continually again and again, and always *totus/totus*, not *partim/partim* (or more precisely, the latter always only in the context of the former).

Therefore, for Luther, the relationship 'in Christ/in us' is not what it was for Calvin. It is not primarily a relationship between the categorical and the relative. It is primarily a relationship between the categorical truth about us in one form (*totus*) and that same categorical truth in another (*totus*). It signifies that what is already perfectly true for us in Christ is also perpetually true for us ever anew in a very different form here and now. Sin's *total* abolition by the righteousness of the crucified Christ is true for us at once perfectly 'in Christ' and then also perpetually 'in us' through the whole course of the eschatological interim. The perpetual advent of grace to baptized sinners, continually forgiving and counteracting their sin, is a kind of permanent revolution or perpetual resurrection from the dead, in other words, as Luther liked to say, a daily baptism – until at last, at the final consummation, Christ will come to dwell as perfectly *in nobis* as we already dwell perfectly in him. 'You have died,' as Luther liked to quote Paul at this point 'and your life is hid with Christ in God' (Col. 3: 3).

A Tale of Two Simultaneities: Karl Barth

Karl Barth's soteriology cannot be well understood if it is not seen that he makes a bold and innovative attempt to combine the two 'simultaneities' we have been considering – Calvin's *simul* and Luther's *simul*. What Barth attempts to combine, in other words, is the simultaneity of justification and sanctification, on the one hand, along with *simul iustus et peccator*, on the other. This enterprise is enormously ambitious, and it is no less complex; only the outlines can be presented here. Barth makes essentially three moves. First, he reconsiders the meaning of our participation in Christ. Second, he reconsiders the meaning of Christ's presence to faith. Finally, he reconsiders the meaning of sanctification. This first move gives him Calvin's *simul*, and the last move gives him Luther's, while the middle move mediates between the two. The overall effect is to create a new framework for the meaning of salvation that incorporates Calvin's *simul* into Luther's. Barth agrees with Luther, in other words, that *simul iustus et peccator* is, so to speak, a grammatical remark in Wittgenstein's sense. It is not just one soteriological truth among others. It rather constitutes the framework of sense and nonsense for soteriology as a whole. It makes explicit the norms that are implicit in God's revelation and enactment of our salvation in the history of the covenant as fulfilled in Jesus Christ. By granting primacy to Luther's *simul*, however, and incorporating Calvin's *simul* into its frame, Barth incurs certain losses. Whether these losses are irretrievable will be touched on in the conclusion.

The First Move: Reconsidering our Participation in Christ

Our participation in Christ, Barth proposes, can be considered in two ways. First, in the sense of active participation, everything depends on faith. Without faith there can be no active participation in Christ, nor can there be a true acknowledgement and reception of his benefits, nor can there be the thanks and praise proper to him, nor can there be repentance and newness of life. When Luther and Calvin speak of participation in Christ, it is this active sense that is usually meant. Barth calls it being in Christ in the strict and proper sense (*CD* IV/2, p. 555). Unlike Luther and Calvin, however, and unlike much of the Catholic tradition both before and after them, Barth does not believe that faith itself effects our participation in Christ or, more precisely, that without faith we fail to participate in Christ in any sense at all.

Second, therefore, in the sense of objective participation, everything depends on grace, and in particular on the operation of grace apart from us prior to faith. Because of the prior operation of grace, Barth believes, our objective participation in Christ precedes our active participation through faith. Jesus Christ is the one great inclusive human being. We are not outsiders to participation in Christ until we happen to become insiders by faith. We are, rather, all insiders by grace whether we recognize it yet or not. Faith does not transfer us from the outside to the inside, but instead enables us to see the staggering fact that, by the prevenient grace of God, we were inside without knowing it all along.[9]

Barth describes the objective participation of all humanity in Christ:

> 'In Christ' means that in him we are reconciled to God, in him we are elect from eternity, in him we are called, in him we are justified and sanctified, in him our sin is carried to the grave, in his resurrection our death is overcome, with him our life is hid with Christ in God, in him everything that has to be done for us has already been done, has previously been removed and put in its place, in him we are children in the Father's house, just as he is by nature. All that has to be said about us can be said only by describing and explaining our existence in him; not by describing and explaining it as an existence we might have in and for itself .... For by Christ we will never be anything else than just what we are in Christ. And when the Holy Spirit draws and takes us right into the reality of revelation by doing what we cannot do, by opening our eyes and ears and hearts, he does not tell us anything except that we are in Christ by Christ. (*CD* I/2, p. 240)

Of course, many questions arise at this point. What of those who never make the transition from objective to active participation? Moreover, if our participation is objective before it becomes active, doesn't our active participation become inevitable or unnecessary or trivial? These and similar questions are important, but they would take us too far afield. Barth's doctrine of universal objective participation breaks with almost the entire Latin theological tradition, including perhaps above all, the ever-dominant Augustinian tradition. One has to go all the way back to early Greek fathers such as Athanasius to find relatively comparable associations of the phrase *in Christ* with the word *all*. Barth boldly allots certain New Testament passages such as

1 Corinthians 15, 2 Corinthians 5, Romans 5 and Romans 11, where similar universalistic associations occur, a weight of significance that they have not enjoyed for centuries. It should not be surprising if, for many conscientious believers, Barth's position, at least initially, should seem implausible or counterintuitive or fraught with unfortunate consequences.

The simultaneity of justification and sanctification, Barth thinks, takes place at the level of our objective participation in Christ before it ever takes place at the level of our active participation. He thereby forcibly shifts the whole axis of salvation (justification and sanctification) away from what takes place in us existentially (*in nobis*) to what has taken place apart from us preveniently in Christ (*extra nos*). This shift is one of the most striking and momentous moves in his soteriology. It can be regarded as the logical fulfilment of a general, though still somewhat unsteady, move in this direction by Reformation soteriology in general. The very idea of justification by faith alone, as we have seen, involved a strong emphasis on the unequivocal perfection of our righteousness in Christ. The idea of free imputation, articulated as vigorously by Calvin as by Luther, entailed that our perfect righteousness in Christ was the stable basis, and not the uncertain goal, of whatever might or might not take place in us existentially between the times. Reformation soteriology, in other words, had shifted the decisive locus of salvation, in principle, from the existential to the Christological level. Peter Martyr Vermigli got the Reformation's massive soterio-logical shift, whose significance can scarcely be exaggerated, exactly right when he said: 'We are more perfectly in Christ than he is in us' (quoted in McLellend, 1957, p. 148). To speak about our reality in Christ was not just another way of speaking about his reality in us. We had died and our life was hid with Christ in God (Col. 3:3). Christ himself was our wisdom, righteousness, sanctification and redemption (1 Cor. 1:30). Reformation soteriology represented a sea-change in which the eschatology of our salvation was grounded, focused and centred no longer in ourselves, but in Christ alone.

Reformation soteriology, however, was clearer about how our being in Christ pertained to justification than about how it might pertain also to sanctification. Calvin, as we have seen, tended to situate sanctification very strongly in the gradualisitc relativities of the existential level, whereas Luther for his part had tended to absorb sanctification into justification without keeping them properly distinct. That was roughly the state of the question as Barth faced it. Little had been done to resolve these matters in any truly fundamental way since the Reformation. It was in this situation, as it were, that Barth stepped into the breach. Like Calvin but unlike Luther, he kept justification and sanctification distinct. More nearly like Luther but unlike Calvin, however, he did so only while also relocating sanctification primarily away from the *in nobis* to the *in Christo* level so that the precise form of sanctification now matched that of justification very closely. It was precisely in Christ that our sanctification took place 'simultaneously' with our justification so that, as Calvin had rightly said, there was never any justification without sanctification, nor sanctification without justification.

Justification and sanctification were, for Barth, two ways of describing reconciliation as a whole. Although they took place in Christ simultaneously, we cannot apprehend them simultaneously, but only sequentially. Nevertheless, in itself 'the *simul* of the one redemptive act of God in Jesus Christ', Barth states, 'cannot be split up into a temporal sequence' (*CD* IV/2, p. 507). In no sense do justification and sanctification constitute two *parts* of a larger whole, because each is itself the whole – Christ's one work of reconciliation – seen from a particular vantage point (*CD* IV/2, pp. 499–500). In the one life history of Jesus Christ as fulfilled in his cross, the humiliation of the eternal Son of God had taken place for our justification in and with the exaltation of the earthly Son of man for our sanctification. Humiliation and exaltation were not two different stages of his life history, but two different aspects of it that had occurred continuously and simultaneously (in various ways) throughout its course from beginning to end. The appropriate mode of descriptive adequacy for the two countervailing aspects of this one reconciling occurrence was dialectical. It was not a matter of one truth in two parts, but of the whole truth of reconciliation cohering simultaneously in two forms that were mutually necessary but also apparently diametrically opposite in operation and movement.

The central theme of Reformation soteriology, as Luther repeatedly urged, was that Christ alone is our righteousness and life. Barth then developed that theme as follows. Through our Lord's humiliation as the Son of God, and at the level of our universal objective participation in it, the great exchange took place whereby he assumed the full abysmal guilt and burden of human sin, even to the point of dying on the cross condemned in our place, in order that, by his sinless obedience, he might give us his perfect righteousness before God. This humiliation grounds and constitutes our justification.

At the same time (*simul*), through our Lord's exaltation as the Son of man, and again at the level of our universal objective participation in it, that same great exchange occurred in another aspect. The God who had validated our Lord's entry into the death of godless sinners (as God had continuously validated him throughout the entire course of his faithful obedience on earth) was also the God who had exalted him, and us with him, into the freedom of eternal life, which is communion with God. This elevation grounds and constitutes our sanctification. In him, in his one saving history of reconciliation as fulfilled on the cross and made manifest by his resurrection, our justification has taken place in and with our sanctification, even as our sanctification has taken place in and with our justification. Having assumed our sin and death, he has at the same time given his righteousness and life. When he died, we died; when he rose again, we rose with him. When he died our death as sinners, he at the same time clothed us with his righteousness; and when God validated his obedience unto death, he at the same time exalted us with him from our bondage to sin and decay to the glory of eternal life.

In short, that is how Barth appropriated Calvin's *simul*. By reconsidering our participation in Christ, by regarding it as objective before it ever becomes active, Barth could affirm Calvin's simultaneity of justification and sanctification – while avoiding any such precarious equivocations as 'double acceptance'. Though subsisting simultaneously as a whole in two forms, there is only one ground of our reconciliation with God (and therefore only one ground of our acceptance by God), and that ground is the humiliation of the Son of God as it took place in and with the exaltation of the Son of man.

The Second Move: Reconsidering Christ's Presence to Faith

Christ's presence to faith, Barth averred, must not be conceived abstractly. It must not be conceived in disconnection from his life history there and then, in which our salvation was enacted, and in which we were objectively included. Nor may his presence be conceived in disconnection from his universal future in which what has been hidden to the ages will at last be revealed, and he will be manifest to all things as what he has been all along – the world's Saviour, the Lord of heaven and earth. Above all, however, the work of reconciliation, which he accomplished for us there and then, must not be conceived as less than it is. It must not be conceived as though it were somehow unfinished, insufficient, repeatable or in need of repetition. It must not be conceived as though in any sense imperfectly accomplished. The reconciliation achieved in and by Jesus Christ, Barth states, stands for ever as an 'unsurpassable action' and an 'intrinsically perfect' work (*CD* IV/3, p. 7; see also p. 327). In him, in his life, death and resurrection, the world's reconciliation with God has taken place 'once for all, totally, universally, radically, and with definitive newness' (ibid., p. 323). Only God incarnate, only Jesus Christ, could save us from our sins, and only on that basis might we participate in and with him in eternal life. Once he has accomplished his unique and perfect work, it needs no repetition, no supplementation, no synthesis with some other (or supposedly other) saving (or supposedly saving) work. Whatever our relationship at the existential level to this reconciliation may be, it cannot possibly involve any of these things. The presence of the risen Christ can only mean his self-presentation to us in the once-for-all perfection of his finished and saving work.

In short, for Barth, Christ's presence to faith cannot be considered apart from its profound interconnection with his life history in the past and also his future glorious manifestation. Even more importantly, nor can it be considered apart from the intrinsic perfection of his one saving work, as accomplished in his life history, and in which we have already been included in advance before ever we come actively to partake of it. 'One has died for all; therefore all have died. And he died for all, that those who live might live no longer for themselves but for him who for their sake died and was raised' (2 Cor. 5:14b–15 RSV). Barth takes the perfect tense of such New Testament statements – here 'one *has died* for all' and 'all *have died*,' such that *all have died in the one* – very seriously.

Christ's presence, therefore, cannot be separated from his past and his future.[10] The *Christus praesens*, we might say, cannot be separated from the *Christus adventus*, the Christ who lived and died there and then, nor from the *Christus futurus*, the Christ who will return in glory at the end of all things. No soteriology, Barth proposes, can be adequate which separates the *Christus praesens* from either the *Christus adventus* or the *Christus futurus*. The *Christus praesens* is so related to the *Christus adventus* and the *Christus futurus* as to constitute a complex unity-in-distinction. These are finally three forms of one and the same Lord Jesus Christ, who in each form of his presence to faith is present as a whole. The three mutually coinherent forms are related without separation or division, and without confusion or change. At the same time, an asymmetrical ordering principle obtains. The *Christus praesens* and the *Christus futurus* are both fully grounded and determined by the *Christus adventus*. It is the *Christus adventus* – the Jesus Christ who in his life history has perfectly accomplished our salvation – who defines and constitutes the identity of his other two forms. This asymmetry means that the order from *Christus adventus* to *Christus praesens et futurus* is irreversible. To be sure, the Christ of ecclesial encounter and experience is the *Christus praesens* in his coinherence with the *Christus adventus* and the *Christus futurus*. The order of encounter and experience (*ordo congressendi et experientiae*), however, must be distinguished from the orders of being and knowledge (*ordo essendi* and *ordo cognoscendi*). The *Christus adventus* – Jesus Christ in his life history and its saving significance – is ontically and noetically prior to, and determinative of, the other two coinherent forms of his post-resurrection manifestation and impartation – so ordered that they comprise the one threefold form in which he lives and moves and has his being.[11]

The *Christus praesens* is the risen Christ. It is Christ's resurrection that makes him not only our contemporary, Barth thinks, but also the contemporary of all times and places, whether before his life history or after it. What needs to happen – and in Christ's resurrection and ascension what does happen – is for the reconciliation he accomplished to be made contemporaneous with the rest of history. Easter involves Christ's 'transition to a presence which is eternal and therefore embraces all times' (*CD* IV/1, p. 318). 'His history did not become dead history. It was history in his time to become as such eternal history – the history of God with the human beings of all times, and therefore taking place here and now as it did then' (ibid., pp. 313–14, translation revised). 'He is present here and now for us in the full efficacy of what … he was and did then and there' (ibid., p. 291). The resurrection means Christ's 'real presence' to us now, and 'our contemporaneity to him' in what he perfectly accomplished there and then in our stead (ibid., p. 348). It means 'the contemporaneity of Jesus Christ with us and of us with him' (*CD* IV/2, p. 291). It makes him 'the Contemporary of all human beings' (*CD* III/2, p. 440, translation revised).

In and with its real historicity – which means his actual life and death – the history of Jesus Christ is a self-transcending event. By the power of his resurrection, it 'bursts through its isolations. It transcends its temporal and spatial limits' (*CD* IV/3, p. 324). It fills and controls all times and places. What our Lord accomplished in his life history 'is too great to be limited to the one event which took place there and then'. It is 'too high, too deep, too comprehensive' to be enclosed in history like any other transient event (ibid., p. 324). Because Christ is risen from the dead, no time or place, no human life, is bereft of his real presence (in whatever form or forms it may take, whether general or particular, manifest or hidden, incognito for the time being or openly known). Christ does not save us by his mere abstract presence. He saves us by his presence as the Crucified in whom we have been, and are, reconciled to God, as the one who lived, died and rose again there and then for our sakes.

The risen Christ is present in the perfection of his one reconciling work. His work of reconciliation is not the mere precondition for some new work other than itself, for some further saving work, for some supplemental work that supposedly enlarges and completes it. His one work of reconciliation continues to take place here and now, but only as that which has already taken place once for all and perfectly there and then. What takes place in and with his presence here and now is, as it were, analytic rather than synthetic. It is always a secondary and dependent form of his one saving work in its finished perfection. It is the outworking through time of what it already contains inherently in itself. What takes place in and through Christ's presence to faith is not the combination of Christ's reconciling work with some other work, some new and further work in us, some second and additional work, some sequel that completes and perfects it as though it were not already complete and perfect in itself. Certainly in its modes of self-presentation to us, it is ever new, endlessly engaging and inexhaustibly rich, and yet it is always also indivisibly one and the same. Because Christ's work is in his person and his person in his work, the presence of Christ is always the presence of his perfect reconciling work.

Therefore, just as Calvin emphasized that Christ cannot be divided into pieces (as Luther had done before him), so Barth also emphasizes that the risen Christ is 'whole and undivided' (*CD* IV/2, p. 502), that he is not present to faith in any partial or divisible way, and thus that his presence always means nothing less than the presence of 'the one totality of the reconciling action of God' (ibid.). Very unlike Calvin, however, Barth argues that Christ's perfection and indivisibility mean that reconciliation in Christ is never a matter of degree. Like Luther, Barth holds that the relation between salvation *in Christo* and salvation *in nobis* is not to be described as a relation between the perfect and the imperfect, but rather as a relation between salvation's perfection in one form (*in Christo*) and that same perfection as it comes to us in another (*in nobis*). In particular, although, unlike Luther, Barth upholds and appropriates Calvin's *simul* respecting justification and sanctification, he departs from Calvin's teaching that sanctification grows into us gradually by degrees. But what could possibly be the alternative?

That there is only one work of salvation, that it has been accomplished by Jesus Christ, that it is identical with his person, and that being perfect it needs no supplementation but only acknowledgement, reception, participation, anticipation and proclamation for what it is – these are the great themes of Barth's soteriology. We have been made to participate in Christ by grace, Barth maintains, before we ever do so actively by faith. Our objective *participatio Christi* already involves us as whole persons. Otherwise we would not be totally righteous in Christ, as Reformation doctrine has significantly urged as the right reading of the New Testament. Otherwise we would not have died when he died – '*we know that our old self was crucified with him so that the sinful body might be destroyed*' (Rom. 6: 6) – nor would we also have risen with him when he rose from the dead – '*you have been raised with Christ*' (Col. 3: 1). What the Bible calls death, Barth contends, is not mere sickness. What it calls darkness is not simply twilight. What it calls incapacity is not merely weakness. What it calls ignorance is not just confusion (*CD* II/1, p. 105). The relation between what the Bible calls light and darkness, life and death, sin and righteousness is not a matter of degree (*CD* IV/2, pp. 497–98).

Christ's own active *koinonia* with us, in life and in death, precedes our active *koinonia* with him. His prior and total inclusion of us in himself and in his work by grace is precisely what we actively and properly acknowledge when he then dwells in us by faith. Faith does not receive Christ, Barth believes, without receiving him in the perfection of his saving work, but in receiving him in the perfection of his work, faith enters into living communion with Christ. Faith thus acknowledges him for who he is, shares actively and rejoices in what had previously been shared only passively and objectively, eagerly anticipates the final revelation and impartation of his perfect work, even though it remains hidden here and now apart from faith, and so bears witness to Jesus Christ, the *Christus praesens*. For the *Christus praesens* is none other than the *Christus adventus*, in whom the world has been reconciled to God, and the *Christus futurus*, who will be unveiled at the end of all things for what he now is, always has been, and ever shall be – the ruler of all (*pantokrator*).

To sum up: Barth reconceives the presence of Christ to faith by seeing it as determined by two primary factors – *participatio Christi* and *perfectio Christi*. *Participatio Christi* means our prior inclusion in Christ by grace (objective *koinonia*) as then provisionally fulfilled by our subsequent inclusion by faith (active *koinonia*). *Perfectio Christi*, on the other hand, means the intrinsic and unsurpassable perfection of Christ's one reconciling work as it presents itself to faith in and with the *Christus praesens*. Our *participatio Christi*, in either form, is always determined by the *perfectio Christi* – the perfection of his work in his person, and the perfection of his person in his work, in whose enactment we were included by the election of grace. Precisely because the *Christus praesens* always means the presence of the *perfectio Christi* in whom our *participatio* has been secured graciously in advance, Barth can have Calvin's *simul* without his equivocations with respect to justification and sanctification. For our justification and sanctification are simultaneously present in Christ to faith as the two forms of Christ's one reconciling work. Those forms took place simultaneously in his one life history with equal perfection (and not the one less than the other, nor either by means of any contributing 'inferior causality' from us). As it turns out, however, it is this same reconception of Christ's presence that also forms the basis which gives Barth Luther's *simul* as well.

The Third Move: Reconsidering the Meaning of Sanctification

Sanctification takes place, for Barth, at two levels – in Christ and in us. In Christ, as we have seen, our sanctification has taken place perfectly, once and for all. At the existential level (*in nobis*), as we have also seen, our relation to this perfect sanctification is one of acknowledgement, reception, participation, anticipation and proclamation. From the standpoint of the previous tradition, the pressing question will focus especially on the question of reception. What can it possibly mean to receive sanctification, if not to receive it by degrees? Barth's answer to this question is striking and takes the same form as Luther's. It means to receive sanctification not more and more, by a process of gradual growth, but again and again, continually from without and ever anew. It means to receive it by the perpetual inbreaking of grace to faith.

The sanctification that is ours in Christ (by objective *koinonia*), Barth maintains, comes as such to those who receive Christ by faith (by active *koinonia*), even though those who receive Christ by faith remain sinners in themselves, not partially but categorically (*totus*). Like our objective participation, our active participation in sanctification is also totally the work of God. The holiness of the community that results from the sanctifying action of Christ is, Barth states, something that comes to it 'not as an inherent quality but as the character he will give it in the fulfilment of this action' (*CD* IV/2, p. 512). Sanctification is thus a Christocentric and eschatological event. It does not come by degrees, but it does come continually and provisionally here and now as what it will one day be openly and definitively – the liberation of the sinner from bondage to both sin and death. Sanctification exalts the sinner from bondage to freedom, and from death to life, as these have already occurred by way of objective *koinonia* in Christ. For as the exalted Son of man, Christ himself *is* our sanctification, and the sanctification that has taken place in him is ours continually by grace through faith (ibid., p. 514). Through faith, through our active participation in Christ, it is ours, and so becomes ours ever anew. The sanctification that confronts us and includes us as Christ's perfect work (*opus perfectus*), also comes to us from him again and again as the perpetual operation of grace in our lives (*operatione perpetua*).

Sanctification does not impart a new, non-sinful nature within us. Whatever regeneration may mean, it does not mean something like the implantation of a seed of holiness in us that grows ever more luxuriantly into good works. It means that even as sinners we are given the freedom to obey God despite our sinfulness (ibid., p. 499). It means that a new form of life is given and made possible for the community of faith, and so also for each member within it, not because the community is gradually ceasing to be sinful, but precisely despite its remaining as sinful in and of itself. In the perpetual gift of new freedom, the community actually begins to do what it in itself it cannot do. It adopts new attitudes and practices that separate it from the surrounding culture. It breaks with the 'irresistible and uncontested dominion' of various historical, cultural and spiritual forces (ibid., p. 546). Bondage to material possessions, to social status, to reliance on coercion and force, to tribalism, nationalism and narrow family interests, to the self-justifications of religious piety – in relation to such concrete but elusive and life-sapping forces as these sanctification means freedom (ibid., pp. 546–53). This freedom is possible for those who in themselves remain sinners only as it is actually given, but by the grace of our Lord Jesus Christ it does not fail to be given, continually, again and again.

What Barth says about sanctification at the level of existential appropriation thus parallels very closely what Luther says about the existential appropriation of justification (or at least Luther's dominant and most distinctive note). Barth states explicitly that he intends to construct his doctrine of sanctification in 'direct analogy' to the doctrine of justification. He writes:

> How much false teaching, and how many practical mistakes, would have been avoided in this matter of sanctification if in direct analogy to justification we had been bold or modest enough to give precedence and all glory to the Holy One and not to the saints ... to the royal man Jesus, as the only One who is holy, but in whom the sanctification of all the saints is reality. (ibid., p. 515)

On this basis Barth makes Luther's *simul* his own. 'Luther's *simul* (*totus*) *iustus*, *simul* (*totus*) *peccator*,' writes Barth, 'has ... to be applied strictly to sanctification and therefore conversion if we are to see deeply into what is denoted by these terms, and to understand them with the necessary seriousness' (ibid., p. 572). He grants that this point is hard to grasp:

> It is certainly hard to grasp that the same human being stands under two total determinations which are not merely opposed but mutually exclusive; that the same human being, in the *simul* of today, is both the old man of yesterday and the new man of tomorrow, the captive of yesterday and the free man of tomorrow, the slothful recumbent of yesterday and the erect man of tomorrow. (ibid., p. 572)

It may seem much better to say that the believer is still partially old and already partially new. Nonetheless, we are badly advised, Barth states, if we abandon the *totus/totus* relation for a *partim/partim*, 'because we fear the severity of the antithesis' (ibid.). For, from the perspective of a properly Christocentric eschatology of participation, descriptive adequacy requires us to say that 'the new human being is the whole human being; and so too is the old' (ibid.). In a striking parallel to Luther, which leaves nothing to be desired in showing how thoroughly Barth assimilates Luther's *simul* into his doctrine of sanctification, Barth describes the believer's situation as nothing less than '*simul peccator et sanctus*' (ibid., p. 575).

What sanctification under the sign of Luther's *simul* means in practice, Barth maintains, is attempting neither too little nor too much. On the one hand, 'there is order and sequence in this *simul*. There is direction – the movement to a goal' (ibid., p. 573). Sin persists in the life of faith, but, by the perpetual operation of grace, sin nonetheless has no dominion (cf. Rom. 6:14). In our conversion God frees us from sin's dominion once and for all, and then continually again and again. The new form of life is possible as it is made actual. On the other hand, humility is still very much the order of the day. Sanctification is not the final state of redemption, but only its provisional anticipation. 'Let us be honest,' says Barth. 'What are we with out little conversion, our little repentance and reviving, our little ending and new beginning, our changed lives?' (*CD* IV/2, p. 582). How can we possibly apply the great categories of the New Testament directly to ourselves? How can we possibly say of ourselves that we have passed from death to life, from darkness to light, that our old humanity has died and that the new is risen from the dead? We cannot say these things of ourselves directly, Barth suggests, but only indirectly. We can say them because of who we are in him, because of our sanctification 'as fulfilled and effectively realized in him' (ibid., p. 583). We can say them because we have been included in his work by grace and actively partake of it by faith. For that reason, and despite the sin in us that remains, 'we are borne by the great movement by which he has fulfilled' (ibid., p. 584).

To sum up: for Barth as for Luther, our *participatio Christi* is fully bound up with the *perfectio Christi*, on the one hand, and the *imperfectio peccati*, on the other. Barth applies this grammar to sanctification in a way that clearly departs from Calvin and echoes Luther, but in the end is distinctively his own. Because, by definition, sin and sanctity are mutually exclusive, and because even after baptism we still remain sinners in ourselves, we are sanctified not by the gradual growth of Christ into us, or of us into Christ, as Calvin supposed, but by the perpetual operation of grace in the life of faith, which breaks the dominion of sin. This perpetual operation is rooted in our active participation in Christ, who, in the strict and proper sense, is and remains our sanctification in himself. Just as sin's guilt was removed by the humiliation of the Son of God for our justification by the gift of our participation in his righteousness, so sin's bondage was removed by the exaltation of the Son of Man by the gift of our participation in his new and unending life in communion with God. In either case the pattern is the same. Christ has included us in himself, in his person and work, as whole persons by grace. This inclusion reaches its fulfilment when we are moved to participate in it actively, first provisionally by faith, and then finally in the great consummation by sight.

Conclusion

When Barth shifted his focus from Calvin's emphasis on the gradual to Luther's emphasis on the perpetual, he incurred certain losses. Calvin had seen the gradual operation of grace more clearly than the perpetual, and Luther had elevated the perpetual operation of grace over the gradual. But both Reformation theologians retained a definite place for the gradual in a way that Barth simply did not. Von Balthasar may or may not be correct to suggest that the 'real and vibrant' history of humanity with God is to be sought at the existential level or directly in the life of faith. Barth would have vigorously disputed that aspect of von Balthasar's point. He would have countered that the real and vibrant history von Balthasar is seeking took place for our sakes in Jesus Christ. Nevertheless, unlike both Calvin and Luther, Barth clearly devotes little attention to the possibility of growth and progress in the Christian life. It is important to see that Barth does not eliminate this possibility entirely. 'To live a holy life,' he wrote, 'is to be raised and driven with increasing definiteness from the centre of this revealed truth, and therefore to live in conversion with growing sincerity, depth and precision' (*CD* IV/2, p. 566). What is striking, however, is how seldom such statements appear in his dogmatics, and how underdeveloped they remain. Barth left a large logical space at this point that remains to be more adequately filled.

At the existential level Luther sees grace confronting faith in three ways: once and for all, again and again, and more and more – in that diminishing order of significance. In Calvin (who also accepts the once and for all), the again-and-again aspect recedes from prominence in favour of a strong emphasis on the more and more. By contrast, in Barth (for whom the once and for all is also strong), the retrieval of *simul iustus et peccator* entailed a corresponding re-emphasis on the again-and-again aspect so characteristic of Luther, while the more-and-more aspect in Barth greatly recedes from view. For ecumenical theology, it is Luther's overall scheme that would seem to hold the most promise – not only for integrating the countervailing emphases of Calvin and Barth, but also for doing greater justice to the gradualism of non-Reformation soteriologies (for example, as in Roman Catholicism and Eastern Orthodoxy) than the unsettled questions of the Reformation managed ever to do, and that still remain urgent after Barth.

Notes

1 I would like to express my gratitude for the help I received on the Calvin section of this essay from Rinse Reeling Brouwer, Anthony N.S. Lane, and the late Heiko A. Oberman.
2 Quotations will be from the Battles translation (Calvin, 1960) unless otherwise indicated.
3 In Allen's translation (Calvin, 1928); further quotations from this translation will be marked 'Allen'.
4 As Brouwer has helpfully pointed out to me, Calvin had another reason for treating sanctification first before he turned to justification. Although parrying Roman Catholic polemics undoubtedly played a role in this arrangement (III.16.1–4), another important reason seems to have been a difference with certain colleagues. Unlike Luther, Melanchthon and Bucer, Calvin wanted to show that repentance was a consequence of faith, not a condition for its possibility. 'Repentance,' he urged, 'not only immediately follows faith but is produced by it .... Those who imagine that repentance precedes faith, instead of being produced by it, have never been acquainted with its power' (III.3.1, Allen revised). Compare this, for example, with Melanchthon's contrary though irenic comment: Apology, art. 12, 45 in *The Book of Concord* (Tappert, 1959, pp.187–88). Unlike his colleagues, Calvin redefines 'repentance' significantly to include 'the whole of conversion to God' (*totam ad Deum conversionem*) (III.3.5). Nevertheless, the material point remains that, for Calvin, justification and sanctification were given to faith simultaneously and inseparably, though also variously, so that the order of their presentation was discretionary.
5 Note that Calvin can speak of sanctification from two distinct, though complementary, vantage-points. On the one hand, it is the communication of Christ's righteousness to us (III.2.24), while on the other, it is our being drawn into conformity with Christ (III.6.3), and in particular with his death and resurrection (through *mortificatio* and *vivificatio*).
6 For qualified but still Augustinian–Thomistic-sounding phraseology in Calvin, see, for example, III.14.20, 21. For phraseology more reminiscent of Scotus and Ockham, see III.17.15, where Calvin approves, though critically transcends, the Franciscan idea of 'accepting grace'.

7   St Thomas Aquinas, *Summa Theologiae* 1a2ae, Question 114, 5.2 (Aquinas, 1972, p. 215, translation revised).

8   As Brouwer has suggested to me, a favourable interpretation of Calvin might still be possible despite the ambiguities and uncertainties in the odd passages I have cited. Perhaps an asymmetry may be discerned within both the *duplex gratia* and the *duplex acceptio*. In the case of double grace, the imputation of righteousness (justification) would not be on the same level nor serve the same function in salvation as righteousness' existential impartation (sanctification), so that the former would take precedence over the latter. A similar pattern could then be posited for double acceptance. Precedence would be granted to acceptance on the basis of the imputation of Christ's righteousness. Divine acceptance on the basis of sanctification would then again have a different status. As Calvin suggests at one point, good works serve to praise God insofar as they come from God and go back to God despite their manifest shortcomings. In this way 'the generosity of God ... bestows unearned rewards upon works that merit no such thing' (III.15.3). Acceptance on the basis of sanctification could be interpreted in light of this divine generosity. While I find this suggestion to be attractive, I think it best not to let it obscure the very real ambiguities. The openings that Calvin unwittingly left to moralism were not without significance as the Reformed tradition subsequently developed.

9   Calvin's famous statement at the beginning of *Institutes*, Book III, as quoted earlier, is therefore, from Barth's standpoint, at best a half truth: 'As long as Christ remains outside of us, and we are separated from him, all that he has suffered and done for the salvation of the human race remains useless and of no value for us' (III.1.1). Christ's relationship to us, Barth would counter, does not so entirely depend on our relationship to him. We may be separated from him, but he is not separated from us, not even as long as he remains outside of us. For the salvation of the human race, he has indeed suffered and done many things – indeed, all that is necessary. And what he has suffered and done is fulfilled only when we acknowledge, receive and participate in it actively by faith. Nonetheless, what he has suffered and done for human salvation is not merely *sufficient* for our salvation until we receive it, nor (even worse) is it merely *potentially* sufficient, subject to our continual fulfilment of certain conditions. In some strong eschatological sense it is already *efficacious* – not just for some but for all. In that strong prevenient sense it does *not* remain useless and of no value for us before it finally moves us to faith. For it continually overcomes, or is disposed to overcome, our lack of faith. Even in the best of cases our faith is very weak. Who is there who does not have to say each day, 'Lord, I believe, help my unbelief'? Who is there who does not have to ask each day for forgiveness? Those lost sinners who come to participate in Christ by faith are, for Barth, a sign of hope for the whole sorry human race. Although we do not know exactly what form the fulfilment of this hope will take (and in particular *whether or how* it will exclude all final tragedy and loss), the universal efficacy of Christ for human salvation may under no circumstances be gainsaid. The inordinately restrictive, and inadequately Christocentric, logic of the Augustinian tradition, which Calvin here and elsewhere notoriously exemplifies, represents not only a failure to think through with full consistency the Christocentric eschatology of the Reformation, but also to do real justice to the great breadth and fullness of New Testament hope. 'After this I looked, and behold, *a great multitude which no man could number*, from *every* nation, from *all* tribes and peoples and tongues, standing before the Lamb, clothed in white robes, with palm branches in their hands, and crying out with a loud voice, "Salvation belongs to our God who sits upon the throne, and to the Lamb"' (Rev. 7: 9–10, emphasis added). Who can doubt that the prevailing Augustinian tradition, in Protestant no less than Catholic circles, has put a great damper on the Church's joyful reception and witness to so great a hope?

10 In Barth's eschatology the relation between the perfect tense, the present tense, and the future tense is a *totus/totus/totus* relation. The one *parousia* of Jesus Christ may be said to be totally past, totally present and yet also totally future. Its substance, scope and content remain constant in the midst of its three basic and very different forms: (i) resurrection; (ii) outpouring of the Holy Spirit; (iii) final consummation and universal revelation (*CD* IV/3, pp. 292–96, 910–15).

11 Cf. Hans W. Frei: 'His identity and his presence are given together in indissoluble unity. But the proper order for understanding this fact is to begin with his identity ... ' (Frei, 1975, p. 149). To this we

might add that, with his identity and presence, Christ's future is also indissolubly given. 'The future mode of his presence will be a significant, incorporative summing up of history' (Frei, 1975, p. 160). Again, the order for understanding remains the same. His identity in all three forms is defined strictly by the *Christus adventus* – by his being in the saving act of his one life history, by his person as enacted in his work, and his work as incorporated in his person, by his self-enactment there and then of his identity and mission as the world's incarnate Saviour and Lord.

References

Aquinas, T. (1972), *Summa Theologiae*, vol. 30, ed. C. Ernst; New York: MacGraw-Hill.

Calvin, J. (1928), *Institutes*, trans. J. Allen, Philadelphia: Presbyterian Board of Christian Education.

Calvin, J. (1960), *Institutes of the Christian Religion*, ed. J.T. McNeill, trans. F.L. Battles, Philadelphia: Westminster.

Frei, H. (1975), *The Identity of Jesus Christ*, Philadelphia: Fortress Press.

Luther, M. (1960), 'The Disputation Concerning Justification (1536)' in L.W. Spitz (ed.) *Luther's Works*, vol. 34, Philadelphia: Muhlenberg Press

McLellend, J.C. (1957), *The Visible Words of God: An Exposition of the Sacramental Theology of Peter Martyr Vermigli*, Edinburgh: Oliver and Boyd.

Oberman, H.A (1986), *The Dawn of the Reformation*; Grand Rapids, MI: Eerdmans.

Tappert, T (ed.) (1959), *The Book of Concord*, Philadelphia: Fortress Press.

von Balthasar, H.U. (1992), *The Theology of Karl Barth: Exposition and Interpretation*, trans. E.T. Oakes, San Francisco: Ignatius.

Wevers, R.F. (1992), *A Concordance to Calvin's Institutio 1559*, Grand Rapids, MI: Diagramma.

CHAPTER 6

Exile, Freedom and Thanksgiving: Barth and Hans Urs von Balthasar

Ben Quash

In the prison of his days
Teach the free man how to praise.
(*In Memory of W.B. Yeats*, W.H. Auden)

Barth and von Balthasar began the task of conversation with each other in Basel in 1940, when von Balthasar arrived back in his native Switzerland from Munich, to take up the post of university chaplain. Barth was already there as a professor in the Protestant faculty, and von Balthasar (having read and been inspired by the early volumes of his *Church Dogmatics*) longed to meet and talk with him in person. From that point onwards, we are looking at theologies that cross-fertilize. We are dealing with a von Balthasar who in the 1940s dragged Barth's *Church Dogmatics* II/1 around with him in his briefcase wherever he went ('like a cat carrying a kitten', said Barth),[1] and a Barth who regularly attended von Balthasar's lectures on 'Karl Barth and Catholicism' at the end of the decade, in order, as he put it, 'to learn more about myself' (Busch, 1976, p. 362). These were theologians who paid real attention to one another on substantive issues, and not with the 'weary bourgeois tolerance' which Barth lamented in so much ecumenical dialogue. It is this seriousness which nourished the extraordinary fruitfulness of their dialogue.

Above all, von Balthasar seized on Barth's firm insistence on the distinctiveness of the Christian revelation, the seriousness of its call to a radical newness of faith and life, and consequently the disturbing and challenging character of the Christian presence in the world. His thought was governed by these emphases all through his life, even as he filtered them through a thoroughly Catholic ecclesiology. He concurred with – indeed, was profoundly influenced by – Barth's drastically Trinitarian vision, and his affirmation of the utter sovereignty of the divine initiative. We begin by outlining these broad convergences.

The Priority of God, the Uniqueness of Christ, and the Importance of the Church

It is important to register that we are not dealing here only with two isolated theological titans who share an unusual, slightly freakish, bond of sympathy. There is a background to this dialogue and also to all the convergences that we will see between von Balthasar and Barth. There are bigger, and fascinating, parallel movements in Catholic and Protestant theology – movements of which von Balthasar and Barth are prominent representatives, but not sole proprietors. Erich Przywara, for example, was a profoundly important shaping influence on both von Balthasar *and* Barth. No one should underestimate the influence that he had on Barth's thought at a crucial stage in its development. In the 1920s Przywara frequently published articles on contemporary theological trends in the Catholic theological journal *Stimmen der Zeit*, and Barth often figured in these. It was Przywara who criticized in the early Barth a certain 'one-sidedness', which closed off the possibility of any unity between God and human beings. Barth, said Przywara, puts

> … in the place of the 'analogy' between God and the creature the pure 'negation'. If the *analogia entis* of the Catholic concept of God means the mysterious tension of a 'similar-dissimilar', corresponding to the tension of the 'God in us and above us', then in the Protestant concept of God, the 'similarity' has been completely crossed out. (Przywara, quote in McCormack, 1995, pp. 320–21)

In remarks like these, Przywara highlighted the lack of an adequate doctrine of the incarnation in Barth's early theology (McCormack, 1995, p. 321), and this criticism hit home: Barth devoted serious attention to it. As McCormack puts it, 'if an overriding stimulus to Barth's future development were to be sought in the winter of 1923/4, then the first place to look would be his encounter with Catholicism' (ibid.). So the cross-fertilization which we see between Barth and von Balthasar has its precursor in this earlier encounter, and the more mature incarnational Christo-centrism of Barth's *Church Dogmatics* – a Christocentrism which was to be one of the things which Barth and von Balthasar most vigorously held in common – owes much to the influence of this Silesian priest.[2]

What Barth looked for in a dialogue partner – and von Balthasar (like Przywara before him) had it – was a proper sense of the sovereignty of the divine initiative. This had to be the first and the last principle of convergence, around which all the others would congregate. Barth recognized this principle in Przywara's *von Gott her* ('from God's side') though he later questioned the adequacy of Przywara's adherence to it. And because of what Barth read and approved of in such texts as Karl Adam's *Das Wesen des Katholizismus* (for example, the statement that God is 'the real I of the Church' (Barth, quoted in McCormack, 1995, p. 382) and contemporary Catholicism's preservation of the Trinitarian and Christological doctrines of the early Church), he was bold to assert that 'in its presuppositions for the Church, in spite of all contradictions, it is closer to the Reformers than is the Church of the Reformation' (ibid.), this being a characteristic shot fired in his running battle against liberal Protestantism.

To understand what is at stake in Barth's concept of God, we need to be clear, despite the inadequacy of the terms, that Barth was a theological 'realist', though he never for a moment denied the role of the knowing activity of the human subject. He did not, in other words, completely dismiss subjectivity in his haste to get at the object. But he did think in terms of a divine 'objectivity'. He was what Bruce McCormack so effectively characterizes as a '*critical* realist'. He accepted Kant's critique of metaphysics, because he accepted the validity of Kant's epistemology, at least 'where it touched upon knowledge of empirical reality' (McCormack, 1995, p. 130). But, that said, he still maintained that 'the divine being [is] real, whole, and complete in itself apart from the knowing activity of the human subject; indeed, the reality of God precedes all human knowing' (ibid., p. 67). Von Balthasar was in profound agreement with Barth here, as is shown by his assaults on certain brands of mysticism (those which suggest the identity of divine and human in the depths of the human subject) and their issue in Idealism and Romanticism of various kinds. It could be said that the whole of *Herrlichkeit* – and, in particular, the opening volume and the volumes on the history of metaphysics (vols 4 and 5) – are an exercise in critical realism.

Barth never lost his commitment to the *von Gott her*. What did happen was that he moved from an early stress on a relatively formal notion of revelation breaking in on us as the wholly other 'Word of God', to a more substantial, historically-extended appreciation of the incarnate form of God's full revelation in Christ. The *Word* is spoken in the man *Jesus*. A stringent actualism, we may say, undergoes a kind of critical correction. To use McCormack's words, '[t]he covenantal dealings of God with humankind in history are grounded in the eternal decision in which God determines Himself in Jesus Christ to be gracious. Where this is presupposed, it is then understood that the acts of God take place against the background of a history' (ibid., p. 456). The absolute opposition of eternity and time (the negation of time by eternity) gives way to a notion of time's assimilation to eternity – but only by the sovereign initiative of God.

The crucial foundations of a dialogue with von Balthasar are laid in this development in Barth's thought. What we see emerging is a conception of revelation that allows it to make use of creaturely conditions – time and space, form and matter. Certainly, this conception is accompanied by an insistence that 'the content of revelation can never be cut off from the *act* of revealing, that is, from the God who freely and sovereignly *chooses* to reveal himself (von Balthasar, 1992a, p. 48). But there is an increased sense that the assertion of this freedom need not entail (always and in principle) a hostility or destructiveness towards created terms.

Revelation, then, has a form (Christ's form), part of which is an historical *Tendenz* (Christ's history). And all things – *all* things – are made sense of in relation to this form. Creation is only understood when recognized as the outer ground of the covenant made eternally in Christ. No useful doctrine of creation can be 'fleshed out without reference to the covenantal purposes of God' and no worthwhile anthropology can be devised independently of 'reflection upon the true, restored humanity disclosed in Christ' (McCormack, 1995, p. 454). Thus, what is called Barth's 'Christocentrism' (which von Balthasar, as is often said, shares) is born. Von Balthasar puts it like this: 'in everything that pertains to [the] world – the riches offered by creation: science, art, technology – [Barth] never for a moment abstracts from the light that Christ radiates upon these riches' (von Balthasar, 1992a, p. 197). And there could be few more evocative characterizations of von Balthasar's own perspective than that. It expresses the comprehensiveness of a vision which for him, as for Barth, is illuminated by the light of Christ. But it expresses the particularism of the Christological commitment, too. Von Balthasar, paraphrasing Barth with approval, writes that:

> Whenever a person thinks he knows what life is all about because of an acquaintance with the general, then we know right away that he lacks the ear for the message of the special and particular. Or, to phrase it with more nuance: whoever wants to start with the general must do so in the strictest obedience: by interpreting everything in view of the particular, expecting wisdom and direction from its concrete indications. (Ibid., p. 195)

Like Barth, von Balthasar knows Christ to be the *concretissimum*, and not latent or passive but vibrantly active as such, in a personal history which animates and gives meaning to everything else: that means 'the vibrancy of both Scripture and tradition and the development of dogma' (ibid., p. 16), as well as the life of the creation in its ordering to (or for the sake of) the covenant between Christ and his Church.

The dynamism of both men's theological vision indicates that the actualism of the early Barth, though made less contrary by his incarnational corrective (or enhancement), still pertains. This, too, is not a point of difference from von Balthasar, but rather the opposite. For both men, aesthetics is ordered to dramatics. *We see the form* because *God acts*, and summons us to respond. The form we see is far from inert. Inertia in such an encounter must, in shame, be attributed to our sin. Barth's seeing, like von Balthasar's, is a moment in a drama 'in Christ', between the believer and God, and his theology then seeks to convey it: 'Barth focuses on the Word, fully and exclusively, that its full splendour might radiate out to the reader. Who but Barth has gazed so breathlessly and tirelessly on his subject, watching it develop and blossom in all its power before his eyes?' (ibid., p. 26). In this concern with the actual, von Balthasar is delighted to associate Barth with Catholic thinkers who follow the same trajectory, including one of his own inspirations, Maurice Blondel. Both Blondel and Barth, von Balthasar notes, wanted

> ... to be pioneers of the concrete and historical aspects of ontology ... their intent was entirely theological: they wanted to draw all intraworldly being and essence (whose self-sufficient validity they did not deny) to the concrete, personal and historical Logos. (Ibid., p. 341)

Amongst contemporary Catholic thinkers, von Balthasar invokes others who articulate a kind of actualism: Guardini, Michael Schmaus, and F.X. Arnold.[3]

That these are very significant areas of convergence between von Balthasar and Barth should begin to become apparent by now. And we can add yet more. There is the fact that both men are convinced that theology must be done from within the Church – that is, in the place where revelation is being heard (or 'seen') – and responded to in the community of the redeemed. Barth, like von Balthasar, could insist that '[t]heology is ... a function of the Church' (quoted in McCormack, 1995,

p. 416). Barth, too, was increasingly, and perhaps surprisingly, ready to give a high status to the ecclesial mediation of revelation (while never taking any initiative away from God). As early as the time of his *Göttingen Dogmatics* (that is, 1924–25) he could write of how, in McCormack's words, 'it is impossible ... for the Scriptures to come to us as the Word of God unless there be an authoritative canon and text, Fathers and dogmas and teaching office. These factors form the "empty canals" through which the Word comes to us' (McCormack, 1995, p. 348; cf. Barth, 1991, pp. 245–46). Von Balthasar is thoroughly committed to this idea, which he develops extensively in terms of the 'objective Spirit' of divine revelation as manifested in the Church as institution.

Finally, and also related to Barth's understanding of the Church, we see von Balthasar appreciating in his Protestant partner a real openness to the Catholic roots of Protestant doctrine (most especially in Anselm and Thomas), so much so that he can be acclaimed not so much a theologian of the Reformation as a theologian of the Church:

> The Church for which Barth is writing his *Dogmatics* has not been founded at the Reformation: no one can found the Church but Christ. That is why Barth avers that he has just as much right as we do to lay claim to the pre-Reformation witnesses and documents of the Church. They are for him the witnesses of the understanding of Scripture and revelation of the *Una Sancta,* the one and holy Church, which will endure as the visible/invisible Body of Christ through all time .... In Barth's *Dogmatics* theology attains a breadth of subject matter and historical range that is coextensive with the Catholic understanding. (von Balthasar, 1992a, p. 23)

Von Balthasar means to give Barth high praise when he writes in his assessment of his theology that he is 'a theologian and not a reformer' (ibid., p. 382).

All this is to show, in broad terms, the shared range of influences and some of the main convergences between Barth and von Balthasar. They are significant. What will interest me in the remainder of this essay, however, is something more specific (although, to be sure, something thoroughly rooted in their mutually sympathetic doctrines of God, their respective commitments to the particularity of the revelation in Christ and the universality of its reach). What will interest me is one very striking set of convergent themes in Barth's and von Balthasar's work – themes which seem to me to set a continuing agenda for contemporary theology. The convergence of the themes, however, does not entail straightforward agreement between the two thinkers in the way they choose to proceed. On the contrary, sharp but theologically generative differences are opened up by Barth's and von Balthasar's common concentration on the interlinked ideas I hope to outline.

The first idea is *exile*. Both Barth and von Balthasar see the human condition as one of alienation – a sense made perhaps more marked than in theologies of the previous century by the series of catastrophes and uprootings which afflicted Europe in their lifetimes. Both also felt the Church being threatened by something like a new Dark Age. This fuels the urgent intensity of their respective work, and their conviction that

Christian life can only be strongly *different* from its surroundings – a kind of subversion. They both see the human figure – the Christian especially – as in exile, and this exilic state is the state Christ adopts in his great work of salvation. For Barth, the exilic motif finds expression in 'The Way of the Son of God into the Far Country'; for von Balthasar, in the descent into hell. Christians who participate in Christ on these terms will find the world both more a place of exile and yet simultaneously more the place where Christ is to be found and served.

But their second concern is with *freedom*. The subversion which the Christian engages in (for both theologians) is the subversion that comes about through a liberating obedience to Christ. We are set free to live in response to the command of God (for Barth); to realize our God-given 'mission' (for von Balthasar). Freedom is perhaps the keynote of Barth's ethics, as well as of von Balthasar's extraordinarily sustained contemplation of the possibilities of drama in relation to theological speaking and Christian living. In fact, it is likely that one of the principal inspirations behind his *Theodramatik* was that he wanted to *intensify* Barth's vision of freedom, feeling that much of what Barth had to say about the radiant horizon of eschatological hope, and about the relation of human action to the divine action, tended to negate human creativity and the urgent call to cooperate with God. All was subsumed (von Balthasar felt) into a great and triumphant divine 'yes' to which humans could contribute little. The second main section will therefore look more closely at whether von Balthasar was justified in levelling this criticism at Barth and will examine what *Theodramatik* can actually be said to *add* to Barth's theology of freedom. It will argue that Barth has richer resources to resist von Balthasar's criticism than he is given credit for, and that von Balthasar is vulnerable in his own way to a denigration of creaturely creativity.

In concluding the examination of these themes, there will be an opportunity to ask whether an abiding common aim remains perceptible in the two theologians' work, despite the differences opened up by the way they each work out their understanding of freedom. The answer, I will argue, is 'yes', because, for both men, the freedom that is conceived of finds fruition in *thanksgiving*. 'Teach the free man how to praise' – that is what both theologians set out to do, despite their conviction that the human state is a state of exile. Barth's theology – and therefore his ethics – is full of a sense that praise is the vocation of the human creature. Thanksgiving, too, is a dominant theme in von Balthasar's theology of the cross – and this is one of the things that makes him so different from Moltmann. Christ on the cross is engaged, above all, in an act of praise – of self-relinquishment motivated by joy at the Father's reciprocal gratitude and joy. This is a powerful and challenging theme, which opens onto a full-blown Trinitarian theology.

Theologies of Exile

Underlying this section is the conviction that concepts of exile and restoration are profoundly eschatological when handled by Christians. They occur in the theologies of Barth and von Balthasar for the same reasons that both theologians are concerned to re-articulate the claims of eschatology at the heart of the doctrine of Christ, in continuity with all that the New Testament witness seems to demand. They also occur with an intensity that was almost certainly informed by historical experience.

The twentieth-century revival in the strength and centrality of eschatology for Christian theology is well documented. The idea that Jesus Christ's eschatological motives and expectations were a dispensable addendum to the core of his message – just a bit of window dressing – was dismantled by a succession of scholars, amongst whom Albert Schweitzer is one of the most cited. The impact of the Great War on Europe's perception of its historical development as a continuous advance towards a more enlightened and freer future also played its part in changing the focus of Christian hope. Only in this light can we fully appreciate Barth's challenge in the *Epistle to the Romans* – his announcement that the revolution of God is (in Jüngel's paraphrase):

> ... a concrete event which does not proceed from this world but breaks into this world from the beyond. This event transforms the entire human race, not just particular individuals. It is a 'divine worldwide revolution!' ... Barth asserts an eschatological immediacy: neither 'trust in God,' nor 'solving the riddle of life,' nor 'certainty of salvation' can be divorced from eschatology. (Jüngel, 1986, p. 33)

Salvation had to be rethought in the face of the collapse of the nineteenth-century myth of progress – both what salvation was *from* and what it was *for*. Barth and von Balthasar develop Christologies to which the belief in the need for eschatological renewal is intrinsic, and in which Christ's action is seen to be relevant to and potent in the present only because of its decisive eschatological character. These Christs can be contrasted with the exemplary Christs of the previous two centuries: Christs who reassure us that salvation dovetails neatly with our human aspirations and projects (our moral ones most of all), and that we have it in us to lead a good life like his.

Before looking at the outworkings in Barth's and von Balthasar's thought of this shift in twentieth-century theological perceptions, it is worth looking at how their lives were affected in very immediate ways by events that made 'aliens' of them. These events, too, play a part in shaping the eschatological vividness of their work, and in particular of their Christologies.

The Exilic Biographies of Barth and von Balthasar

The remarkable thing about Christians, says the early Christian text, the *Letter to Diognetus*, is that they 'differ from other people neither in land nor speech nor custom, for they do not inhabit their own cities somewhere', and yet at the same time they demonstrate 'the amazing and admittedly strange establishment of their own republic' (*Letter to Diognetus*, 5.1–6.2).

In Barth and von Balthasar we are dealing with theologians who – despite significant time spent in Germany – lived for most of their lives in their native country, Switzerland. Like the people referred to in the *Letter to Diognetus*, they were superficially entirely at home. They could not be identified by land or speech or custom as 'out of place'. The turmoil that affected Europe in the 1930s did not remove them to any foreign land; rather, it brought them back to the country of their birth, where both of them remained until they died – Barth in 1968, von Balthasar 20 years later. And yet they can, in certain respects, be considered exiles. It is this distinctive experience (and what I think are its 'reverberations' in their respective Christologies) that I want to look at in this section.[4]

On 8 July 1935 Karl Barth and his family took up residence at St Albanring 186 in Basel. It was a sort of homecoming – his new home was just a short distance, in fact, from the place of his birth. But it was also a move which reflected complicated circumstances, and provoked mixed feelings. He was more than a little reluctant to leave Bonn. 'I have spent the liveliest and richest years of my teaching life here', he said at the time (quoted in Busch, 1976, p. 262). 'I was almost somewhat depressed when I returned home to Basel, where I was surrounded by narrower questions than I was there' (ibid.).

In his student days, and also when he first took up an academic position in Göttingen, Barth had felt something of a foreigner in Germany, and some of his early political restraint may be attributed to this uncertainty about his status as a German speaker yet not a German citizen. On the other hand, after having lived and taught there, he never lost the sense that he was part of Germany and Germany part of him. By the late 1920s he was clearly well at home, ready to defend his involvement in the fight against National Socialism[5] against those who accused him of not having the capacity to 'feel' like a German. At the beginning of 1926 his status in the Prussian civil service in fact gave him German citizenship as well as Swiss. Barth wrote: 'I had become a person with dual nationality, so occasionally I was able to join in "Deutschland, Deutschland, über alles ..."' (quoted in Busch, 1976, p. 189). Meanwhile, Switzerland was not always friendly to him. In 1927, for example, he was vigorously attacked in the Berne press for his supposed pacifism and general lack of patriotism. This played a part in Barth's decision to stay longer abroad. 'A number of Swiss in earlier periods have felt happier here than in their homeland', he wrote.[6]

The sequence of events by which Barth's teaching position in Bonn was made untenable, by which he was banned from public speaking in Germany, and by which his books were prohibited, is well known. On 7 November 1934, he made the decision to refuse to give the oath of allegiance to the Führer in the prescribed form. On 22 November he left the *Reichsbruderrat* over the appointment of Bishop Marahrens as head of the VKL – a man who had publicly declared his support for the Nazi *Weltanschauung*. Barth was suspended on 26 November. He objected at the Bonn court on the following day. On 20 December the disciplinary chamber filed his dismissal with the administration in Köln. Barth did in fact successfully appeal. Even so, on 21 June of the following year he was pensioned off by the secretary of higher education for the Reich and left for Basel more or less immediately.

Barth's is therefore a paradoxical sort of exile. Returning to Switzerland, with Germany and the German situation in his blood, he was at home and in exile simultaneously. Being in Switzerland at this time felt to Barth like swimming against the stream. He felt isolated and constrained in many ways. And yet, 'Switzerland's frontiers were mine too':

> I considered it my most immediate and important duty to play my part in seeing that theology should be carried on, thoroughly and 'as if nothing had happened', in at least one place in an insane Europe – in our Swiss island, and especially in our border city of Basel from which one could simultaneously look over into triumphant Germany, which later suffered so much, and conquered France, which later rose again. And as never before, I was glad to be in a position to serve this cause, which was worthwhile, enduring and full of promise, no matter what happened. (Barth, 1966, p. 52)

Of course, the condition of being 'at home' and yet also 'in exile' in relation to the Swiss–German political situation is not strictly comparable with the condition of being both 'of this world' and 'not of this world' in an eschatological sense. I think, though, that in Barth's positive way of handling his constrained position in Switzerland we have an insight into his attitude to that more general state of exile which, for him, is the Christian condition. Christian life in a fallen world requires not escapism, but rather that the Christian 'keep busy on the home front'![7] The Christian's duty is to live simultaneously *within* and *contrary to* the 'insanity' of his or her surroundings. To recall the *Letter to Diognetus*, we are to live in the present 'exile' in a way that confidently demonstrates 'the amazing and admittedly strange establishment of [our] own republic'. As Dietrich Bonhoeffer suggested when he developed his ethical categories of 'ultimate' and 'penultimate', living in a way that assumes a set of responsibilities that exceed any intra-mundane claims upon one will make one a distinctive kind of ethical agent. An eschatological consciousness will have specific effects in particular, practical situations. What Barth and Bonhoeffer also show, conversely, is that particular situations (like that of many people living in the Germany of the 1930s) will frequently inform, shape and intensify an awareness that one has an accountability to God which is not reducible to other kinds of accountability.

There was another experience of alienation in Barth's life which preceded the 1930s but had a powerful effect on him. It should not be ignored because it is perhaps a more direct cause of the eschatological turn in Barth's thought than his subsequent encounter with Nazism and may therefore play an earlier part in shaping his tendency to talk in terms of exile and restoration. This was the break with his former teachers and colleagues, which forced itself on him on 1 August 1914 – the day the First World War broke out. He witnessed his German teachers signing a manifesto in support of the war policy of Kaiser Wilhelm II and Chancellor Bethmann-Hollweg – an event which he described as being like 'the twilight of the gods':[8] 'a whole world of exegesis, ethics, dogmatics and preaching, which I had hitherto held to be essentially trustworthy, was shaken to the foundations' (quoted in Busch, 1976, p. 81). Barth found himself no longer at home in the world of theological scholarship he had once inhabited happily. He found himself in exile where once he had been at home. The fact that his departure from Germany was not the beginning but the continuation of the experience of being an outsider is one we will return to.

In turning to von Balthasar, it can be seen that the decisive experience of exile for him, too, was exile from a community that once sustained him (in his case, the Society of Jesus), rather than exile in response to the more obvious political forces that raged in Europe and caused him to return to his native country. These latter forces were not irrelevant to him, of course. Von Balthasar's citizenship was, in many ways, a citizenship of Catholic Europe rather than just of Switzerland. He lived and studied in Germany (Berlin and München) and France (Lyons) for vital periods in his formation. His doctoral dissertation, *Apokalypse der deutschen Seele*, was an account of German philosophical and literary thought which seemed almost a forewarning of the apocalyptic neo-paganism which was to erupt in Germany under Hitler, and which he viewed as the debased issue of Idealism's totalitarian disregard of individual dignity and freedom. One of his great influences (and one of the people with whom he was in closest sympathy) was, as has already been hinted, Henri de Lubac – a brave resister of the Vichy state, who took a leading part in denouncing Nazi ideology and anti-Semitism. When, in 1940, von Balthasar retreated to Switzerland – accepting the post of student chaplain at the University of Basel and beginning his friendship with Barth – he was not, of course, forced (as Barth was) out of a prior post (until that point he had been editor of the above-mentioned journal *Stimmen der Zeit* in Munich). But he saw that, in Switzerland, he would have the freedom to work on texts from literature, philosophy and the theological tradition that he hoped to keep alive for a future Europe – the Europe that he hoped would emerge after the barbaric tide which swept around Swiss borders had abated. That was one of the attractions of returning there. Central to his activity when he first arrived in Basel was the work of editing the 'European Series' of the Klosterberg collection: 'a wartime attempt to save Europe's cultural heritage' (Henrici, 1991, p. 15) in the form of 50 short anthologies.[9]

The more personal experience of exile in von Balthasar's life (parallel in some ways to Barth's break with the 'liberal' school) was undoubtedly his departure from the Jesuits. It happened because of his foundation (with Adrienne von Speyr) of a secular institute – a society of consecrated life for laypeople, who continued to live in the world, have jobs and so on: 'Neither the local bishop nor the Jesuit superiors supported the venture, and the Society made it clear, after an interview with its Dutch Father General J.B. Janssens, that Balthasar must choose between the Jesuits on the one hand and his collaborator and spiritual children on the other' (Nichols, 1998, pp. xvii–xviii). Von Balthasar issued this statement to his friends:

> I took this step, for both sides a very grave one, after a long testing of the certainty
> I had reached through prayer that I was being called by God to certain definite

tasks in the Church. The Society felt it could not release me to give these tasks my undivided commitment .... So, for me, the step taken means an application of Christian obedience to God, who at any time has the right to call a man not only out of his physical home or his marriage, but also from his chosen spiritual home in a religious order, so that he can use him for his purposes within the Church. Any resulting advantages or disadvantages in the secular sphere were not under discussion and not taken into account. (Cited in Henrici, 1991, p. 21)

The departure from the Society of Jesus was traumatic for von Balthasar, and the years of his greatest theological productivity which followed (during which he wrote his immense trilogy) were spent in the climate of being at home and not at home – still within the Church, still a priest, but mistrusted by many, on the fringes of ecclesiastical life, and without an official academic post. He played no role in Vatican II, but watched and wrote from the margins of the great new developments in Catholic life.

The Exilic Christologies of Barth and von Balthasar

We now look directly at the Christologies of these two men, in order to suggest how the themes of exile present in their work – along with their eschatological framework – can be considered as a characteristically twentieth-century phenomenon, of which they are leading representatives. I do not want to make unjustifiable claims for the influence of their respective biographies on the way in which Barth and von Balthasar chose to develop their Christologies. I do, however, think that there is call to look very seriously at the dominant role that models of exile play in their presentation of Christ's work. For it is a fact that the descent into hell, for von Balthasar, and what Barth calls 'The way of the Son of God into the far country', are absolutely central to the way in which their thoroughly Christ-centred theologies unfold.

In the Christology of *Church Dogmatics* IV/1 we see Barth describe a movement in God's own being – a movement into all that is against or which seeks to contradict God. Barth uses the term *Fremde* ('foreign sphere') here: 'it is only in the New [Testament] that we see what suffering and death really means, as it becomes the work of God Himself, as God gives Himself to this most dreadful of all foreign spheres' (*CD* IV/1, p. 175). Yet it is only by looking at the way of the Son of God into this foreign sphere – the country that is far from God – that we learn what is truly divine. And it is only by the abasement of Christ's humanity there that humanity is brought home. The 'homecoming' of the Son of Man *coincides* with the way of the Son of God into the far country. The way into exile is walked, transformatively, triumphantly, as the royal road to God.

How does this work? Principally – at this stage of Barth's account – through Christ's exercise of human obedience – his uniquely *free* exercise of human obedience, his exercise of that obedience which other (sinful) human beings cannot manage, but which the covenant between God and man requires. In other words, God reconciles the human *vocation* and our *performance* of this vocation at the place where they are out of joint; he is free at the place of our unfreedom: 'He went into a strange land, but even there, and especially there, He never became a stranger to Himself' (ibid., p. 180). The image of a son going into a far country echoes, of course, the story referred to in English as 'The Prodigal Son' ('The Lost Son' might be a more recognizable description to a German audience). That this is a text drawing on the Jewish paradigm of exile and restoration seems beyond doubt (not least because of the central emphasis it places on the importance of repentance prior to return). Barth has chosen to express a key part of his doctrine of Christ's reconciling work in terms of this paradigm, and he does so vividly. He addresses the *lostness* and the *foreignness* of the human condition apart from God, and then shows how God enters into precisely this condition. He claims for God's Son – for Jesus Christ – that passage to the furthest extreme of degradation which the parable tries to represent. Christ sets the limits to the extension of our lostness, occupying the place where the lowest pitch is reached and the reverse movement set into operation. Christ's entry into this sinfulness and death (the 'limitations' of man, in Barth's terminology: his 'weaknesses', his 'perversities', 'the evil society of this being which is not God and against God' – ibid., p. 158) is therefore unique, unparalleled and transformative. No one goes further from the order and beauty of his Father's house than he; no one travels further to get back to that order and beauty once again.

The importance of exile and restoration imagery for Barth's Christology is apparent here. The Christ he depicts in *Church Dogmatics* IV/1 is the Christ who, both in his earthly life and in his death, makes his hidden, royal way into the place of our exile. And there are consequences for Christians entailed by discipleship of this Christ, in his definition of the place of our exile and his royal freedom in relation to it. Within the eschatological horizons opened up by the life, death and resurrection of Jesus Christ, those men and women who want to live obediently in the covenant and in fellowship with Christ will find themselves able to live differently (*boldly*), expressing not only a this-worldly citizenship and a this-worldly hope, but an eschatological one.

Von Balthasar does *not* talk of Christ going into the far country, like the son in the parable. He talks instead of Christ descending into hell, in a daring and unusual twentieth-century revival of a traditional theological theme which had almost entirely been abandoned. Von Balthasar's theology is like Barth's in that it stresses the whole trajectory of Christ's descent and ascent, humiliation and glorification, as what saves and reconciles humanity to God. The principal difference is that von Balthasar makes more explicit than Barth the fact that this trajectory has as its furthest point not simply the event of the cross, but the very *state of being dead*. Christ sinks like a stone into solidarity with the corpses of the dead – and he does so, we should note, *even though* the victory of the cross has decisively been won. This is not a contradiction. In fact, Christ's solidarity with the corpses is precisely the announcement that the victory has been won. His going to the furthest extreme of deadness is the proclamation that the Son of God *can* reach those in this state; that he can go to the furthest limit of human experience and beyond. Because he is with the dead, they *are saved*.

Barth's Christ is never allowed to appear before us in such a passive state – but there can be little doubt that this descent into hell (which he calls, in his chapter heading in *Mysterium Paschale*, 'Going to the Dead') is von Balthasar's way of expressing that movement of exile and homecoming which Barth testified to in his 'The Way of the Son of God into the Far Country'.

Von Balthasar, like Barth, uses the language of 'territory' to describe Christ's work. '[T]he total depotentiation of the enemy', he writes, 'coincides with a forcible entry into the innermost terrain of his power' (von Balthasar, 1992b, p. 155). Elsewhere, drawing heavily on Gregory of Nyssa, he talks about Christ travelling through the deepest hell, as one not bound by any of the bonds of sin, but 'free among the dead' (ibid., p. 176). He then draws, with Gregory, the analogy between this movement into the depths of Holy Saturday and the movement of the Redeemer into the lostness of the sinful human heart: a spiritual descent into the *corda desperata*.

There is a question – which cannot be dealt with here – about whether von Balthasar's transposition of Christ's archetypal exile into a quasi-mythological sphere removes it from its proper place in the sphere of political action, in which Christians have to make ethical decisions. I have discussed this elsewhere (Quash, 1999, pp. 167–69), and it may be an area in which von Balthasar does not compare well with Barth. There is always a risk in the Christian appropriation of the Jewish exile/restoration paradigm that it will become either too 'otherworldly' or too individualistic, and this danger may be present in von Balthasar's link between the descent into hell and a spiritual experience within the heart.

Certainly, Barth draws more explicit connections between his vision of eschatological citizenship and a proclamation of the *Letter-to-Diognetus*-style divine republic in a 'this-worldly' ethical mode. On the one hand, he does not hide behind the institutional Church. He does not conceive our dual citizenship in terms of a straightforward 'Church–state' dualism, and he does not allow one to retreat from secular politics into an ecclesial sanctuary. On the other hand, and equally firmly, he does not remove eschatological citizenship from the area of real social relations, and make it a matter for the private self.[10] The freedom attained in Christ is expressed in a willed solidarity with the world and the frightened exiles within it, and, in remaining committed to the world in this way, the world is itself transformed. He argues that the way in which we act towards our neighbours is intrinsically related to how we witness to our citizenship 'above'. He believes that our 'exiled' state is the proper *medium* for enacting our eschatological citizenship.

Despite the fact that there are significant differences of emphasis between these two theologians, both of them think out their Christologies through a strong paradigm of exile and restoration. They go on to infer from this a model of Christian discipleship in which Christians can be free in Christ even when constrained by the world, and to be 'at home' in Christ even when in exile in the world – though only through an obedience like his.

Eschatology Renewed

After this relatively close look at features of Barth's and von Balthasar's Christologies, I want to finish by setting them back again within that wider context, which helps to make sense of their decision to use exilic motifs. As I suggested before, exile/restoration imagery has always gone hand-in-hand with eschatology for Christians, in a way that seems to stem from Christ's own teaching. As has been argued in particular by Tom Wright, the first Christians, like all first-century Jews, were shaped by the deeply ingrained self-perception that they were still in some way exiled (even when they were living in their own country). The dispersion and the continuing foreign domination of Israel were, of course, considered part of the evidence. But the exile was also considered to be evident in the failure on the part of many Jews to obey the Law – in other words, in the continuing gap between vocation and performance on Israel's part. This explains why calls for repentance are so characteristic of the many Jewish groups in Jesus' day, who believed that the exile perdured and hoped for national deliverance. For these Jewish groups, the paradigm forged during the Babylonian exile, whereby the loss of homes and homeland was interpreted as a consequence of breach of the Covenant, and the whole of Israel's past (in the Deuteronomic history) retold on that basis, was now projected forwards, as well as backwards, and made the framework for understanding the present situation in Israel. An agonizing reappraisal of national life was entailed by this, to which various groups responded in different ways – Jesus and his followers among them. Jesus' distinctive adaptation of restoration language and imagery seems to have been uniformly eschatological. Not tied to Torah observance in any traditional sense, the reconstitution of Israel was linked to response to an urgent eschatological imperative (to which repentance was crucial), and this urgent eschatological imperative in turn was linked to Christ's own person.

The need for an 'agonizing reappraisal of national life' – and more than that, an agonizing reappraisal of European civilization – is what makes the theologians of the first part of this century comparable to the Jewish people of Jesus' day. Like the Jewish people of Jesus' day, they came face-to-face with the experience of occupation or dispersion and the wholesale failure of many of God's people to be faithful to their calling ('a gap between vocation and performance'). This is, I believe, what explains in part their renewed attention to eschatological thought, in line with the Jews of the inter-testamental period and also the first Christians. The impact of the First World War on Europe's perception of its historical development as a continuous advance towards a more enlightened, more mature, freer and more moral future played its part in shifting the focus of Christian hope away from the merely immanent workings of history towards a divine judgement and redemptive action that were beyond its ordinary processes. History no longer seemed to have within it the key to its own interpretation, nor the capacity to make itself come out right in the end.

If we are to understand the Christologies of Karl Barth and Hans Urs von Balthasar properly, then, in my view, we can only do so in the context of an awareness of the events which underlay the massive revival in the strength and centrality of eschatology for Christian theology in the twentieth century. Their large-scale recovery of 'exile and restoration' motifs is part of that wider turn to eschatology. They therefore typify features which can be found in twentieth-century theology in Europe more generally. They are men who experienced the turmoil of a European culture in crisis, and it is to this experience that their dramatic Christologies (Christologies conceived in terms of a restoration – after exile – that is, in crucial part, 'supra-historical') are a response.

All this is to say that, although it may be difficult to draw a *direct* line between (on the one hand) the move made by Barth and von Balthasar from Germany to Switzerland, and (on the other) the motifs of exile that occur in their Christologies, there is a strong case to be made for an *indirect* link. In both the lives and the theologies of Barth and von Balthasar a certain turbulence was being registered: their biographies and thought were together affected by what was in the background of their work over several decades, not just by specific events. What happened in Europe in the 1930s was part of a bigger picture in which the historical optimism of the West was put under unsustainable pressure. And as mainstream Western theology responded to this turbulence with a renewed interest in eschatology, the classic paradigm of exile and restoration was almost inevitably at the forefront of the various motifs that once again gained currency. Karl Barth and Hans Urs von Balthasar give voice to this paradigm with a force hard to equal in the twentieth century. In so doing, they are men of their time – and perhaps still of ours.

But their registering of the exilic character of Christian existence – its quality of tension with its surroundings – is put in service of something very particular. Not despair, but hope that out of this prison ('the prison of his days') the human being can make a 'way' – a way of freedom and praise of a wholly new order. Participation in Christ, in the view of both these theologians, will be a participation in the exile that puts an end to exile. Both depict Christ opening the way to freedom in places of unfreedom. To this theme we now turn.

Theologies of Freedom

The question of freedom is one of the hardest questions to examine where Barth and von Balthasar are concerned: at different points both appear to make very similar statements about the relationship between creaturely obedience and freedom, but there remains a distinct difference in what they are in fact prepared to countenance on the creature's part. Both have what von Balthasar acknowledges is an 'Augustinian concept of freedom', in that authentic freedom is construed never as a kind of abstract free will apart from the invitation and attractiveness of God, but only as 'a form of living within that mysterious realm where self-determination and obedience, independence and discipleship, mutually act upon and clarify each other … . [T]his domain is that of the Trinity, which grace has opened up for us' (von Balthasar, 1992a,

p. 129).[11] Both share this, and yet, as John Riches and Noel O'Donoghue have stressed, there seems in Barth a more narrow construal of the obedience of faith as *passivity* without any genuinely active dimension of creaturely cooperation (a kind of 'monergism') and, on the Catholic side, greater room for 'a creative response to the enabling divine grace (a kind of 'synergism') (Riches and Quash, 1997, p. 144). This, at least, is how von Balthasar presents the contrast at a number of points in his book on Barth. One of the substantive criticisms of Barth developed at the end of that book is precisely this: that genuine mutuality between God and people is excluded. The creature – the human being – can exercise no really significant initiative. He or she is posited by God as a largely formal presupposition (*Voraussetzung*) of what he has elected to do in Christ. In other words, a basic identity characterizes the divine activity, which only seems to unfold into relationship for a moment before folding back into identity again. The divine–creaturely relationship is thus entirely subsidiary to the unified working of the divine will. Barth, concludes von Balthasar, 'ends up talking about Christ so much as *the* true human being that it makes it seem as if all other human beings are mere epiphenomena' (von Balthasar, 1992a, p. 243).

This has wider ramifications, if true, for the whole way in which nature and history are construed. 'Monergism' would rob them also of a certain integrity. If there is no initiative on the part of the creature then, as von Balthasar puts it:

> ... nothing much really *happens* ... because everything has already happened in eternity: for example, there is Barth's wariness, or, at best, an overly delicate application of ontic categories, in his treatment of grace and justification. Then there is his ascription of the effects of the sacraments to the cognitive order alone, since he rejects the Catholic and Lutheran doctrine that the sacraments effect and cause real change. And finally he transposes both forms of time (or aeons) into a pretemporal eternity, where sin is ever-past and justification ever-future, and rejects all talk of growth, progress – even of a possible lapse and loss of grace and of faith. In short, Barth rejects all discussion of anything in the realm of the relative and temporal that would make for a real and vibrant history of man with his redeeming Lord and God. (von Balthasar, 1992a, p. 371)

Linked with this suppression of historical contingency – the deployment of what I have called elsewhere (following von Balthasar), an 'epic' rather than a 'dramatic' perspective – there is what is sometimes described as Barth's triumphalism (though he reacted in horror and surprise when Berkouwer called his 1954 book *The Triumph of Grace in the Theology of Karl Barth*).[12] Barth (von Balthasar suspected) presumed too easily that he had got his eschatological bearings, even while warning others of 'eschatological arrogance' (cf. ibid., p. 186). The question von Balthasar poses is whether this is merely a manifestation of the 'courage of faith', properly disciplined by an acceptance of the provisionality of all theological statements and the need for perpetual critical reservation, or whether it is the very unexistential perspective of a 'vast panoramic view' (something that Bultmann also criticized in Barth, calling it 'spectator theology' – see McCormack, 1995, p. 405). Von Balthasar reacts strongly to Barth's suggestion that reprobation and judgement can be regarded as merely provisional not because he wants hell to have a large population, but because he thinks we do not have a standpoint from which we can peep into it and draw such conclusions. He does not want to see what he calls the 'existential character of faith and Christian life' (von Balthasar, 1992a, p. 221) swallowed up in 'the high-spirited superiority of a victorious, all-conquering Yes' (ibid., p. 208). 'Theology', he says, 'must put the accent between the totality of victory and the total seriousness of decision exactly where revelation puts its. By doing so, theology resists the temptation of presuming to be the "enlightenment" of revelation' (ibid., p. 224). To do so would be to overstep the legitimate boundaries of theology and begin doing 'metaphysics'. Without losing his basic idea that all evil is 'still fundamentally conquerable', Barth (says von Balthasar) needs 'to be much more flexible at the … places where he presses down, ties up and locks in'; he has 'gone a bit too far into the light'; his tone 'veritably thrums with a hymnic certainty of eventual victory' (ibid., pp. 244, 358, 354).

Von Balthasar, it seems, advocates a far more radical existential irresolution – an arena for human possibilities to determine themselves in various directions: 'out of respect for human nature, human freedom and human decisions (a respect that God himself shows), the eschatological climax must remain an open question … there are many more transitions and nuances here than seem to be the case in Barth' (ibid., p. 363). Von Balthasar does not think he is disagreeing with Barth on any principle, here. He knows that Barth is quite serious in his repudiations of direct and systematic statements about the ways of God, all of which must stand under the sign of failure. But he thinks that, in constructing 'something from a relatively few passages of Scripture that must be considered as the necessary background in all the other statements about the relation between God and man', and even more than that in the *tone* he uses to say what he says, he leaves himself a hostage to those who want too complete a theological overview. Von Balthasar is anxious in his own work to offer a corrective to this (and, as I suggested earlier, it can be argued that the whole project of *Theo-Drama* is just such an attempt):

> Redemption comes to us respecting our incarnate lives in time, leaving room for us to continue to change as we follow in the footsteps of the incarnate Lord. The steps we take in this discipleship have their own inherent meaning and weight. God takes our decisions seriously, working them into his plans by his holy providence. (Ibid., p. 378)

Von Balthasar's theodramatics is, amongst other things, an extended meditation on the nature of the human being as free – as a genuinely dramatic agent capable of initiative, imagination and self-gift. It is a self-declared assault on all those forms of metaphysics (including the secular varieties of the modern period, like Marxism) that downplay the creative irreducibility of individual persons and their capacity for the exercise of free will. At the heart of the second volume of *Theo-Drama* is a section entitled 'Infinite and Finite Freedom' that is essential to an understanding of the whole work because of the way in which it seeks to steer a path between the assertion of a false autonomy on the part of human beings[13] and an obliteration of the importance of personhood. For in von Balthasar's view, intrinsic to the definition of personhood (and therefore at risk in its obliteration) are the mutually necessary elements of love and freedom. A person fully realizes her personhood when she is able to love in freedom and when she is made free by love.

That von Balthasar's more 'synergist' approach safeguards the integrity of human freedom to a degree not achieved by Barth is pretty much an accepted conclusion, and we can choose to rest satisfied with it. But I want to show what happens when we pay closer attention to the presuppositions each theologian is working with, and to what ends. The contrast may not be as straightforward as it looks.

The first sign that the conventional contrast is too easy is the sheer prominence of the idea of freedom in Barth's theology. As was shown in the previous section on exile, Barth's analysis of human need in *Church Dogmatics* IV/1 centres on the human being's unfreedom – we might say, on the insurmountable gap between vocation and performance. This is because his analysis of God's answering of that need is construed very substantially in categories of freedom – freedom from illusion, ignorance, anxiety and fear, and freedom for obedience, courage, joy, peace and thanksgiving. The analysis of the need is typified in the following passage:

> [The human being] chooses a freedom which is no freedom. He is therefore a prisoner of the world-process, of chance, of all-powerful natural and historical forces, above all of himself. He tries to be his own master, and to control his relations with God and the world and his fellow-men. And as he does so, the onslaught of nothingness prevails against him, controlling him in death in an irresistible and senseless way and to his own loss. This is the *circulus vitiosus* of the human plight presupposed and revealed in and with the grace of God. And there is no man who, whether he experiences it or not, is not in this plight. (*CD* IV/1, p. 173)

This is the alienation which imprisons and kills us. It is not the alienation into which Christians are invited in their union with Christ. The way and example of Christ call for an embrace of exile not because we must, not because we are unfree, but because we are free, and because we can. Like the Christ in whose life Christians share, we love the world in freedom, are free in love for the world and are therefore not prisoners. Sharing in Christ gives Christian life what Barth calls 'this direction, this tendency, this dynamic, this pull ... from the heights to the depths, from riches to poverty ... from triumph to suffering, from life to death' (ibid., p. 190). Sharing in Christ (who was 'lord over' the contradiction of human existence at the same time as subjecting himself to it – ibid., p. 185), Christians are enabled to be free in places of unfreedom; to be at home in exile; to praise in prison.

Barth's use of the category of freedom to structure much of his theological anthropology is perhaps most marked in III/4 of the *Dogmatics*, where he examines the human vocation under the headings 'Freedom before God', 'Freedom in Fellowship', 'Freedom for Life' and 'Freedom in Limitation'. Each of these is an aspect of freedom in Christ. Many quite specific ethical issues are dealt with under these headings (work, marriage, war and abortion amongst them), and in each case the strategy Barth adopts is to set these apparently burdensome questions in a context that transforms the way they appear to us. He does not allow them to present themselves to us merely (or even principally) as fearful, as enemies to be overcome, or potentially crushing weights to be laid on our shoulders, or (indeed) as paralysing difficulties that threaten to make prisoners of us. He shows how the transformation effected by Christ permits us to see these issues as opportunities for radical interpretation and action – for witness. The implication in each case is that we can act with a freedom that comes from a larger hope than those without Christ can know. So, for example, our work is seen not to be the most fundamental thing on which we must depend to safeguard our life. And genuine faithfulness in the lifelong bond of marriage is seen to lead not to constriction, but to a liberating mutual affirmation of persons, in the image of the divine love. And knowing that human life is the gift of God's freedom and grace means that human beings: 'will not always desire to be as comfortable as possible in relation to it. They will not always take the line of least resistance in what they think and do concerning it. Those who live by mercy will always be disposed to practise mercy' (*CD* III/4, p. 418). This will have consequences for how we treat our own lives as well as those of others – the unborn amongst them (for they are entitled to be regarded as potential objects of mercy too).

Barth's emphasis on freedom in sections like these concentrates on freedom not as a presupposition of human ethical action, but as an effect of being occupied in the service of God – of being called or appealed to. Freedom is assimilated very closely to joy in these passages, and just as joy is not a presupposition of action so much as something that emerges *in* and *because of* action,[14] so it is for freedom. What comes first is a call (or 'command', to use a word Barth favours). This accomplishes a transformation of our lives from a condition in which all things, including our own actions, seem under the sway of arbitrariness (arbitrariness being a kind of imprisonment). And the transformation from this condition of arbitrariness brings with it liberation, or freedom. This is not a freedom in which the human being is sovereign or solitary, it is the freedom in which God is always 'above him as the Creator, Giver and Lord of his life' (*CD* III/4, p. 407). This is the freedom of the children of God, who step out into freedom when they commit themselves to Christ, thinking of Christ and not their freedom when they do so, and gaining freedom accordingly: 'When he is called by this Word of God to the active life, he is thereby set before the clear meaning and distinct purpose of his life, and he thus becomes a free creature' (ibid., p. 481).

Barth's reference to the active life in this passage prompts a further reflection on what has become the standard (and questionable) contrast between Barth and von Balthasar – particularly when taken in conjunction with Fergus Kerr's discussion in his book *Immortal Longings* of what Barth and von Balthasar respectively suppose to be the human being's deadliest sins. Von Balthasar takes the fairly conventional line that Prometheanism – overreaching pride – is the principal problem. Again and again, when dealing with the philosophers of Enlightenment and their successors throughout the modern period, it is their self-assertion that he condemns. There is in them no obedient attention to the form from which the glory of God breaks forth. Barth, however, as Kerr points out, is prepared to allow the picture to be a good deal more complex. Yes, he devotes a good deal of time to the problem of the pride of man, and (later) to his falsehood as well. But additionally, and importantly, there is another type of sin – one that most stands in the way of the active life. For human beings are faced with a great divine invitation to participate in the new possibilities opened up by the resurrection, and one of the key things that holds them back is *Trägheit* (sloth): 'Barth spells this out as sluggishness, indolence, slowness, inertia.' Sin is 'not merely "heroic in its perversion" … the sinner is also "a lazy-bones, a sluggard, a good-for-nothing, a slow-coach and a loafer" …. [For Barth] inertly drifting is (if anything) a worse sin than shameless self-assertiveness' (Kerr, 1997, p. 41 quoting *CD* IV/2, p. 404). So, whilst von Balthasar laments self-assertion (a kind of illegitimate *attempt* at freedom), Barth is just as keen to condemn the *refusal* of freedom.

The perplexity here is that Barth, the supposed monergist, the man whom von Balthasar criticizes for sometimes 'threatening the reality of the creature' and 'swallowing up the reality of the world' into a 'monism of the Word of God' (von Balthasar, 1992a, pp. 91, 94), is in fact the advocate of a kind of joyous liberation in the creature. The command of God, for Barth, is an invitation to living as the 'free, open-hearted, willing, spontaneous, cheerful, bright and social being' which God intends her to be (*CD* III/2, p. 340 quoted in von Balthasar, 1992a, p. 118). Barth viewed the so-called constraints under which the creature stands as permission to be free. When confronted with what God would have us be, it is inconceivable to Barth that we, in our right minds, would resent it or see it as an obstacle to our freedom. Surely it is just a gracious possibility: 'You had no right to expect to do or to be this (or indeed anything) but look! you *may* do and be it!'

Von Balthasar, meanwhile, though entering the lists against Barth ostensibly in the cause of the relative integrity of creaturely freedom, is nevertheless the one who dwells at far greater length on the creature's need to cultivate receptivity or disposability: *Gelassenheit* (this quality is definitive, for example, of Mary's role in the Theo-drama).

An unusual new angle is opened up here, therefore, on the established Barth–von Balthasar contrast, and it should make us think a second time about what each theologian *actually* stands for when it comes to creaturely freedom and integrity and therefore, more widely, the nature–grace debate. We may well find that we have cause to undercut von Balthasar's own presentation of what makes him different from Barth. There can be no doubt that both Barth and von Balthasar order freedom to obedience, but there is a fine but important difference in how they do it, and in what they bring to the discussion in terms of presuppositions and concerns. The difference between them can, I think, be suggested in a kind of formula. Barth wants the creature to have the *obedient* embrace of *freedom*. Von Balthasar wants the *free* embrace of *obedience*. Barth presupposes that there is initially not much to speak of in the creature – all is owed to the positing work of the Holy Spirit. The creature becomes interesting as a subject only when he or she stands under the divine call or injunction and responds appropriately. He characterizes the divine call as 'a *subpoena* summoning the whole person, a writ claiming man's entire existence, body and soul' (von Balthasar, 1992a, p. 141). But from this initial restriction of what we might think of as creaturely entitlements or faculties, there opens up a great domain of freedom *in Christ* – life in a dynamic and open space (which is how he envisages the Church): 'We can live life with head held high, with a free heart and a clear conscience, proclaiming to God, "Lord, how good are your works!" (Psalm 104: 24)' (*CD* III/3, quoted in von Balthasar, 1992a, p. 112).

So Barth says 'obedience' in order then to be able to say 'freedom'. He is not weighed down or preoccupied by questions about some general or abstract or neutral free will in the human. He is not terribly interested in the way that human subjectivity is structured, apart from in the hearing of the Word.[15] He is not bothered with trying to explain how absolute and relative freedoms can coexist: 'we have no idea or concept for describing it', he says (quoted in von Balthasar, 1992a, p. 133). It surprises him that people can *not* have faith, but he does not agonize over why this is. He concentrates on the *de facto* occurrence of God's speaking and people's hearing. The Word of God, says Barth, 'brings powerfully to light the forgotten truth of creation' – so why speculate about any other supposed 'truths' the creation may have laid claim to apart from this Word's 'striking against it'? A 'natural theology', he says, is, 'justified – indeed, necessary – inside revealed theology', but why concern oneself with a 'natural theology apart from revealed theology? It is inconceivable in any case' (quoted in von Balthasar, 1992a, p. 96). People answer Christ's call: why look anywhere else if we want to see the meaning and implications of created freedom?

When we understand this, we will perhaps see Barth as less 'epic' than von Balthasar supposes him to be, and more the 'joyous partisan' that he himself hoped to represent. He did not feel the need to defend a set of human entitlements *in principle*, when he could celebrate countless human endowments *in fact*. As we noted before, he says 'obedience' in order then to be able to say 'freedom', and to say 'freedom' in quite a specific and distinctive way in the context of a theological ethics. Von Balthasar, in my view, says 'freedom' in a rather more general way in order then to be able to say 'obedience' rather specifically – that is, rather ecclesially. The reason, perhaps, is that he (unlike Barth) *does* regard freedom as a presupposition of action rather than developing anything akin to Barth's rather idiosyncratic use of the idea as something analogous to joy. Like the Idealist philosophical tradition on which he draws, he seeks to treat it as a formal theme in its own right and as something that can be identified and examined in all human beings, whether or not they have explicitly committed themselves to Christ or acted in response to a divine summons. He is much tenser and more preoccupied about conditions in the human being which are notionally 'prior' to the gracious encounter with God. He wants to safeguard (indeed, sometimes simply presupposes) certain things about human subjectivity *in principle*, so that they can be asserted in aid of a distinctively 'Catholic' point of view. This is so even though, with Barth, he accepts that 'there is *in fact* no slice of "pure nature" in this world' (von Balthasar, 1992a, p. 288). To achieve his aim, he expends enormous time on the issue in his book on Barth, tracing formal conceptions of nature as that which is the subject of 'being graced' even though accepting – with Barth, as well as with de Lubac and others – that in practice nature is inseparable from grace, and that both the *regnum gratiae* and the *regnum naturae* are 'the Kingdom of the Son' (ibid., p. 88). Von Balthasar, throughout his work, is prepared to dwell at greater length on the character of human subjectivity and selfhood, including Christ's own subjectivity – the significance of his obedience in exercising a human will and so on. The great importance he accords to *Gelassenheit* as a mode of creaturely obedience already contains within itself (implies) the 'self' of 'self-surrender' – and this is revealing. 'Self-surrender' is not a Barthian phrase in anything like the degree to which it is a Balthasarian one. In talking of self-surrender one presupposes a certain possession of self. Thus we find in von Balthasar references to a 'primal, secure self-possession' (von Balthasar, 1990, p. 211) and statements that 'we possess an inalienable core of freedom that cannot be split open' (ibid., p. 210).

And von Balthasar extends this assumption of a degree of self-possession in individuals to apply to the Church, too. Yes, her 'relational otherness to Christ is a freedom *of* dependence .... But it really is a freedom', he says. In the Church, too, as in the case of individuals, distance is presupposed for the sake of nearness; autonomy is presupposed for the sake of love; irreducible otherness is presupposed for the sake of genuine union.[16] Freedom is presupposed for the sake of obedience. This is what makes bride imagery so important to von Balthasar's doctrine of the Church as compared with body metaphors, for instance.

Von Balthasar's anxious defence of a formal human autonomy issues in a much more specific call for ecclesial obedience than we ever find in Barth. It is here, curiously, that some of the general preconceptions about von Balthasar's 'conservatism' have their roots. Von Balthasar is eloquent about the importance of practical disciplines of self-denial. The saints whose lives he illustrates invariably manifest this quality of being ready to receive an imprint. The archetype of the Church's soul, Mary, is the most perfectly receptive of all Christians (though von Balthasar tries to give a distinctively activist twist to this apparently passive depiction of a mission: even here, we see him far more concerned than Barth with the ways in which subjectivity and will function). Renunciation is tremendously important, and so is respect for the shaping structures of objective Spirit – that is, the institutional Church. These, when accepted obediently, will direct this renunciation and make it fruitful.

What shall we say in conclusion to this question? We may, despite arguments put forward here, still feel uncomfortable with the freedom Barth talks about. For all the *rapprochement* von Balthasar argues for, Barth resists that most crucial aspect of Catholic (and, more particularly, Balthasarian) anthropology, the ability of the creature to *participate* in Christ's work, his sufferings and merits. For von Balthasar, it is important that we can 'be "with" [Christ's] being "for" us ... thereby helping to be "for" others' (Balthasar, 1992a, p. 243). It is a corollary of von Balthasar's assertion of the human being's ability to receive an imprint that he has room (a room which Barth seems not to have) for an abundance of transpositions of Christ's work, and even his characteristics, into the lives of the saints. Individual missions interact with the mission of Christ and share many of its features, so that they become vehicles of revelation in their own (relative!) right.

We ought also to allow, nonetheless, that despite von Balthasar's protestations, there is a persisting difference – often only a difference in style but sometimes, too, in the topics that are accorded attention – between an early proclamation of creaturely dignity which paradoxically ends in a slightly tetchy summons to worldly individuals that they submit to authorized patterns of behaviour (von Balthasar's line), and a blithe disregard for the creature's claims on integrity which equally paradoxically celebrates wholeheartedly what the creature is once it is claimed by God (Barth's line).

Taking stock of what has emerged so far in this study of some of Barth's and von Balthasar's common concerns, it can be said that their parallel way of addressing the human state of exile is to stress the extraordinary freedom that can be manifest when this state of exile is conceived as a being in Christ. What has subsequently emerged, however, is that they each take a different tack when examining exactly what such freedom consists of, and when building it into their respective theological anthropologies. In the concluding section of this essay, I will evaluate whether this divergence in the way in which the two theologians describe freedom means that what at the outset seemed a remarkable similarity in the movement of their thought in fact leads them to radically different places. My intention is to show that this is not so, although they remain utterly distinctive voices with significantly different visions.

Conclusion

An evaluation of the dialogue between Barth and von Balthasar could rest satisfied with pointing to specific fruits of that dialogue, in ecumenical documents for example. It is not fanciful to point to certain ways in which Barth's thought influenced crucial sections of the constitutions of the Second Vatican Council. Aidan Nichols wonders whether *Dei Verbum* was a response 'provoked in part by Barth's criticisms of the Catholic Church's inclination to "control" the wholly other truth' (Nichols, 1993, p. 544). Perhaps even more significant is the anthropology of *Gaudium et Spes*, which is profoundly Christological, in a way that both of the Swiss theologians would have wanted to endorse, whatever reservations they had about accommodations elsewhere. At least as important a feature of their joint legacy is the example they give to ecumenical theology in terms of method. At their most brilliant, these two thinkers represent a reverential, though not uncritical, recovery of the full depth and breadth of the Christian tradition. What we can learn from them as they do this is the fact that the arena in which differences are aired ecumenically will always most productively be the doctrine of God – Trinity, Christology, redemption and so on – and only then and in the light of that, the Church and sacraments. The necessary ecumenical debates will be carried out well only in so far as Catholicism and Protestantism speak together about their understanding of their common Lord and God, humbly submitting to him and living from the hope he gives.

But it is in their all-consuming passion to describe what this 'living from the hope he gives' will actually *mean* that they offer most – not just in the narrower sphere of theological discussion and Church councils, but in witness to the variously confused, disturbed, weary, sated, melancholy and restless citizens of the earthly city amongst whom they live. And it is in this all-consuming passion that they prove themselves to have a vast amount in common, despite their differences of tone and emphasis, some of which came to the fore in the previous section. Above all, theirs is a common concern with *thanksgiving*. It is a disposition seen by both as genuinely fundamental to holy human living. It is the mark of Christ's free exiles and acts as a deeply subversive force in a world that has forgotten how to give thanks, or does not know what it ought to give thanks for, or to whom.

In Chapter 16 of the Book of Acts, Paul and his companions are flogged and imprisoned for interfering with someone's profit margin. They heal a slave girl whose 'prophetic' gifts were a nice little earner for her owner. The world and its interests lock them in, quite literally.[17] Paul and Silas, in their dungeon, beaten up as they are, pray and sing hymns to God. That is not the reaction of hopeless men. And, indeed, their hope is rewarded, for the prison cannot hold them. The Gospel they have been preaching will not be held back, constrained, made a captive, by the corrupt forces that have put them in gaol. However much the world's thrall seems unbreakable, the servants of this Gospel *are actually free* in Jesus Christ. The truth of their freedom – veiled while they sat in chains – is now witnessed to as the chains fell off. Their true status as free men in Christ is displayed.

Two things in particular seem extraordinary about this. First is the fact that – freed though they are – they do not use their freedom for instant escape, though that is certainly a route available to them. Amazingly, they remain in the prison cell – *freely*. When the gaoler (terrified that his prisoners *have* escaped) prepares to take his life, Paul shouts out, 'Do not harm yourself; we are all here.' The freedom attained in Christ, illustrated here, is expressed in a willed solidarity with the world and the frightened dungeon-dwellers within it. The freed men stay in the prison, making their prison a *way*. The second extraordinary thing is the fact that what they were devoting themselves to before their chains fell off and the doors flew open – and continue to devote themselves to subsequently – is thanksgiving and praise.

In this biblical episode, we find an illustration of the way in which the themes of exile, freedom and thanks come together in Barth's and von Balthasar's own visions. Freedom-in-exile is also freedom-for-praise. In stressing this, they go to the heart of a particular and radical vision of Christian discipleship in a world that is deeply informed by Scripture. Moreover, they show themselves to be very closely aligned with each other. (This is so even though for von Balthasar, and not for Barth, the full realization of 'freedom-for-praise' will almost always include an embrace of the authority of the Catholic Church and quite possibly an intense personal participation in Christ's sufferings as his 'form' is transposed into oneself. For Barth it is presumption to claim for oneself a tragic share in the unique work of Christ's passion.)

Barth's theology – and therefore his ethics – is full of a sense that praise is the vocation of the human creature. '[T]he praise of God', he writes, 'is in some measure the climax of all human action Godwards'. It is an 'original necessity':

> Not only God's servants (Psalm 113:1), not only His saints (Psalm 145:10), not only Zion (Psalm 147:12), not only the house of Israel (Psalm 135:19) shall and may praise the Lord, but also the nations (Psalm 66:8, 117:1), all flesh (Psalm 145:21), everything that hath breath (Psalm 150:6), heaven and earth and sea (Psalm 69:34), sun and moon (Psalm 148:3), the angels of God (Psalm 103:20), all His works (Psalm 103:22). The praise of the man who knows God might seem small and insignificant amid this mighty chorus. But the writers of the Old and New Testaments certainly did not look at it like that. They understood the call to the whole creation to praise God as a summons directed with even more urgency and obligation to man. (*CD* III/4, p. 74)

The Sabbath commandment (to take just one example) is ordered to celebration – celebration that is joyous and free (ibid., p. 52) – and, in the same way, thanksgiving is held up as the only proper mode in which to bear the quite unwarranted and overwhelming gift to man by God of *glory* (a fascination von Balthasar inherits if ever there was one):

> [The human being] lives as the creature of God, the child of God his Father, and therefore in the honour and glory with which God clothes him. What follows from this? It follows that man can be honourable and have his glory only in pure thankfulness, in the deepest humility, and – we say it openly – in free humour …. In relation to this honour, then, what is left to man but pure thankfulness? (ibid., p. 664)

The importance of the theme of thanksgiving for von Balthasar, meanwhile, can be traced in what is perhaps initially to us a surprising place: in his discussion of the cross as an act of *Eucharist*. Indeed, he invites us at certain points to view the cross as the consummate act of thanksgiving and as the pattern for Christian participation in Christ: the Eucharist of Eucharists. (He does this despite the fact that elsewhere he dwells at length on the suffering and horror of the cross.) For von Balthasar, the cross is Christ's Eucharist, and it is therefore an act of thanksgiving and self-offering, even when it takes on the outward form of suffering. Though a relinquishment, it is almost an occasion of joy. Here von Balthasar opens up a powerful vision of the way in which Christ's outpouring to death on the Cross is really the secondary outworking of a more primal outpouring, a joyous, reckless outpouring which is at the very heart of God. Von Balthasar chooses to say, with the Orthodox theologian Sergii Bulgakov, that 'there is an initial *kenosis* (or outpouring) within the Godhead that underpins all subsequent *kenosis*' (von Balthasar, 1994, p. 323). In this light, we see that 'the doctrine of the Trinity is the ever-present, inner presupposition of the doctrine of the Cross', to use von Balthasar's words (ibid., p. 319).

How does this *kenosis* within the godhead work? What is it? Does it involve the Son, whilst Father and Spirit remain impassive? And does it involve suffering? The answers to these questions, in von Balthasar's vision, are that it does *not* involve the Son alone, and that something greater than suffering is at work – the something he describes as *eucharistia*, or Eucharist, or (in human terms) thanksgiving. 'The immanent Trinity' writes von Balthasar 'must be understood to be that eternal, absolute self surrender whereby God is seen to be, in himself, absolute love; this in turn explains his free self-giving to the world as love' (ibid., p. 323). Who is doing this eternal 'surrendering'? The answer is: Father, Son and Spirit – all of them. Even the Father, the source of godhead, is pouring himself out without reserve. It is, we might say, the *Father's* self-utterance in the generation of the Son which is the initial *kenosis* within the godhead. 'For the Father strips himself, without remainder, of his [divinity] and hands it over to the Son; he "imparts" to the Son all that is his. "All that is thine is mine." (Jn 17:10).' The Father, to put it even more radically, *is* this movement of self-giving. He does not just perform it; he *is* it.

The Son's outpouring, therefore, is truly understood as an *answer* to the gift of godhead. It is a gift which is of truly equal substance to the Father's gift, but, because it has the character of an answer, it is not the original or only *kenosis* attributable to God. So the character of this responsive outpouring – which makes the Father the Father just as the Father makes the Son the Son – is the character of eternal thanksgiving (*eucharistia*) to the Father, the Source – 'a thanksgiving as selfless and unreserved as the Father's original self-surrender' (ibid., p. 324). In this return, the Father though uttering and surrendering himself without reserve does not lose himself; rather, the whole divine essence remains in complete, dynamic perfection. The perfection is that of love, the same love that overflows into and accommodates creation, trying, in love, to enlarge creation's capacity to be a new responsive reality, a reality which will also 'magnify the Lord'.

What this vision of divine love dares us to do is to see the cross as its mere extension: to see the mission of the Son in the order of salvation as just part of that *procession* – that joyous abundant flow of the divine being – which is already in God. The cross, in that sense, is utterly godly; it is *fitting* in its recklessness; 'the Son, makes a fitting response to the Father's total gift of himself by freely and thankfully allowing himself to be poured forth by the Father .... Both take place in a generous, eucharistic availability that matches the limitless proportions of the divine nature.' On this account, '[t]he creature's No is merely a twisted knot within the Son's pouring forth; it is left behind by the current of love' (ibid., pp. 329–30). This leads to the fascinating observation, borrowed by von Balthasar, that 'it is just as possible to maintain that Jesus' being forsaken by God was the opposite of hell as to say that it *was* hell' (ibid., p. 336 citing E. Mersch). Hell is hate. The work of Christ is a work of love and of union. The death it requires is the complete opposite of that eternal death which is hell. In other words, the suffering was part of something much greater and had a very specific content and goal: the goal of saving us and so magnifying the divine love – magnifying the Lord.

In this powerful vision of a holiness which consists in free thanksgiving, and which takes with utter seriousness (but not maudlin self-denunciation) the link between this disposition of thanks and Christ's work on the cross, von Balthasar shows himself as close to Barth as at any other point. Here we see the best fruit of their exchange of ideas, their long process of mutual attention and regard, their 'conversation'. As we have seen, they have their differences, and these should not be overlooked. Where von Balthasar speaks of freedom in terms of 'communion' (with other creatures because with God), Barth prefers to speak of freedom in terms of 'fellowship', for reasons well rehearsed in studies of his attitude to the *analogia entis*. Where Barth places the accent on the accomplished work of the cross (its victory on our behalf), von Balthasar dwells longer on it as a continuing pattern of the Christian life, a mould, entry into which accompanies entry into Christ and our receipt of a mission – a mould that serves to conform us to Christ. Like Mary, says von Balthasar, we may find that following Christ leads us to our own (analogous) 'cross'. The dark strand that von Balthasar allows to weave through his account of what it is to be a disciple is not paralleled precisely in Barth's work. But thanksgiving is what issues decisively from both these understandings of discipleship, and thanksgiving is the note allowed to sound longest. In this they encounter us, like Paul and Silas in their prison cell, with an offer that challenges our contemporary situation as much as Paul's and Silas's did theirs, seeking to transform the impoverishment of our self-understanding, our aspirations and our action. Barth's and von Balthasar's theologies together offer continued testimony in our own time to a new and distinctively Christian form of eschatological citizenship, to the dramatic possibility in Christ of living lives that magnify the Lord.

Notes

1 Karl Barth to Christoph Barth, 31 May 1941; quoted in Busch, 1976, p. 302.
2 Many of the facts of the developing relationship between Barth and Przywara are recorded in McCormack's book. Eduard Thurneysen alerted Barth to Przywara's writings in an enthusiastic letter of September 1923: 'Acquire for yourself a copy of Number 11 of *Stimmen der Zeit* .... There you will find a remarkable and extensive essay about us from the side of the Catholic partner' (Eduard Thurneysen to Karl Barth, 30 September 1923, quoted in McCormack, 1995, p. 319). Barth's reaction is set out in the foreword to the fourth edition of *The Epistle to the Romans* in 1924. He laments the failure of his Protestant reviewers to grasp his intentions, but goes on to say that '[s]everal opinions from the Catholic side [Pryzwara foremost amongst them] gave me more to think about. Their reviews have, at least in part, pushed me into an accurate understanding of the matter which concerns us and above all have done so on a level of theological discussion which I could not concede to many of my honourable reviewers on this side of the great divide' (Karl Barth, *Der Römerbrief* (1922); quoted in McCormack, 1995, p. 321). McCormack indicates the likely connection between this 'theological discussion' and Barth's announcement 'for the first time since the massive revision which had resulted

in the second edition of *Romans*, that the book really needed once again to be revised "in head and members"' (McCormack, 1995, p. 322).

In February 1929 Barth invited Przywara to give an address in Münster on the doctrine of the Church, and arranged for him to take part, the following day, in the leading of his seminar on Thomas Aquinas. He was greatly excited by his more sustained interaction with the Jesuit and wrote to Thurneysen:

> Erich Przywara, SJ, gave a two-hour long lecture on the Church which, considered from the point of view of its skilled craftsmanship, was simply a dainty morsel, a masterpiece. He then shone in my seminar, once again for two hours, answering our carefully prepared questions. And finally, he 'overwhelmed' me here for two evenings' worth, just as, according to his doctrine, the dear God overwhelms people with grace (at least within the Catholic Church) so that the formula 'God in-above humankind from God's side' is, at one and the same time, the motto of his existence as well as the dissolution of all Protestant and modernist, transcendentalist and immanentist stupidities and constraints in the peace of the *analogia entis*.' (Karl Barth to Eduard Thurneysen, 9 February 1929, quoted in McCormack, 1995, p. 383).

Przywara was to come and participate in seminars again, so von Balthasar's later involvement in Barth's seminars (for example, on the Council of Trent in 1941) had precedents: he entered a conversation already underway.

Przywara was, of course, by no means Barth's only contact with Catholicism. McCormack writes that

> ... in early 1927, Barth became a regular member of a theological circle composed largely of lay Catholics. The circle even met in Barth's home on occasion. Other members included Dr. Bernhard Rosenmüller ... Dr. G. Hasenkamp ... and the Catholic student pastor Dr. Robert Grosche .... By 1928 the circle had become a regular theological 'institute', meeting every month or two. Papers were presented and discussed on topics such as the idea of appropriations in the doctrine of the Trinity, sin and grace, and the essence of evil. The other members of the circle introduced Barth to two nineteenth-century Catholics with whom he had previously been unacquainted: J.A. Möhler, the founder of the "Tübingen school" of Catholic theology, and Matthias Scheeben. (McCormack, 1995, p. 377)

3 'Revelation tells us what man is,' writes Schmaus, 'it tells us by recounting the *history* of what God has done and is doing for us and with us to establish his reign in us.' (Michael Schmaus, *Katholische Dogmatik* II, quoted in von Balthasar, 1992a, p. 340). 'Dogmas always rest on the *drama* of revelation. The *Word* of revelation cannot be divided from the *deed* of revelation .... Revelation is essentially event, deed, history, and not merely speech, doctrine, word' (F.X. Arnold, 'Glaubensschwund und Glaubensverkündigung' (1950); quoted in von Balthasar, 1992a, p. 340).

4 Whilst the effects of Nazism were very real in shaping the lives and the thought of these two theologians (especially Barth), their experience of 'exile' had other sources as well, as we will see shortly.

5 On 1 May, 1931, he became a member of the Social Democrat Party.

6 To W. Spoendlin, 4 January, 1928; quoted in Busch, 1976, p. 175.

7 To G. Lindt, 2 January, 1943; quoted in Busch, 1976, p. 299.

8 To W. Spoendlin, 4 January, 1915; quoted in Busch, 1976, p. 81.

9 The series was eventually to include poetry from the French Resistance.

10 In this, he is close to some of the earliest Christian writers on the distinctive form of Christian estrangement, such as the writer of the *Shepherd of Hermas*:

> 'You know that you who are the servants of God dwell in a strange land; for your city is far away from this one. If, then you know your city in which you are to dwell, why do ye here provide lands, and make expensive preparations, and accumulate dwellings and useless buildings? He who makes such preparations for this city cannot return again to his own. Oh foolish, and unstable, and miserable man! Dost thou not understand that all these things belong to another, and are under the power of another? ... Instead of lands, therefore, buy afflicted souls, according

as each one is able, and visit widows and orphans, and do not overlook them; and spend your wealth and all your preparations, which ye received from the Lord, upon such lands and houses. For to this end did the Master make you rich, that you might perform these services unto Him; and it is much better to purchase such lands, and possessions, and houses, as you will find in your own city, when you come to reside in it. This is a noble and sacred expenditure, attended neither with sorrow nor fear, but with joy. (*Hermas* III:1)

11 Barth puts it as follows: 'If the freedom of man is the freedom to which the command of God calls him, this freedom is itself perfect obedience. And if the obedience of man is that which the command of God demands of him, this obedience is itself perfect freedom' (*CD* III/4, p. 595).

12 Barth wrote: 'I'm a bit startled at the title, *The Triumph* .... Of course I used to use the word and still do. But it makes the whole thing seem so finished, which it isn't for me. *The Freedom* ... would have been better. And then instead of ... *Grace* I would much have preferred ... *Jesus Christ*' (quoted in Busch, 1976, p. 381).

13 The realization of personhood is only possible because God has 'made room' for it. Autonomy is a false description of it: '[F]inite freedom can only exist as participation in infinite freedom, as a result of the latter being immanent in it and transcendent beyond it; finite freedom can only realize itself in and with infinite freedom' (von Balthasar, 1990, p. 272).

14 Barth remarks, delightfully, that one cannot *try* to be joyful – it's impossible. One finds joy in being occupied in certain sorts of activity (*CD* III/4, p. 68). By analogy, freedom is likewise not something one achieves by an exercise of will. It, too, is discovered in certain sorts of activity (praise and service, for example).

15 It is almost in passing that he acknowledges the existence of 'a measure of creaturely freedom [as contrasted with the freedom of the Spirit], of psycho-physical freedom, of space to breathe and move ... of opportunity for expression and development' (*CD* III/4, p. 500).

16 Von Balthasar says these things about Barth (von Balthasar, 1992a, p. 126), but in fact they say far more about his own way of articulating the question of freedom.

17 There are limits to how far Christianity's adherents can push out the boundaries of the space allocated to them without meeting violent opposition. That the context in Acts 16 is a pluralistic, market-driven social sphere lends itself to potentially interesting comparisons with a modern Western setting.

References

Barth, K. (1966), *How I Changed My Mind*, ed. J. Godsey, Richmond: John Knox.

Barth, K. (1991), *The Göttingen Dogmatics: Instruction in the Christian Religion*, vol. I, trans. G. Bromiley, Grand Rapids, MI: Eerdmans.

Busch, E. (1976), *Karl Barth: His Life from Letters and Autobiographical Texts*, trans. J. Bowden, London: SCM.

Henrici, P. (1991), 'A Sketch of von Balthasar's Life' in D.L. Schindler (ed.), *Hans Urs von Balthasar: His Life and Work*, San Francisco, Ignatius.

Jüngel, E. (1986), *Karl Barth: A Theological Legacy*, Philadelphia, Fortress Press.

Kerr, F. (1997), *Immortal Longings: Versions of Transcending Humanity*, London, SPCK.

McCormack, B. (1995), *Karl Barth's Critically Realistic Dialectical Theology: Its Genesis and Development 1909–1936*, Oxford: Oxford University Press.

Nichols, A. (1993), 'Twenty-five Years On: A Catholic Commemoration of Karl Barth', *New Blackfriars*, **74**(877) (December), pp. 538–49.

Nichols, A. (1998), *The Word Has Been Abroad*, Edinburgh, T. & T. Clark.

Quash, B. (1999), 'Drama and the Ends of Modernity', in L. Gardner, D. Moss, B. Quash and G. Ward, *Balthasar at the End of Modernity*, Edinburgh, T. & T. Clark, pp. 139–71.

Riches, J. and B. Quash (1997), 'Hans Urs von Balthasar', in D.F. Ford (ed.), *The Modern Theologians*, 2nd edn, Oxford: Blackwell.

von Balthasar, H.U. (1990), *Theo-Drama II: Dramatis Personae: Man in God*, trans. G. Harrison, San Francisco, Ignatius.
von Balthasar, H.U. (1992a), *The Theology of Karl Barth: Exposition and Interpretation*, trans. E.T. Oakes, San Francisco, Ignatius.
von Balthasar, H.U. (1992b), *Mysterium Paschale*, trans. A. Nichols, Edinburgh, T. & T. Clark.
von Balthasar, H.U. (1994), *Theo-Drama IV: The Action*, trans. G. Harrison, San Francisco: Ignatius.

CHAPTER 7

The Fulfilment of History in Barth, Frei, Auerbach and Dante

Mike Higton

On 28 January 1969 a memorial colloquium was held in honour of Karl Barth at Yale Divinity School, 40 days after his death. James Gustafson spoke on Barth's ethics, Brevard Childs on his reading of Scripture, and Julian Hartt on the scale of Barth's achievement; Hans Frei presented a piece simply called 'Karl Barth: Theologian',[1] in which he spoke of Barth's 'energetic and logically consistent Christ-centredness', and of his theology's ability to 'haunt and comfort the rest of us with its iron and yet gay consistency, when we are less daring in our ways of doing theology' (Frei, 1993, pp. 174–75). Barth's Christ-centredness was shown, Frei said, in his

> … conceptual unfolding of a rich variety of beings and relations, all of them good and right, and all of them real in their own right, and all of them referring figurally to the incarnate, raised and ascended Lord who has promised to be with us to the end, and at the end. (Frei, 1993, p. 175)

'In casting about for a comparison' to Barth's achievement in the *Dogmatics*, Frei said, he found himself 'invariably drawn to some things Erich Auerbach has said about Dante': there is a 'Dantesque element in Barth' (ibid., p. 168).[2]

> For Barth, the Bible was, in a manner, Virgil and Beatrice in one. The Guide who took him only to the threshold of Paradise, it was at the same time the *figura* in writing of that greatest wonder which is the fulfillment of all natural, historical being without detracting from it: the incarnate reconciliation between God and man that is Jesus Christ. (Ibid., p. 169)

To put this in my own terms, Frei was suggesting that Barth's 'energetic and logically consistent Christ-centredness', a Christ-centredness which 'reached a well-nigh incredible consistency' (ibid., p. 175), can best be understood as a *figural economy*. He suggests that if we understand the *Church Dogmatics* as the exploration of such a figural economy, it becomes clear that Barth's theology is one which fosters, rather than inhibits, attention to the particular, the contingent, the surprising and the different. It becomes clear that Barth's vision of the fulfilment of history is profoundly open to history, that it is profoundly historical.

Hans Frei on Karl Barth

A 'Dantesque' Barth

Frei, then, begins his interpretation of the *Church Dogmatics* by drawing a comparison with Auerbach's Dante.[3] I am not here going to provide an exposition of Auerbach's work – that can be found easily enough elsewhere – but the essentials are clear enough.[4] Dante, in Auerbach's description, portrays a vast array of characters who have found (in their respective positions in the inferno, purgatory and paradise) their fulfilment. That is, each character has become most fully him- or herself precisely as he or she takes up his or her position in a vast choreography which, as a whole, displays divine judgement in circles around the centre, Christ. In Dante, we might say, the 'fulfilment of history' is *displayed* in the arrangement of all natural, historical being according to the scheme of God's judgement, and the valuing or preservation of history is displayed in the richness and density of the portrayals that make up this display. In other words, God's judgement, both in its basic threefold division and in the finer grades that structure the inferno, purgatory and paradise, is seen precisely in and through the diverse concrete lives of multiple distinct creatures, and the reality and individuality of each of those creatures is preserved and even accentuated in this portrayal.

For instance, Virgil in the *Comedy* is not, according to Auerbach, an allegorical figure; he is neither 'reason nor poetry nor the Empire. He is Virgil himself' (Auerbach, 1984, p. 70); better, he is the concrete, fulfilled reality of which the historical Virgil was the figure. The Virgil of the *Comedy* is *more* real, and more really Virgil, than the Virgil of history, because he is a Virgil whose position in God's plans is now made fully clear and who is now most fully able to play his allotted role in demonstrating God's justice. The historical Virgil known of by Dante had prophesied the *pax romana*, had inspired future poets, had prophesied Christ in the Fourth Eclogue, had described the pathway to the dead and was a man of justice and piety; living before Christ he nevertheless stood on the threshold of Christianity, pointing towards it; living as a pagan, he could approach, but not cross, that threshold. It is precisely as the fulfilment of this historical figure that the Virgil of the *Comedy* is elected as Dante's guide, but 'can lead him only to the threshold of the kingdom, only as far as the limit which his noble and righteous poetry was able to discern'. Virgil is now what Virgil was then; only now the full meaning – the full grandeur and limitation – of Virgil's existence is made clear. The *Comedy*'s Virgil is a concrete, living figure who interprets for us the concrete, living Virgil of history. Virgil in the *Comedy* is more Virgil than Virgil (ibid., pp. 68–70).

With Beatrice, the situation is more complex. In Dante's own life Beatrice was always understood as 'a miracle sent from Heaven, an incarnation of divine truth' (ibid., p. 74). We need not bury ourselves in discussion of how the Beatrice constructed in Dante's poetry and imagination, the Beatrice of the *Vita Nuova*, relates to the particular Florentine girl who later married Simone de' Bardi (Auerbach, 1961,

p. 60); her fulfilment in the *Comedy* is the fulfilment of the figure of Beatrice experienced by Dante in his own life and depicted in his poetry. The Beatrice of the *Comedy* is the fulfilment of this genuinely, if not straightforwardly, historical reality[5] and is therefore an incarnation (not an allegory) of revelation – an incarnation of 'that part of the divine plan of salvation which precisely is the miracle whereby men are raised above other earthly creatures. Beatrice is incarnation, she is *figura* or *idolo Christi*' (Auerbach, 1984, p. 75). This is what the experience of Beatrice had been to Dante in life; this is now what the *Comedy*'s Beatrice is more fully and clearly. Once again, the Beatrice of the *Comedy* is more Beatrice than Beatrice, precisely because her position in God's plans is made fully clear, and because she is enabled to play fully her role in displaying God's justice, which the Beatrice of Dante's earlier life had filled only in part.

Virgil, one concrete historical figure amongst all others, acts as a guide to this display; he leads Dante through it to the threshold of that region in which the lives of men and women are made to display the reconciliation of God and creation; as a John the Baptist figure he *points towards* this reconciliation only from a distance. Beatrice, on the other hand – again, as one concrete figure amongst others – is in her very particularity an *embodiment* of the reconciliation to which Virgil can only point: she displays the nature and glory and beauty of it.

When Frei explains his comparison between Barth and Auerbach's Dante, he says that the Bible in Barth can be compared to both Auerbach's Beatrice and his Virgil.[6] That is, Barth saw in the Bible a portrayal of creatures who have their own concrete particularity, but are portrayed in the context of divine providence, and in that fuller context are shown to be both *witnesses* to the reconciliation of God and humanity (the Virgil aspect) and the *embodiment* of that reconciliation (the Beatrice aspect).[7] This witnessing and this embodiment are not functions that diminish, annul or override the concrete particularity of the creatures portrayed and neither are they roles that are external or accidental to the creatures' concrete particularity: rather, they are the confirmation and fulfilment, the establishment and preservation, of that particularity. As such, it is misleading to use terms such as 'function' or 'role', as I have done for the sake of convenience: the witness or embodiment displayed to us by the Bible in its characters is a matter of their identity, their being, rather than of something ultimately distinguishable from them. They *are* witnesses and embodiments precisely as the unsubstitutably particular individuals they are.

One way of expanding this interpretation of Frei's sketch would be to suggest that the Bible portrays many diverse witnesses to reconciliation, but only one embodiment: that is, the role of Virgil is played by a cast of thousands (patriarchs, judges, kings, prophets, apostles; saints and sinners), but the role of Beatrice is played only by Christ. Christ is portrayed as an unsubstitutable individual, but in such a way that, in his very unsubstitutable individuality, he is shown to be the embodiment of divine–human reconciliation; other creaturely actors in the biblical drama are portrayed in all their concrete particularity, but in such a way that their concrete particularity is shown as witness to Jesus Christ.

This is, I think, part of Frei's meaning. However, he ultimately makes it clear that he has a more complex view of the figural economy of Scripture. Frei insists that Jesus, as portrayed in the Bible, is both fulfilment *and figure*. As figured, the reconciliation of God and humanity in Jesus of Nazareth is, and will be, the fulfilment of 'all created reality': all the creaturely reality depicted in the Bible (and, indeed, all other creaturely reality when seen in the light of God's Word) finds its true meaning when it is shown in all its particularity as a witness, as a reality which points away from itself and towards Christ. As *figure*, however, what we see displayed concretely in Jesus is also found repeated in every other concrete form of the divine–human relationship: in each of those concrete forms the incarnation is, as it were, republished and filled out, split in the prism of diverse creaturely reality into a rainbow of incarnate reconciliation.[8]

Figural Imagination and Secular Sensibility

This figural economy was, Frei says, a 'given' for Barth's imagination. This imagination is, of course, a *biblical* imagination – an imagination which feeds upon the many concrete portrayals in the Bible and which passionately believes that these portrayals form a unity, with Christ at their centre (and, although the Bible may not form the same kind of structural unity as the *Comedy*, for the figural imagination it is nonetheless a unity: it is not simply 'the Scriptures', it is one Bible). Barth's imagination is also both a *Christological* and an *eschatological* imagination, and the two are inseparable: it is an imagination which looks for the fulfilment of all creaturely reality in Christ's first and second advents and it is an imagination for which there is therefore a concrete horizon set to creaturely reality – a horizon which both appears in the midst of history and is still to come.

More importantly for our purposes, however, the comparison with Dante allows Frei to specify the ways in which Barth's figural imagination was at the same time an *historical* imagination. On the one hand, recognition of Barth's Christocentric vision as a figural vision allows Frei to describe Barth's imagination of fulfilment in Christ as anything but 'Christomonist': it suggests a vision of the fulfilment of history according to which each particular is seen in relationship to Christ and has its very particularity established and accentuated in that relationship. This is a fulfilment which does not involve the annulment or loss of any figure's concrete particularity; it does not involve the abolition of any figure's creatureliness; it does not involve the erasure of any figure's difference from Jesus of Nazareth. In this fulfilment all figures find their full reality as the individual creatures they are, in unity with Christ, and only in Christ.[9]

On the other hand, however, the comparison with Auerbach's Dante allows Frei to highlight another way in which Barth's figural imagination is an historical imagination, by pointing to a kind of shadow that his figural imagination casts, which Frei refers to as Barth's 'sceptical and secular' sensibility. In order to understand this claim, though, we need to be a little more precise about the nature of the figural imagination. That imagination sees every instance or form of a relationship between God and creation as a figure of the incarnate reconciliation between God and humanity that is Jesus of Nazareth. A figural relationship is not a relationship based on straightforward causal links between the poles of the relationship, nor a relationship based on a process of evolution that includes both poles; rather, it is a relationship grounded solely in God's providential plan. This means, however, that when a figural relationship is displayed like this, there is no further evidence which can be presented to explain *how* this relationship works: the only things that one can do by way of explanation are, first, to refer to the mysterious freedom of God for creation which allows him to call and form witnesses in the midst of creation, and, second, to portray both figure and fulfilment in such a way as to highlight the resemblance or contrast between them. A figural relationship cannot be explained; it can only be displayed (Frei, 1993, pp. 170–72).[10]

In other words, the figural relationship is not an expression of some deeper worldly relation between the events, which could be exposed with the right analytic techniques; there is no hidden variable to which the displayed figural relationship is epiphenomenal. What God does in Christ is not the activation or fulfilment of some prior potential within history which also lies behind the apparently diverse figures of Christ in history. If that were the case, then to establish the existence of the prior potential would be to find the *real* relationship between figure and figured – a real relationship of which the figural relationship was a secondary form. If, for instance, we were to hold that Abraham was a figure of Christ because he partially fulfilled the human possibility of God-consciousness which we see perfected in Christ, then that human possibility would provide the secret, subterranean connection between Abraham and Christ at which the figural relationship merely hinted.

Barth, says Frei, resisted any move which would make the actual, concrete, historical appearance of Christ secondary to some deeper, more pervasive worldly possibility (ibid., pp. 170–71). Such a move would inevitably imply that there was a point at which we could substitute the general name of that possibility for the particular name of Jesus of Nazareth. The 'possibility' of Christ's appearance as the fulfilment of all history is to be found purely on God's side, not on the world's side. There is no site within ourselves, no aspect of the 'human situation', no portion of history, no worldly reality which serves to explain the incarnation's possibility. Christology cannot begin with anthropology or with any such generalizing discipline.

Put another way, we may say that, if history is regarded *remoto Christo*, we cannot expect to find any *praeparatio evangelica*, any capacity or potential for relationship with the divine which could in any way dictate the forms in which God could bring that relationship about. Speaking of Barth's 'slightly bemused and slightly amused but appreciative and even delighted' appreciation of America, described in the introduction to the American edition of *Evangelical Theology*, Frei says:

> It is not only the case, I believe, that Barth took pleasure in the vast variety of this indefinitely expansive human experience in this vast natural context – not only

that he affirmed every part of it, at once in and for itself and for its potentiality as a *figura* of God's fulfilling work. Additionally, I believe he looked with a long, cool scepticism at that scene and every part of it because he believed that none of it shows that figural potential by any inherent qualities or signs of its own – either positive or negative. (Ibid., p. 172)

This negative constraint, however, is the source of a far more positive vision. If this constraint is taken absolutely seriously (and Frei suggests that Barth did take it seriously), history is freed from an unbearable burden; it is freed from having to be the ground of the ways of God, it is freed to be itself, freed to be properly creaturely. If Barth's figural imagination is an imagination which sees the particularity and individuality of history upheld when that history is fulfilled in Christ, its shadow-side is a paradoxically 'secular' vision which sees, *remoto Christo*, only the particularity and diversity, the complexity and contingency of history. This is what Frei means when he says that 'there was in Barth a self-conscious secularity of sensibility far, far beyond' that shown by any apologetic theologian who seeks to find in this world the possibility which God's work fulfils. 'Barth', he says,

... may have explored at once calmly and passionately, at once positively and negatively, that secularity which from a theological stance he would have thought an 'impossible possibility'. He may have explored it far more searchingly than any of his opponents, as well as any of his own modifiers with their little apologetical nostrums, either in favor of or against the 'secular situation'. (Ibid., p. 173)

Figural imagination and secular sensibility go hand in hand.[11]

Any suggestion that Barth was, in his own way, a 'secular' theologian needs, of course, very careful handling if it is not to be patently false. We must, for instance, note that Frei in no way suggests that Barth was in possession of some total secular account of the world, an account which excluded God, or graciously allowed God in at its gaps, or which could be set in paradoxical relationship with a positive theological account. The secular, sceptical vision of which Frei speaks is more like an *absence* of such accounts, a willingness to pay attention to the always disruptive, never containable suddenness of things, a willingness to wait upon the particularity of the world rather than pre-emptively positioning and explaining it. The secular, sceptical sensibility of which Frei speaks is, we might say, a commitment to an unending *learning* of the world which does not know in advance what it will find, and which is not simply recalling or confirming general truths already known.

We should not think, either, that the secular, sceptical sensibility is some universally available default position to which all right-thinking observers would revert if only they would dare to think, dare to rid themselves of religious obfuscation. I have called it the shadow-side of Barth's figural imagination deliberately: it is itself produced by the same light of revelation that makes the figural economy visible. Barth is, in Frei's terms, able to take secularity seriously precisely because, for him, it has been made visible by Christ; in Christ Barth finds a judgement upon all religious accounts of the world, and it is only in Christ that he finds the possibility of a non-religious account of the world.[12]

The secular, sceptical sensibility that Frei identifies is, then, a view of the world *remoto Christo*, only visible in the light of Christ. Is this not simply a contradiction? Is attention to the world *remoto Christo* truly a possibility for Barth? After all, for him, the whole of history is to be interpreted in the light of Jesus Christ, and that light reveals the truth about all history; it is not some colouring lent only accidentally by Christ to a history that makes sense on its own. Nevertheless, that light is cast by Jesus and only by Jesus, and that means that it is cast by one concrete occurrence within history. We are, therefore, better able to imagine the world without Christ than we would be able to if Christ's reality or possibility were somehow a deduction from the world; there is no necessity for Christ on the world's side, and therefore the world may be imagined (temporarily, with fear and trembling) without Christ.

To summarize: Frei uses a comparison with Auerbach's Dante to introduce his account of Barth's figural imagination and secular sensibility. On the one hand, he finds in Barth a ringing affirmation that history is fulfilled in Christ – that in Christ it is made most fully real, that in Christ it attains the full being which it has hitherto lacked; on the other hand, he finds that this fulfilment in no way abolishes the concrete particularity of history, but rather that the figural vision allows that particularity to be taken with utmost seriousness. In Barth, in other words, Frei finds a depiction of the fulfilment of history precisely as history.

Barth's Figural Reading

It is impossible in an essay of this scope to give Frei's proposed reading of Barth anything like a comprehensive testing. In particular, asking to what extent the Christocentric organization of Barth's work has the character of a figural economy would involve working through much of the *Church Dogmatics*. Consequently, I have set myself the more manageable task here of looking at some of Barth's explicit use of figural interpretation, to see whether it can inform and deepen the sketch of figural economy provided by Frei.

Election and Rejection

In the Preface to *The Eclipse of Biblical Narrative*, Frei suggests reading *Church Dogmatics* II/2, pp. 340–409 as one example from amongst a 'vast number' of 'Barth's remarkable use of figural interpretation of the Old Testament'. This passage is part of Barth's presentation of the doctrine of election, specifically the election of the individual; it is the second part of that presentation where, after having treated 'Jesus Christ, the promise and its recipient', Barth turns to 'The elect and the rejected' with the question, 'What is it that makes individuals elect?' (CD II/2, p. 340).

The answer which Barth gives is, of course, that it is God who makes individuals elect: the election of an individual is first and foremost a distinction in the way God stands towards that person; it is not based on any 'attribute or achievement' of that person. However, this election is inevitably displayed; the fact that God stands towards a specific person in this particular way finds its expression or correlate in the calling, guidance, conduct and role of that person in his or her specific history. Indeed, this is part of what election means: election to be a witness to, or a displayer of, the God who elects, and the election by which God elects.

A specific human life does not display this election by becoming subject to an external constraint (such that election would compete with freedom), nor does he or she display election by meeting some formula or following some recipe for what can count as an elect life. Each elect person displays election in his or her own way, by being entirely him- or herself. To use an inadequate analogy, it is as if God were to chose to witness to Godself by telling a story about an individual person, but could only make the story a good witness by making it the story of a full-blooded, consistent, contingent and free individual – that is, by telling the story of a being who reflected, in a creaturely way, God's own nature as free, as one who is what he is. It is as if God could only witness to Godself by telling a story of an individual who was not simply exhausted by some abstract definition of witness, who was not simply illustrative of some general theological theme, but who was a free person able to respond in love to the three-personed God who loves in freedom.

Expressed more precisely, God determines individuals to display their election in irreducibly diverse ways, in ways that are coextensive with their unsubstitutable individuality. The calling, guidance, conduct and role of the elect individual are historical occurrences that take time to unfold; they are inherently temporal. We may recall Frei's insistence that a person's identity as witness or embodiment is not a constraint upon, or accidental to, his or her particularity; it *is* his or her particular, temporal identity.

Although election is not *grounded* in any difference of the elect from other human beings, it is *displayed* in such a difference: it is marked by individuals having proclaimed to them, and responding in faith to, their election in and with Christ. All elect people are, in their own ways, marked out like this from those who are not elect: 'In different ways they repeat and reproduce the solitude of Christ. They are lights in the world because he is the Light of the world' (*CD* II/2, p. 345).

It is not, of course, only the elect for whom '[t]he original and proper distinction of Jesus Christ … is the truth which … transcends, comprehends and illumines their existence' (ibid., p. 349). There are also those, the 'rejected', who attempt to live in denial of this election, who attempt to live as ones rejected by God, yet who can only lie by so doing because God has allowed that role to be filled and exhausted by Jesus Christ (ibid., p. 346). In other words, the witness to God's election in Jesus Christ which God calls into being in history, which God *determines*, is a witness which takes two basic forms: the form of acceptance and the form of rejection. Yet each individual makes this witness in his or her own way, displaying this election and rejection in and through his or her own irreducibly complex and contingent path. The basic distinction of acceptance and rejection, each a form of witness to God's election in Jesus Christ, is worked out and displayed in forms that are coterminous with the peculiar concrete destiny of innumerable individuals.

Barth's whole discussion of the nature of election is in fact a redescription of the results of his exegesis – in particular his exegesis of the Old Testament where the electing and rejecting will of God is displayed precisely in and through the portrayal of elect and apparently rejected individuals and groups caught up for a time in the activity of God, without any diminution or overriding of their particular individuality, without any dissolution of the 'freedom in which they are what they are' (ibid., p. 343).[13] Barth stresses that each individual person who becomes, for a time, the secondary subject of the biblical witness becomes a witness in his or her own peculiar way, but nevertheless becomes a witness to the same Lord. The final word in exegesis of all these diverse figures is the same: 'Jesus Christ'. Barth does not, however, mean to take away what he has just given and suggest that the rich contingency of the Old Testament stories ultimately reduces to sameness; the relationship of all these figures to Jesus does not work like that:

> [W]e do not recognise him in any of these types in exactly the same way as in the others, but ... in all of them we have to recognise him as he is. None of the types gives quite the same witness as the others. None simply repeats the witness of the others. The historical multiformity of individual elect and non-elect, of those placed on the right and those on the left, cannot be ignored, and no sound exegesis can afford to ignore it. It cannot be glossed over. It cannot be reduced to a formula. It cannot be simplified. But this multiformity of historical appearances is *best observed and maintained* if here too the final word in exegesis is actually the name of Jesus Christ, if he is understood as the individual in whom we recover both the unity of that which they all commonly attest, and that which is the peculiar individuality of each. (Ibid., p. 366, emphasis added)

If, then, we ask what Barth means, and how he can justify his talk of election, calling and determination – how he can say that individuals display their election precisely in and through their freedom and how he can say that finding the name of Jesus Christ to be the final word in exegesis, far from undercutting the history-like nature of the biblical stories, is the *best* way to observe and maintain their historical multiformity – if we ask all this, the only kind of answer that Barth ultimately gives is exegesis.[14] Rather than directing us to some metaphysic that could ground the possibility of such a claim, he points to the reality, to the ranks of the elect and the rejected who parade through Scripture.

Selected Figures

After 14 pages of his dogmatic presentation of these ideas, with a few exegetical comments thrown in, Barth continues this section of the *Dogmatics* with an immense block of exegesis, covering 55 pages of small print. He begins with a brief survey, mentioning Cain and Abel, Isaac and Ishmael, Jacob and Esau, Rachel and Leah, Ephraim and Manasseh, Perez and Serah, Israel and Moab, and Midian and Canaan (*CD* II/2, pp. 354–57), before turning to three longer exegeses.

He first concentrates on two rituals in which election and rejection are enacted: the ritual of the two birds in Leviticus 14:4–7 (for the cleansing of a leper) and the ritual of the two goats in Leviticus 16:5–22 (on the Day of Atonement). He suggests that, in each ritual, the Israelite spectator sees 'in a picture' his own relationship to God's election and rejection, which are enacted upon the two goats or the two birds. Barth insists, however, that we look more closely at the detail of the passages and see the differences between them. If we do so, we see that they run in opposite directions. In the ritual for the Day of Atonement, the 'elect' goat is sacrificed, and the Israelite sees in this both that his life is required of him and that God will graciously take his life as an acceptable sacrifice. The other goat, however, the 'unusable' goat, shows in its 'surrender to an utterly distressful non-existence' (ibid., p. 359) the fate from which the elect are saved. In the ritual of the two birds, however, the bird that is sacrificed is killed for the sake of the bird that is released. In the sacrificed bird, the leper sees that his accession to purity occurs only with the death of his impure life; in the freed bird, which is first dipped in the blood of the dead bird, he sees that he is removed from the realm of God's wrath and 'once more a free member of the congregation' (ibid., p. 360).

> If, according to Leviticus 16, the non-elect, those who are separated and rejected, stand in the shadows in order that the grace of God may illumine and continue to illumine the elect, we are taught also by Leviticus 14 that it is to the realm of Azazel that the light of God's grace is poured and streams abroad. Let us gratefully know ourselves to be elect in the picture of the first goat of Leviticus 16 – grateful that we are accepted to sacrifice ourselves, grateful that we may suffer the saving judgment of the wrath of God, which is the wrath of his love, as only the elect can and may do! But let us with equal gratitude recognise ourselves as the non-elect in the picture of the second bird of Leviticus 14 – grateful because there is ordained for us the life for whose painful birth the other is elected, the resurrection for whose sake the elect must go to his death! (Ibid., p. 361)

Having established this interpretation, Barth raises two questions. First, he asks whether the individual Israelite can truly see himself in either the dead or the living animal. Does he really see that his life is handed over to God and found to be an acceptable sacrifice? Does he really see that he has finally been transferred to freedom? Barth suggests that life, as we know it, is more limited than this, both negatively and positively, and that we do not see in the biblical stories of the elect and the rejected this kind of purity, completeness or finality in their election or rejection. The rituals represent election and rejection in a heightened, extreme, 'superhuman' form which 'transcends the human reality known to us' (ibid., p. 362). Second, Barth asks how it is that the individual Israelite can see himself both as simultaneously dying a pure death by the grace of God, and being freed for true life by the same divine grace? How can the unity of the twofold picture portrayed in these rituals be achieved? More generally, looking at the Old Testament narratives of election and rejection, Barth notes that, despite all the fluidity according to which the rejected can appear suddenly as the recipients of God's favour, and the elected as the recipients of his wrath, election and rejection are nevertheless finally always represented by two separate individuals or groups, and the full unity of election and rejection in one individual is not, and cannot be, portrayed, even though it is suggested by the interrelation between the two doves or the two goats and hinted at in the fluidity just mentioned.

In the face of this 'twofold enigma', Barth suggests that there is a provisionality about the Old Testament witness to election and rejection. The two rituals together suggest a form of election and rejection the full actuality of which we cannot find in the Old Testament:

> These data confront us with the following choice. On the one hand, this subject of the Old Testament witness may be regarded as an unknown quantity. This might mean that for some reason it is not yet known to us, whether because it has not yet made itself known, or has in fact taken place but has somehow escaped us. But it might also mean that the Old Testament has no subject at all, that its testimony points into the void, and that in the place to which its stories and sacrificial pictures ... all point, there is, in fact, nothing, so that there is nothing to see, and never will be anything to see. On the other hand, the subject of the Old Testament witness may be accepted as identical with the person of Jesus Christ as he is seen and interpreted and proclaimed by the apostles because he had himself revealed and represented himself to them in this way. (Ibid., p. 363)

Barth is deadly serious here. This is no hermeneutical conjuring trick whereby he, with a twinkle in his eye, will pull a Christological rabbit from a Levitical hat. He believes that his exegesis shows that these Old Testament texts point to an election and rejection greater and more final than any they portray, that there is an eschatological provisionality even about these supposedly static Levitical texts. He believes that a recognition of this eschatological dynamism requires us to ask the further question about what kind of fulfilment will come. Furthermore, he believes that his exegesis does not force the question, but allows that there could be no fulfilment, or another fulfilment, instead of fulfilment in Christ.[15] Nevertheless, he believes that the eschatological provisionality that he has identified is part of the context in which Christ emerges, and by which Christ interprets himself and is rightly interpreted by the apostles. The incompleteness and provisionality of the election and rejection actually found in Israel's past and the promise of the completion and unity of election and rejection found at least in Israel's rituals create a space which Christ occupies and transforms. For those who believe in Christ, '[h]ow can we believe in Jesus Christ and not of necessity recognise Him in these passages?' (ibid., p. 364). As a result, Barth goes on therefore, to declare the figural exegesis that Calvin gave to the Leviticus 16 passage 'correct' (ibid., p. 365).

In his second example, Barth retells the whole drama of Israel's first two kings, Saul and David, turning from a passage in which election and rejection are portrayed in their purity by means of a ritual to one in which they are displayed in the thick of human lives. Barth provides first a reading of 1 Samuel 8, in which the 'folly of the nation' demands a '*melek* of the same kind as all other nations' and God judges the nation by giving them what they have asked for, and yet saves them by revealing that his will for them (concealed until now) is a will for a different kind of king, his anointed one. Saul is both this anointed king chosen by God according to God's good purposes and a king like the kings of the Gentiles who is given by God as a judgement; he is, according to Barth, the former concealed under the latter. This reading enables Barth to give a powerful interpretation of Saul's sin, acknowledging that '[t]o this very day we find it difficult to stifle the sympathy and approval which are more readily felt than their opposite' in relation to his 'microscopic sins' (*CD* II/2, pp. 369–70). Saul's sins are precisely moments in which it is clear that he fulfils the nation's desire for the wrong kind of king; he thus shows himself to be both God's judgement against Israel and the one whom God has rejected, and hides his character as God's salvation for Israel and the one whom God has chosen.

From Saul, Barth turns to the 'remarkable figure of David' (ibid., p. 372). David has the same dual character as Saul, but in his case divine election, rather than rejection, is uppermost. Nevertheless, both sides are still emphatically there; indeed, Saul's sins barely register when measured against David's. At this point, Barth makes no simplistic or easy generalizations:

> Why, if [David] is God's elect, is he not unmistakably differentiated from Saul? For all the beauty of the story, it is confusing and disturbing that Saul's son has the leading role in their covenant before God. And it is still more confusing that the position of the king who is also the son of God is not awarded to David but to his son. It is again confusing that for no very clear reason David is debarred from building the temple. Above all, how confusing it is that in his sin he actually realises in a much harsher fashion than Saul in his sins the picture of the heathen king rejected by God. (Ibid., p. 387)

The difference between Saul and David is not based on any comparative estimate of the weight of each man's sins. The difference between them is purely and simply that in David we see election uppermost and in Saul rejection uppermost; God has determined his relation to each differently, and that determination is seen in the whole course of each man's life as it is displayed in the texts of 1 Samuel. Nevertheless, David only appears as the elect in such a way that the shadow of the rejected *melek* of the Gentiles looms large behind him; Saul only appears as the rejected in such a way that the light of God's anointed ruler plays constantly across his features. This ambiguity, Barth suggests, is never absent from the subsequent sorry history of the kings of Israel and Judah. Once again, Barth finds that there is a riddle here – an eschatological provisionality:

> It is the riddle of the fact of a religious community which is gathered and remains gathered for centuries about a text whose content is necessarily a riddle for them, in itself as well as in its relation to their contemporary situation. For in it they can find only the story of a mistake – and of a mistake which in the text itself is

actually, though not explicitly, admitted. They can find only the story of a
beginning ... without the corresponding development, a broken column pointing
senselessly upwards, or, at any rate, a prophecy so far unfulfilled .... It is only
eschatologically and therefore only as prophecy that they can read and
understand these texts, if at all, as the texts of revelation. (Ibid., p. 386)

And once again, and with the same reserve, Barth finally turns to the question of
figural exegesis:

> [W]e can only again say that the ultimate exegetical question in relation to these
> passages – the question of their subject – is identical with the question of faith:
> whether with the apostles we recognise this subject in the person of Jesus Christ,
> or whether with the Synagogue both then and now we do not recognise Christ.
> The question obviously cannot be settled by the Old Testament passages as such.
> The final result of the passages as such is the difficulty. Again, it is naturally
> impermissible to accept the reply of the apostles solely because we cannot solve
> these difficulties in the exegesis of the text itself, or because, on the other hand,
> we share with them an idea that Jesus Christ is supremely fitted to occupy the
> place where we are pulled up short. The apostles themselves did not reach their
> answer as a possibility discovered or selected by themselves, or as a final triumph
> of Jewish biblical scholarship. They did so because the Old Testament was
> opened up to them by its fulfilment in the resurrection of Jesus Christ, and
> because in the light of this fulfilment Old Testament prophecy could no longer be
> read by them in any other way than as an account of this subject. (Ibid., pp.
> 388–89)

There is no need to describe Barth's third example in the same detail. He examines
the strange self-contained tale of the man of God from Judah and the old prophet of
Bethel found in 1 Kings 13, and finds that similar questions to those which he has
raised in the priestly context of the Levitical rituals, and the kingly context of Saul
and David, are raised in a story of prophets and men of God; once again, he finds that
the story points to a resolution which is not contained in the Old Testament itself and,
once again, he argues that a Christian can find that resolution nowhere else than in
Jesus Christ.

In all three examples we see the same movement. Barth begins by practising an
exegetical ascesis: he refuses to begin by finding Christ in these Old Testament
stories. Instead, he begins by paying careful attention to the texts as they stand, to
their details and their dynamics. He is even perfectly willing to pay attention to the
textual history and the subsequent use of these passages.[16] He deliberately and
explicitly brackets out his Christology and approaches the texts, in the first instance,
remoto Christo; he deliberately and repeatedly reminds us of this ascesis even while
he is reintroducing the Christocentric frame at the end of his exegeses.[17] Only once
the passage has been carefully interpreted *remoto Christo* is the hermeneutical
restriction lifted, and only then does Barth's interpretation become thoroughly
figural. He finds that the Old Testament portrayals, in all their rich detail, both
illumine and are illumined by Jesus Christ not because there is some process of
development linking the two, but simply because God has provided in Christ the

answer and fulfilment to the reality that he established in the Levitical rituals, or in the rise of Saul and David. 'Fulfilment' is seen in the specific ways in which it turns out that these passages point beyond themselves, and Jesus Christ is seen to occupy the space at which they point; it is seen in the always particular ways in which each Old Testament character is made a witness (whether positive or negative) to Jesus Christ.

Note: From the Old Testament to the World

In the discussion above, I have silently made a transition from Frei's suggestion that Barth's figural imagination encompassed the *whole of creaturely reality* to examination of Barth's practice of figural interpretation of the *Old Testament*. This distinction cannot be ignored, however; it is the reason why we cannot directly equate Barth's hermeneutical ascesis in his approach to Old Testament texts with the 'secular, sceptical sensibility' that Frei described, even though they are related. The Old Testament is not simply history; it is a witness to the activity of God in history, and it is a witness that, for Barth, holds a privileged position within the purposes of God. It is also a text that has an ambiguous, questionable relationship to any historical-critical reconstruction of 'what really happened'. For the 'secular, sceptical sensibility' described by Frei, not even a negative preparation for the Gospel can be found by examining history *remoto Christo*; for the 'hermeneutical ascesis' an eschatological provisionality can be discovered in the Old Testament narratives even when they are considered on their own terms: they are found to pose a question which need not, but can, be answered by Christ. If Frei is right, then not even a question to which Christ is the answer can be discovered when history is considered 'on its own terms'.

Nevertheless, this difference does not mean that what we have said about the Old Testament can have no wider applicability, for the God to whom the Old Testament texts witness – the electing and rejecting, calling and judging God – is witnessed to precisely as the God of the whole world. The God who is what God is here is identical to the God of all; God everywhere is therefore what God is here. The same electing and rejecting will which Barth found displayed clearly in the Old Testament texts is displayed everywhere, if only we have eyes to see. The difference between interpretation of the Old Testament and interpretation of the world more generally is that, in the latter case, we have further to travel before we can gain those eyes. Frei's point in describing Barth's secular sensibility is precisely that only once we have been given eyes, once we have been schooled in new ways of seeing, can we find even such negative preparations for the Gospel as Barth finds in the Old Testament. We are faced with having to learn from the biblical witness how to make even the initial interpretation of history which is already present in the Old Testament, and that is very likely also to involve an unlearning of improper interpretations. There is no recipe for success in these matters, and any interpretation we are able to offer is bound to be partial and provisional; nevertheless, Frei wants to claim that, assuming this extra work and extra fragility, a similar kind of figural interpretation can be practised on the newspaper as can be practised on the Old Testament.

The Figural Economy

Hans Frei understood Barth's *Church Dogmatics* as a figural economy – that is, as a portrayal of the 'fulfilment of all natural, historical being' in Jesus Christ, in such a way that the full concrete particularity and contingency of historical being is not undercut or ignored, but preserved and proclaimed in this fulfilment. He understood that this kind of fulfilment was not simply asserted or theoretically described in Barth, but that Barth had found a fitting means for portraying it, for showing it. Explicit figural interpretation is, for Frei, the most revealing way in which Barth does this. If we ask what it can possibly mean for history to be fulfilled without diminution of its particularity, Frei will point us to Barth's exegesis. See how Barth finds Christ to be the subject-matter of these history-like stories without turning away from their history-likeness, he will say; look how he does justice to their contingency, their roughness, their intractability, and finds that they speak of Christ in and through that. That is both a depiction of, and a promise of, the fulfilment of historical being in Christ.

Is Frei right, however? Does Barth's practice display the kind of fulfilment Frei describes? Certainly, it seems that Barth's figural exegesis is meant to inspire a closer attention to the rich detail of each pole of the figural relationship, as well as a revelation of the truth about each pole's particularity, rather than a turn away from either pole towards some abstraction.[18] And the connections that he eventually proclaims are, indeed, not based on any worldly continuity or causality, but solely on the freedom of God – and Barth's employment of this kind of interpretation coheres thoroughly with his constant refusal to dig beneath the actuality of what God has done in history to find some worldly possibility which would ground or explain it.

However, when we examine his figural interpretation closely and ask ourselves what precisely the 'fulfilment' of a figure consists in, we see him proceeding by locating in both the Old Testament figure and the Gospel fulfilment a common *pattern* of election and rejection. Each pole of the figural relationship can be redescribed in terms of this pattern, in such a way that the election–rejection pattern in Jesus Christ appears as the completion of an otherwise truncated pattern in the Old Testament stories. The election–rejection pattern provides, in this case, the *content* of the claim that there is a figural relationship between these poles; the pattern, as it were, *mediates* the figural relationship.

This specification of the meaning of 'figural relationship' raises a question. Is Barth finally substituting a pattern, a diagram, a conceptual scheme, for the history-like narrative? Does his figural practice involve turning away from the unsubstitutable particularity of both figure and fulfilment at the last moment? Our suspicions might be sharpened by noting how readily two of the passages chosen by

Barth lend themselves to a quasi-structuralist reduction to diagrams. The rituals in Leviticus 14 and 16, and the folk-tale-like quality of the story in 1 Kings 13 are, in Frei's terms, less 'history-like' than many Old Testament narratives. They are, to some extent, constructed out of a series of categorial oppositions built into Israelite culture, and it is no surprise to find that Barth's pattern-seeking exegesis provides powerful and largely convincing accounts of these passages. What, though, of the far more unruly story of Saul and David? There is no doubt, of course, that Barth's exegesis is a *tour de force*, nor any doubt that he pays sustained attention to a whole range of details and disruptive elements in the stories; nevertheless, despite its enduring brilliance, it is possible to be left with an irritating worry that Barth succeeded, despite himself, in replacing a messy and uncontrollable history with a calculus, and that his confidence in proclaiming the nature of this story's patterned provisionality and hence his proclamation of the kind of resolution it demands is just a little brash, just a little reductive. We can be left with a suspicion that this story's rich complexity is more than Barth can capture in his ultimately diagrammatic exegesis, that it exceeds his conceptual schema, and that Barth's exegesis does therefore involve a turning away from history at the last moment. This worry might give us pause for thought – suggesting that Frei's interpretation of Barth's intentions is misguided, or that Barth does not finally measure up to his intentions.

However, the exegesis we have examined is part of the supporting material for Barth's dogmatic exposition of just one doctrinal locus: that of election and rejection. Barth returns to this material in his discussion of other loci; for instance, he treats much of the same material in *CD* IV/1, pp. 437ff. in his discussion of pride and discusses an element ignored in the present exegesis in *CD* IV/2, pp. 427ff. in his discussion of sloth. The material we have discussed is not Barth's sole or final interpretation of this passage: it is one reading, for one purpose. Yes, his figural exegesis goes by way of the identification of a pattern – a pattern inevitably less rich than the story it describes – but that pattern is not a *replacement* for the story, it is (in the wider context of the complete *Dogmatics*) *subordinate* to the story.

All figural exegesis, insofar as it finds a relationship between two unsubstitutable particular poles, is bound to involve a moment of abstraction: after all, the particularity of the poles means that they are not identical, that they are first of all themselves, and to find a similarity between them is, therefore, necessarily to find a relationship between them *in some respect*: it is inevitably to bracket at least some of the complexity that makes each pole particular. This need not mean, however, that figural exegesis cannot ultimately do justice to the unsubstitutable particularity, the history-likeness, of the poles; it simply means that we cannot think of any single performance of figural exegesis exhausting the poles, and must always accept the possibility of returning and re-reading these poles.[19]

If we restrict our attention for the moment to the relationship between Old Testament figures and their New Testament fulfilment, we can take Frei's interpretation of Barth to mean simply that the fulfilment of the Old Testament in the New is not its abolition but, rather, a fulfilment that frees us *for* the Old Testament.

That is, it is a fulfilment that sends us back again and again to read the Old Testament 'in its own terms', paying attention to its complex, contingent, disruptive nature. Time and time again we will find that we discover patterns which allow us (but do not force us, unless we have faith in Christ) to link Old Testament and New; we will find, for instance, that we can see patterns of election and rejection running through Old Testament narratives and reaching some kind of culmination in the Gospel depiction of Christ. On that kind of basis, we will be able to erect some more abstract scaffolding – in this case a doctrine of election – but we will have to make sure both that the doctrine is framed in such a way as not to suggest that the pattern we have seen is somehow a replacement for the story in which we found it (hence Barth's careful specification of the relationship between God's election and its always different display in the particular course of individuals' lives) and that we do not suggest that this pattern is the only one that can be found (hence Barth's return to the same stories in other contexts). To claim that Jesus Christ is the fulfilment of an Old Testament narrative is to commit to this endless paying of attention, this endless finding of patterns which partially confirm our commitment, this endless reading of the Old Testament narrative alongside the Gospels.

Frei's claim about Barth's figural economy was not simply about relationships between Old and New Testaments, however. He claimed that 'figura' provided a way of talking about the relationship between all creaturely reality and Christ. This suggests an extension of what we have just said, and also an interpretation of Frei's suggestions about the 'secular sensibility'. To claim that all creaturely reality is fulfilled in Christ is to commit to an endless attention to the particularities of the world, an attention educated by our reading of the Bible. It is to commit to an endless learning of a world which is always surprising, always disturbing, always disruptive of any premature generalization or any too-easy closure. It means committing to reading the world and the Gospel side-by-side – the newspaper in one hand, the Bible in the other – expecting to find patterns linking the two, and expecting never to stop finding such patterns.

Lastly, Frei's suggestions provide us with a way of talking about eschatological fulfilment. If creaturely reality as it now is looks forward to eschatological fulfilment in Christ, then it is not looking for its reduction to Christ, or its sublation by Christ, or its abolition in favour of Christ. Rather, it is looking for a future in which it, in ever new ways, explores and interprets the inexhaustible riches of Christ, refracting and reflecting Christ in ways that are endlessly particular. Precisely by being our fulfilled selves we will be constantly renewed fulfilments of Christ. An individual instance of figural interpretation is a hint, a gesture in the direction of this fulfilment; the ongoing practice of returning again and again to figural exegesis provides a better picture of the fulfilment for which we hope.

Counsels for Reading the *Dogmatics*

My suggestions lead to some counsels for reading the *Church Dogmatics*. First, I suggest that the *Church Dogmatics* be seen as a school of figural interpretation. With its enormous length, its curiously repetitive structure and its constant return to exegesis, the *Church Dogmatics* is not simply a static description of a theological system, but a dynamic attempt to teach its readers to read differently – to become, for example, readers of the Old Testament who have learnt to keep the potential distractions of historical criticism and source analysis in their proper place, who have learnt a second naivete in which the texts can be read 'in their own terms' once more, and who have begun learning that Christian vision by which the figural possibilities of the text once more become visible.[20] In this school, the reader is also learning to read the *world* – learning, that is, to unlearn some of the ways we have had of confining the world in ultimately implausible apologetic structures, learning more positively to see the world with a second naivete which allows it to be itself (that is, to see it with what Frei called a secular sensibility), and learning to see the world's figural potential, visible in the light of Christ. These things can only be learnt by example and practice, precisely because they are endlessly and always particular, beyond any recipe or diagram. Only by seeing figural reading done well, and done repeatedly, and done in an almost endless variety of ways, can we serve the kind of apprenticeship that will allow us to go on producing our own figural readings.

Second, however, my suggestions involve reading the *Dogmatics* in such a way that the priority of the biblical narratives over any single performance of exegesis or commentary is preserved. This counsel could be rephrased more pithily: the *Church Dogmatics* is best read inside out. Frei apparently counselled some of his students to begin the *Dogmatics* with volume IV, because there the dependence of Barth's dogmatic exposition on repeated close reading of the Gospel narratives is most evident; to begin reading there is to see that the whole *Dogmatics* rests upon such reading and rereading (a point that is less evident if one begins with volume I). Or we might suggest regarding the small-print sections as having priority over the large-print sections, because the large-print sections contain the refined results of the exegesis performed in the small-print sections and properly point back to them. A *Dogmatics* without the large-print sections would still have integrity (even if it lacked apparent organization); a *Dogmatics* without the small-print sections is inconceivable. Lastly, we could even suggest that the proper doorway into the *Church Dogmatics* is the Index volume – not the contents section, in which the dogmatic theses are set out in logical order, but the Scripture References index and, above all, the 'Aids to the Preacher' section, in which we see most clearly the nature of the *Dogmatics* as exegesis, repeated exegesis, in which pattern after pattern is unearthed in the same text, and those patterns slowly built into an overall dogmatic structure (*not* a systematic structure) which is in one sense nothing more than a guide to ways of reading and rereading these biblical texts. Only if the *Dogmatics* is read 'inside-out' in these sorts of ways can we preserve the truly figural nature of Barth's achievement as a depiction of the fulfilment rather than the abolition of history.

The third counsel may again be put pithily: we should carefully consider whether we should be reading the *Dogmatics* at all. My message, and Frei's, and (if we are right) Barth's as well, is that we must pick up the Bible in one hand and the newspaper in the other and never put them down – and that no book of theology (even the *Church Dogmatics*) can substitute for either. We must go on reading the Bible and the newspaper in the light of each other, looking for particular ways in which, by the grace of God, we can find patterns linking the two – hints of the fulfilment of history in Jesus of Nazareth. We cannot expect to produce any final reading of either, both because the fullness of the fulfilment for which we hope is an eschatological reality towards which the Bible only points (it is Virgil as well as Beatrice) and because the fulfilment we see embodied in it (it is Beatrice as well as Virgil) is an unsubstitutably particular human being. We can only expect to glimpse the fulfilment of history in an endless multiplicity of figural exegeses which mine, but never exhaust, the texts they interpret. Of course, the Christian interpreter with the Bible in one hand and the newspaper in the other may well have the *Church Dogmatics* on a table beside her and may properly use it as one school in which she can learn to read the materials in her hands. But it is no replacement. The abstractions of doctrine are tools in the art of Christian interpretation, but they do not provide a separate object of consideration in their own right, one to which we could turn when we have penetrated beneath the messy particulars of the Bible or the newspaper. However powerful these tools, the more abstract disciplines of theology are, in the figural vision, subordinate to the practice of exegesis, subordinate to the hunt for the always particular ways in which Jesus of Nazareth both is, and witnesses to, the fulfilment of history. We may well ask, with Frei, 'Has Christian theology succeeded in setting us another task instead of this?' (Frei, 1993, p. 175).

Notes

1 The papers were collected in a special edition of the journal of the Yale Divinity School Association, *Reflection*, **66**(4). Frei's paper (Frei, 1969) was later republished in Frei (1993) but that reprint omitted the discussion involving Frei which was transcribed in the Dickerman volume (Dickerman, 1969).

2 Cf. 'Scripture as Realistic Narrative: Karl Barth as Critic of Historical Criticism', a paper that Frei presented to the Barth Colloquium in Toronto in spring 1974. A transcript of an audio recording of this session has been edited by Mark Alan Bowald, and appears on the Yale Divinity School web site at http://www.library.yale.edn/div/div076.htm.

3 The bibliography lists the main relevant sources under 'Auerbach'. It is unclear whether Frei read the *Dante* book (Auerbach, 1961); he was fascinated by Auerbach and, in the early 1960s, particularly by Auerbach's description of Dante's vision of historical reality. The English translation was published by the University of Chicago Press in 1961, but I have found no explicit reference to it in Frei's works or papers.

4 The first commentator on Frei's comparison of Barth and Dante was a respondent to Frei's paper at the colloquium who said 'the comparison with Dante ... I think was wild – nothing short of that; and it's a way into Barth, I think' (Orff, 1969, p. 13). The best exposition of Auerbach's figural reading is that of John David Dawson (1998).

5 In *Dante: Poet of the Secular World* Auerbach suggests that the encounter with Beatrice was, to some extent, the source of Dante's profound feeling for the figural vision:

In many men of his time, that yearning [for transcendence and transfiguration] was so overpowering as to destroy their perception of the world; the spirit became utterly absorbed in mystical devotion to the transcendent figuration of its hope. Dante's intense feeling for earthly existence, his consciousness of power made that evasion impossible for him. He had seen the figure of perfection on earth; she had blessed him and filled him and enchanted him with her super-abundant grace: in that decisive case he had beheld a vision of the unity of earthly manifestation and eternal archetype; from that time on he could never contemplate an historical reality without an intimation of perfection and of how far the reality was removed from it; nor, conversely, could he conceive of a divine world order without embracing in the eternal system all manner of phenomenal realities, however diverse and changing. (Auerbach, 1961, p. 67)

6   By rendering in its own concrete particularity these various creaturely witnesses and embodiments of reconciliation, the Bible can itself be said to be both a pointer to the reconciliation of God and humanity and, in a sense, an embodiment in writing of that reconciliation. For Barth, the Bible is not simply a pointer to the Word, it is a secondary form of the Word; as Virgil, it leads us to the threshold but, as Beatrice, it reveals to us what lies beyond that threshold. It is no contradiction, then, that Frei begins by saying that, for Barth, it is the Bible itself which is both Virgil and Beatrice in one, even though the rest of his discussion focuses on the figuring or fulfilling roles played not by the Bible itself, but by that which the Bible portrays.

7   It may be pushing the comparison too far, but it is worth noting that the Virgil and Beatrice of the *Comedy* are already the *fulfilment* of the historical Virgil and Beatrice. So, we might say, the characters, events and settings of the Bible are not, for Frei or for Barth, a straightforward repetition in writing of characters, events and settings which took place in history, but are portrayals of the *fulfilment* of those things – the setting of those things in the context of God's providence in such a way as to reveal them as witnesses to, and embodiments of, God's will. These portrayed fulfilments are no less concrete, no less particular and historical; indeed, the concrete particularity of the reality portrayed can be taken with *more* seriousness than is possible in other forms of ancient literature, precisely because of the horizon of divine judgement. All this is a fairly straightforward application of Auerbach's interpretation of the *Comedy* to the Bible; Frei, however, appears to be more concerned with the roles that these fulfilled portrayals of historical characters, events and settings can themselves play as figures of one another: that is, he is concerned with a second level of figural relationships, supervening on that just described. I am not sure that any clear distinction between these two levels of figural relationships can be found in Frei's sketch; it might, however, be an illuminating way of redescribing aspects of Frei's (and Barth's) hermeneutics.

8   There is one more aspect of this complexity, hinted at in Frei's account: the Jesus to whom the Bible witnesses, the Jesus who is the reconciliation between God and creaturely reality, is, for Frei, the Jesus of both advents; he is the Jesus who lived, died and rose, and he is the Jesus who is to come. There is an extent to which the Jesus of the first advent is a figure of the Jesus of the second advent: the second advent will complete, confirm and reveal the first advent rather than simply being a linear extension of it. This makes the figural economy sketched by Frei even more complex.

9   I should mention, at this point, that nothing I have said so far is intended to make that all-too-familiar mistake of assuming that Barth is a universalist: just as in Dante the fulfilment of history is also seen in the inferno, so with Barth the promise of the fulfilment of creaturely being in Christ includes the possibility that that fulfilment will take place in such a way that the 'no' enfolded in God's 'yes' will also be displayed.

10 Similarly, if we are asked how it was *possible* for Dante to combine his vision of the ordered judgement of God on all history with a true flourishing of attention to historical particularity and difference, the answer can only be: 'He did so: read the *Comedy*!' So with Barth: the answer to the 'Christomonism' accusation, the accusation that Barth's attention to Jesus of Nazareth does not allow any other creaturely reality space to be itself, is simply: 'He *does* allow this space: read his figural exegesis in the *Church Dogmatics*!'

11 Frei places the figural vision and the secular sensibility in paradoxical relationship, referring to Barth exploring 'that secularity which from a theological stance he would have considered an "impossible

possibility"', and I can't help wondering whether Frei, despite himself, overdoes the opposition between the two. Are there, in this, hints of an overreliance on Auerbach's Hegelianism (see note 12 below)? In Barth, it seems to me, such an antagonism is rightly excluded.

12 Although Frei does not make it explicit, there is an interesting link between his description of Barth's secular and sceptical sensibility and Auerbach's portrait of Dante as 'Poet of the Secular World' (Auerbach, 1961). Dante, for Auerbach, stood at the cusp of the figural tradition: he was both the author of its final triumph and the unwitting perpetrator of its undoing. He was midwife to a new tradition of secular, sceptical realism which would eventually turn and kill the very figural vision from which it had been born. Auerbach took the inspiration for his analysis of Dante from Schelling and, especially, from Hegel, and it is no surprise to find that Auerbach's Dante simply represents one episode in Western culture's long coming to its humanist senses and that the figural vision, though an essential precondition for the emergence of secular realism, is in the event overcome and replaced by the new synthesis. For Barth, on the other hand, the relationship between the figural and the secular is different: a commitment to the figural account involves the defeat of those religious pretensions or anxieties which would keep us safe from a secular, sceptical vision. Barth's figural vision therefore includes this negative secular vision as a constant minor partner, rather than giving birth to it as an antagonist. A view of the world as having no inherent possibility of communion with God apart from the particular divine act of communion in Christ is a view which lets the world simply be worldly, earthly, *irdischen*, secular.

13 The Bible is, in fact, everywhere concerned with the election of individual men. A human name mysteriously appears and occupies the stage for a time, whose peculiar human life, doing and sufferings in relationship with those of others form for a time the secondary subject and content of the biblical witness, and therefore themselves become a witness to that which is the primary subject and content of this witness. (*CD* II/2, p. 341)

14 Cf note 10 above.

15 The choice between these … possibilities is not an exegetical question; it is a question of faith. It is, therefore, to be distinguished from exegesis. But it is inescapably posed by it; and in the answer to this question, whatever it may be, exegesis is forced (even in the form of a *non liquet*) to speak its final word. (*CD* II/2, pp. 363–64)

16 For instance, he discusses the sources of the 1 Kings 13 story on p. 393, and the 'sacral interest with which these texts were read' on p. 386.

17 The phrase '*remoto Christo*' needs clarification. Barth was, of course, a Christian interpreter first, foremost and always, and we cannot sensibly hope to ask whether he would have been able to arrive at his exegeses, his identification of the patterns and the provisionality in these Old Testament stories, had he not been a Christian interpreter. Whoever the 'he' is in that final clause, it is not Barth. Perhaps we might say that the deliberate ascesis, the *remoto Christo* procedure we are describing, is rather an attempt to produce (as a Christian interpreter, schooled and enabled by Christian interpretation) readings of the text which will be intelligible and perhaps convincing to those who do not share this Christian inheritance. It makes sense to imagine Barth in conversation with a Jewish Rabbi about Leviticus 14, for instance, and to imagine them having enough to say to one another to allow the conversation to continue rather than falter; it is possible to imagine each holding the other to account for his exegesis of the passage, by constant reference back to the text.

18 I realize I have not demonstrated Barth's attention to the particularity of Jesus of Nazareth, witnessed to in the Gospel narratives. We could have looked at Barth's exegesis of the Gospel narratives in such passages as *CD* IV/1, pp. 259–73 on Gethsemane.

19 For Frei's explicit comments on the use of multiple descriptions in preserving the history-like qualities of a narrative, see *The Identity of Jesus Christ* (Frei, 1975), ch. 10.

20 Compare this counsel with Frei's description of the *Dogmatics* in Frei (1978).

References

Auerbach, E. (1953), *Mimesis: The Representation of Reality in Western Literature*, trans. W. Trask, Princeton, NJ: Princeton University Press.

Auerbach, E. (1961), *Dante: Poet of the Secular World*, trans. R. Manheim, Chicago: University of Chicago Press.

Auerbach, E. (1984), 'Figura', trans. R. Manheim in *Scenes from the Drama of European Literature*, Theory and History of Literature 9, ed. W. Godzich and J. Schulte-Sasse, Manchester: Manchester University Press; Minnesota: University of Minnesota, pp. 11–76, 229–37.

Dawson, J.D. (1998), 'Figural Reading and the Fashioning of Christian Identity in Boyarin, Auerbach and Frei', *Modern Theology*, **14**(2), pp. 181–96.

Dickerman, D.L. (ed.) (1969), *Karl Barth and the Future of Theology: A Memorial Colloquium held at the Yale Divinity School January 28, 1969,* New Haven, CT: YDS Association.

Frei, H.W. (1969), 'Karl Barth: Theologian' in Dickerman 1969, pp. 5–12, reprinted in Frei, 1993, pp. 167–76.

Frei, H.W. (1975), *The Identity of Jesus Christ: The Hermeneutical Bases of Dogmatic Theology*, Philadelphia: Fortress.

Frei, H.W. (1978),. 'Eberhard Busch's Biography of Karl Barth', *Virginia Seminary Journal*, **30**, pp. 42–46, reprinted in Frei, 1992, pp. 157–62.

Frei, H.W. (1992), *Types of Christian Theology*, ed. George Hunsinger and William Placher, New Haven, CT: Yale University Press.

Frei, H.W. (1993), *Theology and Narrative: Selected Essays*, ed. G. Hunsinger and W.C. Placher, New York: Oxford University Press.

Orff, R. 'Response [to Hans Frei]' in Dickerman, 1969, p. 13.

CHAPTER 8

'Mend Your Speech a Little': Reading Karl Barth's *das Nichtige* through Donald MacKinnon's Tragic Vision

John C. McDowell

Giving a Tragic Performance

All the World's a stage and we're merely players.

In this famous statement of Shakespeare's Jacques in *As You Like It*, a metaphor is used that can be found well before and beyond sixteenth-century England. Even so, this version of the claim, with its stubborn 'merely', has more of a pessimistic ring to it than do such versions as that in Marcus Aurelius' *Meditations*. This, perhaps, makes it particularly resonant for modern ears attuned to the din of numerous twentieth- and early twenty-first-century catastrophes.

One must ask about precisely this stubborn 'merely', however, since it suggests that Jacques has projected a particular and limited piece of human experience on to a larger canvas in such a way as to close future possibilities for hopeful action.[1] With that 'merely', Jacques crucially proposes that this limited picture is actually an adequate (even comprehensive, or meta-) account of the way the world is. A similar sense of closure, of limitation, or the *seeing from beyond the end of the drama*, also fuels George Steiner's query about the foolishness of action in tragic drama – a drama in which the tragedy or catastrophe will always be the unavoidable result of the action. Steiner argues that this literary genre dramatizes an account of the world as tragic in a mood that he calls 'absolute tragedy', or 'tragedy pure and simple' (Steiner, 1996a, 1996b; cf. McDowell, 2000c), and in Steiner's reading such tragic dramas, those refusing to brighten their dark mood, claim to know what the world is like, provide a meta-perspective, and by their mood thereby create only pessimism.

One response to this account of the absoluteness of the tragic would be to claim that tragedies contain much that complexifies and moderates the essentially bleak and pessimistic mood that Steiner perceives as undergirding them. Steiner recognizes this, of course, which is why he claims that absolute tragedy is so rarely given pure expression even within tragic dramas. Absolute tragedy is unendurable to human sensibilities. In *King Lear*, for instance, while Lear's family lies destroyed and his royal lineage is irreparably interrupted, the kingdom lives on – although how the preceding events have indelibly scarred the state's new ruler, Edgar, makes for interesting speculation.

Nevertheless, as Donald MacKinnon recognizes, the protagonist's frequent achievement of *anagoresis* (self-knowledge) and repentance (the less than 'bleak' material) in these dramas cannot justify or mitigate the absurdity of the waste (MacKinnon, 1979, p. 193). For example, to read the deaths of the central characters in *King Lear* – particularly of Lear's daughter Cordelia – through any kind of 'greater good' framework (that is, to see the tragic as a stage on the way to resolution) would be to trivialize what has occurred. There can be no 'reconciliation' that can justify the catastrophe for these people and their households.

Certainly, tragedies are often much more complex than they are imagined to be. But perhaps the main point to be tackled here is Steiner's sense of '*endings*', of what the *outcome* of the drama is like, or, rather, his depiction of the dramatized 'tragic vision' as possessing a meta-perspective on the course of the world. It is his sense that tragedies must end badly that directs his talk of 'absolute tragedy', and his assessment that the mood of Christian hope stands in direct contrast with its essential optimism. However, such perspectives on 'endings' can only be available to either the *audience* or the *playwright*, *not* to those whose lives are embodied in the drama itself – after all, there is still hope while the story has not ended for the protagonists.[2] (So in Act V, scene III Lear even entertains the possibility of reimbursing his disavowed daughter.[3]) And it is this way of reading tragic dramas from *within* their midst, and not from *beyond the end point*, that makes for interesting theological reflection. It is only when the audience's or playwright's vision is allowed to the actors on the stage that the vitality of their action is destroyed and the tragic drama becomes fundamentally undramatic, with the characters' action powerless to shape the play.

What happens to our reading of the human drama, however, if we insist on a stance *within* the drama's midst, and thereby refuse Jacques' overview? Donald MacKinnon's observations on tragic dramas provide just such a critique of Jacques' pessimism. The latter's is an illegitimate perspective that speaks as if it can observe the drama from some point *beyond* its course, and see therefore how things must *end* badly. MacKinnon thus interrogates the notion of the foreclosure of the dramatic (not only in relation to the literature but also the 'drama of life'). Put in its simplest terms, one cannot see from any point beyond the drama's course as if it has ended. Nevertheless, importantly, he maintains that tragic dramas can express themes and interrogations that are essential to the health of one's description not only of 'the human situation', but also, more controversially, of the ways of God's commerce with the world (MacKinnon, 1966c, p. 109; see also Sutherland, 1990; Steiner, 1995, pp. 2–9).

Now, Steiner's account of Christian hope is structurally similar to his account of absolute tragedy, even if the tenor is in marked contrast: Christian hope, for Steiner, is as essentially optimistic as absolute tragedy is essentially pessimistic. And this suggests that Donald MacKinnon's account of tragedy – both his refusal of its essential pessimism when it is turned into an overview of the world and his refusal to abandon the darkness of tragic drama's questioning – might be an interesting conversation partner for a theology of Christian hope, providing a critique of any easy optimism. It will be my contention in this essay that Donald MacKinnon's handling of tragedy allows us to revisit the question of Barth's supposed essential optimism and helps us see that there are crucially, in Barth's work, resources that can counter any unqualified claim that he was averse to all forms of tragedy, or that he was simply a mirror image of Jacques.[4] In particular, listening to his discussions of evil as *das Nichtige* will allow us to disrupt any simple account of a Barth who undramatically (because the drama is supposedly *finished*), and (crucially) untragically (because this supposed completion is *reconciliation*), flattens history into a 'moment' of Christologically imposed resolution.[5]

MacKinnon's occasionalistic and fragmentary style is too 'open-textured, explorative, questioning, self-critical, and morally concerned', too meditative and impressionistic for his work to be an *antiphony* of Barth's song (Hardy, 1997, p. 276). Nor, however, does he sing a *completely different* song since not only does he have great admiration for his older contemporary, but he is also critically impressed by one whom he describes as 'the one living theologian of unquestionable genius' (MacKinnon, 1968, p. 54). Nevertheless, MacKinnon proves to be a corrective – a corrective that is arguably not entirely alien in its suggestions to the substance of Barth's reflections.

The first part of this essay concentrates on MacKinnon, moving from his sense of the brokenness of theological discourse, through the need for theology to converse widely, to the particular kinds of theological conversation he had with tragic drama. Whilst MacKinnon's sensibility appears to be contrary to that of Barth, the second main section of this essay qualifies and complexifies this difference by reflecting on Barth's treatment of *das Nichtige* in *CD* III/3.

Theologically Performing the Ordinary

Can a Divinity Professor be Honest?

In a little-known article of 1966, MacKinnon asks a question that seems to haunt his work, 'Can a Divinity Professor Be Honest?' (MacKinnon, 1966a, pp. 94–96). His struggle is with how to be true to his academic 'calling', with the integrity to 'follow the argument whithersoever it leads' (ibid., p. 95).[6]

Pressing the implied sense of MacKinnon's writing, one could say, with Barth's *CD* IV/3 and the fragments of the uncompleted *CD* IV/4 (which suggest something important about Barth's own conception of the limitations of the theological task), that falsehood or lack of truthfulness, and consequently also integrity, is more subtle than any simple giving of a *false impression* – the externality involved in the concept of lying. Falsehood in this simple sense is the mask worn to hide one's motives (expressible primarily in the active voice, the deliberate activity of a deceiving agent). Lack of integrity, on the other hand, constitutes a *being false* – the delusion of those themselves lied to. This sense of falsehood points to the construction of one's being in untruthfulness (expressible primarily in the passive voice, of being made); the untruth that 'possesses', shapes and determines the particular motives, consciousness and active deliberations one has and is involved in (Barth, 1981, p. 224f.). This sense of what it is that is false is hidden from one's awareness since it is something gathered, learned, obtained and fallen into, a determinant of one's consciousness, presumed 'natural' to its believer. In Arendt's terms, 'evil' is banal, everyday, and therefore frequently passes without detection.

What characterizes the politics of certain kinds of power-relation (propaganda, totalitarian coercion and manipulation, even certain apologetic strategies) through which these falsehoods are predominantly expressed is their incapacity for *conversation*, as Williams, a former student of MacKinnon, suggests (Williams, 2000, p. 3). One steps back from the risk of conversation into a position of (imagined) invulnerability by displaying the 'control' over the real subject-matter. Williams targets 'the tyranny of a total perspective', which subsumes all knowing into a framework laying claims to comprehensiveness and finality.

Here are shades of *CD* I/1, in which Barth speaks in a more eschatologically nuanced way than does MacKinnon of theology as a 'penultimate' discipline, 'a work of critical revision and investigation of the Church's proclamation in view of the divine verdict', yielding all too human fallible and uncertain results (*CD* I/1, p. 83). As such, theology is *necessarily* fallible, fragile, broken, penultimate, decoloured by sin and resistant to all conceptual foreclosures or 'systematization' (see, for example, *CD* I/1, p. 83; *CD* I/2, p. 483; *CD* III/3, p. 294). Embracing this recognition of one's proper eschatological locatedness will render to theology's broken words the proper service of a humble witness and remind any *theologia gloriae* of its prematurity. In other words, theology cannot escape the risk of bondage to unacknowledged narratives.

Precariousness and vulnerability, or living 'an exposed life', are part of the price paid for being honest, MacKinnon argues. It is a sense of a necessary dis-ease with that which takes refuge in tradition or Christian culture or claims a finality of metaphysical explanation. These refuges temper the sense and tranquillize the pain of exposure (MacKinnon, 1969, p. 34). Instead MacKinnon advocates a 'deliberate cultivation of an interrogative ... mentality', a way of being true that attends to the multiple complexities that resist neat resolutions (which evacuate particularities of their concreteness in generalities), and that therefore acknowledges the substantial limitations involved in our knowing (MacKinnon, 1966a, p. 94).[7] Certainly, he does engage in some speculative constructions and even re-engages in a certain type of metaphysics. But these are carefully disciplined by a deeply challenging and discomforting interrogative style of doing theology in 'the borderlands'. Elsewhere he names this his 'untidy and inconclusive exploration', so that his assessment of R.G. Collingwood could almost have been a self-depiction: 'In the end he raised more questions than he answered; but here certainly he reminds his readers of Socrates, who made his associates face the difficult truth of their own deep ignorance' (MacKinnon, 1968, pp. 167, 174).

MacKinnon Conversing Widely

It is through this resistance to premature conceptual closure, this refusal to capitulate to the self-indulgent temptations of imagining that the way in which one tells one's story is free of unarticulated falsehoods, that humble dialogue with other perspectives and disciplines moves. Barth's concern for the possibility of hearing God 'through Russian Communism, a flute concerto, a blossoming shrub, or a dead dog' (CD I/1, p. 55) is a way of, as he later describes, 'eavesdropping on the world' by entertaining an unpredictable variety of dialogue partners. On one occasion MacKinnon, for his part, even commented that 'many existing religious beliefs, institutions and *performances* ... are fair target not only for disciplined academic criticism but for the kind of merciless satire on T.V. and radio' (MacKinnon, 1966a, p. 96).

His appreciation of the particularities and complexities involved in providing an account of God's commerce with the world enables MacKinnon to judge positively the place of literature within theological and philosophical reflection as explorations of 'living discourse' (MacKinnon, 1974, p. 79).[8] Speaking of the moralist, for instance, he argues that 'his theorizing is impoverished if he ignores the dimensions of human experience to which such writers [as Tolstoy, Dostoevsky, George Eliot and Joseph Conrad] admit him' (MacKinnon, 1968, p. 215).

MacKinnon complains about superficially aesthetic approaches to literature that treat it as pre-eminently a form of entertainment (ibid., pp. 50ff.). Similarly, von Balthasar, theologian of the dramatic *par excellence* and greatly admired by MacKinnon, argues, '"*l'art pour l'art*" is a totally derivative and depraved form of the encounter with beauty: the blissful, *gratis*, shining-in-itself of the thing of beauty is not meant for individualistic enjoyment in the experimental retorts of aesthetic seclusion' (von Balthasar, 1990, p. 29f.).

In other words, MacKinnon's *mimetic* or realist approach to reading enables literature to interrupt, redirect and even transform ways of negotiating the world. It can, moreover, specify the irreducibility of the particularities, complexities and contingencies of living that are resistant to stock formulae and categorization and without which there is a serious diminution in one's understanding. With reference to *Hamlet*, for example, MacKinnon suggests that:

> It can hardly be denied that our understanding of such notions as responsibility, free-will, decision are enlarged, even transformed (or should be enlarged and transformed) by the dramatist's most subtle exploration of the Prince's personal history. And this enlargement the dramatist achieves not by the enunciation of some general principle, but by laying bare, in the subject of his hero, the deepest recesses of the human spirit, the half-acknowledged emotional overtones and undertones which belong to any processes of decision, and which can so easily be overlooked. (MacKinnon, 1968, p. 50)

This could entail the possibility that it 'explore, ... complicate and ... enrich the apparent security of theological concepts' (Wright, 1988, p. 13).

Barth's Musical Time

Critiques of Barth as unconversant with extra-ecclesial affairs – the Barth, perhaps, of a popular reading of 1934's *Nein!* to Brunner – are careless.[9] But in contrast to von Balthasar, for example, Barth's primary theologically aesthetic interest lies less in the dramatic arts than in Mozart's music through which he claimed to hear creation praised (see, for example, *CD* III/3, pp. 297ff.; Barth, 1986, p. 33f.). Appreciation of Mozart is more than either a trivializable matter of taste or something appropriate merely to the scaffolding or cosmetics of Barth's theology (see Gill, 1986, p. 404).[10] Mozart's is 'music which for the true Christian is not mere entertainment, enjoyment or edification but food and drink; music full of comfort and counsel for his needs' (*CD* III/3, pp. 297f.).[11] In 1958 Barth even speaks, albeit unusually, of 'the golden sounds and melodies of Mozart's music ... not as gospel but as parables of the realm of God's free grace' (Barth, 1969, pp. 71f.).[12] Certainly, the Barth disillusioned with the Russian Revolution's trajectory had learned to explode his earlier theologico-cultural pretensions as manifested in the claim of a 1910 article ('Die Christliche Glaube und die Geschichte') that Michelangelo and Beethoven are sources of revelation alongside Paul. And even though he does propose a theologically controlled way of reading cultural products, he provides few concrete examples; he even tends to hesitate to accord Mozart parabolic status since '[a]ll such phenomena are doubtful and contestable' (*CD* IV/3.1, p. 135). Barth follows his famous comment on listening to God even if he should speak through 'Russian Communism ...' with an injunction: 'But, unless we regard ourselves as the prophets and founders of a new Church, we cannot say that we are commissioned to pass on what we have heard as independent proclamation' (*CD* I.1, p. 60f.).[13]

Given this reticence, it would be speculative to ask why Barth privileges this particular aesthetic form, since he provides no reasons as to why it is theologically sensible. Although it would controvert his insistence on the mediating *Word*-iness of Presence, is Barth suggesting something of a sense of an immediateness of experience through music when arguing that 'Mozart does not wish to *say* anything: he just sings and sounds' (Barth, 1986, p. 37f.)?

In any case, although one cannot provide a concrete answer to these questions, given the scant evidence on the matter, it is at least possible to ask whether anything theologically has been lost to Barth's (undramatic) work here. It is worth bearing in mind that, as von Balthasar's *Theo-Drama* makes plain, a theology informed by drama can be a reminder that one's response to the world (whether that be through epistemological reflection or moral action) always takes place *within* the performance. Thereafter, this can express something of the *indeterminacy* and *open-endedness* of the myriad kinds of relation that typify one's living, a living with an *unframeable* anticipation of the event of the eschaton. We might ask, however, whether the fact that the performances of playing or listening to music take time, and a time that does not necessarily work towards an 'end' the form of which may be predicted in the midst of the performance, might perhaps suggest something similar.

MacKinnon's 'Tragic Gospel'

When the names of Homer, Goethe, Dostoevsky and Shakespeare appear in Barth's writings, those of the Attic Tragedians are conspicuously absent. The solitary Euripidean reference, for example, and the Shakespearean allusions, avoid reference to tragedy. Indeed, references to tragedy or the tragic are, on the whole, scant, confined to occasional scattered comments on the sinful human condition or, more accurately, the outworking of humanity's sin and guilt (see *CD* III/1, p. 406; *CD* IV/2, p. 230). Nevertheless, even here Barth prefers talk of humanity's sin rather than 'tragic greatness', fearing that the latter may imply less than the former (*CD* I/2, p. 430).

In contrast the significance of which defies easy assessment, Sophocles and Shakespeare (the latter primarily as author of *Hamlet* and *King Lear*) stand alongside the likes of Aristotle, Kant and Barth in MacKinnon's list of important educators and thinkers on the nature of knowing and living. While von Balthasar's concern is over what is lost to theology when it supports 'the actor's banishment from Plato's *polis*' (von Balthasar, 1988, p. 10),[14] MacKinnon asks more specifically about the exiling of the *tragedians* as presenters and explorers of 'ultimate issues' (MacKinnon, 1966b, p. 109; 1974, pp. 50, 100f.). Plato's move, he maintains, was 'a prolegomenon ... to [the establishment of] a world without ambiguity, a world from which the kind of darkness that Sophocles, for instance, had profoundly understood was expelled. For Plato it was demonstrably blasphemous to query the certainty of a "happy ending"' (MacKinnon, 1979, p. 187).[15]

Christians, he argues, lack the courage to read the Gospels in the light of tragic drama (and, indeed, also lack the courage to admit any modified kenotic *theopaschian* sense of 'God'), and ultimately anaesthetize any sensitivity to the tragic by converting history into a ballet-dance of *ideas*. This process is detectable in theodicies' unwarranted attempts to *resolve* the problem of evil through facile optimisms or teleologies in their 'apologetic eagerness' (MacKinnon, 1974, p. 124; cf. 1995, p. 106). There is a self-deceit in the actions of one who

> ... fashion[s] a God whose role it is to write a happy ending to the human tale. So evil, the macabre and secret source of human waste, is trivialized; so the burden of human existence is lightened by the banishment from our ethical vocabulary of such solemn words and phrases as 'irrevocable', 'too late'. (MacKinnon 1966c, p.176f.)

However, is there not something alien in appealing to the tragic for an eschatological resurrection-faith? Should the Christian not, then, speak with Reinhold Niebuhr of a 'resolution of tragedy' (Niebuhr, 1938, p. 155f.), or at least a transcendence of tragedy, or with P.T. Forsyth of 'the Divine *Commedia* on the scale of all existence' (Forsyth, 1917, p. 76)?

Steiner's commendation of MacKinnon's post-Auschwitz refusal to evade the painful interrogating dimensions of the tragic as putting in question 'the resurrection itself' requires careful handling (Steiner, 1995, p. 6). MacKinnon rather suggestively declares that the resurrection is 'a *prius* of my whole argument' (MacKinnon, 1968, p. 95). What, however, the resurrection does is highlight, and not obliterate, precisely the darkness of the preceding days. It is only in the light of the resurrection that Christians can learn to say, with Pascal, that Christ will indeed be in agony until the end of the world (ibid., p. 96).

Describing his sense of the 'central importance' of categories discernible from tragic drama for Gospel-reading, MacKinnon provides a series of brief and impressionistically sweeping, but nevertheless profound and disruptive, meditative readings that reveal a sensibility in tension with Barth's (ibid., p. 94). He suggests that, as far as the realization of Jesus' eschatological hopes for Israel was concerned, language of (a 'purposive') 'failure' is not inappropriate (MacKinnon, 1979, p. 65); that Judas went his damnable way; that the open-ended horror of anti-Semitism is 'the terrible sequel to the story of the cross' (MacKinnon, 1968, p. 103; cf. 1974, p. 130); that 'victories' are not free from the tragic qualities of waste and destruction; and that all moral planning exhibits a tragic texture.

Hebblethwaite's (1989) accusation that MacKinnon was Manichaean reveals a deep misconception of the appeal to the tragic in MacKinnon. At most, one might speak of a Manichaean *sense* that MacKinnon gives to the dramatic as far as he can partially perceive its being 'dramatized'. In other words, the 'tragic' is so bound up with the 'good' that the world we experience does not lend itself to unambiguous moral evaluation or description. Reading anything more meta-perspectival than that (that is, suggesting that 'this … is the way the world is ultimately') in MacKinnon is deeply problematic. This is supported by several features of MacKinnon's work. First, he complains about trivializing and simplistic talk of 'the tragic sense of life', with its dissolution of ambiguity in a cult of despair. In other words, he does not value any theological use of categories of the tragic in an unqualified manner and for their own sake. Second, his tentative manner insists on 'a certain reverent agnosticism' to this kind of meta-question. This is reflected in his concern for the precise 'sense in which the term "tragic" may significantly be predicated of the Gospel records', and in his reluctance to display any detailing of the eschatological future (MacKinnon, 1969, p. 51). Third, he speaks of Christian hope for 'the ultimate sweetness of things' as 'a message of which our world is in direst need', a world which tends to swing from various forms of facile optimism to debilitating despair (MacKinnon, 1968, pp. 118, 120). MacKinnon cites Barth here as a reminder of joyous hope. The otherwise sympathetic Ford appears not to notice this (admittedly barely audible) voice in MacKinnon. However, Ford's critique has a certain value in contrasting the latter's emphasis on the darkness inherent within tragedy with both Paul's notion of 'sorrowful yet always rejoicing', and Gardener's explication of the 'redemptive' quality and joy in Shakespeare's *King Lear* (Ford, 1989, p. 123).

Nevertheless, any simple appeal to ambiguity in life (sorrow *and joy*, tragedy *and* comedy and so on) can only be a superficial response to MacKinnon's interrogative spirit. It misses the fact that tragic dramas *are not* usually framed in terms of a simplistic optimism–pessimism dualism. MacKinnon is no Schopenhauer in his reading of 'tragedy', and admits that 'tragedy' is only an umbrella term for a complex and multifarious set of plays with an 'open-textured quality' that overlap in their dramatic exploration of themes of waste and meaningless suffering (MacKinnon, 1969, p. 50).[16] If, for von Balthasar, it is beyond human competence to see the lines of intersection between tragedy and comedy (von Balthasar, 1988, p. 437), for MacKinnon tragic dramas involve an indeterminacy of 'endings' whose depth-narratability has its own apophatic constraints, and consequently testify to the unnarratable and unthinkable.

MacKinnon's appeal to the 'tragic' functions interrogatively, then. Tragic dramas' very multiplicity and diversity bespeak the problem of transcripting tragic experience into theory (see Ricoeur, 1967, p. 212). In this way, they disrupt the easy coherences of meta-perspectives on something named 'reality'. Instead of answering any philosophical or theological questions, they acutely raise them, particularly over any created securities of meaning and value. Tragedies 'teach' less by didactic or conceptual means, than, as Ricoeur argues, by 'more closely resembling a conversion of the manner of looking' through a destabilizing interrogation which therein reorients action (Ricoeur, 1992, pp. 245ff.). They teach a 'kind of perpetual moral wakefulness' (in Wyschogrod's phrase), asking about the complexity of motives, the flawed characters we develop, the depths of our unwisdom in decision-making, the manner of possible resistance and the importance of external factors in shaping events, to name a few features of our narrative identities. Highlighted within all this is the fragility of goodness, the precariousness of all that we value, the risky delicacy of human self-control and movement towards all forms of possession (be they psychological, economic, political, intellectual and so on), and our vulnerability to evil.

This is not so much a case of a theology aware of its own blindness, but rather a theology that gropes its way in the dark, stumbling and yet fragilely acting *from the midst* of the drama of redemption.

The Drama of Barth's 'Heroic' Christ

Barth's real interest is revealed in the context of his meagre remarks on tragedy. Talk of tragedy is set within a study of the kingdom's 'total and absolutely victorious clash ... with nothingness' (*CD* IV/2, p. 230). Tragedy has been incarnationally negated. 'Jesus Christ ... breaks down this resistance to grace by Himself appearing as grace triumphant, as the royal removal of our sin and guilt by the action of God Himself' (*CD* II/1, p. 374).

The dramatic element in the conflict between God and sin is itself spoken of in almost Homeric terms, with Christ depicted as 'hero', and without retention of any serious component of the tragic (Barth, 1981, p. 261). The dramatic element here functions to avoid abstracting the God–sin conflict from Christ's history (*CD* I/2, p. 376). *CD* IV/3 roots talk of Christ as 'the Subject of the action, the dominating

Character in the drama, and the Hero in the conflict'. As may be expected given the militaristically triumphant tone, in this discussion 'there can be no question of an equality between the two factors which here confront and conflict with one another' (*CD* IV/3.1, pp. 172, 171f.). Consequently, Barth warns of 'the tragedy of an abstract *theologia crucis*' that changes the story of the cross and resurrection into joyless 'Nordic morbidity' (*CD* IV/1, p. 559). Instead, the story of cross and resurrection, couched in militaristically triumphalistic tones, has a single trajectory.

This extravagant teleological rhetoric (which, however, appears in the context only of redemption-talk and not of creaturely processes and abilities) suggests that Barth is reluctant to engage more substantially with tragic drama for the very reason that he felt attracted to Mozart. Consequently, he criticized Bach's *St. Matthew's Passion* as a travesty and 'abstraction' of Matthew 26–27, a 'tragic ode culminating in a conventional funeral dirge' (*CD* IV/2, p. 252f.). 'Jesus never once speaks in it as the Victor.'

This does not, however, in any way mitigate the fact that, for Barth, the Christian suffers the present's contradiction between the 'old' and 'new', the eschatologically provisional (*CD* IV/3.1, p. 366). '[T]he heavens grow dark … [and] harmony is engulfed in disharmony and teleology obscured by senselessness' (*CD* III/1, p. 372). Hence, suggestively, Barth claims that the act of hope in Christ is a 'comforted despair', something that stands in *contrast* to non-Christian forms of both pessimism *and optimisn* (*CD* IV/1, pp. 633, 636).

Nevertheless, if unqualified, Barth's triumphal discourse could all too easily tend towards an untragic eschatological prediction, since the assertive nature of the discourse suggests that the character of the future is confidently imaginatively ascertained before its universal manifestation, its shape blueprinted proleptically from the knowledge of the victorious past event. This would certainly differ from seventeenth-century federal theologians' or millennialist groups' mapping the exact form of *future history*. Even so, it could tread similar pathways with respect to the *ultimate outcome* of the future, as several critics suggest with their identification of a 'logical' Barthian nod toward the *apokatastasis* (G.C. Berkouwer), or the perceiving of a closure of the future in the immediate presence of the revelational event (R.H. Roberts and J. Moltmann). The drama has already been Christologically resolved, the sting has been removed from existence, and evil's threateningness and the space for human rejection is therefore denied (see, for example, Wingren, 1958, pp. 25, 38, 112, 117; Rodin, 1997, pp. 221f., 223–233).

Whichever account is traced, the problem, then, appears to be substantially more theologically interesting than that of mere inattentiveness to the nuances of tragic dramas, although this is a serious failing in itself.

With this in mind it is worth exploring what Barth was doing in the (in)famous §50 of *Church Dogmatics*.

'Nothing Will Come of Nothing': *CD* III/3 on *das Nichtige*

CD III/3's 'Mythopoetics' of 'das Nichtige'

In *King Lear*'s fateful opening scene the flattery-seeking monarch asks his favoured daughter, Cordelia, how much he is loved. Refusing to associate herself with the treachery of her elder sisters, Cordelia replies with 'nothing'. The tragic train of events is set on its way as the spectator puzzles at Lear's subsequent explosive outburst, appearing almost as a childish tantrum (after all, he is king) and moment of bravado, and moves all too rapidly towards his famous assertion, 'Nothing will come of nothing. Speak again'.

In a sense, Lear's words were unfulfilled. *Something* did come from nothing, and although this something was not a 'thing' in the sense that physical objects are things, the something was nevertheless a dramatic and consequential shaping of the available possibilities for agency.

The 'something from nothing' theme arises in the context of several critiques of Barth's account of evil and sin as 'nothing' in the context of §50 of III/3, '*Gott und das Nichtige*'. How can death, hell and the tragic come from *nothing*ness? Von Balthasar, as we have seen, claims that Barth's tone 'veritably thrums with a hymnic certainty of eventual victory' (von Balthasar, 1972, p. 354). And surely this optimistic mood should be viewed as a move, as are all optimisms, to secure sight into that which is not obviously open for inspection – namely, the future. Hence, von Balthasar continues, Barth has 'gone a bit too far to the light' (von Balthasar, 1972, p. 358).

Reading Barth too unqualifiedly in this way, however, misses something highly significant, something (rather than nothing) that lends a certain tragic texture to his reflections in the complex and difficult, but suggestive, theological microcosm of §50. These reflections on evil are notable steps, and one can read volume IV, and particularly the fragments of what would have been IV/4, as, in some sense, their detailed and dramatized expression (*CD* III/3, p. xii).[17]

Composed in the aftermath of the physical, diplomatic and psychological ruins of post-war Europe, *CD* III will nevertheless disappoint anyone expecting Barth's commentary on, or even explicit theological response to, the cultural landscape of its time. Critics frequently despair of the 'buffoonery' and irresponsibility of one whose mention of the Jews is primarily that of the *Gotteskranken*,[18] whose theological account of women is a patriarchal hangover[19] and whose delving into politics (especially those of the Cold War) is laughably uninformed and arbitrary (see Niebuhr, 1959, pp. 184, 186; Lovin, 1984, p. 41f.). Furthermore, it is often recalled that Barth's response to 1914 was to question his liberal teachers' *theology*. Has the theologian who claimed to hold the Bible in one hand and the newspaper in the other extended his arms to their full span thereby preventing their meeting?

Suggestive of something more culturally significant is Pattison's general observation that 'concern with the void' is regarded by 'a considerable body of opinion' as having been a product of the general angst-ridden *Stimmung* (mood) – and that it is therefore quickly dismissable (*too quickly* dismissable in an any genealogical critique) as being 'somewhat passé' (Pattison, 1996, p. 2). Indeed, what *CD* III represents is a very different style of post-war explosion from that of the 1922 edition of *Der Römerbrief*. Speculation on the different impacts of the two periods on the Barth of 1922 and that of 1945 (*CD* III/1) is tempting, particularly since the latter Barth had, through bitter experience and the way in which he then learned to read the Scriptures, come to *expect* less of people and movements. The Red Revolution of 1917 had affected him deeply. It is, then, somewhat simplistic to complain, as Horton does, that Barth was not as good a prophet for the post-Second World War age of anxiety as he was for the age of overconfidence which preceded it (Horton, 1956, p. 359). Through his developing Christofiguration of theological memory he has learned to *hope*, and this hope theologically undermines the basis of this post-war anxiety and therefore creates a very different mood from that of 1922. Consequently, in 1948 he declares: 'It is easy to be afraid anywhere in the world today. The whole of the Western world, the whole of Europe is afraid, afraid of the East. But we must not be afraid. ... Everything is in the hands of God' (Barth, 1954, p. 99).

The surrounding culture's impact on the Barth of 1947 is most clearly displayed in his discourse of *das Nichtige*, which suggests at least an implicit dialogue (an admiringly critical one) with Heidegger and Sartre (*CD* III/3, p. 334). Pattison attempts to identify the function of this language as being to 'harmonize faith in the goodness and omnipotence of God and a vision of the world as fallen' (Pattison, 1996, p. 7), and this use of the melodic 'harmonize' is very interesting: despite Barth's best intentions, Pattison regards him as characterizable by metaphors of euphonics, or musical harmony.

Undoing Contextless Theodicy

Since systematizing involves a conceptual constructiveness that is insufficiently attentive to the resistant particularities and complexities that attend our explorations into the way things are, MacKinnon utilizes his 'proper respect for the irreducibility of the tragic' to inhibit 'ambitious metaphysical construction' (MacKinnon, 1974, p. 145). 'It is a lesson to be learned from tragedy that there is no solution to the problem of evil' (MacKinnon, 1968, p. 104; cf. Ricoeur, 1967, p. 165).

For theodicy, evil is a 'problem' for theorizing to solve. Ears are trained to hear that the seemingly discordant notes actually offer their own *contribution* to the overarching form and structure of the melody, even though the generalized perspective usually prevents speculation on how specific instances, and/or what have recently been generally named 'horrendous evils' (one should add '*pointless*'),[20] make their contribution. In such strategies, particularly in the 'greater good' theses, discussions of evil's place in the world tend to employ language of 'justification' and 'necessity'.[21] The existence of a good and all-powerful God, so most forms of this story go, can be justified in permitting evil to exist since it is 'necessary' for the achievement of a 'greater good'.

Barth denies the possibility of constructing (the engineering metaphor is apt) a 'theodicy' in this sense. That type of apologetic is not open to the Swiss professor who persistently maintained that apologetics could not be a rationally performed task separable from dogmatic description. He saw apologetics, as performed by 'natural theology', as seeking to construct a 'Being' (or Ultimate 'Thing') from the fragments of our misplaced reasoning from first principles (foundations) – a Being that can only be a 'no-God'.

This is where Barth is frequently misunderstood, and Schulweis' comment on 'theodicy [as] … a symptom of man's enslavement to moral and logical criteria and norms irrelevant to the conduct of the divinely unique One' could accentuate the common suspicion of a Barthian anti-intellectualism and irrationalism (Schulweis, 1975, p. 157). The task Barth believes himself able to perform honestly is something contextually *Christian* outside the framework of which only distorted images and even idols are created, and these are mistaken for the living God. Barth was famously fond not only of Kant's critique of metaphysics but also of Feuerbach's critique of religion. Something similar permeates his discussions in §50 with regard to evil- and sin-talk. They, also, cannot be abstracted from their proper theological grammar without incurring a serious distortion of meaning (see, for example, *CD* III/3, pp. 350f., 365f.), and Barth even implies that something is wrong with appeals to 'commonsense notions of evil' (Peterson, 1998, p. 10).[22] Similarly, discourse of 'goodness' and 'omnipotence' (a theistic 'muscle-word') cannot be decontextualized from their theological reference as happens in the so-called 'classic' definition of the 'problem of evil'.

In proceeding rigorously to 'examine' or give a 'report' of (if such spectatorial metaphors may be used) the nature of sin theologically (or, rather, Christologically or, better still, Trinitarianly) Barth may well provide a description that overlaps with, and can even *analogically* draw from, certain themes of theodicy-projects (*CD* III/3, p. 295). Exploring the nature of sin and evil, expressions of that which is declared to be a problem before God (and not God a problem before them),[23] may well then lead to *certain clarifications* of the sorts of ways in which it is appropriate and inappropriate to speak of God's and creation's relations to evil. Hick, however, fails to understand that this is very different from *systematically* 'strain[ing] after completeness and compactness' concerning evil (*CD* III/3, p. 295), and that done non-theologically, when he claims that Barth's *das Nichtige* discourse is 'an infringement of his ban upon speculative theorizing, and from outside that thought world' (Hick, 1977, p. 135f.).

To return to the musicology metaphor, it would seem more appropriate to argue that Barth's theo-composition allows for the discordant notes (sin, evil and suffering) to be heard after a fashion (even if the nature of this 'after a fashion' is highly controversial), and yet that these notes that are themselves, while not simply reducible to the melody, drawn upon symphonically to make the piece more complex: '[T]he break itself and as such will be reproduced and reflected in our knowledge and its presentation' (*CD* III/3, p. 295).

To change the metaphor, it is not that Barth objects to the use of *words* to *describe* evil, but that he objects to the pseudo-scientific grammar of theodicies. In other words, it is their comprehensive explanatoriness that is particularly the problem.

The Unjustifiability of (Un)resident Evil

Divine conflict: The evilness of evil   When MacKinnon claims that Paul 'writes not as if he would provide a solution, but rather as if he would lay the texture of a problem bare' he displays something of his own way of doing theology (MacKinnon, 1968, p. 156). It is in this laying bare, or for Barth in the provision of a report, that the exposure of the tragic particularities and unsystematizable ambiguities involved in 'reading' the world prevent MacKinnon from voicing any easy talk of 'a synthesis in which reconciliation' is achieved.

Barth's own complaints against theodicy projects, as he perceived and knew them, are also theologically substantive. The focus is similarly on the manner of resolution, or at least toleration, of the relation between 'Creator, creature and their co-existence, and the intrusion upon them of the undeniable reality of nothingness' (*CD* III/3, p. 365). Barth is Trinitarianly compelled to develop a doctrine of God as being-for-creation in such a way that the 'humanity of God' entails that the event of the cross is not a *moment of pathos* within an otherwise impassible Godhead (an episodic reading about which MacKinnon also complains – MacKinnon, 1987, p. 232). Instead, in Barth's post-Second World War sense of the self-determined 'humanity of God', this cross of the One raised is (as well as being the point at which sin is displayed) precisely the point at which God is most identifiable as being God, as an involved-being-for-the-other – a claim to which the kenotic language of 'giving-up' cannot fully do justice.[24] Or, as MacKinnon puts it, kenosis 'is not strange or alien to His being' (MacKinnon, 1987, p. 235); rather, he continues in a discourse that incarnationally rewrites what is meant by divine omnipotence, it is God's 'supreme assertion in the setting of a deeply estranged world' (MacKinnon, 1987, p. 155).

Barth's move is less the simplistic claim that theodicy, by being in its very nature *formed reflection*, trivializes suffering[25] and more a theological complaint that its precise manner of understanding the place of evil in the world domesticates that evil. Hence it is the intolerability of *das Nichtige* that is §50's main concern, something which theodicy is in danger of forgetting. This section opens, for instance, with the striking statement that '[t]here is opposition and resistance to God's world-dominion' (*CD* III/3, p. 289). Consequently, Barth rejects theodicies in which evil and sin are worked into the whole system (either dualistically as necessary antitheses, or monistically in order to contribute to the good), and which therefore entail that these become necessary and/or even good (*CD*, IV/1, pp. 374–87). Specifically, he rejects Schopenhauerian pessimism (*CD* III/1, pp. 335ff.), and anti-dualistic differentiations between *das Nichtige* and creation's *Schattenseitte* (see *CD* III/3, pp. 296ff.). Moreover, he hesitates to discuss demonology because of the temptation to fit Satan into a legitimate and proper place within creation. These various perspectives subtly conceal 'genuine nothingness' and fabricate 'a kind of alibi under cover of which it cannot be recognized and can thus pursue its dangerous and disruptive ways the more unfeared and unhampered' (ibid., p. 299).

It is the radicalness and ruthlessness of *das Nichtige* or, in Ruether's words, 'the evilness of evil' that Barth wants to assert and refuse any possible domestication and justification of (Ruether, 1968–69, p. 6; cf. *CD* III/3, p. 299). This he tends to emphasize in three main ways: by utilizing conflictual metaphors; by acknowledging *das Nichtige* as *atopos* with regard to both Creator *and* creature; and by describing its threateningness.

Bounded conflict   Given his talk of God as free-to-love, whose electing and creating are for purposes of covenant fellowship in grace, and whose participation in the life of his creature culminated in the cross – talk already formed by Christological discourse for Barth even before *CD* II/2 – it is appropriate for Winston to comment that, for Barth, '[t]o know the real God is to know Him as the adversary of evil' (Winston, 1959, p. 55; cf. *CD* III/3, p. 290). *Das Nichtige*, then, is portrayed as 'an alien factor' (CD III/3, p. 289), 'a real enemy' and 'adversary with whom no compromise is possible' (ibid., pp. 301, 302). It is inappropriate to speak of a *causalitas mali in Deo* – the *malum* is antithetical and abhorrent to God – and thereby to 'the totality of the created world' (ibid., p. 302).

This conflict had its origin 'before' creation (understood *logically* rather than simply *temporally*), with the separation of creation and nothingness, and the preservation of the former 'from being overthrown by the greater force of nothingness' (ibid., p. 290). Creation is preserved from falling into 'total peril', or from the ultimate consequences of the conflict's ability 'to overwhelm and destroy the creature' (destroy *absolutely*, it must be added for comprehension) (ibid.). The de-creativeness of *das Nichtige* is always bounded, and therefore *theo-dramatically* limited in its scope, by God's creativeness and, indeed, redemptive re-creativeness (and *CD* IV/3 is good exploration of the nature of the *ongoing* drama of the risen Christ with the multiple manifestations of *das Nichtige*).

A good grammar of creatureliness   According to von Balthasar, the dying sinless Jesus 'proves thereby that sin is so much a part of existence that sinlessness cannot maintain itself in it. But he also proves that sin is not a necessary and inherent characteristic of life. Evil is not a part of God, nor yet a part of essential man' (von Balthasar, 1988, p. 167f.).

Important in this conflictual account, then, is that God's creating is wholly beneficent to creatures, and the result of that creating is wholly good (*CD* III/3, p. 302), something which Barth found strikingly expressed in Mozart's voicing of creation's praising of its Creator (ibid., p. 298f.). However *radical* evil may be, Ricoeur explains, it cannot be as *primordial* [or *original*] as goodness', and hence it becomes 'scandalous at the same time it becomes historical' (Ricoeur, 1967, pp. 156, 203).[26]

For Barth, any aetiology of *das Nichtige* requires a 'protection' of the grammar of creaturely dignity through an insistence that it cannot be sought 'in the non-divinity of the creature' (*CD* III/3, p. 349).[27] Possibly alluding to Nietzsche's talk of Christianity as 'life-denying' and his own philosophy as 'a yea-saying', Barth speaks of his intention to be 'loyal to the earth' by being true to humanity's permanent belonging-to-the-world and by opposing both the sense of the human in conflict with the flux of temporality and any attempt to escape the proper limitations of creaturehood, of one's life-span's definite temporal allottedness, which is ended by death (*CD* III/2, p. 6). Temporality is even attributable to humanity's eternal life (ibid., p. 521). Thus Kerr regards Barth as 'celebrating our finitude' (Kerr, 1997, p. 24; cf. pp. viif., 23). Createdness, declared 'good' by the Creator, is life's *proper* framework: 'we are not in an empty or alien place' (*CD* III/3, p. 48). And, significantly, those words were written at a time when Europe was facing rebuilding after the horrors of Auschwitz and the war's ravaging of the continent.

Thus, as created, humanity has no right (sin is closed off from the human being), reason (what has been created is good) or freedom (freedom is the creature's freedom-for-God) to sin. This is the theological sense of a characteristic comment, which cannot be read in context as a paternal rendering of God–creature relations: 'The creature is not its own. It is the creature and possession of God', and not 'capable of sin' (*CD* III/3, pp. 359, 356). Consequently, as explicated earlier in *CD* II/2, humanity is not divinely fore-ordained or equipped to sin but is rather, destined towards blessedness and eternal life (*CD* II/2, pp. 170, 171; cf. *CD* III/1, p. 263f.).

The conflict of *das Nichtige*, then, is not only with God but also with creatures. Sin is 'detrimental', and harmful to the extent of disturbing, injuring and destroying 'the creature and its nature' (*CD* III/3, p. 310). Barth speaks of it as a 'denaturalizing' 'self-alienation' (Barth, 1981, p. 213).

It is this oppositional/conflictual perspective that facilitates the use of negative language: *das Nichtige* (nothingness); negativity; a substanceless antithesis (*CD* III/3, p. 302); an 'ontological impossibility' (*CD* III/2, p. 146); *unmögliche Möglichkeit* (impossible possibility) (*CD* III/2; *CD* III/3, p. 351); 'the absurd (irrational) possibility of the absurd (irrational)' (*CD* III/3, p. 178); an 'inherent contradiction' (ibid., p. 351); and a possibility passed over and rejected *as a legitimate reality* by God. In other words, as *das Nichtige*, it has no autonomous *being* like that of creatures. Rather its quasi-reality stands in a relation of negation or privation to the 'good', a description recalling Augustine's post-Plotinian *malum est privatio boni* (ibid., p. 318). It is therefore a nullity that is only parasitical on, and not in any way identifiable with, the good that is 'reality' (or 'being') (*CD* II/2, p. 170f.).[28]

The gatecrasher   As that to which God gives 'an absolute and uncompromising No' *das Nichtige* is the 'uninvited' enemy, an unwanted intruder into created life (*CD* III/3, pp. 292, 310). But, what is the nature of this 'uninvitation'? According to Hick there are grounds for suspecting that Barth, in a sense, made nothingness *logically necessary* for his scheme of creation and redemption (see Hick, 1977, p. 138). Barth, in his way of opposing any Manichaean-style dualism, grounds *das Nichtige* in God's activity of election and creation, albeit in the qualified sense that it is that which God does not elect or create (*CD* III/3, p. 351f.). Moreover, in a discussion of Genesis 1: 2 he appears to equate *das Nichtige* with the chaos from which God's creating was separated (ibid., p. 352).[29]

Hick tentatively claims that Barth maintains the *O felix culpa* in the sense that evil 'exists' in order 'to make possible the supreme good of redemption' (Hick, 1977, p. 139). And, indeed, Barth does unwittingly appear to imply sin's inevitability in creation, when, for instance, he declares that 'God wills evil only because He wills not to keep to Himself the light of His glory but to let it shine outside Himself' (*CD* II/2, p. 170).

This suggests that, in a very real sense, the responsibility for *das Nichtige* lies with God. Fiddes, for example, argues that the notion of 'the *opus alienum* of God comes down heavily on the side of the *opus* of God. It is too much 'his own' and not enough 'most alien' …. It is simply his own, though hapless, work' (Fiddes, 1988, p. 218f.).[30]

To address this question fully one would need not only to explore Barth's treatment of divine omniscience and its relation to creaturely agency, but also his dialectical talk of the nature of eternal temporality as a simultaneity inclusive of a successiveness (see McDowell, 2000a, ch. 5). At least it can be recognized, theologically, that for Barth it is *creation*, and not *evil*, that exists as the presupposition of redemption, or in order to make it possible. Moreover, Barth's theology does not appear to be a 'problem-oriented approach' (that is, postulating the incarnate history as a response to sin), although this statement must be qualified by noting that he *never* abstractly discusses the question of an incarnation in a sinless world because creation *is* sinful, and therefore the incarnation is always placed within that context in a manner reminiscent of Revelation 13: 8 (*CD* II/2, p. 122; *CD* IV/1, p. 36). Consequently, he speaks of the world's reconciliation, resolved in eternity and fulfilled on Calvary (*CD* IV/2, p. 314). Hence, the Incarnate's conflict with sinfulness cannot, without some copious qualification, merely be the temporal playing out of the exclusion of *das Nichtige* in creation.

It is vital to note that Barth does not suggest that *sin* is *necessary* in any theological sense because *das Nichtige* is something which God, as Creator, is somehow responsible for bringing into its own 'improper way' (*CD* III/3, p. 351). In this discourse, and indeed perhaps surprisingly so given the popularity of various types of reading of Augustine's ('free will'!) 'theodicy', Barth moves to prevent the question of the primordial *unde malum* being directed towards the creature. Sin cannot be conceived as a possibility of humanity's created nature since that would imply that it is grounded in the will of God as a means to the end of human nature (see ibid., p. 292).

The is-ness of the inessential and insubstantial   In a somewhat curious statement, however, Barth declares that '[i]t "is" because and as so long as God is against it'

(*CD* III/3, p. 353). Is Hick right, after all, to suggest that *das Nichtige* is not nothingness but some-thing, an aspect of the 'good' and not that which God has declared to be creation's enemy?

On the contrary, by giving *das Nichtige* its 'is-ness' as that which is rejected, the *opus Dei alienum* (understood only in the light of the *opus Dei proprium*) declares what it is that is not good, that is not part of his creative intention, and denies it the divine right of becoming something. It deprives it of the status of the 'is-ness' of an 'autonomous existence independent of God or willed by Him like that of His creature', or of creative intentionality (ibid., p. 353). 'Only God and His creature really and properly are. But nothingness is neither God nor His creature' (ibid., p. 349).

This is what gives to *das Nichtige* 'its ontic peculiarity. It is evil' (ibid., p. 353; cf. p. 354). It is the 'perverse and perverting' antithesis whose relationship to creation is 'actual' but absolutely negative, offering only menace, 'damage and destruction', corruption and death, so that it must never be expressed in terms of synthesis (ibid., pp. 354, 310). It can never contribute anything to the goodness of creation.[31] Hence 'To sin', Jenson argues, 'is to achieve precisely ... nothing' (Jenson, 2000, p. 2; cf. Barth, 1981, p. 214).

Only the most theologically insensitive and philistine of commentaries could charge Barth with a denial (a logical denial, since it is contrary to his intentions) of the threat of *das Nichtige* simply because of the way he names it, apparently making it 'a mere semblance' (*CD* III/3, p. 353). As his treatment of the cross suggests, for example, he certainly does not *intend* (although his practice may be another matter) to minimize sin's demonic energy, as Wingren, Berkouwer and others imply (see *CD* IV/3, p. 177; Wingren, 1958, p. 110; Berkouwer, 1956, pp. 232, 272).[32]

The functioning of Barth's careful linguistic crafting of axiologically rich negativity-talk cannot permit such a reading, however one prescribes how nothingness language (usually contemplated in the context of the *thing*-ness) 'logically' operates (see Hendry, 1982–83, p. 274f.). It may be *not-being*, but it is certainly not *non-being*, although its disruptiveness leads precisely towards the annihilation of the beingness of being. It is *something* even though it is not *some thing*, but attempts to have its own kind of existence (see Wolterstorff, 1996, p. 587). Since, then, 'God takes it into account', 'is concerned with it' and treats it 'seriously' it 'is surely not nothing or non-existent' but 'in a third way of its own nothingness "is".... Nothingness is not nothing.... But it "is" nothingness' (*CD* III/3, p. 349).

The sense of *privatio*, defined as 'the attempt to defraud God of His honour and right and at the same time rob the creature of its salvation and right' (ibid., p. 353f.), or the parasitic disruptiveness of the Good, contributes further to the disabling of any striving for explanation (see MacKinnon, 1979, p. 193). This refusal is what an exasperated and uncomprehending Hick calls 'leaving the problem hanging in the air, without presuming to settle it' (Hick, 1977, p. 143), although Winston unfortunately implies too much of the contrary when unqualifiedly claiming that 'Barth attempts to resolve, or at least alleviate, the obvious contradiction between God's sovereign goodness and the existence of evil' (Winston, 1959, p. 55). Barth recognizes the 'absurdity' of evil, and thereafter he deposes philosophical drives for conceptual systematization in theodicy projects by taking a view of the iconoclastic interrogative subversion of the tragic that is not dissimilar to that of Ricoeur and MacKinnon.[33] He declares that nothingness 'is altogether inexplicable' because it 'is absolutely without norm or standard'.

> For this reason it is inexplicable, and can be affirmed only as that which is inherently inimical.... Being hostile before and against God, and also before and against His creature, it is outside the sphere of systematisation. It cannot even be viewed dialectically, let alone resolved. (*CD* III/3, p. 354)

Instead, he communicates the irrational facticity of what MacKinnon names the 'surd element in the universe' (MacKinnon, 1995, p. 109).

It is worth registering that all this could arguably be *conducive* towards a MacKinnon-like 'phenomenology of moral evil', 'a descriptive study aimed at achieving a *Wesenschau* into the substance of the thing' (MacKinnon, 1966c, p. 176f.). Midgley similarly argues that some kind of analysis of the 'immediate sources of evil in human affairs' is needed, rather than an aetiology and theodicy defensive of God's beneficent existence. '[W]e have to grasp how its patterns are continuous ... with ones which appear in our own lives and in the lives of those around us' (cited in Webster, 1998, p. 65). As *CD* IV/4's posthumously published fragments indicate, such descriptiveness would operate by focusing one's prayerful attentions on the sources of evil in human affairs (distinguishable from cosmological sources/origins) and acting against them in a Christo-regulation of human agency.[34]

Barth, like MacKinnon with his agnostic preference for paradox over synthesis, in view of the mystery of the paradox of the existence of evil alongside the sovereignty of God in the world, refuses to try to justify God. Rather, God justifies himself in the event of encounter. Barth is content with placing evil under the scaffold of God's 'unwilling' and its Christic 'having-been-overcome.' The question of the reason for God's 'permission' of the existence of that absurd opposition is left an unresolved mystery expressible only in paradoxical terms. But 'permission' is certainly a category that Barth was not averse to drawing on (*CD* III/3, p. 367). And, indeed, it is a category that could support Ricoeur's perception of a residual nod to the ancient tragic experience of the 'tragic god' in the Edenic narratives (Ricoeur, 1967, p. 311; cf. p. 327).[35]

Being irresponsibly responsible, or being unable to not dispose of sin   In a statement concerning the stealing of the blessedness of being by sin, Barth suggests a highly significant 'nevertheless' in his discourse about what it means for sin to lack the 'right' to exist. The creature, he emphasizes, cannot be exonerated from all responsibility for its existence, presence and activity. On the contrary, the threat of *das Nichtige* has to become inexcusably and inexplicably *acted* out as sin, as human acts, for evil to be spoken of as a pervasive actuality or *factuality* (see *CD* III/3,

p. 310).[36] The intrusion of *das Nichtige* is ontologically unfounded, yet it can be referred to only in the bizarre, extremely foolish and irrational acts of agents. As Barth argues, 'the covenant-partner of God can break the covenant ... [and is] able to sin, and actually does so' (*CD* III/2, p. 205).

Here Barth seems to have learned not only from Augustine, but perhaps also from Kant, who argued that although there is no conceivable ground from which the moral evil in us could have come, it is a universal feature of our experience of human agency.

However, Barth's 'enfleshing' of *das Nichtige* in his treatment of sin here might seem too voluntaristically conceived, a moralizing narrowness[37] of

> personal act and guilt ..., refusal of the gratitude ... [one] owes to God, [one's] arrogant attempt to be his own master, provider and comforter, his unhallowed lust for what is not his own, the falsehood, hatred and pride in which he is enmeshed in relation to his neighbour, the stupidity to which he is self-condemned, and a life which follows the course thereby determined on the basis of the necessity thus imposed. (*CD* III/3, p. 305)

In this paragraph Barth has announced several themes more fully elaborated later in *CD* IV: sin as the enemy; the sin best named as the evil action of pride (IV/1); the evil inaction of sloth (IV/2); and falsehood (IV/3). There is a suggestion here that Barth is negating the distorting social and systemic context of sin, one's own frequently unconscious complicitous collusion with it, its complex remodulation of the fluid structures of the self and therein the erotics of that self. It would, for instance, take some nifty manoeuvring to remove the sin of 'pride' from its *active* grammatical sense, as several feminist critics demonstrate.

Highfield, however, defends Barth because of the latter's 'zeal to avoid any tragic interpretation of sin in which sin is viewed as a fate which we have to endure rather than something we do freely and knowingly' (Highfield, 1989, p. 83).

Being lorded over, or being predisposed to sin However, maintaining an *exclusively* voluntarist account seems an odd position to take for one whose early engagement in socialist praxis impacted on his reading of the Bible. Highfield's comment is misleading, then, and not merely because he misunderstands the complex interplay of themes of agency and fate in both Greek and Shakespearean tragic dramas. Perhaps to recognize this is to take a theology of sinning out of the constrictive environment of simple blame-seeking, and instead renovate the phenomenology of moral evil that MacKinnon has called for, with an ethics of compassion and hopefulness.[38]

Webster more accurately argues that Barth recognizes the meandering of his sin-talk towards 'the vicinity of Pelagius', and consequently complements it 'with some consideration of its supra-personal aspects, and of the enmeshing of the individual's will in a web of cause and effect not of his or her own creation' (Webster, 1998, p. 73f.). Webster is also right to point to 'a remarkable section on "the Lordless Powers" released by the human person in alienation from him- or herself' (ibid.). In fact, the tone of this has already been registered in *CD* III/3 when Barth announces that sinners 'have become the victims and servants of nothingness, sharing its nature and producing and extending it' (*CD* III/3, p. 306; cf. p. 352). Hence, 'nothingness is not exhausted in sin' but 'is also something under which we suffer in a connexion with sin which is sometimes palpable but sometimes we can only sense and sometimes is closely hidden' (ibid., p. 310).

An exploration of these themes makes possible a markedly different account, one more sensitive to the factors that *tragically* shape our being founded in this hamartiosphere. It would give sense to a comment like Ricoeur's that 'sin pervades all registers of life', or Farley's that 'sin modifies the very structures of the self [and] distorts our temporality, our biological aggressiveness, and our passions for reality and the interhuman' (Ricoeur, 1967, p. 246f.; Farley, 1980, p. 127). Even the Adamic myth, according to Ricoeur, suggests through its anguine antagonist (its serpent figure) a certain *thereness*-of-evil anterior to, and even regulative of, subsequent *peccability* (Ricoeur, 1967, p. 257f.). It is part of the tragedy of the story that it leaves the motivation of the voluntary sinful act shrouded in mystery, Farley continues, and yet this is suppressed by any 'theology of sin' which 'interprets the origin of sin as a sheer act of will' – even though such voluntarism does perceptively recognize 'that human evil or sin is ontologically contingent; it takes place with human self-making' (Farley, 1980, p. 129f.)

Demonic legion   Webster interestingly implies that Barth's post-Augustianian account 'of evil as ultimately *privatio*' masks this emphasis on sinning and the need for '*description*, informing us of what is the case, by naming and delineating what it is that sinners do' (Webster, 1998, p. 71f.). In one sense, this is misleading since it suggests that, like other opponents of the *privatio boni*, who claim that *privatio* is an 'underestimating [of] evil', Webster might have missed the controlled point it attempts to make in metaphysical terms.[39] After all, when commenting on Augustine, Barth claims that '[i]t is not only the absence of what really is, but the assault upon it. ... It seeks to destroy and consume it, *tendit ad non esse*, as the fire threatens to consume fuel, and is in process of doing so' (CD III/3, p. 318).

But, perhaps in another sense, an important point is being made by these critics. Horne speaks for many when he declares that *privatio* 'conveys a frustrating sense of abstraction: the atmosphere of the philosopher's study, remote from the experience of violence, cruelty and hatred of the real world' (Horne, 1996, p. 43). Perceiving evil as *privatio boni*, according to Horne, would constitute 'a failure ... of the imagination ... to come to grips with the realities of experience' (Horne, 1996, p. 52). Similarly, although somewhat overstating his case, MacKinnon sweepingly declares that 'it only has to stated clearly, and worked out in terms of concrete examples, to be shown to be totally inadequate as an analysis either of moral or physical evil' (MacKinnon, 1969, p. 44).

Rather than critique it for its 'philosophical' air, however, it would be better to argue that resources for evil-discourse need to be extraordinarily rich and wide-ranging and cannot be limited to what is, at the very least, an abstract and formal configuration of metaphors. Even talk of 'evil' and 'sin' is an abstraction that overtaxes these terms with the multiplicity of the realities they denote.

If nothing else, the suspicion is worth noting that the mistake of numerous commentators on §50 consists in not noticing that Barth also multiply elaborates on this theme elsewhere, especially in his more consciously dramatic sections.[40] Indeed, he even speaks of only 'provisionally' defining the disruption as 'nothingness' (*CD* III/3, p. 289). In other words, as the important section on 'The Lordless Powers' demonstrates, he has not frozen his metaphors into any single or abstract way of describing; he even begins to describe the multiple visages of *das Nichtige* in positive ways (see Horne, 1996, p. 106). Even Augustine, Horne is forced to recognize, 'had more to say on the subject' (ibid., p. 43). Nevertheless – and recognizing this is vital for gaining a sense of what Barth is doing – this 'saying' is only used for the purpose of delineating his vision of what Christians, whose hope is Christomorphic, should be setting their faces against in order to follow God's rejecting of *das Nichtige*. The cross militates against an idealistically anaemic view of humanity's place within a world corrupted by *das Nichtige*.[41] Barth's is, as Webster rightly argues, 'an ethical account of wickedness':

> Barth's theology takes with great seriousness the command for rebellion against sin: the defeat of sin is not merely a vicarious achievement, passively received from the hands of an omnipotent Lord, but a summons to us to recover our agency and assume the liberty in which we stand. (Webster, 1998, p. 76)

The fitting stance for the creature is, then, not to ask whether God meets our accreditation requirements for a god worthy of recognition as such, but to accept the proffered privilege of enlistment in the cause of the healing of the nations.[42] This is to speak, with MacKinnon, of a sympathizing 'with the Marxist insistence that such things [as cancer] call not for explanation but for elimination' (MacKinnon, 1968, p. 156). No place can be unhoped for. Even the 'lordless powers' 'cannot be ontologically godless forces' (Barth, 1981, p. 215):

> [E]ven today we still live in a world that has been basically dedemonized already in Jesus Christ, and will be so fully one day. But in the meantime it still needs a good deal of dedemonizing, because even up to our own time it is largely demon-possessed, possessed, that is, by the existence and lordship of similar or, at times, obviously the same lordless forces which the people of the New Testament knew. (Ibid., p. 218)

Conclusion

Barth's conversations do not always appear on the surface, and his perspective on tragedy, whilst his grasp of its particular literary expressions may be simplistic and observably limited, is best displayed not so much through his occasional lapses into speech concerning it, but by his insufficiently qualified Christological dynamic.

Leaving this comment there may prove misleading, however. There simply is more to Barth than recognizing the weakness that his [non-]reading of tragic drama may imply. Certainly his developed perspective cannot be named 'tragic' if that is understood as an undifferentiated account of what makes tragedies tragic, a hermeneutic that can fill our ignorances concerning something grand variously disguised as 'life', 'existence', 'history' and so on. But then neither can MacKinnon's. Barth's discussion is always theologically framed, with God's gracious history in Jesus Christ being the point at which not only is evil most readily perceivable to the theologically disciplined eye, but at which it is pronounced (through the resurrection of the executed Christ) unfinalizable. In other words, talk of evil is contextualized within a criteriological perspective informed by the grace of the reconciling God (which, in turn, sees evil through the category of 'sin'). What this entails for Barth is that *hope* is most truly Christian when, contrary to what appears to be appropriate, it refuses to let any part of 'creation' be unhoped for. This sense of the ontological radicality or, better, being-without-home of evil prevents its reduction to banality or, better, its seeming-to-live-ordinarily-in-every-home. It is not insignificant that the section on 'The Lordless Powers' is set firmly, not merely in the vicinity of a lament over the dishonouring of God's Name, but in the midst of an ethically engaged response invoking God as 'Our Father'. Hence MacKinnon reveres Barth for being theologically hopeful, and it is instructive that MacKinnon does not set him in his sights when critiquing others for not taking the tragic seriously. The implication is that, for Barth, taking the tragic seriously would necessitate interrogating it in the hope of resisting it. This means that Steiner is right to set the Christian hope for redemption in tension with the tragic. Gorringe illustrates the sense of this perspective with reference to Barth's Münster lectures on ethics of 1928–29:

> It was the eschatological cast of Barth's whole theology which challenged this mood [of hopelessness in post-1928 Weimar] throughout, and the promise of the renewal of all things, the affirmation of all created reality, which grounded the political imperative. In no way was it an expression of a mood which expected nothing of the present, and everything of the future. (Gorringe, 1999, p. 94)

Steiner is wrong, however, in proceeding to claim that therefore Christianity cannot, with its eschatology, permit the tragic to play any meaningful role, for Steiner does not understand the nature of Christian 'hope' as something resistant to any conceptual finalizing of its eschatological discourse, although he does understand the tragic, like Barth, in terms of endings. First, as Steiner did come to notice, MacKinnon himself reminds us of the theological complexity of the tragic dimension, of a hope without the secure enclaves of even pious talk of triumph. Indeed, 'all our hopes', MacKinnon says in 1946, 'are set' in 'the descent of Christ into the tomb' (MacKinnon, 1946, p. 12).[43] In MacKinnon is put into practice a profound sense of the provisionality and hubristic brokenness of thought and action, culminating in the almost tortuous, tentative and stammering bringing of Christ's reconciling action to speech and practice. The redeeming action of God in Christ has not yet been resolved. An awareness of that does not lead MacKinnon into using 'cross' and the 'tragic' as purely interpretative categories, and therefore as categories that reinforce social and political status quos by imagining the inevitability of evil, as West wrongly accuses him of doing (West, 1985, p. 434). The recognition of the existential relevance of tragedy and *hubris* is not the same as fatalism, a distinction West fails to recognize, along with the interrogative character of MacKinnon's oeuvre.

Second, Barth's own treatment of evil suggests possible illumination through categories amenable to a tragic sensibility:

> [W]e have here an extraordinarily clear demonstration of the necessary brokenness of all theological thought and utterance. There is no theological sphere where this is not noticeable. All theology is a *theologia viatorum*. It can never satisfy the natural aspiration of human thought and utterance for completeness and compactness. It does not exhibit its object but can only indicate it. (*CD* III/3, p. 293)

Taking the tragic tragically, then, entails holding open the categories within which it is spoken of, while realizing that its discourse is fundamentally reflection on *active* hoping for something other.

Steiner, however, is on to something else when he claims that Christian theologians are resistant to the tragic. At least this is the case if this is taken as an observation about theological practice, an observation concurring with MacKinnon's own critique. Barth's folds appear too neat on occasions, and that cannot be solely accounted for by mere simplistic resort to any personal psychology of a generally untragic sensibility. Victorious rhetoric cannot be separated from his sensibility as if reading Barth could involve knowing him better than he knew himself or problematically searching for the kernel within the chaff. For Barth, it is of the nature of the Gospel to provide this resistant reading. Yet, MacKinnon reminds us, meditation on the Gospel may also require something significantly different from what Barth provides here at this point. The problem may well lie, then, more in the manner of his reading of the cross, than in what von Balthasar accuses him of – that Barth 'ends up talking about Christ so much as *the* true human being that it makes it seem as if all other human beings are mere epiphenomena of Christ' (von Balthasar, 1972, p. 243).

Perhaps the recognition that Barth 'was always the champion of the concrete against, for instance, the abstract or merely possible' needs to be revised by the claim that he betrayed himself by undetermining the specificity of the cross, instinctively, and perhaps Hegelianly, providing a certain rhetorical kind of narratable legibility with attendant eschatological implications beyond the bounds of any unstructurable nescience over the futural (MacKinnon, 1968, p. 283f.).

The implication, then, is that, although this MacKinnon-like rereading may be assumed to arise internally from a Barthian corpus, taking it seriously may ultimately demand a theology that not only sounds, but also looks, quite different from Barth's, without whom it may also not be what it must become – that is, if it is to do justice to the specificity of God's history as a history with a particular instance of human pain at its core, and if hope is not to topple over into something less hopeful, such as optimism.

That said, however, one needs to be suspicious not merely of the apparent way in which Barth hid the tension, but also of any systematic or single-layered readings of him. Hence MacKinnon, citing an informal conversation with Olive Wyon, declares that 'for all the massiveness and intellectual power of his argument, one is in the end dealing with a poet rather than an exegete' (MacKinnon, 1966b, p. 108).

This poetic depiction might be appropriately set in more musical terms, and the *Church Dogmatics*' style may suggest how harmony may be disrupted:

> I suggest that we listen to something jolly from Mozart, a little song which is almost frivolous – almost so – but which I like to hear from time to time because of its refrain: 'Silence – I will say no more.' Yes indeed. I will say no more ... we also need to be able not to think that we always have something to say. Let us listen then. (Barth, 1977, http://www.religion-onine.org)

Notes

1 One should also, of course, interrogate Jacques' depiction of the world as simply a stage for human thespians, a stage that does not have much to do with who the actors really are. A much richer picture of the interactions between the world's actors and their environments than any simple stage metaphor will allow needs to be developed. As Hans Urs von Balthasar explains about his own use of the 'stage' image as a metaphor for the world, 'this stage was inaugurated as an integrating feature of the action itself' (von Balthasar, 1998, p. 111).

2 This parallels the recognition that pessimism is not simply to be *identified with*, although it is certainly *one* possible expression (the assertive or positivistic one) of, a broad-ranging nihilism.

3 Shakespeare, 1972, V.111.8 – the 'come let us away to prison' speech.

4 For suggestions of what the 'tragic' might look and not look like see McDowell (2000c).

5 Interestingly, although without further exploration, von Balthasar discusses Barth's *das Nichtige* in the context of his 'The Final Act as Tragedy', and does this in his part-volume on eschatology (von Balthasar, 1998, pp. 205ff.).

6 It is true that this article acknowledges little sense of a responsibility to the ecclesial dimension to MacKinnon's reflections, the struggle of knowing how to appreciate one's epistemic mediatedness and contextuality while seriously engaging as widely and honestly as possible with non-ecclesial sources for reflection. But that questions of ecclesial contextuality were not too far away is suggested not only by the reflections on ecclesial practice that he provided in other writings of the period, but also by the general ecclesial advice he offered.

7 In a statement pregnant with implications for any theodicy project, MacKinnon describes an anxiety of 'official Churches ... always to secure apologetic victories' that therein constitutes a loss of integrity (MacKinnon, 1966a, p. 95).

8 Here he refers to parables, but his descriptions can be applied equally to his use of drama, those open-textured forms which, by their indirection, 'hint, or more than hint, at ways in which things fundamentally are'. Consequently, they illuminate human life by 'inducing deeper self-criticism, by puncturing make-believe, by renewing simplicity, etc.', and open possibilities for human action (MacKinnon, 1974, p. 94). A parallel between parables and drama is explicitly made when MacKinnon argues that one can 'receive what is offered to us in tragedy as parable' (MacKinnon, 1966b, p. 109).

9 Barr (1993) is representative of this reading of Barth. However, Barth's perspective is far removed from any simple Christ-against-culture model, and this move constitutes no softening of his suspicion of natural theologies (*pace* Brunner, 1951; Palma, 1983).

10   See Barth, 1986, p. 23 for something suggestive of the opposite.

11   Significantly, the assessment in *CD* III/3, at p. 299 appears deliberately to echo Jesus' closing of his parables (for example, Matt. 11:15).

12   Gill records that when he remarked on the portraits of Calvin and Mozart hanging side-by-side in Barth's study, Barth announced: 'My special revelation [Calvin]. And my general revelation [smiling at Mozart]' (Gill, 1986, p. 405).

13   An important point is being made here about the necessary reticence appropriate to a theology that entertains consciousness of its eschatological provisionality – a point that verges on being lost in Reinhold Niebuhr's style of theological nationalism (Niebuhr, 1938, p. 53; cf. Barth, 1954, p. 81ff.).

14   It is important to note, at least as a way of qualifying Plato's so-called 'aversion to the dramatic', that Plato's dialogues themselves are redolent of a certain type of 'drama' in their manner of conversation (see von Balthasar, 1988, p. 138; Roochnik, 1990).

15   Echoes of MacKinnon's disdain of the way of the politically cultured post-Constantinian state church rebound here.

16   MacKinnon speaks, in Wittgensteinian mood, of being able to 'at best … discern a family resemblance between' tragic dramas, provided one avoids 'a blind indifference to the multiple complexity of those works which we class together as tragedies' (MacKinnon, 1969, p. 42). 'It would be a grave mistake to generalize about tragedy as if there were an "essence" of the tragic that we could extract and capture in a manageable formula. The world of Racine is very different from that of Shakespeare, and both alike from the worlds explored by the ancient Greek tragedians' (MacKinnon, 1979, p. 186).

17   Hans Schwarz's exclusive concentration on §50 is problematic (Schwarz, 1995, pp. 163–68).

18   See, for example, Rogers (1999, chs 6 and 7); and Marquardt cited in Sonderegger (1992, p. 146). In 1949 Barth explained the continued grace of God to the Jews, and declared that the Jew 'is the mirror in which we see ourselves as we are, i.e. we see how bad we all are' (Barth, 1954, p. 198).

19   Assessments differ as to whether this was a correctable 'lapse' into cultural patriarchy, or rather a 'necessary' product of an 'irredeemable' theology. See, for example, Ward (1998); Rogers (1999, pp. 6 , 8); Sonderegger (2000); Ruether (1983, p. 98).

20   See Adams, 1989. Stephen Wykstra points out that talk of waste and meaninglessness is person-specific, and therefore cannot rule out the possibility that, within the divine perspective, there are no pointless sufferings (Wykstra, 1984, p. 80f.). This, surely, begs the question of whether talk of the justification of suffering is itself not also person-specific, and is ironic in utilizing an argument that Immanuel Kant had considered, even in 1791, detestable to human moral sensibilities (Kant, 1998, p. 19f.).

21   Strangely Hebblethwaite declares that '[t]he Judaeo-Christian … sees the problem of evil first and foremost as involving a demand for explanation and justification' and cites Job and Ivan Karamazov (Hebblethwaite, 1976, p. 7). But would an *explanation* even have been sufficient for them?

22   See Webster (1998, p. 69): 'Barth's Christological determination of sin is not so much an attempt to dislocate "theological" from "empirical" reality, as an argument born of a sense that human persons are characteristically self-deceived.' Theologically speaking, Webster's second subclause inverts Barth's move – Barth's 'Christological determination of sin is … an argument born of a sense that' God's commerce with the world has been disclosed in the person of Jesus (see *CD* IV/2, p. 387) and in its light the nature of human being.

23   Schulweis's claim about Barth's *anthropo*-dicy rather than *theo*-dicy (since *humanity* needs justification) requires qualification lest it suggest that theodical *strategies* can be properly inverted (Schulweis, 1975).

24   Similarly, even Moltmann's more subtle divine passibilism slips when claiming a 'divine self-emptying love [in which] the Son of God *abandoned his divine identity*' in the godforsakenness of the cross (cited in Bauckham, 1987, p. 70, emphasis added; cf. Moltmann, 1974, p. 25ff.). However, Moltmann's notion that the cross is indicative of the triune relationality is more to the point (see, for example, Lapide and Moltmann, 1981, p. 54).

25   Some examples of this particular complaint are MacKinnon (1974, p. 169) and Tracy (1998, p. 114).

26   Burns complains that 'most [recent theological and philosophical attempts to understand the nature of human evil] ... still tend, if mutedly, to cling to the notion of mankind's essential moral goodness' (Burns, 2000, p. 292). If 'essential' here has reference to the eschatologically creative will of God (the theological *reality* of human being), then Burns demonstrably lacks understanding of evil's nature within a theology of grace. If it refers to the phenomenon of the human (the *actuality* of human beings), then he seriously misunderstands Ricoeur's *theological* point. It is significant that when Ricoeur speaks of the 'anteriority of innocence' he does so in the context of the Adamic myth of the Fall (see Ricoeur, 1967, pt II ch. 3; citation from p. 251).

27   Unlike Allender, for instance, one needs to be careful with the language of the 'evil person' lest it be forgotten that, even in sin, human beings are elected creatures (see Allender, 1999).

28   René Girard writes of: 'the absolute need that demons have to *possess* a living being in order to survive. The demon is not capable of existing apart from that possession' (cited by Webster, 1998, p. 76). According to Augustine, although evil is not a substance it *appears* as a substance (*De morbis manichaeorum*, 2.5.7).

29   This, it must be re-emphasized, is not Barth's equation of *das Nichtige* with the *Schattenseite*, although Ruether feels that 'this frontier has a way of becoming blurred' in Barth's explication (Ruether, 1968–69, p. 14). Hick understands Barth to be thinking of what has 'traditionally' been called metaphysical evil – namely finitude, imperfection, impermanence, and the fact of having been created *ex nihilo* and being thus ever on the verge of collapsing back into non-existence. However, Barth views these as necessary limitations and imperfections that are not to be counted as *evil* (see, for example, *CD* III/3, p. 74 on physical death 'as a natural limitation').

30   Rodin pushes this conflict further into the eternality of the Godhead 'which is then played out in the creaturely sphere' (Rodin, 1997, p. 89f.).

31   This contrasts with a perspective, such as that of Sanford, which can associate 'evil' with an accompanying shadow – this shadow, he claims, 'contains many valuable qualities that can add to our life and strength if we are related to them in the right way' (Sanford, 1981, p. 51). This confuses and conflates the *Schattenseite* of creation with *Böse* no less than does Hick's account. Blocher more adequately declares that 'Evil is disorder; it oppresses and is oppressive' (Blocher, 1994, p. 11). As such, 'evil is an unjustifiable reality'. And yet Blocher fails to comprehend talk of 'nothingness': 'evil is "something" which occurs; it is not merely "nothing", as we know only too well'. However, and here is the problem, who is this 'we'? If it is anyone able to be dissatisfied with the way things are, then the difficulties involved in delineating what it means to speak of 'sin' and 'evil' in the first place are naively overshot, as are the strategies and conditions of self-deception operative in our (un)natural environments. If, on the other hand, the reference is to those whose learning is done through Christ, then it needs to be asked what kind of 'something' Christ revealed 'sin' and 'evil' to be.

32   For a better description, see Hartwell (1964, p. 120).

33   On Barth's being critical of theodicy strategies, see Wolterstorff (1996, p. 584).

34   Barth announces that he 'can speak of them [the 'Lordless Forces'] only in consciously mythological terms' (Barth, 1981, p. 216), although he does proceed to name them in terms of political absolutisms, mammon, ideologies, technology, sport, pleasure and transportation.

35   Barth's theme leads Wolterstorff to speak of a 'trade-off': 'God trades the good of stopping *das Nichtige* in its tracks for the greater overall good which ensues from permitting it to continue its incursions for a while' (Wolterstorff, 1996, p. 605). On Schleiermacher's understanding of evil, Robert Merrihew Adams argues that 'it is not in its own right an object of divine (or other) causality; but he is quite clear that this does not remove the evil from the scope of the divine causality (§81.1, p. 331f./I, pp. 487–89). It merely qualifies the way in which it does not fall within the scope of the divine causality. It does not get God off the hook, if that were needed' (Adams, 1996, p. 564).

36   Wolterstorff notes that Barth comes close to the free-will account, which Barth proceeds to reject on the basis of its misconstrual of freedom as freedom of choice (Wolterstorff, 1996, p. 604).

37   This emphasis remains popular for Christian groups that critique the narcissism of contemporary Western therapy cultures – they deceive themselves in their therapies for the healing of the socially

depleted and self – the self whose healing of externally imposed sickness constitutes self-relief, satisfaction and victimhood, rather than responsibility. Of course, the background to this voluntarism may be in the 'spiritualizing' tensions that have dogged Western cultures since post-Platonic philosophy (see Farley, 1980, pp. 77, 79).

38 Alistair McFadyen's study, which deals with the complex interplay of socio-psychotherapeutic and classical (as well as feminist) accounts of evil that take sin-talk beyond simple and generalizable moral guilt–blame grammar, provides a very interesting challenge to dominant voluntarist portrayals of sin and evil (McFadyen, 2000).

39 Mallow reads Barth's *das Nichtige* carelessly because of a misappropriation of the nature of Barth's noetics:

> Barth's statements to the effect that sin is operative in man only because of his blindness and ignorance seems to greatly underrate the place of sin in today's world. He seems to be saying that man needs only to understand his contingent and dependent nature in light of what God has done in Christ in order to recover his self-mastery and re-orient his life. (Mallow, 1983, p. 98)

40 Quite simply, Stephen H. Webb is incorrect to declare that Barth 'is forced … to view evil as purely privative (*das Nichtige*)' (Webb, 1996, p. 102).

41 Blocher indicates his misunderstanding of what Barth is doing in his Christological hermeneutic when he claims that any drawing 'theology of sin from Christ and the cross *directly*' that does not 'listen to Scripture as a whole …, and only then perceive how precisely the doctrine is proclaimed and, so to speak, reinforced in the Christ-event' is problematic (Blocher, 1997, p. 17).

42 Barth's approach, then, fits more the specifics of Surin's picture of 'Theodicies With a "Practical" Emphasis' (Surin, 1984). The danger with this description, however, is that it could set the 'Theodicies With a "Theoretical" Emphasis' too comfortably alongside this more 'Practical' one, implying that they are indexibly two different and competing species of the *same thing*, and thereby mask the incommensurability (suggested by Barth's disruption of the formulas of theodicy projects).

43 It needs to be noted, however, that language of 'descending' can suggest an *activity* whereas in the 'act' of *being dead* Jesus was *inactive*.

References

Adams, M.M. (1989), 'Horrendous Evils and the Goodness of God', *The Aristotelian Society: Supplementary Volume*, **63**, pp. 297–310.

Adams, R.M. (1996), 'Schleiermacher on Evil', *Faith and Philosophy*, **13**, pp. 563–83.

Allender, D.B. (1999), 'The Mark of Evil', in L.B. Lampman and M.D. Shattuck (eds), *God and the Victim: Theological Reflections on Evil, Victimization, Justice, and Forgiveness*, Grand Rapids, MI: William B. Eerdmans, pp. 36–60.

Barr, J. (1993), *Biblical Faith and Natural Theology: The Gifford Lectures for 1991*, Oxford: Clarendon Press.

Barth, K. (1954), *Against the Stream: Shorter Post-War Writings*, ed. R.G. Smith, London: SCM.

Barth, K. (1969), *How I Changed My Mind*, ed. J. Godsey, Edinburgh: The Saint Andrew Press.

Barth, K. (1977), *Final Testimonies*, ed. E. Busch, Grand Rapids, MI: Eerdmans.

Barth, K. (1981), *The Christian Life: Church Dogmatics IV/4 Lecture Fragments*, trans. G.W. Bromiley, Edinburgh: T. & T. Clark.

Barth, K. (1986), *Wolfgang Amadeus Mozart*, trans. C.K. Pott, Grand Rapids, MI: Eerdmans.

Bauckham, R. (1987), *Moltmann: Messianic Theology in the Making*, Basingstoke: Marshall Morgan and Scott.

Berkouwer, G.C. (1956), *The Triumph of Grace in the Theology of Karl Barth*, trans. H.R. Boer, London: Paternoster Press.

Blocher, H. (1994), *Evil and the Cross*, trans. D.G. Preston, Leicester: Apollos.

Blocher, H. (1997), *Original Sin: Illuminating the Riddle*, Leicester: Apollos.

Brunner, E. (1951), 'The New Barth', *Scottish Journal of Theology*, **4**, pp. 123–35.

Burns, R.M. (2000), 'The Origins of Human Evil', *Scottish Journal of Theology*, **53**, pp. 292–315.

Farley, E. (1980), *Good and Evil: Interpreting a Human Condition*, Minneapolis: Fortress Press.

Fiddes, P.S. (1988), *The Creative Suffering of God*, Oxford: Clarendon Press.

Ford, D.F. (1989), 'Tragedy and Atonement', in K. Surin (ed.), *Christ, Ethics and Tragedy: Essays in Honour of Donald MacKinnon*, Cambridge: Cambridge University Press, pp. 117–30.

Forsyth, P.T. (1917), *The Justification of God: Lectures for War-Time on a Christian Theodicy*, London: Latimer House.

Gill, T.A. (1986), 'Barth and Mozart', *Theology Today*, **43**, pp. 403–11.

Gorringe, T.J. (1999), *Karl Barth: Against Hegemony*, Oxford: Oxford University Press.

Hardy, D.W. (1997), 'Philosophy Through History', in D.F. Ford (ed.), *The Modern Theologians: An Introduction to Christian Theology in the Twentieth Century*, Oxford: Blackwell, pp. 252–85.

Hartwell, H. (1964), *The Theology of Karl Barth: An Introduction*, Philadelphia: Westminster.

Hebblethwaite, B. (1976), *Evil, Suffering and Religion*, London: Sheldon Press.

Hebblethwaite, B. (1989), 'MacKinnon and the Problem of Evil', in K. Surin (ed.), *Christ, Ethics and Tragedy: Essays in Honour of Donald MacKinnon*, Cambridge: Cambridge University Press, pp. 131–45.

Hendry, G.S. (1982–83), 'Nothing', *Theology Today*, **39**, pp. 274–89.

Hick, J. (1977), *Evil and the God of Love*, 2nd edn, London and Basingstoke: Macmillan.

Highfield, R. (1989), *Barth and Rahner in Dialogue: Toward an Ecumenical Understanding of Sin and Evil*, New York, Bern, Frankfurt am Main; Paris: Peter Lang.

Horne, B. (1996), *Imaging Evil*, London: Darton Longman and Todd.

Horton, W.M. (1956), 'How Barth Has Influenced Me', *Theology Today*, **13**, pp. 359–60.

Jenson, R.W. (2000), 'Introduction: Much Ado About Nothingness', in C.E. Braaten and R.W. Jenson (eds.), *Sin, Death, and the Devil*, Grand Rapids, MI: Eerdmans, pp. 1–6.

Kant, I. (1998), 'On the Miscarriage of all Philosophical Trials in Theodicy', in *Religion Within the Boundaries of Mere Reason And Other Writings*, trans. and ed. A. Wood and G. Di Giovanni, Cambridge: Cambridge University Press, pp. 17–30.

Kerr, F. (1997), *Immortal Longings: Versions of Transcending Humanity*, London: SPCK.

Lapide, P. and Moltmann, J. (1981), *Jewish Monotheism and Christian Doctrine: A Dialogue Between Pinchas Lapide and Jürgen Moltmann*, trans. L. Swidler, Philadelphia: Fortress Press.

Lovin, R.W. (1984), *Christian Faith and Public Choices: The Social Ethics of Barth, Brunner, and Bonhoeffer*, Philadelphia: Fortress Press.

McDowell, J.C. (2000a), *Hope in Barth's Eschatology: Interrogations and Transformations Beyond Tragedy*, Aldershot: Ashgate.

McDowell, J.C. (2000b), 'Learning Where to Place One's Hope: The Eschatological Significance of Election in Barth', *Scottish Journal of Theology*, **53**, pp. 316–38.

McDowell, J.C. (2000c), 'Silenus' Wisdom and the "Crime of Being": The Problem of Hope in George Steiner's Tragic Vision', *Literature and Theology*, **14**, pp. 385–98.

McFadyen, A. (2000), *Bound to Sin: Abuse, Holocaust and the Christian Doctrine of Sin*, Cambridge: Cambridge University Press.

MacKinnon, D.M. (1946), 'The Tomb Was Empty', *The Christian Newsletter*, **258**, pp. 7–12.

MacKinnon, D.M. (1966a), 'Can a Divinity Professor Be Honest?', *The Cambridge Review*, **12**, pp. 94–96.

MacKinnon, D.M. (1966b), in *The Resurrection: A Dialogue Arising From Broadcasts by G.W.H. Lampe and D.M. MacKinnon*, ed. W. Purcell, London: A.R. Mowbray.

MacKinnon, D.M. (1966c), 'Subjective and Objective Conceptions of Atonement', in F.G. Healey (ed.), *Prospect for Theology: Essays in Honour of H.H. Farmer*, London: James Nisbet & Co., pp. 169–82.

MacKinnon, D.M. (1968), *Borderlands of Theology And Other Essays*, London: Lutterworth.

MacKinnon, D.M. (1969), *The Stripping of the Altars: The Gore Memorial Lecture Delivered on 5 November 1968 in Westminster Abbey, and Other Papers and Essays on Related Topics*, London: Collins.

MacKinnon, D.M. (1974), *The Problem of Metaphysics*, Cambridge: Cambridge University Press.
MacKinnon, D.M (1979), *Explorations in Theology 5*, London: SCM.
MacKinnon, D.M. (1987), *Themes in Theology: The Three-Fold Cord*, Edinburgh: T. & T. Clark.
MacKinnon, D.M. (1995), 'Teleology and Redemption', in T.A. Hart (ed.), *Justice the True and Only Mercy: Essays on the Life and Theology of Peter Taylor Forsyth*, Edinburgh: T. & T. Clark, pp. 105–109.
Mallow, V.R. (1983), *The Demonic: A Selected Theological Study. An Examination into the Theology of Edwin Lewis, Karl Barth and Paul Tillich*, Lanham, NY and London: University Press of America.
Moltmann, J. (1974), *The Crucified God: The Cross of Christ as the Foundation and Criticism of Christian Theology*, trans. R.A. Wilson and J. Bowden, London: SCM.
Niebuhr, R. (1938), *Beyond Tragedy: Essays on the Christian Interpretation of History*, London: Nisbet and Co.
Niebuhr, R. (1959), *Essays in Applied Christianity*, New York: Meridian Living Age Books.
Palma, R. (1983), *Karl Barth's Theology of Culture*, Pittsburgh Theological Monographs 75, Allison Park, PA: Pickwick Publications.
Pattison, G. (1996), *Agnosis: Theology in the Void*, Basingstoke and London: Macmillan Press.
Peterson, M.L. (1998), *God and Evil: An Introduction to the Issues*, Boulder, CO and Oxford: Westview Press.
Ricoeur, P. (1967), *The Symbolism of Evil*, New York: Harper & Row.
Ricoeur, P. (1992), *Oneself as Another*, trans. Kathleen Blamey, Chicago and London: University of Chicago Press.
Rodin, S.R. (1997), *Evil and Theodicy in the Theology of Karl Barth*, New York, Bern, Frankfurt am Main, Paris: Peter Lang.
Rogers, E.F. (1999), *Sexuality and the Christian Body*, Oxford: Blackwell.
Roochnik, D. (1990), *The Tragedy of Reason: Toward a Platonic Conception of Logos*, New York and London: Routledge.
Ruether, R.R. (1968–69), 'The Left Hand of God in the Theology of Karl Barth: Karl Barth as a Mythopoeic Theologian', *Journal of Religious Thought*, **25**, pp. 3–26.
Ruether, R.R. (1983), *Sexism and God-Talk: Towards a Feminist Theology*, Boston, MA: Beacon Press.
Sanford, J.A. (1981), *Evil: The Shadow Side of Reality*, New York: Crossroad.
Schulweis, H.M. (1975), 'Karl Barth's Job', *The Jewish Philosophical Quarterly Review*, **65**, pp. 156–67.
Schwarz, H. (1995), *Evil: A Historical and Theological Perspective*, trans. M.W. Worthing, Minneapolis: Fortress Press.
Shakespeare, W. (1972), *King Lear*, ed. G.K. Hunter, Harmondsworth: Penguin.
Sonderegger, K. (1992), *That Jesus Was Born a Jew: Karl Barth's 'Doctrine of Israel'*, University Park, PA: Pennsylvania State University Press.
Sonderegger, K. (2000), 'Barth and Feminism', in J. Webster (ed.), *The Cambridge Companion to Karl Barth*, Cambridge: Cambridge University Press, pp. 258–73.
Steiner, G. (1995), 'Tribute to Donald MacKinnon', *Theology*, **98**, pp. 2–9.
Steiner, G. (1996a), 'Absolute Tragedy', in *No Passion Spent: Essays 1978–1996*, London: Faber and Faber, pp. 129–41.
Steiner, G. (1996b), 'Tragedy Pure and Simple', in M.S. Silk (ed.), *Tragedy and the Tragic: Greek Theatre and Beyond*, Oxford: Clarendon Press, pp. 534–46.
Surin, K. (1984), *Theology and the Problem of Evil*, Oxford: Basil Blackwell.
Sutherland, S. (1990), 'Christianity and Tragedy', *Literature and Theology*, **4**, pp. 157–68.
Tracy, D. (1998), 'Saving From Evil: Salvation and Evil Today', in H. Häring and D. Tracy (eds), *The Fascination of Evil, Concilium*, London: SCM, pp. 107–16.
von Balthasar, H.U. (1972), *The Theology of Karl Barth*, trans. J. Drury, New York: Anchor.
von Balthasar, H.U. (1988), *Theo-Drama I. Prolegomena*, trans. G. Harrison, San Francisco: Ignatius Press.
von Balthasar, H.U. (1990), *Theo-Drama II. The Dramatis Personae: Man In God*, trans. G. Harrison, San Francisco: Ignatius Press.

von Balthasar, H.U. (1998), *Theo-Drama. Theological Dramatic Theory V: The Last Act*, trans. G. Harrison, San Francisco: Ignatius Press.

Ward, G. (1998), 'The Erotics of Redemption – After Karl Barth', *Theology and Sexuality*, **8**, pp. 52–72.

Webb, S.H. (1996), *The Gifting God: A Trinitarian Ethics of Excess*, New York and Oxford: Oxford University Press.

Webster, J. (1998), *Barth's Moral Theology: Human Action in Barth's Thought*, Edinburgh: T. & T. Clark.

West, P. (1985), 'Christology as "Ideology"', *Theology*, **88**, pp. 428–36.

Williams, R. (2000), *On Christian Theology*, Oxford: Blackwell.

Wingren, G. (1958), *Theology in Conflict: Nygren, Barth, Bultmann*, trans. E.H. Wahlstrom, Edinburgh and London: Oliver and Boyd.

Winston, A. (1959), 'Barth's Concept of the Nihil', *The Personalist*, **40**, pp. 54–61.

Wolterstorff, N. (1996), 'Barth on Evil', *Faith and Philosophy*, **13**, pp. 584–608.

Wright, T.R. (1988), *Theology and Literature*, Oxford: Basil Blackwell.

Wykstra, S. (1984), 'The Humean Obstacle to Evidential Arguments from Suffering: On Avoiding the Evils of "Appearance"', *International Journal for Philosophy of Religion*, **16**, pp. 73–93.

CHAPTER 9

The Eclipse of the Spirit in Karl Barth

Eugene F. Rogers Jr

Where Barth Allows the Son to Eclipse the Spirit

Karl Barth allows the Son to eclipse the Spirit when he allows his fear of Schleiermacher to overshadow his admiration for Athanasius. It is an odd critique. One would not usually accuse someone of ignoring a topic he has named in the title of an independent book,[1] or a topic named in the titles or thesis statements to *more than a score* of sections totalling some 2100 pages,[2] or a topic to his treatment of which more than one scholar has devoted an entire book (Thompson, 1991; Rosato, 1981), or a topic integral to one he is credited with reviving. Yet many critics have argued, persuasively, that despite books, sections, monographs and the Trinitarian revival, Karl Barth has managed substantively to ignore the Holy Spirit, or to reduce it to a function of Jesus Christ – 'the power of Jesus Christ'.[3]

Indeed, that is a formulation all too similar to one that Gregory Nazianzen had warned about. The danger, in words of Gregory's that Barth had certainly read, is that we should 'give essence to the Father and deny personality to the others, and make them only powers of God, existing in him and not personal' (Nazianzen, 1983, Or. 32.32). Barth's defenders might note that Gregory's warning applies only to the Spirit as a power of the Father. But we read further in Gregory, 'Give him [the Holy Spirit] to the Son, and number Him among the creatures .... You dishonor the Son in your opposition to the Spirit. For he is not the maker of a fellow servant, but he is glorified with one of co-equal honour' (Nazianzen, 1983, Or. 32.12). Or say we read in Barth that the Spirit is the 'act of communion' between the Father and the Son (*CD* I/1, pp. 470–71). Never mind the *Filioque*: Gregory has warned against certain kinds of 'act' language too, denying that calling the Spirit an 'Activity of God' amounts to protecting the Spirit's deity; rather, according to Gregory, it makes the Spirit an accident of God (Nazianzen, 1983, Or. 32.6).[4] Anticipating another of Barth's possible replies – that the predominance of the Son over the Spirit arises from his exegesis – Gregory notes that one can make such mistakes of reticence 'out of reverence to Scripture' (Nazianzen, 1983, Or. 32.5).

The Spirit is announced as an actor in a *Leitsatz* in *CD* I/1 as 'the Lord who sets us free' (*CD* I/1, p. 448). But when Barth comes to explicate that thesis, he repeats it once, 'The New Testament answer is that it is the Holy Spirit who sets man free for this and for the ministry in which he is put therewith,' and then in the very next line begins an exegetical section with the line '*Christ* has "set us free for freedom"'. Now, there is nothing wrong bringing in the other persons whose economic act is indivisible, and certainly nothing wrong with quoting from Galatians. But it is odd that Barth only repeats the *claim* that the Holy Spirit is the one who sets us free, and gives no reason to think we could not explicate the setting free with reference to Christ alone. The reference to the Spirit could be omitted without loss. A sin of omission can be overlooked, unless it seems to be part of a pattern. The Spirit, Barth announces, brings freedom, but the account of freedom in *CD* III/4 has only 14 mentions in 700 pages, of which only one (pp. 320–23) introduces an extended treatment. 'The Promise of the Spirit' in *CD* IV/3.1 (pp. 274–367) takes 20 pages to mention the Spirit, abandons it for another 50 pages, and finally reaches the title topic on page 351, just for 18 pages out of 93, or less than 20 per cent. The same could not be said of Barth's treatments of Jesus Christ – indeed, not even of Barth's treatments of Jesus Christ in the sections announced to be about the Spirit. One wonders if Spirit–talk appears for variety or ornament. One also worries that an intra-Trinitarian, as well as a rhetorical, problem may underlie these textual features: that the Spirit has no gift to give the creature which is not Christ, because the Spirit has no gift to give Christ.

Everywhere in these passages, the Spirit is the condition for the possibility of the human knowledge of God. With that I have no quarrel. Yet if it is Christ who, in exegesis and elaboration, sets us free, and the Spirit is only our freedom, we have the same problem with which Protestants charge Thomas Aquinas. They worry, famously, that grace has become a thing, a human possession. Of course, this charge is fatuous. In Thomas Aquinas, grace is not possibly a human possession of a sort that could undermine God's prevenience, but is the Holy Spirit itself. And yet, if that charge is justified at all, even on the grounds that Thomas ought to have written differently in order to head off a possible misunderstanding and to have spoken of the *Holy Spirit* as dwelling in the heart instead of impersonal, lower-case, common-noun *grace*, then one might say the same about Barth's freedom. He calls it the work of the Spirit, then expounds it as an impersonal, lower-case, common-noun thing.

My title speaks of the 'eclipse' of the Spirit in something of a conceit. Citing Athanasius, Barth calls quite rightly for the Spirit to have its own 'autonomy' at the beginning of the *Dogmatics,* in *CD* I/1, and returns to it at the end of the *Dogmatics* in *CD* IV/4. The Spirit shines in *CD* I/1 and again in *CD* IV/1 – and appears elsewhere as a sort of penumbra. The *Dogmatics* begins and ends with some of the most promising pneumatological insights in the history of theology. In *CD* IV/4, as in *CD* I/1 §12.1, the illumination of the Spirit is more than a penumbra bearing witness to the objectivity of Jesus Christ; there it is something 'not automatically given with the fact that Jesus is present as the revelation of the Father', something 'added to the givenness of the revelation', a 'special element' 'not identical with Jesus Christ, with the Son or Word of God' (*CD* I/1, pp. 449, 451). In *CD* I/1, as Williams helpfully paraphrases the passage, 'it is the Spirit who constitutes revelation as historical, capable of being responded to by individuals in specific contexts' (Williams, 2000, p. 118; citing *CD* I/1, p. 330).

> The *pneuma* is the miracle of the presence of real human beings at God's revelation .... Without God's being historically revealed in this way, revelation

would not be revelation .... The fact that God can do what the biblical witnesses ascribe to him, namely, not just take form and not just remain free in this form, but also in this form and freedom of His become God to specific human beings, eternity in a moment, this is the third meaning of His lordship in His revelation. (*CD* I/1, p. 331)

In *CD* IV/4 the Spirit returns to grant human beings a 'history': 'In the Holy Spirit the history manifested to all human beings in the resurrection of Jesus Christ is manifest and present to a specific human being as his own salvation history' (*CD* IV/4, p. 27).

In the middle of the *Dogmatics,* however, Barth covers the illumination of the Spirit with the material objectivity of the Son. The Son, in a phrase that Rowan Williams has used to title a book, becomes a 'ray of darkness'. There is a mention of the Spirit as the creator of history in *CD* III/1. But, in just one place in the thousands of pages that separate *CD* I/1 from *CD* IV/4, Barth protests of Christological statements and pneumatological statements that:

> Both statements denote one and the same reality. But neither renders the other superfluous. Neither can be reduced to the other. Hence neither is dispensable. Again, neither can be separated from the other. Neither can be understood as except as elucidated by the other. (*CD* IV/3.2, p. 759)

And yet that is just what happens from *CD* I/2 straight through to *CD* IV/3. Christological statements render pneumatological ones superfluous. Pneumatological statements are reduced to Christological ones. Pneumatological statements are dispensed with. Christological statements are separated from pneumatological statements for hundreds of pages. Christological statements are understood as true without elucidation by pneumatological statements. Throughout the middle of the *Dogmatics,* with few exceptions, the Spirit does appear to be automatically given with the fact of Jesus and identical with him, or, in a development of that common-noun element, percussively and repetitively identified with the 'power' or the 'promise' of Jesus Christ.[5]

Why Barth Allows the Son to Eclipse the Spirit

Both sides in the debate about whether Barth's pneumatology is or is not adequate have tended to neglect a salient fact: Barth does this kind of thing in other cases, too. That is, he performs the rhetorical manoeuvre of announcing one topic and pursuing another. There is good reason to think that, when he deploys this strategy, he does so with deliberation and a certain mischievous delight. Take, for example, another famous case, one that causes similar discomfort in the reader but which has largely received theologians' acclaim. In his marvellous reworking of the doctrine of election, in which Barth makes it safe to be a Calvinist again, the reader expects to hear about the predestination of the individual. But Barth thinks that the question 'Am

I saved?' or, worse, 'Is that one saved?' is a terrifically bad question. It's narcissistic, and it distracts the Christian from Christ. It's as if a prosecutor has asked a defence witness, 'When did you stop beating your wife?'. The defence attorney can object; the judge can sustain the objection; the court reporter can strike the question from the record; but the question once voiced has infected the jury, and the defence attorney must do *something* else, something to *distract* the jury from the question, in order effectively and successfully to *un*ask it. That is Barth's strategy in the doctrine of election. First, he presents the reader with 100 pages on 'The Problem of a Correct Doctrine of the Election of Grace'; here he distracts the reader from the question 'What about me?' or 'What about her?' with the proclamation of the Gospel that 'God is for man too the One who loves in freedom' – a proclamation about God, not about the human being. But in the next section he does not then turn to the human individual. Rather, he distracts the reader further with another 100 pages about 'The Election of Jesus Christ'. Now that he has recast the doctrine of election as one about God's attributes of love and freedom, and about what is basically the doctrine of atonement in Jesus Christ, one expects finally to reach the election of the individual. But, no, now there comes a third 100 pages on another topic, 'The Election of the Community', which, for all its supersessionist problems, teaches Christians the much-needed lesson that most of them are Gentiles. By this time, the jury has pretty well forgotten the 'have you stopped beating your wife' question, and it must seem safe to meet it head-on, because now at last we get a section that bears the title, 'The Election of the Individual'. But no. Here, again, we get nothing about you and me. Rather we get biblical typology: Cain and Abel, Saul and David, Judas and Paul, along with such delightful obscurities as Serah and Perez, the scapegoat and the offered goat, the bird slain and the bird flown. The reader who makes it to the end has not only forgotten the original question, she has undergone Barth's *therapy* against it. It will not arise again. She has not only been advised – as Augustine, Luther and Calvin all suggest – to look for her election not in herself but in Christ, she has been *caused* to do so by Barth's exposition, and his refusal to expound.

It is not too difficult to see that something similar is going on with the Holy Spirit. Here, too, Barth wants to unask what he thinks is a terrifically bad question. Despite the fact that Schleiermacher's theology is manifestly Christocentric in its explicit statements, Barth diagnoses it as covertly anthropocentric, and anthropocentric for a pneumatological reason: the Spirit of the Lord has become identified with the spirit of the human. The Holy Spirit is, indeed, the root in God of the human response, and Barth's account of the knowability of God and the readiness of the human being as movements of God to God in the Spirit is brilliant: the human response exists as God's taking us up into the Trinitarian dance – even, although Barth does not say so, as the beginning of theosis. Barth sees the human response to God primarily, although he does not put it this way, in terms of deification. That is, only God can properly respond to God; only God the Spirit can appropriately celebrate the love between the Father and the Son. *If* the human being should do so *too*, that cannot be a human reaction autonomous over against God; rather, it is already a participation in the divine, in the divine autonomy, indeed in the autonomy that the Spirit exercises 'over against' the Father and the Son (*CD* IV/4, p. 76). But the human response is also, in the post-Schleiermacher climate, all too susceptible of reversal, of becoming the door by which God becomes a human projection and so Feuerbach wins. Better, in that case, deliberately and forcibly and therapeutically to turn every question about the Spirit into a question about Christ, because the doctrine of Christ has an objective density that better (Barth thinks) resists the attempts of post-nineteenth-century human beings to assume that theology is about themselves. Thus Rosato does not consider as a flaw the fact that the *Church Dogmatics* does not so much describe the Spirit as display its work.

If this is so, then Barth's constant referring of the Spirit to the Son also has its proper place. The Spirit in the New Testament constantly leads or follows or rests upon the Son. The Spirit apart from the Son can be faceless, 'concealed by the deity which He reveals to us, by the gift which he imparts' (Lossky, 1957, p. 162).[6] According to Vladimir Lossky, the Spirit

> ... mysteriously identifies himself with human persons whilst remaining incommunicable. ... the Holy Spirit effaces himself, as person, before the created persons to whom he appropriates grace. In him the will of God is no longer external to ourselves.... [T]his divine person, now unknown, not having his image in another hypostasis, will manifest himself in deified persons: for the multitude of the saints will be his image. (Ibid., p. 172ff.)

And Ephrem the Syrian says that when we look into the oil of the Spirit anointing the head of the Christian, it reflects the manifold faces of Christ:

> Oil is the dear friend of the Holy Spirit ...
> Christ has many facets, and the oil acts as a mirror to them all:
> from whatever angle I look at the oil, Christ looks out at me from it
> (Ephrem the Syrian, 1983, pp. 48–49, 51; the whole poem is relevant)

Those are strategies according to which even the East, with its vaunted emphasis on the Spirit, cannot fault Barth's reticence, but must respect it.

But it is almost as if Barth finds the still, small voice defenceless. He has to hide it from Schleiermacherian excess. Can we regard him as capable of that?

It can be right if the still, small voice is really only the voice of the human spirit. But suppose it is, indeed, the voice of the Lord, the giver of life, who with the Father and the Son is worshipped and glorified. Or put it another way: I like the way in which Barth's doctrine of election unasks the anthropological question. But I dislike the way his Christological treatments undo the doctrine of the Spirit. Why the difference? To refuse the question of the human is different from refusing the question of the Spirit. There is even the notorious warning about 'blasphemy against the Holy Spirit'. The questions are the same only if one allows Schleiermacher to set the terms and *concedes* the reduction of the holy to the human. Should the human, on the other hand, be elevated to the level of the holy, then even Barth's doctrine of election would have to be improved.[7]

In the following sections we will be taking Barth at his word, that pneumatological statements are never superfluous or reducible to Christological ones, never dispensable, never separable from them, and always require their elucidation to be understood as true.

When in Doubt, Turn to Athanasius

Just as Barth names Athanasius as his only predecessor in his otherwise innovative doctrine of election, which names Jesus Christ as the electing God, 'the beginning of all God's ways and works', so Barth refers to Athanasius also at a crucial point in his doctrine of the Spirit.[8] 'It was again Athanasius who saw the connections and spoke the decisive word in this regard' (*CD* I/1, p. 467). Barth refers here to Athanasius's defence of what Barth calls 'the deity and autonomy' of the Spirit. If it is the 'autonomy' of the Spirit that Barth has so often been accused of slighting, it is Athanasius who succeeds in doing what Barth intended to do: articulate the autonomy of the Spirit *in* its connection to the Son. In Athanasius, that is, we find a defence of Barth's *intention,* to articulate 'the deity and autonomy' of the Spirit, *simultaneous with* a defence of Barth's *practice,* never to speak of the Spirit apart from the Son. From Athanasius we can learn how to do Barth better than Barth. In these passages, Father, Word and Spirit all do one work by exercising their intra-Trinitarian pattern in the economy: 'For what the Word has by nature, as I said, in the Father, that He wishes to be given to us through the Spirit irrevocably' (Athanasius, 1983, III.25.25; cf. also Athanasius, 1951). Note the passive voice. The Son does not give, but the Son wishes the Father to give through the Spirit. Even God's self-giving involves a dance of courtesy, bidding and gratitude. God's self-giving characteristically incorporates us into that dance or pattern. Indeed, in another passage Athanasius presents his argument as a prayer by the Son to the Father about the Spirit. That is, he does not describe the pattern but displays it – in terms of an intra-Trinitarian conversation he overhears in the Gospel of John:

> 'And when they shall be so perfected', [the Son] says, 'then the world knows that thou hast sent me, for unless I had come and borne this their body, no one of them had been perfected, but one and all had remained corruptible. Work thou then in them, O Father, and as thou hast given to me to bear this body, grant to them thy Spirit, that they too in it may become one, and may be perfected in me.' (Athanasius, 1983, III.25.23)

There are several features to note in that dense passage. First, it correlates the Spirit and the Son in such a way that the role of each is ineliminable. The Son bears a human body so that human bodies may bear the Spirit. This thesis fittingly corresponds to the famous version, according to which 'the Word became human that we might become divine' (Athanasius, 1971, ch. 54) because, of course, it is the body that 'humanifies' the Word and the Spirit that deifies the human through the work (or transfiguration) of the body. Christ enacts the work with the bearing of the body, and the Spirit appropriately completes or perfects it when the body bears the Spirit. Put differently, the Spirit rests on one who has taken on the identity of the Son. The passage exemplifies the rule of Gregory Nazianzen, that the Son is the enactor (*demiourgos*) of the work and the Spirit the perfector or perhaps applier of it (*teleopoios*) (Nazianzen, 1983, Or. 34.8).

Nor is the human bearing of the Spirit an automatic or mechanical consequence of the Son's bearing of a body. (To call the Spirit the 'power' of Jesus Christ is, among other things, to deploy a mechanical metaphor.) Rather, another intra-Trinitarian initiative intervenes. The Son *bids* the Father to *grant* human beings the Spirit, as the Son had bid the Father to grant him a body. The body is a gift to the Son; the Spirit is a gift to the body; but each gift is free, not mandated, following in its characteristic pattern. As John Milbank explains, the gratuity of a gift depends on an *interval* rather than a mechanism (Milbank, 1995); it is more nearly musical than mechanical. Athanasius displays a moment, or interval, of gratitude by the Son for the gift of a human body; an interval of pleasure by the Father at the Son's stewardship of the gift; an interval of prayer by the Son that the Father give the gift of the Spirit even unto others in response, but in free response, to the Son's own gift of his body for them. These intervals are not spatial or temporal, but space and time make room for their created imitation. They are intervals that constitute a music or dance that is God's life. To join God's life is not to get caught up in intellectual complications, but to get caught up into inter-personal interrelations, exchanges, intervals, musical spaces or dances of gift and gratitude.[9] To be theologically musical – which Barth is to the highest degree – is to be able, by the inspiration of the Spirit, to imitate, or harmonize with, or accompany that music. It's just that there are some notes – call them grace notes – that Barth has missed.

What's missing, to sum up, is the Trinitarian *interval* between the Son and the Spirit. If the Spirit is the power of the Son without, or with scarcely any, audible remainder, then the interval has closed up; we have one note. Barth lacks the Son's *bidding* of the Father and the Father's *giving* – freely and not automatically, but characteristically and harmoniously – of the Spirit.

Barth anticipates and leaves room for the Athanasian interval by quoting the relevant passages from John in *CD* I/1, but that's all. The rest lies open for us to fill in. The closest Barth comes to filling it in does not appear until his account of baptism in *CD* IV/4, which we will come to later.

This Athanasian insight throws light on a number of uncompleted themes in Barth. First, the 'autonomy of the Spirit' that Barth intends to display is not, as he would be first to assert, an empty, nineteenth-century volition or subjectivity, an autonomy for anything at all. Rather, the particular autonomy of the Spirit is the autonomy of a *gift*. Nor is it just any gift, but a gift that belongs in a particular, interpersonal pattern of exchange, the gift bidden by the Son and granted by the Father. We know what kinds of gift the Son is likely to pray for, because we know the prayers to the Father that he makes incarnate. That formulation does not mean, however, that the Spirit is once again without an (intra-Trinitarian) action appropriate to it, of its 'own'. For, if the action of the Spirit is bestowed by the Father upon the Son, then it is also the case that the Spirit (in the Trinity, as in the economy) consents or is willing or adds gladness, celebration or glory to the giving of the Father, so that the gift is joyous, or 'not intolerable', as Barth puts it, to God (*CD* III/1, p. 59). Since the Spirit consents or adds gladness and joy to the gift, we might even say, with Robert Jenson (1982), that in so doing the Spirit 'frees' or 'liberates' the Father for the giving. Certainly, we would *not* want to say that the Spirit resists or hinders the good-pleasure of the Father, or that the Father forces or constrains the Spirit, or that the Spirit recoils from the Son, or that the Son drags the Spirit, unwilling, to himself. So, by the Spirit's willingness or encouragement, the Spirit eases or empowers or, indeed, bestows liberty on the Father for giving. To say this of the Trinity is simply to acknowledge that if the Spirit liberates human beings to respond to the Father and witness to the Son, that is not an arbitrary or capricious role for the Spirit to play, but one that the Spirit exercises antecedently in the Trinitarian life. The 'autonomy' of the Spirit is the autonomy – the gratuity – of a gift, a particular gift, which the Father bestows, the Son receives and the Spirit conveys with the witness of gladness or frees, even under conditions of finitude and sin, to be tidings of great joy.

If the autonomy of the Spirit is the gratuity of the gift, which is not empty but liberates the Father and therefore us with good news, and if it needs an interval for its gratuity, so that it comes not automatically but musically, then Barth is right to associate the this-worldly activity of the Spirit with history – indeed, the history of prophecy, Gospel and Church. The interval between the Son and the Spirit in the Trinity is the condition for the possibility of history, of human freedom and doxology rather than human mechanism, in the economy. Earlier, I concluded that, despite his talk of history and witness and God's very eventfulness, Barth tends to close that interval, when he makes it of the 'essence' (and not the freedom or the witness or the gratuitous celebration) of the Spirit to join the Father and the Son,[10] when he turns so consistently from the Spirit to the Son, insisting that the Spirit is the 'power' of the Son and leaving the impression that Spirit-talk is dispensable if Son-talk is sufficiently robust. If so, it may be this closing of the interval – or, to put it more kindly, this simplification of the melody for discrete, post-Schleiermacher purposes – that accounts for the impression, especially strong in Barth's wonderful doctrine of election, that, despite its 'actualism', everything is over and done with, that universal salvation follows irresistibly if not explicitly from the election of Jesus Christ. If this impression – rebuttable but persistent – signifies anything, it is because Barth's Trinitarian theology leaves little or no contingent interval for the Son to bid the Father rather than exercise his 'power', or for the Spirit to consent with gladness rather than arrive in due course. In the economy, that leads to a picture in which it is hard to articulate how that interval makes room for the operation of *human* gladness and witness at the advent of the Son, over long periods of history, stretches of geography and varieties of experience. The interval of the Spirit *makes* the history to which Barth refers and *guarantees* its contingency, unpredictability, novelty and surprise: the Spirit makes all things new, crowning the Father's initiatives with a surplus of gladness in the Trinity as in the economy. The guarantee of the Spirit in the economy, that history will continue to surprise, and geography will continue to vary, and personality will continue to delight, does not have to undermine the infallibility of election, but allows the Spirit time and space and psychology to overcome the resistance that we so richly, if vainly, afford it. But the worst consequence is not a narrowing of the interval for human gladness; Barth wants to keep that open. What's worse is that the narrowing of the interval for human gladness results from a virtual closing of the interval for the *Spirit's* own proper gladness at the Father and the Son.

Before the Eclipse, or the Athanasian Interval Open in Barth

In speaking of an 'eclipse' of the Spirit in Barth, I suggested that the most promising bits of pneumatology in Barth come at the beginning and at the end, in *CD* I/1 and *CD* IV/4, with a few references in between that constitute little more than glimmering reminders of those interventions. But those promising sections are promising precisely because they preserve and elaborate the Athanasian interval. In order to go on from Barth, we need to develop those insights in ways that Barth leaves open but ceases to pursue.

Consider some programmatic statements from *CD* I/1 and their peculiar form. In these passages, Barth does not so much read the this-worldly or economic activity of the Spirit back into the Trinity. Rather, he reasons that, because God is faithful and reliable, the Spirit's activity here below must arise from the Spirit as he truly is, so that the Spirit's role in the Trinitarian life provides the condition for the very possibility of the Spirit's earthly role. It sounds oddly Kantian, but is in fact patristic. It is the patristic argument for the deity of the Spirit: the Spirit must be God, because otherwise it could not deify.[11] Barth makes this move in the context of the Spirit's work in revelation. But the point here is that we can learn to apply the move also elsewhere, to other aspects of the Spirit's work:

> The Holy Spirit does not first become the Holy Spirit, the Spirit of God, in the event of revelation. The event of revelation has clarity and reality on its subjective side because the Holy Spirit, the subjective element in the event, is of the essence of God himself. What he is in revelation he is antecedently in himself. And what he is antecedently in himself he is in revelation. (*CD* I/1, p. 466)

Again:

> The Spirit is holy in us because he is so antecedently in himself. (Ibid., p. 467)

> God the Holy Spirit is 'antecedently in himself' the act of communion, the act of impartation, love, gift. For this reason and in this way and on this basis he is so in

his revelation. Not *vice versa!* We know him thus in his revelation. But he is not this because he is it in his revelation; because he is it antecedently in himself, he is it also in his revelation. (Ibid., pp. 470–71).

Later on, Barth comes to state the general rule (and to the delight of Lindbeck disciples, he actually calls it a rule):

> But we have consistently followed the rule, which we regard as basic, that statements about the divine modes of being antecedently in themselves cannot be different in content from those that are to be made about their reality in revelation .... The reality of God in his revelation cannot be bracketed by an 'only,' as though somewhere behind his revelation there stood another reality of God. (Ibid., p. 479)[12]

> The recognition of this communion [in God] is no other than recognition of the basis and confirmation of the communion between God and the human being as a divine, eternal truth, created in revelation by the Holy Spirit .... Conversely, in this fellowship in revelation which is created between God and the human being by the Holy Spirit there may be discerned the fellowship in God himself, the eternal love of God. (Ibid., p. 480)[13]

The kind of reasoning on display here can also improve what Barth says about the *Filioque*. By making community of the *essence* of the Spirit, Barth protects the *Filioque* at the expense of the Spirit's freedom and work. If the Spirit *must*, by necessity of origin, be the bond between Father and Son, then the Spirit is no longer free by necessity of character or divine goodness to guarantee the bond between Father and Son as a *gift*. And if the Spirit is not the giver of gifts and the exerciser of freedom 'antecedently in himself', then he cannot be so also for us. But Barth wants to affirm, with Augustine, that the Spirit is gift *par excellence,* and with Aquinas that 'Gift' is the Spirit's most proper name. And Barth wants to affirm, programmatically in the *Leitsatz* for this section, that the Spirit is appropriately 'God who sets us free' (ibid., pp. 448, 456). It is to protect the Spirit's role 'antecedently in himself' as the giver of gifts, the guarantor of communion, and the one who sets free, that we must count the Spirit as a Trinitarian person equal to the Father and the Son, and not because of some nineteenth-century notion of Trinitarian subjects as centres of consciousness or independent agents.

These theses share a particular logical form, one that Barth displays superlatively well, and that we might well learn from him. In each case, the phrase 'in that' or 'for that reason,' relates two complete clauses. The clause introduced with 'in that,' or the sentence referred to with 'for that reason' both supply the condition for the possibility of something. Here we see how Barth turns not just Schleiermacher, but also Kant, on their heads. Barth is always concerned with the conditions for the possibilities of things, but such conditions always turn out to be Trinitarian. What puts Barth's theology on 'the secure path of a science' is not an abstract feeling of absolute dependence, as in Schleiermacher, but something Barth describes with the compliment 'concrete' – some *Trinitarian* presupposition. In the twentieth century there was much talk of collapsing the immanent Trinity into the economic one. Barth disallows this. The distinction is necessary to preserve the gratuity and character of God's action in the world. The pattern is always the same and very instructive: the condition for some human possibility is always a divine possibility. Furthermore, it is a possibility arising out of God's concrete relations as Father, Son and Spirit. In almost all cases, we can be more particular than that. The condition for the possibility of some human reality arises out of concrete relations between the Father and the Son. This happens often enough to prove frustrating for critics. I want to suggest a pattern of reasoning that Barth pursues so rarely that we may wonder if he avoids it; and yet it is parallel, and he opens the way for it. What happens when we systematically pose the question, 'What human possibilities are illuminated by God's concrete relations between the Father or the Son *and the Holy Spirit*?' If we see that the triune God makes us witnesses to his glory in the economy, then that is so because the Spirit witnesses to the love between the Father and the Son 'antecedently' in the triune life.

The Eclipse, the Closing of the Athanasian Interval, or What We Do Not See

The Bible tends to appropriate the offices of witnessing, and glorifying, to the Spirit. Theologically, one would expect Barth to say, 'In that the Holy Spirit witnesses to the love between the Father and the Son already in God's own life, it becomes manifest and worthy of belief that God did not wish to enjoy Himself only but also to consummate His creatures'. (I mimic the dense formulation of *Dogmatics in Outline:* 'In that God became human, it has also become manifest and worthy of belief that He did not wish to exist for Himself only and therefore to be alone' (Barth, 1949, p. 50, *Leitsatz*). Or, more simply, consider a thesis like this: 'In that the Holy Spirit glorifies the love between the Father and the Son, we, too, may glorify God and enjoy Him forever.' But we do not get these pneumatological emphases. The closest we get is the *Leitsatz* that goes, very promisingly, like this: 'When it is believed and acknowledged in the Holy Spirit, the revelation of God creates human beings who do not exist without seeking God in Jesus Christ, and who cannot cease to testify that He has found them' (*Leitsatz* to §18, *CD* I/2, p. 362). But what follows has to do with Scripture and Christ, the reference to the Spirit being more of a *Schmuckzitat*. Similar disappointments occur when we get sections entitled 'Jesus Christ, the True Witness' or 'The Glory of the Mediator'. Why not 'The Holy Spirit, the True Witness'? or 'The Glory of the Holy Spirit'? Offices that the Bible and tradition appropriate to the Spirit, are treated Christologically by Barth.

Note that this is not necessarily wrong. Because the actions of the triune God *ad extra* are indivisible, any action of God with a creaturely object is the work of all three persons, so that it is not wrong to say that the Son witnesses or glorifies, just as it is not wrong to say that the Son creates or the Father redeems. Reappropriation of divine works *ad extra* to Trinitarian persons less often associated with them can be a sign of robust Trinitarian thinking. Particularly in his attempt to overcome Schleiermacher, Barth had a strong impulse to refer human possibilities to an objective basis in the second person. He is more of a Basil ('some are orthodox in mind only, while others venture to be so with the lips also' – Nazianzen, 1983, Or. 32.5) than a Gregory Nazianzen, who writes: 'We will get us up into a high mountain, and will shout, if we be not heard, below; we will exalt the Spirit; we will not be afraid; or if we are afraid, it shall be of keeping silence, not of proclaiming' (Nazianzen, 1983, Or. 32.3).

It is true that that Holy Spirit is *responsible* for the human reception of revelation. But the Holy Spirit is not therefore *reducible* to the subjective. Precisely if the Holy Spirit is the (relatively) independent *witness* to the revelation by the Father of the Son, then the Spirit has its own objectivity. Yet we can recognize this objectivity as such only if we see the Spirit as an actor united to the other persons, not their act. The Spirit has the objectivity of a witness, not the subjectivity of a response. A witness responds, of course. But a witness responds as a real third party, not automatically or mechanically or predictably, but as one who sovereignly gives a gift and freely performs a service to the Truth. The same might be said of a celebrant or a guarantor or a transfigurer: one who adds something new and unexpected to bring the revelation to perfection as a gift to the others. If there is in the Trinity no joyful waiting in trust and thanksgiving upon the Spirit to work, but a grinding mechanism, then in humanity too the response is not free and no eucharist.

After the Eclipse, or the Athanasian Interval Reopened

Barth *licenses* the procedure of Trinitarian deduction more broadly, not only with respect to the Son, but also with respect to the Spirit, even if he pursues there it only with reticence and hardly with gladness. In his 'Concluding Unscientific Postscript on Schleiermacher', written right at the end, in 1968, we read:

> As to a clarification of my relationship to Schleiermacher, what I have occasionally contemplated for here and now – and thus not only with respect to a theological event in the kingdom of glory (which will then form the triumphal ending to my history with Schleiermacher), but, so to speak, with respect also to a millennium preceding that kingdom – and what I have already intimated here and there to good friends, would be the possibility of a theology of the third article, in other words, a theology predominantly and decisively of the Holy Spirit. Everything which needs to be said, considered, and believed about God the Father and God the Son in an understanding of the first and second articles might be shown and illuminated in its foundations through God the Holy Spirit ... isn't he the God who in his own freedom, power, and love makes himself present and applies himself? (Barth, 1982, pp. 277–78)[14]

Consider these theses, which sound like Barth, and might have been written by Barth, but were not, or not quite:

> The Holy Spirit rests on the elect of the Father. For that reason the Spirit witnesses and celebrates this election not only in God but also in the baptism of Jesus and finally in us, electing further witnesses to the good pleasure of the Father in the Son.

> In that God the Spirit burns at Pentecost, it has also become manifest and worthy of belief that God does not wish to enjoy and glorify himself only and therefore to be without a created participant and witness of it.

The traditional name for this aspect of the Holy Spirit's work is illumination or manifestation (see Gregory Nazianzen on baptism). The difficulty with calling it 'revealedness', as Barth famously does in *CD* I/2, § 16, is that it becomes unclear just how what the Spirit does in the Trinity is the condition for the possibility of its work in the economy. Do we say that the Spirit reveals the Son to the Father? That sounds odd. That the Spirit illuminates or manifests the Son in the Trinity, and therefore also in the economy, sounds less odd. I think the key is to look at the glimpses of the intra-Trinitarian life that we see in the New Testament. The Spirit hovers over the Son in Mary's womb at the annunciation; the star illuminates his birth at the nativity; the dove descends upon him at the baptism; the Spirit drives him into the wilderness; the cloud overshadows him at the transfiguration; the paraclete is invoked at the Last Supper before Jesus declares the bread to be his body; the tongues of fire appear over the heads of the disciples in the upper room. In all these cases we see a pattern: the Spirit comes to rest upon the Son. The baptism and the transfiguration give us clues about how the intra-Trinitarian basis of the New Testament observances might be articulated. The Spirit blesses the Son; the Spirit transfigures the Son; the Spirit witnesses to the Son. In the Trinity the Spirit characteristically presents the Father and the Son with the gift of response – witness, celebration, transfiguration – with an overplus or surplus or Sabbath beyond a dyadic love. It is not necessary, but graciously appropriate, that what the Spirit does in the Trinity should include us in the economy – especially if the Spirit's role is to add something to love, to witness, glorify and multiply it. In the pattern from Romans 8:11, it is gratuitously appropriate that the Spirit should do that by including us in the witness to, and glorification of, the love of the Father and the Son. In the economy the Spirit's blessing of the Son takes the form of manifesting and illuminating him also among us.

We find confirmation that Barth practises, even if he does not fully elaborate this pattern. Consider these theses, which do appear in Barth: 'The role of the Holy Spirit in God is the condition for the possibility of human knowledge of God in redemption' (*CD* I/1, pp. 466–89); 'The role of the Holy Spirit in God is the condition of the possibility of human glorification of God in creation' (*CD* III/1, pp. 56–60); creation is 'for his own supreme glory and therefore in the Holy Spirit' (*CD* III/1, p. 59). Here we find confirmed the claim that it is appropriate to the Spirit to glorify God first of all *in se* and then in us; the Spirit 'does not hinder their fellowship but glorifies it'. But, here, Barth also makes one of those surprising turns that makes him worth reading on the Spirit even when one suspects his elaboration of being a little crabbed.

For 'the execution of this activity' – the creation of the world by the Son and in the Spirit – 'is history' (ibid.).

The reference to history suggests a great deal that Barth lets go without saying. But we can imagine something like this. The Spirit in Genesis hovers over the face of the waters; it moves in creation, and it moves over a creation perceived as fluid. Its movement and the movement of creation in response to its blowing is historical. The prophets proclaim in the Spirit the Lord's response to the concrete history of Israel. The Spirit in Luke inaugurates the birth of Jesus Christ in history. The Spirit drives Jesus into the wilderness for a history of temptation. At Pentecost the Spirit initiates the history of the Church – and so on. It is appropriate to the Spirit to arrange concrete, particular circumstances and states of affairs, the messy details of history, to suit the divine purpose. It is appropriate to the Spirit to apply (*applicator*) the work of the Son to concrete, particular people. If it is appropriate to the Spirit to empower (*liberator*) the human response to the Word, then it is appropriate to the Spirit to do so historically (*CD* I/1, p. 451, quoting *Synopsis purioris theologiae*). If Barth has confessed a tendency to '*immer etwas hegeln*' – always to somewhat wax Hegelian – then here we see both the always and the somewhat (Welker, 1983). It seems natural to Barth to associate *Zeit* with *Geist* – but then he doesn't do much with it. 'That its existence should not be intolerable to God but destined to serve His greater glory – the creation of this essential condition of its existence is the peculiar work of the Holy Spirit in creation' (*CD* III/1, p. 59).

Aha! That's what we want! It is the appropriate role of the Spirit to add something even to the good-pleasure of the Father and the work of the Son. It is that Spirit should *glorify* that good-pleasure and that work: that it should witness, celebrate, and secure them, and that it should do so not only in the triune life, but also among us. *Were* it not so, if it should go *un*witnessed, *un*celebrated, *un*secured, Barth implies, there would be something amiss with the love in God, something stale or static. Not that God for that reason needed creation – by no means! Creation remains gratuitous because the Spirit can celebrate and innovate already in the Trinitarian life. The Spirit's creation of additional witnesses to God's life is therefore neither necessary nor arbitrary, but characteristic, not least because the Spirit's work creates them, again, not in some arbitrary way but in the image of the Son and for the sharing in their life. In short, the Spirit creates witnesses in order to bear testimony to the Son also in us. Thus it is fitting how the Spirit blows the waters – in creation, at the Red Sea, in Mary's womb, on the Sea of Galilee – to make a theatre for God's glory, or for the glory of the Son. Thus it is fitting how the Spirit moves hearts – among the judges, prophets, and kings, in the demons and the disciples, at Pentecost and in the present – to raise up witnesses to God's glory, or for the glory of his Son Israel. The Spirit makes us witnesses, because the Spirit makes us apt for the celebration that makes up the triune life.[15] The Spirit's creation of history is therefore no mere Hegelian abstraction, but Christologically concrete. We may sum up: the Spirit rests upon the Son in the economy, because the Spirit rests upon the Son antecedently in the Trinity.

In *CD* IV/4, 'Baptism with the Holy Spirit' and 'Baptism with Water', the idea that the Holy Spirit 'applies' the work of Christ to individual human beings returns – an idea with New Testament roots, patristic development and Protestant Orthodox repitition. In 1 Corinthians 12:11, the Spirit 'apportions' (διαιροῦν) 'to each one his or her due' (ἰδίᾳ ἑκάστῳ). This recalls the rule articulated by Donald Winslow in his study of Gregory Nazianzen, that 'what Christ has accomplished universally, the Spirit perfects particularly' (Winslow, 1979, p. 129). Note that (unlike some trans-lations) there is no Enlightenment 'individualism' here, but particularity – a particularity of the sort Barth favours. In the Corinthians passage, this apportionment or particularization takes place in the explicit context of baptism. Appropriately, it is in his belated treatment of the sacraments, at the end of his career, that Barth's doctrine of the Spirit becomes lively again, almost as lively as in his treatment of revelation, of the Spirit's witness to the revelation in Christ. If one reads *CD* I/1 and *CD* IV/4 together, one can almost see the witness of the Spirit to the revelation of the Son precisely in the baptism of the Son in the Jordan; indeed, that is how the Syriac tradition explains the puzzle of why Christ had to be baptized at all:

> How fearful and full of awe is this moment when the supernal beings stand in silence upon this baptismal water – thousands upon thousands of angels, ten thousands of Seraphim hover over this new mother, holy baptism, the spiritual mother who gives birth to spiritual sons who enter into the bridal chamber of life that is full of joys … . They stand by the river Jordan to receive the Son of God who has come to perfect baptism. The Holy Spirit descends upon him from the uppermost heights, not to sanctify him, but to bear witness to him. (Jacob of Serugh, II, pp. 332–34)[16]

The other thing to note about 1 Corinthians 12:11 is the verb. It not only suggests the apportionment of the witness to Christ's work at baptism, it also bears the translation 'the Spirit distributes', suggesting the distribution of the elements of the Eucharist. So at baptism and at the Eucharist we see a characteristic, twofold activity of the Spirit: the Spirit *distributes* gifts and *gathers* the community.[17] What the Spirit distributes particularly, it also builds up corporately (and that's why no modern individualism comes in question). 'To put it again in a single sentence: In the work of the Holy Spirit the history manifested to all human beings in the resurrection of Jesus Christ is manifest and present to a specific human being as his own salvation history' (*CD* IV/4, p. 27). Indeed, if in this history Jesus is himself the baptizer (as opposed to John) with the Spirit (*CD* IV/4, p. 76), then we may rewrite our latest theses about the Spirit intra-Tinitarianly: as Jesus distributes the Spirit to particular parts of the body, so the Spirit returns the gift by building up his body. But his body is now built up in a different way. By the gift of the Spirit, the historical body slain and resurrected for the community becomes historically – over time and in particular human beings – the corporate body in history. That the body of Christ *continues* to have a giftfulness and corporate life is the Spirit's gift to the Son. The gift to the Son – and to the Father – is the inclusion of us particular human beings in the pattern of the Trinitarian life. Through the Spirit in baptism we begin, and through the Spirit at the Eucharist we anticipate, a new participation of human beings in the Trinitarian life – a participation which the humanity of Christ does not exhaust but which opens it up, gives it more to do, greater significance, not mechanically but historically, by taking up a myriad human lives and acts. This is indeed the Athanasian interval filled out, the Spirit adding its personal more, its surplus, something that exceeds the work of Christ and, in its exceeding, something that frees and makes new.

Perhaps the eclipse *just is* an interval, a temporary disappearance of the Spirit that trusts in the Son, and may, on account of that trust, insist upon its freedom. If so, it is precisely the frame of *CD* I/1 and *CD* IV/4, with little puffs of reminder, that marks the interval as one not of abandonment but of the waiting upon another that provides time and space for gift.

Notes

1 Barth's *Come Holy Spirit* is a book of early sermons (1920–24), of which only one turns out to treat the Holy Spirit, and then as the making-present of Jesus Christ (Barth, 1978, pp. 171–82).

2 §12, 'God the Holy Spirit', I/1 (1975), pp. 448–90; Chapter II, Part III, 'The Outpouring of the Holy Spirit', §§16–18, I/1, pp. 203–456; §62, 'The Holy Spirit and the Gathering of the Christian Community', IV/1, pp. 643–739; §63, 'The Holy Spirit and Christian Faith', IV/1, pp. 740–79; §67, 'The Holy Spirit and the Upbuilding of the Christian Community', IV/2, pp. 614–726; §68, 'The Holy Spirit and Christian Love', IV/2, pp. 727–840; §72, 'The Holy Spirit and the Sending of the Christian Community', IV/3.2, pp. 681–901; §73, 'The Holy Spirit and Christian Hope', IV/3.2, pp. 903–42. The Holy Spirit is also announced in the *Leitsätze* or thesis statements of §9, 'The Triunity of God', I/1, pp. 348–83; §15, 'The Mystery of Revelation', I/2, pp. 122–201; §16, 'The Freedom of Man for God', I/2, pp. 203–79; §17, 'The Revelation of God as the Abolition of Religion', I/2, pp. 280–361; §18, 'The Life of the Children of God', I/2, pp. 362–456; §19, 'The Word of God for the Church', I/2, pp. 457–537; §25, 'The Fulfilment of the Knowledge of God', II/1, pp. 3–62; §26, 'The Knowability of God', II/1, pp. 63–178; §28, 'The Being of God as the One who Loves in Freedom', II/1, pp. 257–322; §64, 'The Exaltation of the Son of Man', IV/2, pp. 3–377; and §[74], 'The Foundation of the Christian Life', IV/4, pp. 2–218.

3 For example, Jenson (1993; here, p. 303, in reference to IV/3); and Williams (2000, pp. 107–27, esp. pp. 107, 117–18, 120–21). I have elsewhere prosecuted that sort of critique myself (Rogers, 1998). But here I want more to explain than establish the phenomenon.

4 It might be all right if each of the persons was the act of the others, but we don't get that.

5 Rosato argues differently. Counting the sections from III onwards that announce the Spirit, as actually about the Spirit, and noting programmatic statements in favor of pneumatology from 1947 onwards, Rosato charts a pneumatological turn from around 1947. It is a reading *in optimam partem*. What remains to be explained is why those treatments are remarkably unpneumatological for another 20 years.

6 See Lossky (1957, pp. 161–62 and 172–73) referring to Nazianzen (1983, Or. 32.26–27). This is pointed out by Williams (2000, p. 123). Williams also points out that Aquinas, for example, finds 'Spirit' a weak and non-specific word at *ST* I.36.1 and II-II.14.1 (Williams, 2000, p. 126).

7 As Jenson has done in his doctrine of the Holy Spirit as the electing God (Jenson, 1984, pp. 134–39) and I have suggested (Rogers, 1998).

8 For more on Barth and Athanasius, see Jennings (1993). The turn to Athanasius seems more important when we consider Rowan Williams's claim that Barth's importance in twentieth-century theology is a result of Barth playing Athanasius to the Deutsche Christen's Arius (see his 'Postscript: Theological' in Williams, 1987). Note, too, that in accusing Calvin of substituting, in his doctrine of election, a

metaphysical principle for Jesus Christ as 'the beginning of all God's ways and works', Barth recalls Calvin to the debate between Athanasius and Arius over the interpretation of that Psalm, and places him – although Barth is uncharacteristically too polite to say so – on the Arian side.

9   For the language of being 'caught up' in the Trinitarian life, see MacKinnon (1940), and his students – for example, Williams (1996, p. 59).

10 In defence of the *Filioque* (*CD* I/1, pp. 479–80).

11 For example: 'If he is in the same rank with myself, how can he make me God, or join me with Godhead?' (Nazianzen, 1983, end of Or. 32.4). Or 'If he is not to be worshipped [that is, as God], how can he deify me by baptism?' (Or. 32.28).

12 Barth rises to the explicit statement of a rule in a mildly polemical context. He claims that this rule tells for the *Filioque* and against the Eastern view. But that's silly. Barth and Eastern Orthodoxy disagree on this matter not because they follow different rules about the relation of the immanent and economic Trinity, but because they read the Bible and the history of the Church differently. The East also believes that revelation is reliable because there is no god behind God. The theologian guilty of that is more likely to be one much closer to home – namely, Calvin.

13 Again, Barth presents this as a defence of the *Filioque*. But in the East, too, one can say that the Holy Spirit guarantees the communion between the Father and the Son antecedently in God, and therefore among us, without that being necessitated by the *Filioque*. Rather, the guarantee of communion is the Spirit's free – and utterly reliable – gift to the Father and the Son, and therefore his even more free and still reliable gift also to us.

14 Rosato helpfully collects several earlier statements of this type (Rosato, 1981, pp. 3–5). Still, I think we ought to take Barth at his word that such statements of his have been 'occasional' and not 'predominant', 'intimations' and not 'decisive'.

15 '*Nos aptare Deo*' 'the Spirit makes us apt for God'. Barth quotes from Irenaeus (*CD* I/1, p. 451, citing Irenaeus, *Contra Haereses*, III.17.2).

16 Cf. SA I in Assemani 291–92, in Brock, 1979, p.134.

17 Lossky puts this a little differently. According to him, Christ 'lends His hypostasis to the nature,' while the Holy Spirit 'gives His divinity to the persons. Thus, the work of Christ unifies; the work of the Holy Spirit diversifies.' Yet, in case that seems too neat, he immediately qualifies it: 'Christ creates the unity of His mystical body through the Holy Spirit; the Holy Spirit communicates Himself to human persons through Christ' (Lossky, 1957, p. 167).

References

Athanasius (1951), *The Letters of Saint Athanasius Concerning the Holy Spirit,* trans. C.R.B. Shapland of *Ad Serapion*, New York: Philosophical Library.

Athanasius (1971), 'On the Incarnation of the Word', in R.W. Thomson (ed.), *Contra gentes and De incarnatione*, Oxford: Clarendon Press.

Athanasius (1983), 'Four discourses against the Arians', trans. A. Robertson, in P. Schaff and H. Wace (eds), *Athanasius: Select Works and Letters*, Nicene and Post-Nicene Fathers, 2nd series, vol. IV, Grand Rapids, MI: Eerdmans, pp. 306–447.

Barth, K (1949), *Dogmatics in Outline,* trans. G.T. Thompson, London: SCM.

Barth, K (1978), *Come Holy Spirit*, Grand Rapids, MI: Eerdmans.

Barth, K (1982), 'Concluding Unscientific Postscript on Schleiermacher', trans. G. Hunsinger, in K. Barth, *The Theology of Schleiermacher,* ed. D. Ritschl, Grand Rapids, MI: Eerdmans.

Brock, S.P. (1979), *The Holy Spirit in the Syrian Baptismal Tradition,* The Syrian Churches Series, vol. 9, Poona, India: Anita.

Ephrem the Syrian (1983), 'Hymn on Virginity', no. 7, in *The Harp of the Spirit: Eighteen Poems of St. Ephrem*, Studies Supplementary to *Sobornost*, trans. S.P. Brock, London: Society of St Alban and St Sergius.

Jacob of Serugh (1903), *Homiliae S. Isaaci Syri Antiocheni*, ed. P. Bedjan, Paris.

Jennings, W. (1993), 'Reclaiming the Creature: Anthropological Vision in the Thought of Athanasius of Alexandria and Karl Barth', PhD dissertation, Duke University.

Jenson, R. (1982), *The Triune Identity*, Philadelphia: Fortress Press.

Jenson, R. (1984), 'The Holy Spirit', in C.E. Braaten and R.W Jenson (eds), *Christian Dogmatics Volume II*, Philadelphia: Fortress Press, pp. 101–78.

Jenson, R. (1993), 'You Wonder Where the Spirit Went,' *Pro Ecclesia*, **2**, pp. 296–304.

Lossky, V. (1957), *Mystical Theology of the Eastern Church*, Cambridge, MA: Harvard University Press.

MacKinnon, D. (1940), *God the Living and the True*, Signposts 2, Westminster: Dacre Press.

Milbank, J. (1995), 'Can a Gift be Given? Prolegomenon to a Future Trinitarian Metaphysic', *Modern Theology*, **11**, pp. 119–41.

Nazianzen, Gregory (1983), 'Orations', trans. C.G. Browne and J.E. Swallow, in P. Schaff and H. Wace (eds), *Cyril of Jerusalem/Gregory Nazianzen*, Nicene and Post-Nicene Fathers, 2nd series, vol. 7, Grand Rapids, MI: Eerdmans, pp. 203–422.

Rogers, E.F. Jr (1998), 'Supplementing Barth on Jews and Gender: Identifying God by Anagogy and the Spirit', *Modern Theology*, **14**, pp. 43–81.

Rosato, P.J. (1981), *The Spirit as Lord: The Pneumatology of Karl Barth*, Edinburgh: T. & T. Clark.

Thompson, J. (1991), *The Holy Spirit in the Theology of Karl Barth*, Allison Park, PA: Pickwick.

Welker, M. (1983), 'Barth und Hegel', *Evangelische Theologie*, **43**, pp. 307–28.

Williams, R. (1987), *Arius*, London: Darton, Longman and Todd.

Williams, R. (1996), 'The Body's Grace', in C. Hefling (ed.), *Our Selves, Our Souls and Bodies: Sexuality and the Household of God*, Boston: Beacon Publications, pp. 58–68.

Williams, R. (2000), 'Word and Spirit', in *On Christian Theology*, Oxford: Blackwell, pp. 107–27.

Winslow, D.F. (1979), *The Dynamics of Salvation: A Study in Gregory of Nazianzus*, Cambridge, MA: The Philadelphia Patristic Foundation.

CHAPTER 10

Et Resurrexit Tertia Die: Jenson and Barth on Christ's Resurrection

Katherine Sonderegger

Few theologians can muster as much theological passion for Christ's resurrection as does Karl Barth, but Robert Jenson runs a close second. Christ's resurrection anchors Barth's massive second part-volume of the Doctrine of Reconciliation – indeed this event, strictly speaking, *is* the doctrine of sanctification – but the resurrection cannot in fact be reserved to any single volume of the *Church Dogmatics*. 'That Christ lives' is a governing maxim of the entire *Dogmatics*, a rule of faith that undergirds and orders the whole, much as 'Christ's act becomes ours' or 'the supernatural becomes natural' governs Schleiermacher's *Christian Faith*. We could not begin to grasp Barth's complex treatment of historical criticism of the Bible, or his doctrine of revelation, or his massive reconsideration of the creature's election in Christ, or of divine world governance without acknowledging the maxim of Christ's resurrection, structuring the whole. Indeed, 'maxim' is hardly strong enough. Barth writes that 'we are not concerned here with the precedence, victory or triumph of a principle, even though the principle be that of grace; we are concerned with the living person of Jesus Christ' (*CD* IV/3, p. 173). He acknowledges a living Lord who summons, instructs, commands and saves, not simply in theology but *to* it, and to the theologian. The *Church Dogmatics*, in its length and breadth, serves but one purpose: to acknowledge, with every strength, theology's present, commanding, resurrected Lord.

So, too, we find in Robert Jenson's two-volume *Systematic Theology* a pronounced concentration on the resurrection of Christ from the dead. A rival to Barth in concentration, Jenson outstrips Barth in his striking accent on the apocalyptic and eschatological in Christ's resurrection. Jenson's *Systematics* makes the eschatological the hallmark of his system: the doctrine of last things may begin with Christ's resurrection but extends into the doctrine of Church and sacrament, the nature of creaturely existence and, most strikingly, into the doctrine of Trinity itself. Indeed, Jenson makes the resurrection his formal principle in theology: 'God is the One who raised Jesus from the dead' or alternatively, 'Jesus, who ... is raised from the dead'. Like Barth – but unlike him, too – Jenson anchors his analysis of higher criticism in the event of resurrection, as he does the treatment of the scriptural canon, the nature of divine promises and, most sharply, the nature of deity itself. For Jenson, the governing theme of all religion is the relation of time and eternity; and it is the particular gift and power of the Gospel that it joins time and eternity, through Christ's passion and resurrection, into the passion, liveliness and Spiritual freedom of God. Such joining is the deification of the creature and the joyous theme of theology.

So far – to borrow Jenson's idiom – so very good. But not everything follows the same course in these two dogmaticians. Karl Barth and Robert Jenson hold material positions often similar to each other, and in the Object of their theologies – the Triune God – hold identical. But the thought-form of their dogmatic work and the purpose of their theologies – the 'dogmatic principal and task' in Barth's terms – differ significantly and shape, in turn, the content of their doctrines. The difference emerges, in striking fashion, in their doctrines of the resurrection and ascension. That alone would justify attention to these theologians' formal principles and self-definitions. To be sure, theological method or 'prolegomena', as Jenson has it, does not offer the best road into theological work and, when empty of content, is surely the driest. But there is no escaping the technical demands of academic theology, and the conceptual ordering and expression of doctrine – even unstated – shape theological content, often against the theologian's intent.

In every systematic work, decisions are forced upon the theologian: decisions about the sources and content of doctrine, certainly, but, more urgently, decisions about the purpose, means and norm of theology itself. Such decisions, lying so deep in the theological act itself, take the helm of doctrine and set it early upon its course. What appears to lie ahead – the distant objects of theology – obeys the old travellers' law: how we set out determines what we see ahead. Such a law threatens theologies that make the future or the eschatological event central to their Christologies, for it is the axiom of these theologies that the future, not the past, determines the present. This puzzle, again, would justify an attention to theological principle and task. When we consider the resurrection of Christ from the dead in Barth's and Jenson's work, then, we must ask: How have the differing 'formal principles and tasks' of these theologies shaped the 'material principle' and content? Can these theologies say what their authors intend about the risen Christ, and what the Church must hear? How does theological method secure, shape and express dogmatic content?

Method and Obedience

We begin with Karl Barth. And despite a remarkable flowering in technical analysis of Barth's development and prolegomena, the dissertation of the young Yale theologian, Hans Frei, remains unrivalled in the field; so we begin there, too.[1] After his disenchantment with academic Liberalism, Frei writes, Barth intended to express a new conviction of the dangerous and sovereign freedom of God, a freedom over, but also a freedom towards, sinners and their piety (Frei, 1956, ch. I §B, esp. pp. 125–31). But it was no small task to find a thought-form and conceptual system adequate to his new intention. Frei discerns in the young pastor a desire to speak with confidence of God's victory over sin and death and notes that Barth turned to biblical realism for the content. As the realists Barth drew upon – Hermann Kutter and Christoph Blumhardt

– were social democrats, Barth's radical politics could enter, at last, into his theology, but at a price. Barth, Frei argues, had either to set aside his technical thought-forms, learned from Schleiermacher and Kant, and plunge boldly into raw proclamation, or attempt to find new technical concepts to express his new-found passion for the freedom of a gracious God (ibid., pp. 88, 105–11, ch. II §L, ch. III, §C). Barth did not long rest content with bare proclamation. But where, then, would he find such concepts?

Again and again, Barth returns to the thought-forms of his academic training: to various forms of Kantianism; to radical scepticism; to Idealists of inner emigration, such as Kierkegaard. As late as 1929, Barth lays out the technical landscape of theology within or beside the contours of modern European philosophy: realism and idealism, 'Fate and Idea' (Barth, 1994).[2] Such division between theology and philosophy echoes – indeed, may depend on – Schleiermacher's own geography of dogmatics and dialectics. That 'theology has its own theme', a favourite byword of Barth and Barthians, could be just as well ascribed to Schleiermacher – a fact more readily noticed by Barth than by his descendants. Barth was haunted, Frei argues, by the fear that, even after the agonized battle of the 1920s against Schleiermacher, against his thought-form and method, Schleiermacher alone would remain standing at the battle's end, his opponents silenced or worse, paying unwitting tribute to his victory. Barth had reason to worry.

His opposition to liberal thought-form was cast, from the second edition of the *Romans* forward, in the concepts of his enemies: the idiom of German Idealism. And, as Barth had occasion to learn, it is the particular genius of that method that contradictions to it affirm it. Barth's intention was always – and this is Frei's central thesis – to point to a stark and overmastering divine grace, but his concepts and formal principles kept hemming in or reversing the proclamation of the gracious freedom of theology's Lord (ibid., ch. I §B, esp. pp. 94–98). That was the constraint imposed upon theology by the liberal or 'relational'[3] method – or so Barth saw it. But it was *Barth's* particular genius, Frei concludes, to overcome – not oppose – the liberal method and in that way to combine at last his biblical realism, his cultural criticism and his technical array of concepts. Barth's break with liberalism did not conclude in his discovery of theological realism; that, Barth believed, he inherited from his earliest liberal days from Schleiermacher.[4] Rather, his break can be discerned by his attempt to order thought-form by content and intention. By 1930 Barth believed that he had found, in the act of 'obedience', a means of mastering thought-form by its divine object and content. Barth's desire to speak of the living and astonishing Lord now found concept and method in the 'analogy of faith', a faith that was sheer gift, not presupposition or coordinate of the divine giver. So Frei – but not just Frei. For Barth himself will lay out his own methodological preoccupations that echo, confirm and present under new idiom, Frei's main claims.

Barth himself speaks of this final emergence from the liberal method as the discovery of the proper 'formal and material principles' of dogmatics, enunciated first in his *Christian Dogmatics* of 1927 (Barth, 1982), rewritten in the early 1930s as

Volume One of the *Church Dogmatics*. Critical to the entire revolution in Barth's thought, signalled in these volumes, is the decision to move the question of theological method from the formal to the *material* side of the enterprise. Indeed, we would no longer need to debate the role, emergence and gravity of analogy in Barth's early work, were we to focus more clearly on the decision to move dogmatic method to its home in the material task of theology. For this reason, theological method takes pride of place in academic theology in the modern era. In it, the thought-forms, concepts and rational ordering of the discipline were made explicit, coordinated with one another and justified. Method made theology academic – and Barth was fully in accord with its standards. It is not the thought-form of the method – dialectic or analogy – or even less, the content this method presents, but rather the *location* of this method in the architectonic of the discipline that reveals the allegiance of the theologian. By subsuming method under the material commitments of theology, Barth discloses his movement away from Schleiermacher's method, *Glaubenslehre*, as well as his own *Christliche Dogmatik*, as well as his movement towards the position of his maturity in the *Church Dogmatics*.

It is tempting, however, to misunderstand Barth's movement away from his liberal past and also tempting to imagine that Barth considered nineteenth-century academic theologians as mere water carriers for the strictures and systems of European philosophers – for Descartes, Hegel and, above all, Kant. But that is to caricature Barth's interpretation of his own past and to overlook the preservation of philosophic thought-forms in his theology. The common conviction of modern theology in the nineteenth century was not that philosophy set the terms for theological debate. Nothing so crude as that. From the seventeenth-century scholastics onwards, philosophical method – and that meant, by and large, epistemology – defined the task of scientific, warranted knowledge of self and world; Schleiermacher only made that definition explicit. The *object* of theology was never knowingly set by philosophy, nor the field in which theology worked, nor the orthodoxy by which dogmatic statements were judged. Each object its own method: that was the theme of Schleiermacher's work on academic disciplines and the view shared on all sides in the university. The point, rather, was that theology entered the lists as an academic discipline, and the technical concepts and problems of the human sciences had to be acknowledged, addressed and comprehended by theologians – from their own vantage-point, to be sure – if theology were to be intelligible to its generation.

Again, Barth fully shared this academic point of view; indeed, he never abandoned it. Throughout the *Dogmatics* Barth intended to address his contemporaries, to take up the critical problems the human sciences presented, and to acknowledge the standards of coherence, rationality and historical warrant that university faculties honoured. We could never explain the long, detailed excurses on academic debates from anthropology, psychology and sociology; the retention of Idealist concepts such as dialectic, limit, autonomy and heteronomy; the detailed exegeses of philosophers such as Nietzsche, Heidegger and de Beauvoir; reflections on historians and higher critics of all kinds. From these can we not see that Barth was a child of his generation, and a full member of the academy. To the measure that dogmatics was an exercise of the intellect, it must share, acknowledge and conform itself to the standards of intelligibility imposed on reader and writer alike. To that measure, Barth remains a true heir of nineteenth-century German academic theology.

But Barth breaks decisively with his inheritance when he moves the discussion of theological method from the formal to the material task of dogmatics. Here Barth shows himself to be not the academic but, rather, the Church theologian, committing himself to the particular freedom that proclamation of the Gospel gives, not in that way repudiating his standards of rationality, coherence and intelligibility, but rather deepening them. The distinctive note of *spaciousness* in Barth's theology – the ability to range freely over doctrines, to survey a wide field of history and the arts, to speak in the mixed idiom of Scripture, of high and low culture and, above all, to speak confidently and fearlessly without academic scrupulousness and anxiety all stem from Barth's recognition that method *follows*, and does not precede, content. Barth develops this insight at the conclusion of volume I/2 of the *Dogmatics*, §24.2, 'Dogmatics as a function of the teaching Church'. 'We understand by dogmatic method,' Barth writes there, 'the procedure which dogmatics must adopt if it is successfully to handle its material task, i.e., the unfolding and presentation of the content of the Word of God' (*CD* I/2, p. 853). Here Barth once again picks up the theme he treated in the earlier section on dogmatic norm, this time from a second side: the Word of God, which is the Object and norm of doctrine, now, in its content, becomes theology's material task and method. Preserved from the *Christliche Dogmatik* is the Kantian thought-form in which these tasks are laid out: theonomy, heteronomy and autonomy. Dogmatics is principally theonomy: God in his revelation is Objective Law for the Church, and theology is obedience to that commanding and gracious Law. Barth does not shy away from such external commands, despite Kant's strictures. There is no 'as if' about Barth's recognition of Lawgiver or of our obedience! Barth's hard-won breakthrough to God as Object, not simply Subject of our thought, will not allow him to back away from a frank heteronomy between the God who commands, and the hearing Church, which obeys. As the Church hears, it must speak: that is the rise of the 'teaching Church', the Church of proclamation and dogmatics.

But we must ask, what does it mean for Barth to claim that the Word of God 'irrupts, invades and presses to identity' in the Church's word of proclamation, as Barth styles the divine speaking? (ibid., p. 802). Or, to express this in the thought-form of Barth's academic method: how can Word and word coinhere without surrendering human or divine freedom? Barth's preoccupation with God's person-ality dated back to his student days (see, for example, Barth, 1914) and for anyone raised on German Idealism, that personhood meant freedom. God must be able to address the believer – to utter a new command that is not already presupposed in the inwardness of belief. Barth's attraction to images of speech – to 'stepping in front' of the believer, to commanding, addressing, prohibiting and to uttering the novel and strange – all these images underscore the spontaneity of divine personality, a reserve that must be disclosed, not discovered on pious introspection. Human and divine freedom, then, stand sentry to proper method. Has Barth gained entrance to it?

The answer lies in Barth's understanding of obedience. There is little as central to Barth's dogmatic method as the act of obedience; little as crucial to his break from his liberal past. We could say, in fact, that 'obedience' provides the structure and carries the weight of Barth's *Church Dogmatics* if this turn of phrase did not suggest that Barth, over his four long volumes, did little else than analyse a concept and unfold a human disposition or state. To do this would be to hand Barth's entire enterprise over to the 'anthropological' system he detected in Schleiermacher and bitterly opposed – an irony Barth feared, and judging from responses to his work, justifiably feared. No, obedience cannot be a *concept* through which dogmatics is understood or structured; rather, it must be a practice, a human act of faith. Obedience characterizes both the dogmatic norm and method, both formal and material principle, both the hearing and teaching Church. Obedience both accounts for the possibility of error in dogmatics and testifies to the possibility of its truth. It expresses the heteronomy of theology, but also its freedom, its being bound to the Word of God and, in just this way, being free for and against it. Obedience as formal and material principle of dogmatics is the theologian's response to the commanding promise of God, a trust in the identity that the Word presses to enact in human words. And in that very trust, the obedient theologian recognizes and repents of the failure to conform to the promise, of disobedience to the commanding Lord.

What, then, is obedience? How can it join together freedom and fallible knowledge; how can it name a theological method? Strange to any academic theologian's ear is the claim that obedience is a theological method. It jars, because method, to these theologians, is a specimen of epistemology. Like Descartes, academic theologians seek a method by which error can be rooted out and truth discovered or recognized. Method is the means by which proper dogmatic claims may be grounded, ordered and secured. 'Obedience' is not merely a dark horse for such an office; it is not even in the running. Obedience is an act of will or, perhaps better, of the whole person; it is loyal response to command. To be sure, there is a cognitive element in obedience, and that element will figure prominently in Barth's own dogmatic work; but it remains a province of the will, all the same – a bending, conforming and submitting to another. Here is the revolution in Barth's thought: to move method into the material side of dogmatic work is to bring it from the province of epistemology into conation. It makes the proper correlate to method not truth or certainty, but rather freedom. Or to speak in biblical idiom: to the voice of the commanding Lord, it is to answer, 'Here am I; send me!' Or in Calvin's celebrated definition: 'We shall not say that, properly speaking, God is known where there is no religion or piety' (Calvin, 1960, p. 39).

Note that the very things that academic method is to secure in modern theology – the proper knowledge of God, the spurious from genuine command, the faculty or region that receives or responds to God, the conceptual clarity and coherence of doctrine – are simply assumed by Barth. It is often said that Barth did not understand, appreciate or even notice the technical problems of proper method in his dogmatism: he did not see that interpretation or introspection or subjectivity could not simply be wished away. But we may say, for Barth's part, that he simply did not share enough common ground with his critics to disagree. Should a theologian take a human act of will to be proper method in theology, should method be an element of the material principles of theology, then problems of the conditions and faculties of knowledge cannot be basic. They follow and are solved by the primary state: obedience to the Word.

Obedience is the concrete act of assenting to, following and carrying out another's will. This act implies hearing or, more properly, listening. It is an altogether different act, Barth claims, to hear another's words as a neutral or independent investigator than to listen to them as one who will be sent on her way by them. Both acts require hearing accurately, interpreting faithfully, recognizing properly the speaker of the words, but only one listens in order to assent. Only one hears in the words a command; only one believes that proper hearing can be attested only by the deed. Such contrasts are only heightened if the task can be divided between those who read texts and those who listen to a speaker. Barth holds that proper method in theology can only be the ready hearing of a living voice, a hearing that does not *lead* to action but is itself the first moment in an act of faith, a heartfelt handing over of the self to God. This very act Barth styles 'theonomy' and it is the ground of both heteronomy *and* autonomy. And in its wake for every Christian and for the whole Church lies the danger of error, disobedience and hardness of heart.

Proper method in theology – the act of obedience – now correlates with the freedom of the subjects, not their correspondence to each other or to their accuracy or certainty. The failure of the method correlates with judgement and sin, not fallacy or misperception. And the proper relation between Creator and creature, named through this method, is not subject to knower or, even less, object to investigator, but rather commander to servant. This relationship of obedience, following a long Augustinian line, Barth calls freedom. Theology is a spacious discipline, a joyous and beautiful art, not because of its self-certainty or authority or, even less, because of its claim to universality or relevance, but rather because of its gracious freedom to follow the commands of a living Lord. And freedom is a gift of grace. Barth here joins together his Kantianism and Augustinianism: true autonomy is possible only through theonomy. Far from stifling human freedom, obedience to a commanding God is the gift of true freedom. Proper method in theology, then, is a gift of a merciful God; obedience can be possible only because a command is given, and the heart is set free to obey. This movement from gracious Lord to obedient servant – the material principle of dogmatics – is summed up in what Calvin called the promise and what Barth called the covenant: I shall be your God and you shall be my people.

Obedience rests on the divine promise. Theology cannot be confirmed in its authenticity or truth by the completeness of its self-submission: obedience alone cannot warrant dogmatics. Nor can a churchly community – the teaching Church – justify its proclamation and doctrine through its own powers, even spiritual powers:

'The Church teaches. But this fact is not self-grounded or self-effected, nor is it inherently good or inherently capable of improvement. It is not the function of dogmatics to establish this fact, to confirm it, or repeat it at a higher level of gnosis or philosophical reflection' (*CD* I/2, p. 801). Nor can we discern in the character of that obedience theology's reliability or rationality. Barth does not classify obedience as blind or prudent or reasonable. He does not look to see if one obeys automatically, like a 'lifeless corpse which allows itself to be carried to any place' or 'an old man's staff which serves in any manner in which the holder wishes to use it', as Ignatius Loyola famously characterizes true obedience (Loyola, 1991, p. 304).[5] Nor does Barth investigate whether the witness instead weighs the prudence of conformity to command; he is simply not interested in this sort of calculus. Rather, Barth assumes, but does not spell out, that obedience requires the intellect as well as will; it is a love of God that demands one's whole heart, mind and soul. Because God is truth, and Christ is the world's light, there can be nothing blind, chaotic or irrational in the divine command. To obey such a God cannot be mindless or absurd. But the assurance that God is not *mysterium tremendum*, nor obedience fanaticism, does not lie in the character of the human act. Rather it rests in the promise. God alone makes obedience possible; God alone warrants that obedience is rational, fitting and trustworthy. God promises that he will seize the human word and bring it into conformity with himself. He will make that identity, in Jesus Christ, 'visible and palpable' (*CD* I/2, p. 802). He alone promises that obedience to his Word will find its object, and that theological obedience will succeed to knowledge of God. Christ is that 'visible and palpable' Word; obedience to him is true, rational and successful theological doctrine.

Obedience, then, can fail. It can be partial, foolish and stubborn. It can begin in reluctance; it can wander, delay and draw back. Theological obedience can misunderstand. It can be filled with self-deception, pride, human vanity and wish. And because it is the act of sinners, theological obedience will be all of these; it will stand always in the need of deliverance and mercy. For just this reason, theological obedience clings to the divine promise, and not to itself, a brand fit for the burning. And, for just this reason, the Word must come to the theologian fresh each morning. The command to obey cannot be satisfied only once; theology cannot simply repeat an old obedience. Rather, each time the theologian seeks the Word, she must wait for it in renewed obedience, renewed listening, renewed deed. For this reason, Barth rejected the doctrine of biblical inerrancy but not because he rejected the doctrine of inspiration; far from it. Indeed, he considered Scripture a form of secondary command to the theologian: it is a source of 'relative heteronomy' in the formal principles of proper dogmatics. Rather, Barth rejected verbal inerrancy of Scripture because he found in that doctrine a temptation to consider the obedience to the Word as an act completed in the past, satisfied and preserved by those disciples long ago. To consider proper method in dogmatics to be bare repetition of biblical words, teaching or events is, for Barth, to rest not in the promise but rather in a text. It is to fall back, once again, on our own resources, our own possessions and faculties. It is to commit the error of Schleiermacher's method of 'immanent laws' (ibid., p. 799) all over again by his bitterest enemies.

Proper obedience in theology – the proper formal and material principles and tasks – can be only that of a witness. The category 'witness', so fateful in English-speaking theology, carries rather a different flavour in Barth's work. By it he intends the full, proper and supreme act of obedience to the Word. In a powerful part-section, Barth characterizes it in this way:

> [Biblical witnesses] are witnesses. But that means that they are not observers, reporters, dialecticians, partisans. No doubt they are all these other things too. No doubt they have not uttered a single sentence or syllable which does not also reveal them, to a greater or less extent, in these other attitudes. But cutting across all these attitudes, in the form and garments of them all, there is a certain fundamental attitude. This is the attitude of the witness. It is distinguished from the attitude of the interested spectator, or the narrating reporter, or the reflective dialectician, or the determined partisan, by the fact that when the witness speaks he is not answering a question which comes from himself, but one which the judge addresses to him. And his answer will be the more exact and reliable the more he ignores his own irrepressible questions in the shaping of his answer, and the more he allows it to be exclusively controlled by the realities which it is his duty to indicate and confirm. The attitude of the biblical witnesses is decided by the fact that, whatever else may rightly or wrongly be said about their other attitudes, they are in the position and are called to give information upon a question put to them from without. They are called by God in the face of all other men to be witnesses of His own action .... Their starting-point is this speaking and acting of God in its determinate reality, and they think and speak before the face of the same God, who now as Judge asks of them nothing but the truth concerning this reality, concerning His own speaking and acting which has taken place once for all. They speak under this twofold presupposition, with the weight of it, and therefore with the unchecked flow of a headlong mountain stream. Of course, they also describe, narrate, reflect and argue. How can any witness speak without to some extent doing these things too? But these things do not make him a witness. Nor did they make the prophets and apostles witnesses of God's revelation. What makes them its witnesses is the fact that they speak under this twofold presupposition: they believe and therefore speak. It is just this attitude which must be the standard for dogmatics as the model of Church proclamation. (Ibid., p. 817)

How different, for Barth, is the witness than for Locke! We do not seek the character of the witnesses, their veracity, judgement or powers of recall, nor do we expect to find part-warrant for our belief in the strength of these excellent witnesses. Not at all! For Barth, biblical witnesses, like modern-day witnesses in preaching and theology, have only this to say for themselves: they are questioned by a Judge, and so they must speak. They will betray all their human traits, including their fallibility, in their speech, but they cannot do otherwise. They are carried along by the torrent of God's own speech and act.

Witnessing to the Resurrection

Standing at the head of all the divine ways and works is the resurrection of Jesus Christ from the dead. The apostles, modern-day preachers and theologians are principally witnesses to this divine act; to this mighty work, they are called to obedient proclamation. The proper method in theology is obedience; the proper attitude is witness; the proper content that governs that method and attitude is Christ's resurrection. In this sense we may say that, for Barth, all dogmatics is obedient reflection on the reality of the resurrection, the revelation of Christ's own self-attestation.

It is hard to capture in brief compass a doctrine as rich and subtle as Barth's account of Christ's resurrection. Indeed, if our presentation of Barth's dogmatic method of obedience is close to the mark, we should never characterize any section of the *Church Dogmatics* as 'Barth's account', but rather as a particular hearing of the Word that points us, indirectly, to the demand that we readers hear that Word afresh. There could be no biblical event so faithful to this stricture as the narrative of the resurrection and ascension of Christ. Barth's witness to this event is concentrated in the second part volume of the Doctrine of Reconciliation, 'The Homecoming of the Son of Man'. Barth concludes his exposition of the exaltation and sanctification of the creature in Christ with an unfolding of the Easter event as revelation: the disclosure of the crucified Lord as light of the world. Christ's life should not be divided, Barth counsels, between a state of humiliation and a state of exaltation; rather the seamless nature of the one Lord, present in his teaching, deeds, and supremely in his death, is now fully revealed as this very same one in his resurrection from the dead. The noetic character of the resurrection is strongly underscored in Barth's interpretation: Christ reveals himself in his glory to his disciples, and they will know him because of and through this. He calls them to witness to his work of reconciliation, to obey his commandment to make disciples of all nations. The Church – the 'earthly-historical form of Christ's body' in Barth's terms – is the community summoned by this self-witness of Christ. In Christ's own Spirit, men and women hear the word of the living Christ, their eyes are opened, they recognize him. The resurrection is revelation in all these senses.

But Christ's resurrection is no less an event of history for all that. In the preface to *Church Dogmatics* IV/1, Barth notes that, although he is not often mentioned in the work, Bultmann and his 'method and results are always present' and that an 'intensive, although for the most part quiet, debate' moves in the undercurrent of the 'Doctrine of Reconciliation'. This debate is nowhere as central – though once again, quietly – as in Barth's treatment of the historicity of the resurrection. The resurrection and ascension of Christ, Barth tells us, 'are two distinct but inseparable moments in the one and the same event. The resurrection is to be understood as its *terminus a quo*, its beginning, and the ascension its *terminus ad quem*, its end' (*CD* I/2, p. 150). This event is a narrative, a movement, or turning point that took place there and then:

> In the resurrection and ascension of Jesus Christ we have to do with an inwardly coherent *event* .... It takes place after the conclusion of the preceding sequence, and is obviously distinct from it externally, because this sequence ended with the death of Jesus Christ. But it has the same character as what had gone before to the extent that it, too, is an event within the world, in time and space. It, too, takes place in the body, although not only in the body. It, too, was experienced and attested, not only inwardly but outwardly, by certain men. It begins outside the gates of Jerusalem on the third day after that of Golgotha, and according to Acts 1.3 it ends forty days later – again on a hill .... It is an event which involves a definite seeing with the eyes and hearing with the ears and handling with the hands, as the Easter stories say so unmistakeably and emphatically, and as is again underlined in 1 John 1. It involves real eating and drinking, speaking and answering, reasoning and doubting and then believing .... The event is not perhaps 'historical' in the modern sense, but it is fixed and characterized as something which actually happened among men like other events, and was experienced and later attested by them. (Ibid., p. 143, emphasis original)

In this event, Jesus Christ is Lord: 'the termination as well as the initiative lie entirely in his own hands and not in [the disciples]' (ibid., p. 144). He enters rooms through closed doors; he manifests his glory to those who cannot see; he reveals himself to those who cannot recognize him. In these manifestations, he discloses the truth of his incarnate life. He makes witnesses to his purpose, already foreshadowed in his teachings, miracles and death, but now revealed in majesty to those who deserted, denied, and lost hope in him. They will now receive his Spirit; they will now become the Church of Jew and Gentile.

These events, Barth underscores, must be 'miraculous' or, better, 'majestic' in character; they could not be the revelation of Christ were they not. They will not be 'historical in the modern sense'. Rather, they will be historical in the proper and exalted sense: the unfolding of the life, death and victory of God with his creatures, the unfolding of God's own time. The ascension of Christ will be an event in the world's history in this same sense as well:

> The ascension of Jesus Christ is the terminating point of this history of revelation. Jesus went – but where did he go to? We can and must give a twofold answer. It must first be to the effect that he went to the absolutely inaccessible place, to the cosmic reality by which man is always surrounded (for even on earth he exists under heaven) and from which to that extent he derives, but which he cannot attain or enter. The spheres which are accessible to him are earthly spheres, and only earthly spheres .... That is why the fact that he went there – it is again a miracle that can only be touched on lightly – is only stated and not described in the New Testament. How can the fact that he went there be described? ... But here, too, there is another and decisive aspect. The *ascendit ad coelos* of the creed has its meaning and point in the *sedet ad dexteram Dei Patris omnipotentis*. When he went into this hidden sphere he went to God. (Ibid., p. 153)

The exposition of the narrative of revelation must follow the 'reserve' demonstrated by the New Testament witnesses: it must not depict these events or attempt to describe them fully, even less to explain them. Rather, Barth quietly assumes, the proper method, in obedience to the Word, is to unfold the 'meaning and point' of this event. The proper method is followed when a direction, purpose and character is heard, embraced and obeyed. Barth lays out what he holds to be the New Testament witness to heaven, and its glory:

> In biblical terminology heaven is the dwelling place of God in the world which is not built with hands, the place of his throne, from which he exercises his almighty dominion .... And the 'cloud' which parted Jesus from their eyes in Acts 1.9, like the cloud of the transfiguration, is nothing other than the aureole of the original sphere of the divine dominion, the dwelling of the Father as it becomes visibly present on earth, disclosing itself to the Son of God, and in and with him to the Son of Man. The disciples saw the man Jesus received into this 'cloud' .... It belongs to God to come from that place. We can also say that it belongs to man to be from that place – as the creature of the Creator who rules there, as the recipient of the grace of Father, Son and Holy Spirit which he sends from there, as the child of God that he is declared to be from there as the brother of his Son. But we cannot say that it belongs to man to go to that place. The one man Jesus goes, however. This is the conclusion of the history of his revelation .... It is not only God who is now there, but as God is there he, this man, is also there. That this is the case is the hidden thing which is revealed in the ascension of Jesus Christ. (Ibid., pp. 153, 154)

The distance between this description of the unity of Creator and creature, and the unity of 'origination' (*Ursprung*) that dominated Barth's early writing, marks the journey Barth made from the thought-form and method of academic liberalism to the content, method and intention of the *Church Dogmatics*.

How different all this landscape appears to Robert Jenson! From this vantage of Barth's decisions in theological method, we can pick out more readily the landmarks of Jenson's method, thought-form and intention. And they are not Barth's, though they are instructed by him. Jenson pays homage to Barth throughout his *Systematics*, reserving especially strong praise for his doctrine of election. But Jenson endorses many other material positions of Barth's, from his doctrine of sin, to his notion of divine temporality, and his doctrine of Trinity, especially in the unity of economic and immanent Trinity. But no reader of Jenson's complex and innovative *Systematics* will need me to tell them that Jenson's theology is no repristination of Barth.

Jenson's innovations over the tradition are striking and powerful: he rejects substance metaphysics as part of the 'religion of the ancient Hellenes'; he denies to a pre-existent *Logos asarkos* any role beyond that of counterfactual proposition; he assigns to the Holy Spirit the transforming spontaneity of the absolute future, even to the Trinity itself; he rejects any notion of eternity that is timeless, immutable or impassable. Jenson's reading list is genuinely catholic and impressively broad: he makes substantial and creative use of elements of modern physics; he borrows freely from Orthodox liturgists and dogmaticians; he recovers minority traditions, such as the sixteenth-century Swabians, to set up innovative translations of traditional *loci*; and he appeals to musical form – the fugue in particular – to do real work in the doctrine of God. His Christology takes up Chalcedonian themes under the conditions of a 'process ontology', so that Christ's 'humanity and deity must be *communal concepts*' (Jenson, 1997, p. 138). And his reappropriation of Nicene Trinitarianism dictates three 'Identities', rather than a single Divine Nature, as primal to the divine reality, a distinctly Eastern note in the doctrine. But against that, Jenson incorporates a Western theme, elaborating on an Augustinian use of psychological categories, broken open by the maxim that 'there may be *more than one way to be personal*' (ibid., p. 120). And all this in two volumes – a scant 600 pages!

These elements seem clearly unBarthian – the last most strongly – and yet most of these themes can be seen as a *radicalization* of ideas, presuppositions and trends in Barth himself. Jenson certainly sees his own project in this light: he is 'wrenching concepts' out of their original place, reworking and reshaping them, but all in order more faithfully to serve the tradition from which they came. We might turn, then, to other sources for the stubborn difference that remains between Barth and Jenson. We might account for some of this different atmosphere, landscape and tone through Jenson's greater interest in, and reliance on, Rudolf Bultmann and his students, especially Bornkamm and Käsemann. Yet again, we remember Barth's own admission in the preface to *CD* IV that 'Bultmann is always present' there, even when standing in the shadows. We might point then to Jenson's place in the history of doctrine: his ability to make far greater use of the argument, problematic and thought-form of Wolfhart Pannenberg than Barth did – or, I believe, than Barth would, were he working today. It is from Pannenberg, after all, that Jenson receives the 'chief material contribution' Pannenberg makes 'to dogmatic theology': that the identity of the Son consists in relation to the Father, and not to the second identity of the Trinity, the Word (ibid., pp. 126, 127). In the end, however, these different allegiances, I believe, are more sign than cause. In the end, the difference between these two dogmatic theologians lies in their method and the location of that method within the architectonic of their systems. We may get a bearing on this location, and the divergent paths they mark out, by focusing first on a material doctrine: Jenson's account of the resurrection and ascension of Christ.

Like Barth, Jenson recognizes in Christ's resurrection the centrepiece of the Gospel narratives. 'A Gospel' Jenson writes 'is an expansion of the proposition "Jesus, the one who ... is risen"' (ibid., p. 195). It was natural, Jenson continues, that the pre-Easter material receive elaboration, incorporating sayings-material, deeds and wonders, and also – though not supremely, as for Barth – his death. But the resurrection was not elaborated so, at least at first:

> ... the statement of his Resurrection could and did remain abrupt – in the first Gospel, of Mark, very abrupt indeed .... It is noteworthy with what extraordinary freedom the tradents and authors at this point proceeded; constructing any sort of plausible sequence of events from the resurrection stories they adopt, or even discerning one behind them, has regularly defeated scholarly effort. It seems that almost any selection of resurrection stories ... could serve their purpose, since the assertion 'He was raised' *itself* could not in any case be narratively expanded. (Ibid., p. 195, emphasis original)

In all accounts of the Resurrection, however, Jesus is *seen*; it is a 'plastic representation'. The Easter-event should not, for all that, be considered merely visual, an interior episode that, like Berkeley's empiricism, could lead readily to an Idealism about the external act and object. No, the resurrection of Christ should not be identified with a vision, an effulgence of Easter-faith – though faith, to be sure, accompanies the Easter sight – and even less, with a 'mass hysteria – whatever that may be' Jenson icily concludes.

But what, then, do the first apostles in fact see?

> It seems clear that what Peter, the Twelve and Paul saw – if it was not a delusion or invented – was Jesus as an inhabitant of the age to come, as God even now 'reveals' him, lets some meet him in advance .... Jesus is risen into the future that God has for his creatures. What certain persons saw after his death was a reality of that future. (Ibid., pp. 197, 198)

So far we hear, once again, echoes of Barth's own insistence on the event-character of Christ's resurrection, and its narrative structure, an episode that has a beginning and an end. And in thought-form we hear in Jenson echoes of Barth's insistence, familiar to all students of nineteenth-century higher criticism, that the resurrection is an eschatological event:

> Paul calls what he saw a 'revelation' (*apokalypsis*) .... It thus seems to have been Paul's understanding that what he and the other witnesses [note that term!] saw was of the same ontological character as what Zechariah or Daniel or the postcanonical apocalypticists saw, that is, the fulfilling future of creation as it already now comes to the Father in the Spirit and as God therefore can, if he will, show it to us .... [Christ] lives 'in the glory of God'. Christ is risen into the Kingdom, and Christ is risen into God. He is located in the heaven seen by the apocalyptic prophets, and he is located in the triune life. Thus he is himself the presence of God in heaven; he is what makes it heaven. (Ibid., pp. 196, 201)

So far, we might consider this doctrine of the resurrection, like many other material themes in Jenson, as a deepening and radicalizing of Barth. But Jenson presses on. In a brief chapter – the entire compass achieved in some bare dozen pages – Jenson brings forward two problems in the doctrine that have no parallel in Barth.

Jenson considers the resurrection appearances to present an 'antinomy' to Christian thought – Jenson, too, knows his Kant – derived from 'conceptual analysis ... of deceptively simple propositions [laid out] by the 20th-century systematic theologian and ecumenist Peter Brunner' (ibid., p. 198). From the propositions that 'the Risen One is Jesus in the identity of his person' and that 'he lives in the glory of God' Jenson adds the proposition: to be risen 'means he or she is alive'. Now these propositions yield an antinomy when we analytically discriminate the meaning of 'identity' and 'life'. To be alive, Jenson tell us, is to be able 'to surprise us'; the dead cannot do this, though we may never understand them fully. Only those with a future before them can disclose a new word, reveal a new trait, develop a new pattern, taste or skill. But to have an identity – to possess it fully, completely and perfectly – Jenson argues, is to have died: only the dead can be said properly to have a reliable, sturdy and fulfilled identity. The risen Christ is, then, dead and alive; spontaneous and fully rounded out; still at work in the Church and, on the cross, able to breathe his last 'It is finished'. Note that these are conceptual antinomies; Jenson styles them in later chapters 'the antinomy of hope'. And they receive a conceptual resolution: 'We will see the antinomy of hope resolved in *love*: love is at once a determinate reality for which we can hope, and is itself perfected hope for those who are loved, so that when hoped-for love is granted hope truly begins' (ibid., p. 198).

Likewise, we may resolve the antinomy about Christ's resurrected identity: he is love. In his suffering death he completed the life of love; he loved his own to the end. We may be secure in the love – 'unconditionally' at last – because this identity of Jesus as the Loving One is completed in his death. But we need not fear that this is the love that enters now into the past, to the realm where in its darkness all is forgotten, scattered, lost. No, for

> … it is the very substance of love to be full of surprises for the loved one. For to love is fully to affirm the freedom of the loved one; it is to be committed to respond to this freedom with good, whatever the loved one does in it. So long as I live I cannot bind in advance what I will do in my freedom; therefore neither can I know in advance what my lover will do for me. (Ibid., pp. 198, 199)

Unlike the fragile, weak and deceptive loves of sinners, Christ's love is perfect: in his perfected life, he dies in love; in his risen life, he lives to 'will our good in a freedom beyond our predicting' (ibid., p. 199). But this does not mean that we no longer know who Jesus is, for that would make his death of no account. No, Jesus' identity is settled at Golgotha and no further action, presence, history or love in the Church and world alters that personal marker. He is the risen Jesus, the loving one; just so is he our living hope.

And just so, we may resolve the conflict that springs from Christ's ascension, the close of the Easter-event. The narrative of Christ's resurrection underscores that it is a '*bodily* resurrection, with or without the empty tomb' (ibid., p. 201). And a body, Jenson quotes approvingly from Calvin, requires a place, and 'if there is no *place* for Jesus' risen body, how is it a body at all?' (ibid., p. 202, emphasis original). But it is just this conviction – that Jesus' body is located in a spatial heaven – that has been destroyed, Jenson warns, by the Copernican revolution in cosmology. A heliocentric universe, with its uniform ontology, its causal nexus and extension, leaves no room for a heaven, beyond and above the inky skies. There are no subtle bodies to animate spheres, no loftier and more noble spheres to illumine, order and dignify the universe; no area beyond the *primum mobile* to receive an ascending and risen Lord. It is no longer rational – harmonious with the scientific, intellectual and academic canons of the day – to hold that Jesus' glorified body sits in some heavenly place, nor arrived there through some space-travel beyond the planets. Such movement through the 'silence of those infinite spaces' could only summon up 'mocking proposals' by the scientific-minded, and limp evasions by the pious, turning the risen Christ into 'a spook'. Of course, Jenson notes, there were attempts at 'demythologization' before Copernicus. He cites the Scholastic notion of 'supernatural' bilocation by which Christ is fully, physically and locally present in the sacrament on the altar, all the while reigning at the right hand of the Father. But it is left to the sixteenth-century Germans, during the Wars of Religion, to offer the proposal which Jenson endorses.

Johannes Brenz, as full of scorn as any modern rationalist at Christ's bodily ascent through the heavens, proposes that 'Christ's body is ubiquitous ... elevated beyond all location'. That is because God 'is his own place' and relates to his cosmos under different modes and to different ends. Christ's body resides on the altar not because of a divine mode of location, but rather because Christ in his divinity must share the divine omnipresence. And, Jenson adds, Christ's tomb must be empty – though this should be said 'cautiously' – for his corpse would remain as a presence to believers, a relic visited, preserved, enshrined. But as it is, Jenson concludes in one of his haunting turns of phrase, 'if the tomb marked by the Church of the Holy Sepulchre is indeed where Christ lay, then it is empty not by inadvertence but as the Temple of Israel was empty' (ibid., p. 206). For Jenson, these threads tie together this way:

> It is time for theology, taught by the collapse of the Ptolemaic cosmology and the new possibilities this opened and by centuries-long difficulty about Christ's body in the Eucharist, to let what Paul meant by 'body' teach us also what to mean by 'body'. This is what Brenz and his fellows began to do. We must learn to say: the entity rightly called the body of Christ is whatever object it is that is Christ's availability to us as subjects; by the promise of Christ, this object is the bread and cup and the gathering of the church around them. *There* is where creatures can locate him, to respond to his word to them. (Ibid., p. 205, emphasis original)

To be 'available' in Jenson's terms simply *is* to be body: to be present to another is to make oneself available, immediate, palpable and of use. Much as we might, in a rough-and-ready common-sense way, identify matter by its resistance, weight or stubborn shape, so we might analyse the concept, body, as that which presents itself to us. Here we see the confluence of Jenson's intellectual ancestors: his openness to Heidegger-style phenomenology; his respect for Bultmann and the centrality of decision, scientific rationality and self-presence; his incorporation of Hegelian dynamism and concept into the metaphysics of the external world. But more central than these is Jenson's conviction that the risen Christ must be the gathered community, the *totus Christus*, the presence of Jesus in and through his Kingdom. That is 'another way of being personal'.

And, as Jesus simply *is* the second identity of the Trinity, we should expect that the doctrine of Trinity, in Jenson's hands, will carry out the conceptual resolution of the antinomy of hope through the freedom of love and the transformed rationality of 'being personal in another way'. The divine life of the Father, freed up for him by the eschatological Spirit, cannot, in its novelty, alter the identity and rule (*arche*) of the Father, for:

… the Spirit is God coming to us from the last future; he is God coming from and as the Kingdom. The temporal infinity of God is the unsurpassability of this event: such things as the unconditionality of the gospel-promise, the immunity of sacramental presence to the unbelief of worshipers, the impossibility of building the Kingdom by our labors, are not results or illustrations of God's infinity, they *are* that infinity …. The infinity of the Spirit's coming is the inexhaustibility of the relation between Jesus and all that proceeds his advent to establish his Kingdom. It is the inexhaustible richness of the transformation of all temporal events by Jesus' sacrifice and victory …. Nothing in God recedes into the past or approaches from the future. But the difference is also absolute: the arrow of God's eternity, like the arrow of causal time, does not reverse itself … they are like before and after in a narrative. (Ibid., pp. 219, 218)

The name of the Spirit who liberates the Father for the Son, is Love, and that liberated, loving and mutual indwelling is 'Infinite Life,' the triune being that *is* personality in a new way. The resurrection of Christ is the great spiritual *novum* in the narrative of that infinite life:

The Spirit is God as his and our future rushing upon him and us; he is the eschatological reality of God, the power as which God is the active goal of all things, as which God is for himself and for us those 'things not seen' that with us call for faith and with him are his infinity. When credal articles for the Spirit end with resurrection and life everlasting, they merely specify what the Spirit in himself as person is. In himself, God confronts his own future; he confronts that Spirit who is the Spirit 'of' the Father, the novelty of genuine narration. The great occurrence of dramatic causality in God is the resurrection. That the Son once slain would rise is, after the fact, an eternal certainty, but it was not beforehand, and *also not for God*. (Ibid., p. 160, emphasis added)

This is breathtaking architectonic, but it is not Barth's. To be sure, the material commitments to narrative and a repudiation of substance metaphysics lead to startling innovations in classical doctrine. And Jenson's attraction to conceptual analysis and a distinctly late-modern technical array of concepts would lead us to expect novelty over Barth. But more is at stake here. To Jenson's method and, in Barth's idiom, his formal principle, tasks and attitudes, we must turn to see the final unity and difference between these two dogmaticians.

Method and Interpretation

In an opening part, parallel to Barth's treatment of the formal and material principles of theology, Jenson lays out his 'Prolegomena' on the nature of systematic theology and its norms. Here we find much that must remind us strongly of Barth. It is not simply that Jenson places the biblical narrative, as a single, complex story, at the very core of theological norms and sources, nor that, like Barth, Jenson readily speaks of the relative authority of the history of doctrine, nor that Jenson, again like Barth, will be quick to acknowledge theology's objective or 'metaphysical' character. It is that

Jenson, in resonant echoes of Barth, speaks of a 'hearing and speaking Church': 'Given what we *have* heard and seen as the gospel, what *shall* we now say and enact that the gospel may be spoken? ... Theology is critical and possibly innovative interpretation at the turn from hearing to speaking the gospel' (Jenson, 1997, p. 16). Or more striking still:

> The occurrence of the gospel depends on the chain of witnesses who have brought the news from the first witnesses to those who now hear .... Theology's question is always: In that we have heard and seen such-and-such discourse as gospel, what shall we now say and do that gospel may again be spoken? (Ibid., p. 14)

And in a tantalizingly brief note on the problem of error and human freedom: 'Why is *thinking* needed to make this turn? We have heard the gospel and now are to speak it; why not just repeat what we heard? Should not gospel-speakers be qualified primarily by accurate memory or close preservation of documents?' (ibid., p. 14, emphasis original). We might see in these methodological parallels a ground of Jenson's material closeness to Barth, but we need also to account for difference. And here we might pause over the claims that stitch together the sentences cited above.

'Theology' Jenson claims in these same pages 'is an act of *interpretation*: it begins with a received word and issues in a new word essentially related to the old word'. Or, surrounding the observation about 'theology's question': since the Gospel thus always has, and agitates, a conflicted conceptual history of its own, the theological question has a temporal seam. It is in the seam between these questions that there must be thinking, that theology is actual as 'hermeneutic'. Jenson rounds out this observation by the relation of hermeneutics to the role, highlighted in different ways by J.L. Austin and George Lindbeck, of language as grammar:

> If theology is hermeneutics, it is *universal* hermeneutics; the act of interpreting with which it is concerned can turn to anything at all. But when hermeneutics become universal they just so become metaphysics .... Again, if theology is grammar, the very first work to which the label 'metaphysics' was attached was Aristotle's attempt to discern a universal grammar .... We may make a closely related point by noting that if Christian theology is grammar, then it is *prescriptive* grammar .... Every theologoumenon lays down a prescription: speak in this way and *not* in that other way to which we may be inclined. (Ibid., pp. 20f.)

And, finally, Jenson applies his definition of theology as hermeneutics to its role as interpreter of Scripture. Theology cannot be bound to the literal fundamentals of the text; the 'testing' of doctrinal claims must be done against Scripture, but it cannot entail only 'direct comparison'. Rather, both Scripture and theology are to be tested against a task: the advancement of 'church proclamation and devotion'. Jenson sums up:

> The scriptural test of a theologoumenon is its success as a hermeneutical principle: whether it leads to exegetical success or failure with mandated church homiletical, liturgical, and catechetical uses of Scripture .... A theologoumenon that fails to help us in this work, with a text and use to which it is evidently relevant, is in process of refutation. (Ibid., p. 33)

These methodological preliminaries bear fruit in Jenson's doctrine of 'Word and Icons' (Jenson, 1999, ch. 29) where the claim that the tasks of preaching, praying and teaching express and conserve a 'community of interpreters' that is continuous, indeed identical to the original gathered community at Jerusalem, Corinth, Rome and beyond, to the ends of the earth.

But we have travelled some distance from the role and attitude of witness to that of interpreter. What shall we say, in the end, about these two tasks, and their place in the formal and material principles of theology? Here we must be struck by the different descriptions or, better, expositions of the word, witness. Recall that, for Barth, a witness is one who answers before and to a judge: she speaks because she must. Obedience is the material task of the witness: he is to assent, in his frailty and his freedom, to the commanding Word and, in just this way, know his Lord. The attitude of witness, for Barth, is a dogmatic method: not simply disciples but also theologians speak only on the witness-stand. We inhabit a world at some remove from all this in Jenson's exposition. In Jenson's thought-world, witnesses are not those cross-examined but are instead a living tradition. In Barth, witnesses speak under authority; in Jenson, they are authority. For Jenson, the witnesses stand in a line of succession; they are a chain that passes on, from teacher to student, what has been seen and heard. The stagework here is not the courtroom and its examining judge, but rather the classroom or ceremonial hall where the past is handed on and handed over to the generations who come after. Little wonder that Jenson reserves high praise for apostolic succession and the charism of the teaching office, or magisterium. And the task these witnesses set themselves is also at some remove from the task of the dogmatician: they hear and speak at the primary and 'performative' level; the theologian, like the grammarian, *interprets*, though with prescriptive force, the text and traditions, so that they may be put to use once again by the Church in its material and performative tasks. To be sure, Jenson makes use of these first- and second-order distinctions with reserve and qualification. But it remains one thing to witness an event and another to interpret it, and that will make all the difference. We may see, as if in a laboratory opened to our inspection, this work of theological interpretation when we return to Jenson's account of Christ's resurrection and ascension.

The resurrection of Christ presented a conceptual antinomy, the ascension a threat to rationality, both generated by the claim that Christ's risen identity is embodied. The apostles witness a living body, one not immediately recognized but rather disclosed to them as Jesus' own, and then removed from their sight into the heavens. We have seen Barth treat these same passages through a careful redescription, exposition and commentary on their 'purpose and direction'. He listened to them; his unfolding of these events is his act of obedience to them. And, if restatement can be seen as interpretation, Barth will indeed go this far to meet Jenson and his method. But no further. As if on facing pages, we have seen Jenson offer something else: an interpretation and what we might style a conceptual explanation. Jenson's method dictates that the theologian offer a 'new word essentially related to the old word', and that the newness be seized upon through 'thinking', a conceptual reappropriation, transformation and critique of 'antecedent religious and theological understanding' through conversation and debate, all under the direction of the promise. Theologians, then, are interpreters, in a community of debaters, contributors and rejecters. It has been the work of the better part of a century to lay out just what 'interpretation' entails, and it is no easy matter to say just what a 'conceptual analysis' or 'explanation' might be. Wisely, Jenson moves past these thickets quietly, with only a nod in the direction of Bultmann and, more favourably, Hans-Georg Gadamer.[6] But we can gather from his own scriptural interpretations just how he understands these tasks.

To interpret, we can see, is to state an old idea or concept in new terms and, in that way, resolve puzzles, ambiguities and conflicts in the original. This clarification is carried out through the idioms, practices and convictions of the hearing audience; the new meaning is expressed in, but also against, the values, aspirations and history of the contemporary readers. Such work requires thought, because it demands an investigation into the original 'discourse': its semantic field, conceptual idioms, history of argument and ideals. But, even more, interpretation demands a creative, coherent and engagingly plausible translation of these old expressions into the new, such that the wine does not burst the old skins, but puts them to work again. 'If the gospel is indeed to be news decisive for those who, at a time and place, are there to hear it, it must be news about the projected fulfilments and feared damnations by which people's lives are then and there moved, and these are constant across neither time nor space' (Jenson, 1997, p. 15). Now it is clear that such a task could not be carried out in isolation; a community shapes both the original text and its re-presentation. But even a continuous community of interpreters is hard-pressed to say just what identifies a successful interpretation, or just what explanations really are or do. Little wonder that conversation, debate and argument play central roles in interpretation! For Jenson, theological interpretation must give a rational, coherent and faithful translation and clarification of Scripture and doctrine such that Church confession, commitment and sacrament are enriched and carried on.

The resurrection and ascension of Christ – the fulcrum of the Gospels, the identity of God – are the unsurpassed candidates for theological interpretation. What does it mean, Jenson asks, for Christ to rise bodily? How can it be understood that Christ appeared, under his own conditions, and for his own appointed time, and then completed them through an ascent to heaven? How can these events, without parallel in Scripture or religious history, be explained to a new congregation of the faithful, so that the Church's sacraments are made intelligible, fruitful, powerful to save? For these tasks, Jenson turns to the scientific claims of our age – the heliocentric world of modern physics – and to his own meaning-system of personal identity, mutuality and spontaneity. The Easter-event is translated, clarified and given meaning through these interpretations. They express with remarkable conciseness and compression the purpose, ethic and architectonic of Jenson's entire *Systematics*. They innovate radically, but by conserving not dismissing the past. They are traditional and they are strikingly modern. They provoke debate – not least from students and disciples of Barth himself.

For it is no small matter, I believe Barth would say, to move theological method from the material side of the enterprise to the formal; no small matter to make theological method a species of epistemology rather than conation; no small matter to view the theologian as interpreter rather than obedient witness. Why, Barth would ask, should the travel of bodies through space, Ptolemaic or post-Copernican, be a puzzle that theologians must resolve, translate or explain? Why is postmodern physics even a candidate for objection to, or a category for interpretation of the ascension? Barth himself is remarkably silent about or, we may assume, un-embarrassed by the Ptolemaic cosmology. It is not that he rejected the old, or for that matter, the new cosmology; rather, he did not find them germane. Barth would press on: why must scriptural events be characterized through concepts, or discordances be understood as conceptual antinomies? Why have the levels of explanation and interpretation been elevated to the conceptual and systematic? Who is the theologian, Barth would ask, that he or she may assume the task of giving meaning and fresh word to the old? What kind of rationality, coherence and warrant are entailed in these tasks of interpretation and understanding? What kind of freedom has the interpreter exercised in these tasks?

These questions might remind Barth of an academic method he had turned aside: the conviction that the Word and human word must be given together in the awareness, idiom and practice of the recipient, for only in that way can the revelation be intelligible, persuasive and valuable. Hans Frei has termed this method, in its many forms, relationalism, and Barth saw, in this starting point, a priority given to the modes, categories and aims of the pious subject that circumscribed and ultimately controlled the Word, even under the most stringent claims to Orthodoxy and metaphysical realism. Barth did not see his own method as sailing free of academic standards of intelligibility. He, too, sought rationality, coherence and clarity, but he held that they were given not through the secondary act of interpretation, but are rather grounded, given and given again only in the Word itself. Indeed, the very fact that the Word has continuing power, and that the new, meaningful human word is consistent with the old, can be warranted only by divine action, by a fresh speaking of that divine Word not by an interpreter, not even an interpretive community, not even one with spiritual gifts. To be sure, none of these questions and worries that I have placed in Barth's mouth here are new, as readers of Barth know well. Barth lodged these complaints against Bultmann throughout his career, and I believe he would lodge them still. But Bultmann – as, I imagine, Jenson would, too – denied that the dangers Barth feared followed from Bultmann's method, or that the virtues Barth praised followed from his own.

So, as one persuaded by Barth, I might put the matter this way: can a theologian be an interpreter *and* an obedient witness? Barth did not seem to think so, and we might guess that, for different reasons, Bultmann would agree. True, as Barth often said, *methodus est arbitraria*. Each theologian and each generation must find their own way in theology. And yet, Barth warned, the theologian remains responsible. We must, Barth argued, in this freedom and responsibility before the Word, decide between them. And, as Barth had occasion often to repeat, there is no theology secured through method; it is all established by grace and under divine mercy. So, perhaps we should conclude our comparison of the resurrection and ascension of Christ in these two theologians with a classical phrase Barth was so fond of and put to such good use: *Hic Rhodus; Hic salta!*[7]

Notes

1 It is the fate of unpublished dissertations to be read only by specialists. This fate extends even to Hans Frei's magisterial dissertation (Frei, 1956). But it is a measure of Frei's achievement that specialists wish that the dissertation were more widely read, and that, some 50 years later, many consider it still unmatched in technical mastery and insight into Barth's early work.
2 A fine translation by George Hunsinger may be found in Barth, 1986, pp. 25–61.
3 This is Frei's term for any method in which subject and object are given together immediately in individual or collective awareness, as a '*nexus* of Divine–human contact' (Frei, 1956, pp. 27, 28).
4 See his affirmation of Schleiermacher as a realist in 'Schicksal und Idee' and in his entry on Schleiermacher in Barth (1972, pp. 425–73).
5 Ignatius' larger view of obedience is considerably more nuanced than these images suggest. He does not intend all obedience to be invincibly blind; even in the *Constitutions*, from which these analogies are drawn, Ignatius acknowledges that Jesuits cannot obey a sinful command.
6 Gadamer (1965) is cited in Jenson (1997, p. 20; 1999, p. 280). For analysis of and bibliography for explanation, see the entry by Salmon (1993).
7 'Here is Rhodes; jump here!' This phrase, still a favourite of German essayists, stems from Aesop, through Hegel to Marx, where it entered into political vocabulary with a transformed meaning: 'This is the crossroads; now you must decide.' Barth used it in this sense. The history of this phrase, and its transformation in German letters, can be found at the following website, dedicated to the interests of Isaiah Berlin: http://berlin.wolf.ox.ac.uk/lists/quotations/quotations_by_ib.html.

References

Barth, K. (1972), *Protestant Theology in the Nineteenth Century*, trans. B. Cozens and J. Bowden, London: SCM.
Barth, K. (1982), *Christliche Dogmatik im Entwurf* in *Karl Barth Gesamtaugabe*, vol. II, ed. G. Sauter, Zürich: Theologische Verlag.
Barth, K. (1986), *The Way of Theology in Karl Barth*, ed. M. Rumscheidt, Allison Park, PA: Pickwick.
Barth, K. (1994), 'Schicksal und Idee', in *Karl Barth Gesamtausgabe*, vol. III., ed. H. Stoevesandt, Zürich: Theologische Verlag, pp. 344–93.
Calvin, J. (1960), *The Institutes of the Christian Religion*, vol 1, trans. F.L. Battles, ed. J.T. McNeill, Philadelphia: Westminster.

Frei, H. (1956), 'The Doctrine of Revelation in the Thought of Karl Barth, 1909–1922: The Nature of Barth's Break with Liberalism', PhD dissertation, Yale University.

Gadamer, H.-G. (1965), *Warheit und Methode*, Tübingen: JCB Mohr.

Jenson, R.W. (1997), *Systematic Theology. Volume 1*, New York: Oxford University Press.

Jenson, R.W. (1999), *Systematic Theology. Volume 2*, New York: Oxford University Press.

Loyola, I. (1991), *Spiritual Exercises and Selected Works*, ed. G. Ganss, New York: Paulist Press.

Salmon, W. (1993), 'Explanation', in J. Dancy and E. Sosa (eds), *A Companion to Epistemology*, Oxford: Blackwell.

CHAPTER 11

Fighting at the Command of God: Reassessing the Borderline Case in Karl Barth's Account of War in the *Church Dogmatics*

David Clough

'To the memory of one who faithfully fulfilled the office of teacher in the church' is the dedication that begins John H. Yoder's *Karl Barth and the Problem of War*. But in his extended interrogation of Barth's attitude to warfare Yoder does not allow his respect to stand in the way of strong and impassioned critique. He draws on personal conversations with Barth and transcriptions of Barth's conversations with others in addition to Barth's published writings, and there are passages where he makes it clear that he is responding to Barth's comments on the draft of his manuscript. This makes the book an account of an interchange between two theologians, albeit reported by only one of them.

Yoder's account divides my sympathies: I am as troubled as he is by Barth's description in *CD* III/4 of the exceptional case in which warfare is commanded by God, but I disagree with Yoder that the problems here are the result of a fundamental problem with Barth's ethical method. In addition to recounting Yoder's conversation with Barth, therefore, I will also in this essay enter the dialogue as a third participant, suggesting a resolution of the difficulties in Barth's treatment of war with which neither of the other participants would wholly agree.

It may seem surprising that Yoder was prepared to engage so comprehensively with a passage of the *Church Dogmatics* that Barth conceded 'is perhaps not one of the most felicitous' (interview, *Stimme der Gemeinde*, 1963, cited by Yoder, 1970, p. 117). The discussion is fruitful in spite of the infelicities of the text because, in addition to being novel and provocative, Barth's account contains insights that go beyond the tired opposition of pacifism and Just War theory. Yoder is impressed by 'the monumental body of theologically integrated Protestant ethical thought which [the twentieth] century has seen' (Yoder, 1970, p. 15). There are good reasons not to adopt the entirety of Barth's view of the ethics of warfare as expressed in the *Church Dogmatics*, as the following pages will make clear. Engaging with his position, however, is enlightening in key areas and clarifies both the issues at stake and the options available for a theological assessment of war.

In the *Dogmatics*, Barth treats pacifism and warfare in volume III/4. He completed it in 1951, and recent European history had given him ample opportunity both to reflect on the proper attitude of the Church to war, and to act on the result of his convictions. He vigorously supported the war against Hitler and wrote to Christians in England, France, the United States and elsewhere to urge them to do so.[1] Barth discusses war under the heading of 'The Protection of Life', which he describes as the elucidation of the commandment 'Thou shalt not kill'. All human life belongs to God, so respect and protection is demanded for it. The commandment to protect it, however, has its horizon in the will of God the Creator, so the protection of life is limited and not absolute. To think otherwise would be to treat human life as 'a kind of second God' (*CD* III/4, p. 398). Barth notes that the main theme of the section on the protection of life is the exceptional case (*Grenzfall*) where 'the Lord of life may further its protection even in the strange form of its conclusion and termination' (ibid.). He discusses the possibility of this *Grenzfall* in relation to suicide, abortion, euthanasia, killing in self-defence, capital punishment and tyrannicide before turning to a consideration of killing in warfare.

Barth's first words on warfare call for an unflinching realism about the nature of modern national conflict. He identifies three illusions that we can no longer entertain. First, there are no longer uncommitted spectators in a nation at war. All members of a nation are now military personnel and therefore belligerents, directly or indirectly: no longer is war fought by small armies from the 'military classes'. Second, it is now clear that the issue in modern warfare is economic power: 'the struggle for coal, potash, ore, oil and rubber, for markets and communications, for more stable frontiers and spheres of influence as bases from which to deploy power for the acquisition of more power' (*CD* III/4, p. 452). In the past, it was easier to believe that wars were fought for more noble motives, such as honour, justice, freedom and other supreme values, but it is now difficult to believe this sincerely. The armaments industry, with its close links to science and industry, 'imperiously demands that war should break out from time to time to use up existing stocks and create the demand for new ones'. Barth amends the Roman proverb 'if you want peace, prepare for war' to 'if you do not want war, prepare for peace' (ibid.), but claims that the way in which we are possessed by economic power means that neither of these is applicable. We want a form of war even in peacetime, so our mobilization for war, and the outbreak of war, are inevitable. The third illusion Barth identifies is that war requires anything other than 'quite nakedly and brutally the killing of as many as possible of the men who make up the opposing forces' (ibid.). Previously, it was easier to focus on the skill, courage, and readiness for self-sacrifice that war demanded of the individual, and to believe that the individual confronted by an individual enemy was in an unavoidable position of self-defence.

> To-day, however, the increasing scientific objectivity of military killing, the development, appalling effectiveness and dreadful nature of the methods, instruments and machines employed, and the extension of the conflict to the civilian population, have made it quite clear that war does in fact mean no more and no less than killing, with neither glory, dignity nor chivalry, with neither restraint nor consideration in any respect.... Much is already gained if only we do

at last soberly admit that, whatever may be the purpose or possible justice of a war, it now means that, without disguise or shame, not only individuals or even armies, but whole nations are out to destroy one another by every possible means. It only needed the atom and hydrogen bomb to complete the self-disclosure of war in this regard. (Ibid., p. 453)

I interrupt Barth here to question whether the illusions he identified accurately characterize war as it is fought 50 years on. In relation to the first illusion, that there is a meaningful category of non-combatants, the evidence is mixed. Contemporary military techniques used by technologically advanced nations reduce the need for large-scale conscription, so there has been a movement back to smaller professional armies, but the recent increase in smaller-scale wars, such as those in the Afghanistan, the former USSR and the former Yugoslavia, have made combatants of significant proportions of the population. The military–industrial complex continues to require the daily involvement of many citizens in preparations for wars by their own nation, or by others via the lucrative trade in armaments.[2] In addition, the sizeable proportion of tax revenues devoted to military spending by most governments involves all members of society in war preparations at a different level.[3] Barth's observations here are a useful reminder, then, of the involvement of the whole nation in preparing for and carrying out military operations. There is also a clear difficulty, however, in dismissing the distinction between combatants and non-combatants, traditionally known as the principle of discrimination in Just War theory: it removes a widely acknowledged – if less widely observed – check on the conduct of war. If war can be morally legitimate, as Barth will go on to claim, the absence of this principle would inevitably make it more destructive to a wider group of persons than it would be if the principle continued to be observed. While this point is rhetorically fruitful, when spoken by the non-pacifist it is also morally irresponsible.

The second illusion about war from which Barth wishes to free us is that its motive is anything but the acquisition of economic power. Here, again, we have a useful reminder that the criterion of just cause in Just War theory is all too often a fig leaf barely covering the naked pursuit of national self-interest. Almost invariably, a purportedly just cause can be found to legitimize a war fought with baser intentions, and the difficulty of judging intentions from the outside make it difficult to gainsay such claims. We will make significant gains in realistic understanding of national motives if we accept that gaining economic power is very often the motive for war. This is not Barth's point, however. Barth wants us to accept that there is no other motive but gain of economic power for war. Were this a face-to-face conversation, we could argue about whether motives for particular wars could be subsumed under this description. As I write in August 2003, the motives for the war in Iraq waged by the US and UK governments continue to be hotly debated. Motives seem inextricably mixed here: most nations would accept the right of the US to use limited force in self-defence, yet given the scale and breadth of US military aggression in its so-called 'War on Terror' it is hard to escape the conclusion that its aims are much wider than this. It is not hard, however, to find examples of military actions where attributing economic gain as the sole motive is implausible, such as the US military support of the UN distribution of famine relief in Somalia in 1992–93, or the current deployment of African peacekeeping troops in Liberia. Again, therefore, Barth's attempt to disabuse us of the illusion that war can be fought for noble motives is a valuable reminder of the need for an hermeneutic of suspicion in assessing motives for going to war, but its force is weakened by overstatement.

Barth's third illusion, that war is always total war, falls into a similar category. The refined objectivity of the methods used to kill has gone far beyond that of the 1950s, so that the act of initiating an attack that will kill and maim on a small or large scale can resemble participation in a video game. We have not yet thought through the implications of this for a theological assessment of war. Barth's claim, however, that war is always nations set on the complete destruction of each other, is unconvincing. We have certainly seen recent examples of this kind of total war: the systematic rape of Bosnian and Croatian women in the early 1990s; the massacre of the Tutsi people in Rwanda in 1994. Yet there are also counterexamples: neither Argentina nor the UK was set on the complete destruction of the other in the war over the Falklands/ Malvenas, and the US could have entirely destroyed the nation of Iraq at the end of the first Gulf War, but did not. Barth's third illusion is perhaps the least plausible of the three.

Having stated these reservations about the three illusions about war that Barth identified, I will return to Barth's contribution to the discussion. Following this blunt assessment of contemporary warfare, Barth states that the *Grenzfall* in relation to warfare must be stated with even stricter reserve than in the other cases of killing he considered previously. This is so for three reasons: first, war involves a whole nation in killing, making everyone responsible for whether this is commanded killing or forbidden murder; second, it involves killing those who are only enemies in the sense that they are fighting for their country; and, third, war demands almost everything that God has forbidden be done by millions on a broad scale. 'To kill effectively, and in connexion therewith, must not those who wage war steal, rob, commit arson, lie, deceive, slander, and unfortunately to a large extent fornicate, not to speak of the almost inevitable repression of all the finer and weightier forms of obedience?' (*CD* III/4, p. 454).

All affirmative answers to the question of whether war can be commanded by God 'are wrong if they do not start with the assumption that the inflexible negative of pacifism has almost infinite arguments in its favour and is almost overpoweringly strong' (ibid., p. 455). Barth agrees with those who lament the Church's change of political theology after Constantine: 'in a kind of panic at all costs to give the emperor or other ruler his due there has been a complete surrender of the wholesome detachment from this imperial or national undertaking which the early Church had been able in its own way and for good reasons to maintain' (ibid., p. 456). For Barth, the mistake here is in eschatology: the Church's justification of war is an indication that 'the realities and laws of this passing aeon ... have come to be rated more highly than the passing of this world and the coming of the Lord. The criterion has thus been lost without the application of which there can be no controlling Christian will and action within this passing aeon' (ibid.). We have lost a sense of the 'unheard-of and extraordinary' idea of killing for the state: the primary task of Christian ethics in this context is 'to recover and manifest a distinctive horror of war and aloofness from it' (ibid.).

The exercise of power is an *opus alienum* for the state, Barth claims: the state possesses power and is able to exercise it, but Christian ethics must always challenge the state with the question of whether the exercise of power is necessary. The normal task of the state is 'to fashion peace in such a way that life is served and war kept at bay' (ibid.): it is when a state does not pursue this normal task that it is compelled to take up the abnormal task of war. It 'requires no great faith, insight nor courage' to condemn war absolutely, or to 'howl with the wolves that unfortunately war belongs no less to the present world order, historical life and the nature of the state than does peace':

> What does require Christian faith, insight and courage – and the Christian Church and Christian ethics are there to show them – is to tell nations and governments that peace is the real emergency to which all our time, powers and ability must be devoted from the very outset in order that men may live and live properly, so that no refuge need be sought in war, nor need there be expected in it what peace has denied. Pacifists and militarists are usually agreed in the fact that for them the fashioning of peace as the fashioning of the state for democracy, and of democracy for social democracy, is a secondary concern as compared with rearmament or disarmament. It is for this reason that Christian ethics must be opposed to both. (Ibid., p. 459)

Barth suggests that 'the cogent element of truth in the pacifist position' will benefit if it is not presented as the total truth 'but is deliberately qualified, perhaps at the expense of logical consistency'. The consistency of theological ethics 'may for once differ from that of logic' (ibid., p. 461).

Yoder objects, as we will see, to the concept of the *Grenzfall* in Barth's ethics, but up to this point he has been sympathetic to the substance of Barth's discussion of war. When Barth turns to his critique of pacifism, however, Yoder is compelled to speak. He applauds Barth for taking a position 'very near that of Christian pacifism … nearer in fact than of any really prominent theologian in the history of European Protestant dogmatics' (Yoder, 1970, p. 19), but notes that Barth has little understanding of the pacifist position he all but endorses. Yoder suggests that Barth's knowledge of Christian pacifism when he wrote *CD* III/4 was restricted to the writings of Leo Tolstoy, acquaintance with the school of Leonhard Ragaz and one book by G.J. Deering. Barth seems to believe, Yoder says, that the pacifist he opposes is a legalist, that the state should immediately abandon violence, is not specifically Christian in his position and takes principles from the Decalogue or the Sermon on the Mount as exceptionless norms. Yoder disclaims this 'absolutist' pacifism and claims that his dispute with Barth

... is therefore not a debate between pacifism and militarism, nor even between pacifism and non-pacifism. It is rather a debate to be carried on within the pacifist camp, between one position which is pacifist in all the general statements it can make but announces in advance that it is willing to make major exceptions, and another position, nearly the same in theory, which is not able to affirm in advance the possibility of the exceptional case. (Ibid., pp. 51–53)

After this interjection from Yoder, we will follow Barth a little further. After describing the horror of war and the Church's responsibility for building peace, Barth moves on to describe the *Grenzfall* in which war may be commanded by God. The first criterion he provides to identify this possibility is that the existence or autonomy of a state must be attacked, so that a nation finds itself forced to choose to surrender or assert itself. Barth then asks why this possibility should be allowed and responds 'that there may well be bound up with the independent life of a nation the responsibility for the whole physical, intellectual and spiritual life of the people comprising it, and therefore their relationship to God'. He continues:

It may well be that they are forbidden by God to renounce the independent status of their nation, and that they must therefore defend it without considering either their own lives or the lives of those who threaten it. Christian ethics cannot possibly deny that this case may sometimes occur. The divine command itself posits and presents it as a case of extreme urgency. (*CD* III/4, p. 462)

In a surprising single sentence in a small-print paragraph, Barth adds, 'I may remark in passing that I myself should see it as such a case if there were any attack on the independence, neutrality and territorial integrity of the Swiss Confederation, and I should speak and act accordingly' (*CD* III/4, p. 462). Barth makes three further brief points about this exceptional case in the three pages he devotes to it. First, he suggests that a nation may be called to go to war to help a weaker neighbour, as well as if its own existence is threatened. Second, he recognizes that if a state is to be ready to go to war in these cases, it must prepare itself to do so even in peacetime, and arm itself accordingly. Third, Barth claims that the 'distinctively Christian note in the acceptance of this demand is that it is quite unconditional. That is to say, it is independent of the success or failure of the enterprise, and therefore of the strength of one's own forces in comparison with those of the enemy'. If war 'is ventured in obedience and therefore with a good conscience, it is also ventured in faith and therefore with joyous and reckless determination' (ibid., p. 463).

I cannot help interrupting Barth here. This passage makes clear the distance between Barth and the Just War tradition. Barth dispenses with the criterion of probable success in Just War theory, which states that you must be likely to succeed in your objective for going to war. If observed, this principle reduces bloodshed by avoiding conflicts that are fruitless, which accords with the overall aims of Just War theory: to reduce the number of wars and the damage done by them. These laudable and humane objectives are vital if the legitimacy of war is to be affirmed in a Christian context, and for Barth to set them aside puts the wars he foresees as permissible exceptional cases into the category of holy wars, or crusades, rather than just wars. Christians must either reject war or help to win support for principles that minimize the damage it does. Barth does neither here.

Barth's final word on the subject of war in this volume is in relation to conscientious objection: he supports conscientious objection so long as it is in relation to particular wars, rather than absolute, and calls on the Church to guide individuals in these decisions, which may require the Church to counsel individuals not to fight for the state:

> In doing so, it might have to accept the odium of unreliability in the eyes of the government or majority. In certain cases, it might have to be prepared to face threats or suffering, bearing for its part the total risk of this kind of revolutionary loyalty. But there have been prophets before, and where does the Church learn that it is absolved from facing the same risk? (Ibid., p. 469)

In relation to this passage Yoder notes the implication that:

> ... since the necessary war is very rare and cannot in fact be seen and decided upon in advance, the church should always be ready to enter corporately the ranks of the opposition, expressing here faithfulness to what the state *should be* though her insubordination to what the state *is*. (Yoder, 1970, p. 45)

Having attended carefully to Barth's position, with only infrequent interruptions, let us now listen to Yoder. His central contention is that Barth's use of the category of *Grenzfall* is mistaken, and the mistake is particularly evident in the 'non-Barthian' way Barth uses extra-biblical categories to resolve the question of whether war could be commanded by God. Yoder questions the need for the attention Barth gives to exceptional cases in ethics: 'Why should it not be possible for a general statement in Christian ethics to have the same validity as a general statement within some other realm of Christian dogmatics?' (ibid., p. 61) The concept of the *Grenzfall* means that Barth expects exceptions in advance; the *Grenzfall* 'does not emerge unpredicted at a point where concrete problems turn out on inspection to be otherwise insoluble; the concrete cases are, rather, found to fit the place prepared for them by the systematic exposition' (ibid., p. 65). Barth, Yoder claims, is wrong that pacifists are less free to obey God: 'the pacifist who in his ethics claims to be bound to the general line of God's revelation without being able or authorized to predict exceptions is no less free for obedience than the theologian who in dogmatics is also bound to the general line of God's revelation in an affirmation about the nature of Christ or about the essence of the Church' (ibid., p. 62). Yoder asserts that, if human finitude means that it is impossible to affirm with complete certainty that God has always forbidden all killing, it must be even less possible to affirm that there are places where God will affirm killing (ibid., pp. 72–73). This leads him to his strongest charge against Barth:

> ... the *Grenzfall* is not a formal concept with validity in the discipline of ethics. It is simply the label which Barth has seen fit to attach to the fact that, in some

situations, he considers himself obliged to make a choice which runs against what all the formal concepts of his own ethics would seem to require. Barth has not constructed in the *Grenzfall* a reliable method of theological ethics in which it would be possible to found either logically or with relation to the revelation of God in Christ the advocacy of certain deviant ways of acting, such as killing when killing is otherwise forbidden. He has simply found a name for the fact that in certain contexts he is convinced of the necessity of not acting according to the way God seems to have spoken in Christ. (Ibid., p. 73)

Yoder substantiates this charge in his consideration of Barth's delimitation of the exceptional case of warfare commanded by God. Barth's claim that a nation may be commanded to fight to ensure its survival is very surprising to Yoder. It reintroduces the idea of a *Volk*, with an independent moral value and a special relationship to God, which Barth rejected decisively earlier in the *Dogmatics* (Yibid., p. 80).[4] Yoder argues that the consequences of admitting the possibility of warfare are disproportionate to its status as an exceptional case. In particular, 'to say that the state should be constantly prepared for war is like saying that an honest man should always be prepared for lying or a faithful husband for divorce; it confuses an extreme eventuality with normality, thus demonstrating the inadequacy of the *Grenzfall* as a tool for straight thinking' (ibid., p. 107). Respect for life itself, Yoder argues, is a philosophical abstraction from the biblical texts, which Barth then uses to justify the destruction of life (ibid., p. 112).

Yoder concludes that 'between Barth and an integral Christian pacifism the only differences lie at points where Barth did not finish working out the implications of his originality' (ibid., p. 118). Widening the discussion, he draws on two pieces of evidence to support his view. First, in volume IV/2 of the *Dogmatics*, Barth briefly revisits the topic of the use of force in his consideration of Jesus' directions to his disciples. Here he observes that Jesus attests to the kingdom of God 'as the end of the fixed idea of the necessity and beneficial value of force'. The kingdom 'invalidates the whole friend–foe relationship' in its call for love of the enemy. There can be no question of a general rule here, but:

> ... for the one whom Jesus, in His call to discipleship, places under this particular command and prohibition, there is a concrete and incontestable direction which has to be carried out exactly as given. In conformity with the New Testament one cannot be pacifist in principle, only practically. But let everyone give heed whether, being called to discipleship, it is either possible for him to avoid, or permissible for him to neglect becoming practically pacifist! (*CD* IV/2, p. 530, incorporating Yoder's revised translation, 1970, pp. 116–17)

The second piece of evidence that Barth might have revised his treatment of warfare in III/4 is from a comment he made in 1962 concerning it, to which I have already referred: 'Of course that was all written in 1951. ... I cannot yet completely reject it even now. Nevertheless I would say, that it is perhaps not one of the most felicitous passages in the *Kirchliche Dogmatik*. ... I first spoke 99 percent against war and the military. I hope this impressed you!' In the same interview, he condemned the mischievous use of the text by some German politicians to prove the possibility of a modern just war (interview, *Stimme der Gemeinde*, 1963, p. 750ff., cited and trans. Yoder, 1970, p. 117n.).

Now that I have recounted the substance of the discussion between Barth and Yoder, I will enter the conversation more directly to offer my own assessment of the position we have reached, and a suggestion for a way forward. There are two aspects to Yoder's criticism of Barth here: first, a general criticism of the structure of Barth's ethics, centred on the concept of *Grenzfall*, and, second, a specific criticism of Barth's discussion of warfare. I agree with the specific criticism, but dispute the general one. Barth's use of the *Grenzfall* here is different from the way in which he uses it in discussing other cases of the protection of life. In each of the accounts of suicide, abortion, euthanasia, killing in self-defence, capital punishment and tyrannicide, Barth emphasizes the reasons why the command of God will almost always require the protection of life, but he finally allows the possibility of rare exceptions. The openness to these borderline cases does not threaten the line of argument up to that point, and Barth does not call for deliberate preparation for the exceptional case. Yet in the case of war, the *Grenzfall* overturns and negates Barth's argument that, in 99 per cent of cases, the command of God forbids warfare.

Comparison with Barth's treatment of killing in self-defence is particularly instructive. Barth argues that self-defence is 'almost entirely excluded' by Pauline texts and the Sermon on the Mount. The latter puts the attacker in the same category as the beggar and the person who seeks a loan. Self-defence may be natural, but is forbidden to the Christian except in rare cases. Where Christians have been 'strictly disciplined', 'thoroughly disarmed' and 'clearly pointed to peace', it is then possible that they may hear the exceptional command to defend a third party or themselves (*CD* III/4, pp. 427–37). If we were to follow the pattern of Barth's discussion of warfare, we would then go on to spell out the consequences of this exceptional case. If we are to be free to defend others and ourselves when we receive the *Grenzfall* command here, then we must be appropriately prepared. Training in self-defence will clearly be required, and our readiness for self-defence would be further enhanced if we ensure that we are armed at all times and regularly devote time to training in the use of firearms. Barth does not follow this path in the case of killing in self-defence because it is so obviously counterproductive. The command of God will almost always be to refrain from self-defence, so the preparation we require is to learn how to keep ourselves from following our instincts to strike back and how to resolve conflicts peacefully. Spending time in self-defence training and always carrying a firearm to be ready for the exceptional case where a forceful response is commanded by God would make it difficult or impossible to retain a commitment to not resisting one's attacker. Careful preparation for the exceptional case guarantees that it will be unexceptional.

This example is unfortunately not the caricature it seems to be. Barth's treatment of the *Grenzfall* case in discussing warfare is exactly analogous to training and carrying weapons for personal self-defence. He rejects retaining standing armies as a national policy, but requires preparation for war in peacetime if a country has decided only to go to war when commanded by God in an emergency.[5] This is in spite of Barth's earlier harsh criticism of national preparations for war in peacetime and its connection with the military–industrial complex, and his statement that the task of the Christian Church and Christian ethics 'is to tell nations and governments that peace is the real emergency to which all our time, powers and ability must be devoted from the very outset' (ibid., p. 459). We cannot devote all our powers to the emergency of peace and, at the same time, devote some of our powers to making sure that we are in a position to win a war if peace fails. The great economic and human resources such preparations for war demand is one of the most powerful arguments in favour of a national policy of pacifism. According to Barth's discussion, the exceptional case in which we are called to war implies an exceptionless norm that requires us to expend substantial resources on war preparations. Yoder's comparison with an honest person preparing to lie, or a faithful spouse preparing for divorce – or, better, infidelity – is precisely to the point. Barth's treatment of the exceptional case here overturns and renders irrelevant the 99 per cent he intended to speak against war and the military. His recommendation of routine preparation for war means that he cannot support his contention that war is an *opus alienum* of the state: it has clearly become the *opus proprium* he rejected.[6]

One way of resolving these difficulties in Barth's account of war would be to work back from this *de facto* acceptance of war preparations and weaken his earlier commitment to the insights of pacifism and the importance of preparations for peace. This option would clearly be against the major line of argument of this passage. Only three of the 20 pages on war in the English translation of *CD* III/4 are devoted to explicating the exceptional case: the other 17 emphasize the horror of war, the importance of building institutions for peace and the role of conscientious objection.[7] The recommendation of practical pacifism in *CD* IV/2 and the interview Yoder cites from *Stimme* provide further evidence against this line of interpretation. As I have suggested above, to permit warfare while dismissing non-combatant immunity and the criterion of probable success is irresponsible. Thus the only coherent move to make in this direction is to adopt Just War theory, which cannot be reconciled with Barth's position that pacifism has almost infinite arguments in its favour.

A second alternative in interpreting Barth here is that offered by Yoder: reject the concept of *Grenzfall* and embrace the exceptionless ethical demand of pacifism. This option is counter to Barth's deepest meta-ethical commitments. All ethical absolutism is idolatrous, according to Barth: Christians must be obediently open to whatever God's command may require of them. Yoder bridles at being labelled an absolutist (see above), but the nub of his difference with Barth is that he does not share Barth's concern that a rigid ethical system can interfere with attentive listening to God's command. Abandoning the idea that God might call us to something new would solve the difficulty with Barth's account of war, but at the cost of the greater part of his view of the relationship between theology and ethics.

The difficulty I have identified with Barth's account of war in the *Dogmatics* is not with his treatment of pacifism or the structure of his meta-ethics, but with his treatment of the exceptional case in relation to warfare. A more promising way of overcoming the difficulty addresses this issue directly. Barth must allow the possibility of the use of force in response to God's command, but he need not treat this possible scenario as he does. Returning to the example of self-defence, we have seen that Barth allows that self-defence may be commanded in the *Grenzfall* case, but he does not recommend preparations for this eventuality. In the context of warfare, Barth stipulates that the exception is harder to justify because of the scale of the evil war creates, which means that preparations in this case would be for a possibility even rarer than self-defence. If we add to this the fact that Barth considers that in peacetime we must devote all our energy to peacemaking and that preparation for war demands substantial human and economic resources, we have a persuasive case that Christians cannot support preparations for the exceptional case in which they may be called upon to go to war: they are too busy with the emergency of peace to prepare for the distant and unlikely prospect of war, and know that war preparations are incompatible with serious attempts to build a peaceful order. This means there is no mandate to prepare for war. There remains the almost unthinkable possibility that God will call Christians to engage in large-scale killing of their fellows, but this *Grenzfall* case no longer transforms the rest of the existence of the Christian. It is true that a nation governed on this basis will be less likely to succeed in war if it is ever called upon to fight, but the Christian vocation is to peacemaking, not to amassing state-of-the-art tools for killing and destruction and not to consigning a significant section of society to manufacturing these armaments or to full-time training in using them without qualms. This development of Barth's position results in a consistent account in which his view of the nature of modern warfare and the insights of pacifism are respected, and the *Grenzfall* case is restored to its position at the fringe, rather than the centre, of his thought. The interpretation is in accordance both with his suggestion of a position of 'practical pacifism' in *CD* IV/2 and with the evidence from the *Stimme* interview that he intended to write 99 per cent against war and the military. It also facilitates the task Barth assigns to Christian ethics here: 'to recover and manifest a distinctive horror of war and aloofness from it' (*CD* III/4, p. 456).

The reinterpretation of Barth's treatment of the *Grenzfall* case in relation to warfare is important because it allows us to hear both his bleak analysis of the reality of modern warfare and his call to the Church to address the emergency of peace without being distracted by his strange account of the borderline case. We do well to pay attention to his reminder that all members of society are complicit in military preparations, that the real issue in warfare is frequently economic power, and that our possession by economic power in the shape of the military–industrial complex demands our continuous preparation for war. In particular, we need to reflect further on the meaning of the Christian vocation to be peacemakers, which Barth characterizes as telling 'nations and governments that peace is the real emergency to which all our time, powers and ability must be devoted from the very outset' (ibid.,

p. 459). This is a strong and countercultural message at a time when the dominant strain of the churches' contribution to the debate on the legitimacy of wars is a continual sober blessing of national military actions and the preparations that precede them. Barth challenges us to imagine a world in which we devote resources to serious efforts at peacemaking: the £50 billion-plus spent on the 2003 Iraq war gives some sense of the possibilities here. He also helps us see beyond this extraordinary scale of expense to the immense and demonic economic forces that lead us to accept it. Such powers and interests will not be easily defeated, but the development of Barth's account of war in the *Dogmatics* I propose helps us to see clearly that the role of the Church is to prophesy against them, and to call nations to recognize the constant emergency of peace.

Notes

1 Barth's wartime letters are available in Barth (1945). Several are translated in Barth (1941). Busch's biography (Busch, 1976) gives an account of Barth's activity in this period, and Will Herberg provides a short survey of a few of the letters (in Herberg, 1968). Yoder includes a critique of Herberg's essay in Yoder (1970, pp. 119–31).
2 For example, in the UK, 672 000 of my fellow citizens (4 per cent of the UK working population) are employed either by the Ministry of Defence, or in arms-related industries (source: *UK Defence Statistics 2000*, published by the Ministry of Defence, London).
3 For example, in 2001 the UK devoted over 6 per cent of its public expenditure to the military (source: *Budget Report 2001*, H M Treasury, London).
4 Barth wrote:

> In this connexion we must consider one of the most curious and tragic events in the whole history of Protestant theology. It took place in Germany in the years between the two world wars. I refer to the novel elevation on a wide front, if with varying emphases, of the term 'people' to the front rank of theological and ethical concepts, and the underlying assertion and teaching that in the national determination of man we have an order of creation no less than in the relationship of man and woman and parents and children. (*CD* III/4, p. 305)

5 Switzerland required, and still requires, national service of all its male citizens, currently between the ages of 20 and 42. During this period, regular training in the use of firearms is required and arms are kept in the home.
6 See Yoder (1970, p. 106): 'Is is realistic, in terms of social psychology and in the light of the experience of highly armed nations, and is it straightforward use of language to retain such phrases as *ultima ratio* and *opus alienum* when readiness for war is thus organized?'
7 While I am in strong agreement with Yoder that Barth's treatment of the exceptional case undermines his statements against war, Yoder is inaccurate in claiming that 'Barth uses almost as much space defending, defining, and demonstrating the necessity of the extreme case as he does in drawing clearly the main line of his arguments' (Yoder, 1970, p. 103). Given that Barth wished to delimit an exceptional case, the problem is rather the brevity of his description of it.

References

Barth, K. (1941), *The Christian Cause*, New York: Macmillan.
Barth, K. (1945), *Eine Schweitzer Stimme 1938–1945*, Zollikon-Zurich: Evangelischer Verlag.

Busch, E. (1976), *Karl Barth: His Life From Letters and Autobiographical Texts*, trans. J. Bowden, Philadelphia: Fortress Press.

Herberg, W. (1968), 'The Social Philosophy of Karl Barth', in *Karl Barth, Community, State, and Church: Three Essays*, Gloucester, MA: Peter Smith, pp. 11–67.

Yoder, J.H. (1970), *Karl Barth and the Problem of War*, Nashville: Abingdon Press.

CHAPTER 12

Afterword

David Ford

'We should carefully consider whether we should be reading the *Dogmatics* at all.' Mike Higton's provocative counsel goes to the heart of a proper theological ambivalence about 6 million words of theology. Should we not do what Barth did (work with the Bible in one hand and the newspaper in the other) rather than return to what he said? The answer is, of course, that we should, like Barth, do both. He read a great deal of dogmatics and other genres of theology, and John Webster and George Hunsinger in their chapters have shown how fruitful his work as a theological historian of theology is.

Yet Higton's counsel is not to be dealt with so blandly. It alerts us to the recurrent temptation not to allow primary sources to claim our primary attention. Higton stresses the 'messy particulars of the Bible or the newspaper', their immersion in the complexities of actual history. Immersion in the *Church Dogmatics* can easily reduce the freshness and seriousness of our engagement with Scripture and contemporary life. The *Dogmatics* is so much more ordered, better-digested and generally encouraging. It may take patience to read, but nothing like the sort of patience required to hear, study and meditate on Scripture, let alone relate Scripture to the many dimensions of what is going on in our world. The practical result of Higton's counsel should, ideally, be to engage with Scripture and our responsibilities in the world at least as thoroughly as Barth did, using the *Dogmatics* and other theologies and discourses as secondary aids.

That point might be put in terms of conversation. The primary focus of our conversation – in prayer, in the Christian and theological communities, and interiorly in our thinking – is on what is testified to in Scripture, on the life and thought that has sprung from that over the centuries, and on what the Spirit is opening up through it today. But the nature of that testimony (and, above all, of the God who is central to it) is such that we are led into a potentially endless variety of further conversations.

Here Eugene Rogers' daring and delightful development of Barth's theology of the Holy Spirit suggests a theological account of what this book attempts. The Holy Spirit is not only the witness, celebrant, guarantor and transfigurer but also the one who distributes gifts and gathers the community. In so many of those roles the Spirit is about speech-giving and speech-receiving, and a good deal of the quality of a community's life is in its conversation. Good conversation displays just those features that Rogers describes: a sense of gratuity, surprise and joy; endless variation and abundance; a capacity for reticence; a dynamic that consummates relationships without ending them; and an expansiveness that adds more and more to love. One might add other dimensions such as argument, discernment and judgement. Winslow's profound statement in relation to Gregory of Nazianzus, that 'what Christ has accomplished universally the Spirit perfects particularly', might be developed in the style of Barth's expositions of the Gospels (especially in *Church Dogmatics* Vol. IV) by exploring the role of conversation and debate in the ministry of Jesus Christ and then asking what the perfecting in the Spirit of that might be like in each of our families, communities and other settings.

To give conversation the role in theology that this book does can be quite subversive. It offers us a Barth whose commitment to conversation, and endless engagement in it, is likely to disturb those whose use of Barth tends to be to close conversations. Webster's Barth insists on a fresh look at Schleiermacher and the nineteenth century; Hunsinger's Barth leads us to rethink central issues in the Reformation in such a way that the Reformation can speak back; and Quash's Barth allows us to appreciate some rich convergences and irresolvably profound differences on very basic matters between Barth and von Balthasar. I am sure I am not the only reader to have longed for more – perhaps something about those seminal intensive conversations with Eduard Thurneysen before the commentary on Romans was written, or on the decades of collaboration with Charlotte von Kirschbaum, or on the pivotal argumentative relationship with Rudolf Bultmann. There is scope for much more in this vein – and perhaps the core longing is for a full, critical biography of Barth.

This book also, however, insists that we go beyond Barth's own conversation partners. Gorringe draws in several culture theorists; Ward speculates about Barth in relation to a range of other discourses under the heading of apologetics, a practice about which Barth had serious reservations; and McDowell takes up MacKinnon's concern with tragedy. There is something of Barth's own practice of theological freedom in this – a concern to do the sort of thing he did, rather than just say what he said.

But what results from all this conversation? The obvious, tautologous answer is: conversation with new partners. That is itself a major matter. The authors have been drawn into theological conversation, apprenticed to a master. It is no accident that, by my reckoning, at least five of the chapters in this book have origins in doctoral dissertations. There can be few better ways of learning the trade of theology than to grapple with Barth. It is not just that it is an education to read him at length. It also stretches supervisors/advisers. The sheer scope and quality of Barth's theology provokes conversations about one key topic after another.

I was first introduced to Barth by Hans Frei at Yale in the 1970s when I was deciding on a topic for doctoral research in Cambridge. I had more or less decided to study another theologian until, at the last moment, a friend made me admit how deep Barth had gone and that, even though a doctorate on Barth appeared impossibly difficult, I would always regret it if I did not attempt it. In retrospect, the three years spent on Barth were almost as important for the conversation with others about him as for reading the primary and secondary literature. The key conversation partners were

Hans Frei, my supervisors Stephen Sykes and Donald MacKinnon, and Eberhard Jüngel in Tübingen. It was an induction into diverse theological traditions whose common strand was their appreciation of Barth. The result was, of course, a dissertation, but more significantly it was a set of complex responses to Barth and the initiation of interior and exterior conversations that still continue. Perhaps the most fascinating of these have been with a series of doctoral students over a 20-year period – seven have done topics that were on Barth's theology or had it as a major component. None has regretted their demanding choice. They have led me into appreciating and criticizing Barth in ways I would never have imagined, but if I were to choose one key lesson learnt through all this it would be: while reading Barth, have the Bible in the other hand. That is the basic text for Barth, and no appreciation of him, or criticism of him, or development beyond him will ring true unless it engages afresh with the Bible and does so at least as truly and wisely as he. His greatest theological achievement is to help us read Scripture better, to be gripped and transformed by God through the testimony of Scripture, and to have new and fruitful conversations around Scripture. His main inadequacies and failures are likewise in this area. The way beyond him is primarily through the abundance of truth into which the Holy Spirit leads as we listen to Scripture. But, immersed in the *Church Dogmatics*, it is beguilingly easy not to devote to the Bible the sort of energy and sustained attention that Barth gave to it.

I conclude with some reflections on that early statement by Barth in the preface to the first edition of his commentary on Romans, quoted by Higton and McDowell in their Introduction: 'The understanding of history is an uninterrupted conversation between the wisdom of yesterday and the wisdom of tomorrow.' Wisdom is a pervasive biblical theme, of importance far beyond the texts where it is explicitly mentioned. One of the delights of the present volume has been the wisdom of many of its insights into Barth. These are, at times, even distilled into proverb-like form – some of my favourites are: Hunsinger's description of the confrontation of grace with faith in three ways, 'once for all, again and again, and more and more'; Quash's contrast of Barth's 'obedient embrace of freedom' with von Balthasar's 'free embrace of obedience'; Higton's counsel 'that the *Church Dogmatics* be seen as a school of figural interpretation' where we would be wise to serve an apprenticeship; and Sonderegger's question, 'can a theologian be an interpreter *and* an obedient witness?'

That question, and Sonderegger's agreement with Barth's apparently negative answer to it, raises for me the counterquestion: surely God's wisdom requires that a theologian be *both* an interpreter *and* an obedient witness? It would be a long argument to support a positive answer to that question, but perhaps the key issue lies, unsurprisingly, in who God is. Sonderegger describes Barth shifting emphasis from the cognitive to the conative in focusing on obedient witness, and it would be possible to see this mirrored in him centring his doctrine of divine attributes on love and freedom. Both love and freedom are more associated with 'will' than with 'intellect', and this shift in a classical balance is hardly redressed by not including wisdom among the perfections. Schleiermacher had love and wisdom as his culminating divine attributes: might he have been wise in this? The 'wisdom of tomorrow' might well find that the 'wisdom of yesterday' about wisdom itself has a good deal to contribute, not only about the divine attributes and the inextricability of interpretation from witness, but also about many of the other disputed matters discussed in this book, such as culture, apologetics, growth in sanctification, and tragedy. Meanwhile, the book has made its own most worthwhile contribution to that 'uninterrupted conversation', and it is to be hoped that it will act as a model for further conversational, 'theology in the Spirit' not only with Barth but with many others.

Index of Names